The Essence of Japanese Cuisine

The Essence of Japanese Cuisine

AN ESSAY ON FOOD AND CULTURE

Michael Ashkenazi and Jeanne Jacob

PENN

University of Pennsylvania Press
Philadelphia

First published in the United Kingdom by Curzon Press

First published 2000 in the United States of America by
University of Pennsylvania Press
Philadelphia, Pennsylvania 19104–4011

10 9 8 7 6 5 4 3 2 1

Library of Congress Cataloging-in-publication Data

Ashkenazi, Michael.
The essence of Japanese cuisine : an essay on food and culture / Michael Ashkenazi and Jeanne Jacob.
p. cm.
Includes bibliographical references and index.
ISBN 0–8122–3566–5 (alk. paper)
1. Cookery, Japanese. 2. Japan–Social life and customs. I. Jacob, Jeanne. II. Title.

TX724.5.J3 A87 2001
641.5952–dc21

00-023031

For Oren, Erez, and Maayan,
who participated vicariously in the making, and more importantly,
the research for this book.

Contents

Acknowledgements

TO PROTECT THE privacy of some informants we have used pseudonyms and disguised identifying characteristics in the text. Nonetheless, we cite some who deserve special mention for their invaluable assistance while we researched and wrote this book.

Our thanks go first and foremost to the many interviewees and informants who gave of their time and substance. We also owe two institutions particular thanks: the Japan Foundation for funding research in Japan, most recently in 1996, and the staff of the Ajinomoto *Shoku Bunka Sentā* (Ajinomoto Food Culture Centre) and particularly Mr. Kubota Yutaka, the Vice President of the Ajinomoto Foundation for Food Culture who gave us encouragement and a free run of one of the most exciting food libraries in the world.

In Yuzawa, Akita Prefecture, we are indebted to countless people. Foremost is Okuyama Shunzō, friend and counsellor of many years, who once again acted as informant, mentor, opener of many doors. He and wife Miyako hosted and fed us, and, more importantly, stimulated discussion and examination of many of the ideas expressed here in person as well as through correspondence over the years. Other members of the Okuyama clan – Yukiko and Yoko – assisted us in Tokyo. Fujiwara-san of Fujiwara Miso is thanked for taking time off to explain in detail the process of manufacture, and for an informed tasting session of his product and others. The members of the Yuzawa Rotary Club, and of the Yuzawa South Rotary Club were as welcoming as always and opened many doors for us. Mr. Kurata of Kurata Confectioneries provided much valuable information as well as introductions.

In Hokkaido we owe thanks to Mr. Yoshida Shigeki for introducing us around Abashiri and spending long sessions exploring ideas of food and drink. We are also grateful to Mr. Tomura Makoto of *Gyaran* and Sakai-san of Sakai Trading for their time and attention. Many others in Hokkaido helped in gathering data and suggesting avenues of inquiry.

In Tokyo, Hiroko and Akiyo Nakatani and their children Sachiko, Nobuko and Yutaka, Jeanne's family in Japan through the YWCA Mothers Scheme, introduced her to Japanese home cooking and living. They have continued in their role for many years, and helped in collecting material for this book, enlisting friends, colleagues, and relatives to provide us with information, all of which is useful and much of which was delicious.

Yano Tetsu and the members of the SF Translation Group have continued to open our eyes (and many doors) to the wealth of possibilities in Japanese cuisine since our student days. We thank them for their friendship and support which always make our stays in Japan not only culinarily interesting but intellectually stimulating. Without them, and particularly without the kindness and concern of Asakura-san, we would have been much more impoverished spiritually and culinarily.

Tanaka Tosui took precious time off her calligraphic work to introduce and guide us to the gastronomic treasures of her community in Toshima-ku. We are grateful for her hospitality and kindness throughout.

Mr. Yamamoto Toshio, chef and manager for his time and hospitality and sharing with us his breadth of knowledge regarding the food business in Japan.

Mr. Mabuchi Mutsuo, First Secretary of the Japanese Embassy in Israel, later seconded to the Tokyo Metropolitan Government, and his wife Haruko, who invited us to their home and helped ensure the success of our research in many ways.

Mr. Noda Koichiro, author, film-maker, gourmet, and great conversationalist deserves thanks for a memorable dinner and no less memorable exposition on Japanese food.

Ms. Mori Kazuyo who several times took time off from her busy schedule to discuss traditional Edo cooking and her own business enterprise.

Ms. Nakajima Miho of *H2O* provided many useful hints from her own experience as editor.

To Aracoeli Soriano, networker par excellence, a million thanks for taking care of us in many ways whenever we're in Tokyo, and for introducing us to her favourite restaurants and to Morieda Takashi, who in turn must be thanked profusely for his many connections in the Japanese cooking world.

Outside Japan we owe thanks to the staff of the Japan Centre at the University of Birmingham where several drafts of this book were written and particularly to Dr. Chris Watson, the director. Michael's colleagues at Gyosei College are thanked for encouragement and for comments and hints that helped in the writing of this book. Adrian of Macintosh Support UK deserves thanks for his courtesy and help in restoring our confidence in Apple Co. which enabled us to complete this book. The members of the H-JAPAN, H-ASIA and the l-food-japan mailing lists have freely offered advice and information on references and sources when requested.

We are grateful to Dr. Kazuko Okazaki-Luff, Mr. Gordon Brooks and Ms. Momoko Thompson for reading earlier drafts of this book. Their comments contributed greatly to the book's style and substance.

From innumerable people we have received advice and commentary on the ideas behind this book and on its writing, as well as their hospitality, and we are grateful for their contribution to this book. We claim responsibility, however, for any errors of omission and commission, for which we apologise in advance. We can only restate what has been a truism in any cuisine: *chacun à son goût*, and we are, of course no exception: this book is unquestionably from our *personal* views (albeit, aided by original research and a great deal of reliance on others' efforts and research) of Japanese food.

Illustrations

Between pages 112 and 113.

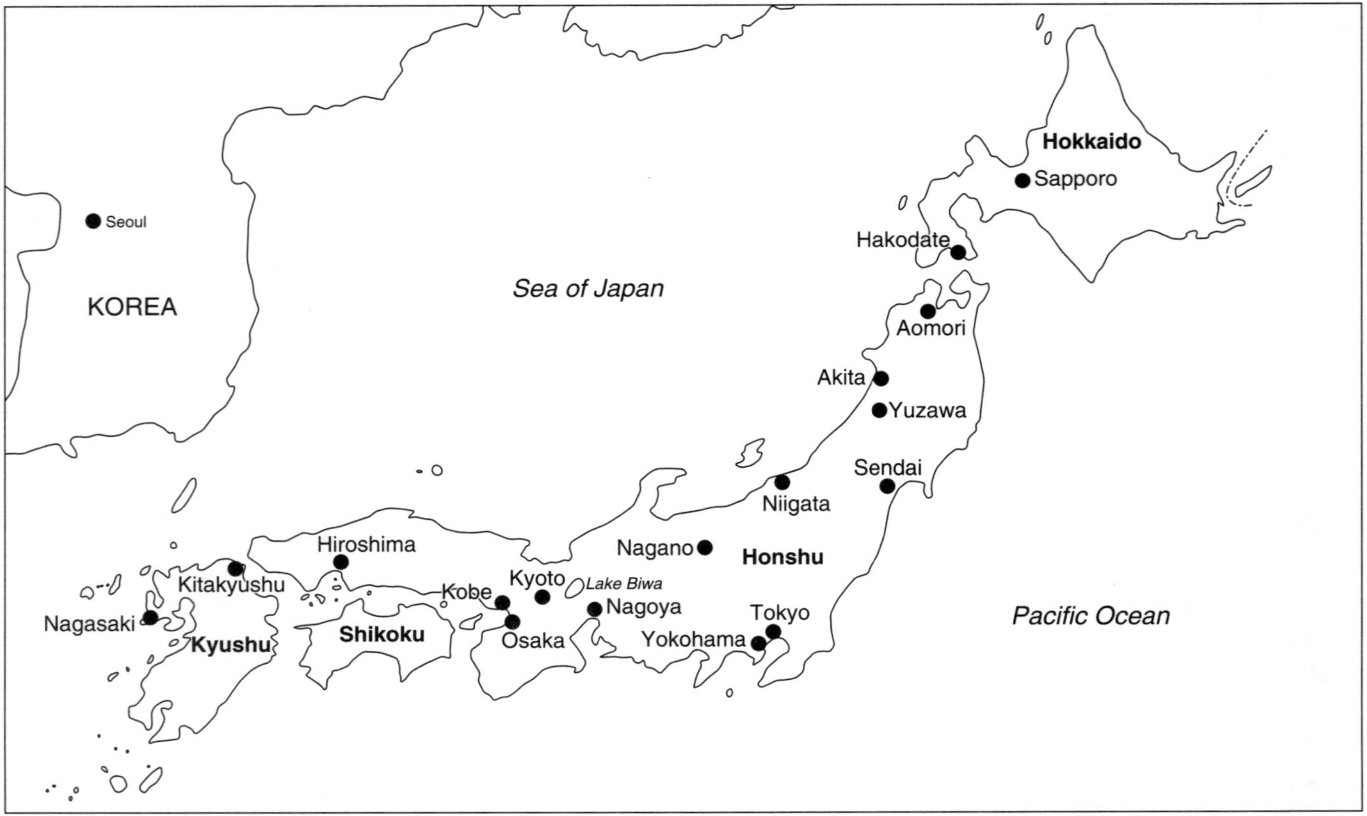
Hokkaido
Sapporo
Seoul
Hakodate
KOREA
Sea of Japan
Aomori
Akita
Yuzawa
Sendai
Niigata
Nagano
Honshu
Hiroshima
Kitakyushu
Kyoto
Lake Biwa
Kobe
Nagoya
Tokyo
Nagasaki
Shikoku
Osaka
Yokohama
Kyushu
Pacific Ocean

Map of Japan

1 Redefining Japanese Food

ANYONE WITH AN appreciation of fine cooking can recount memorable meals. Most of ours had been set in Japan, and we started to wonder what it was that set apart these meals from others. What elements contribute to a diner's enjoyable experience of Japanese food? Are these different for non-Japanese food, and why? Without a clear idea of what a Japanese fine dining experience is like, it is impossible to analyse it. Here is a recreation of one of those meals.

We met Yukiko at the entrance to Shinjuku station, from which it was a short walk to the restaurant she had chosen. Yukiko was an interior co-ordinator for a major home construction company and her excellent taste naturally extended to food. Several years before she had introduced Jeanne to an innovative restaurant, and the fusion of Mediterranean techniques with Japanese ingredients and condiments served on handcrafted stoneware plates was impressive. Prepared as we were, our expectations fell short of reality.

It was the end of August, and summer's oppressive humidity had abated somewhat, and even in the confines of Shinjuku's monstrous forest of buildings, tepid breezes, if not precisely cool, were a relief. Shinjuku – one of Japan's, if not the world's, greatest entertainment quarters – is all excitement. Kilometres of fluorescent lights, enough to light a medium-sized city, millions of people, hundreds of smells, shops and bars and entertainment places announcing their wares with pictures, photos, wax models of food, beckoning touts.

We followed Yukiko into the entrance of an inconspicuous five-storey building sandwiched between two others whose glass fronts reflected a garishly lit *pachinko* parlour on the other side of the street. As the door closed behind us, we also left the raucous atmosphere behind us and entered a completely different setting. From the awesome Teshigahara-style flower arrangement whose size (and spotlights) dominated the marble foyer, through the muted grey and pink kimono of the maitre d' who welcomed us, all signalled contemporary and vibrant elegance.

The restaurant, Tsunohazu, occupied the entire building, and we were ushered to a lift that whisked us to our floor. Our room, narrow and long, had a long bar of highly polished black wood running the length of one wall. Lining the other wall were low enclosures that framed booths for parties of four. There was a small flower arrangement and a scroll in a *tokonoma* (decorative niche). Most Japanese restaurants with Western-style chairs rarely feature decorative niches in addition to the main floral arrangement at the entrance. Exclusive gourmet establishments *(ryōtei)* do. Tsunohazu was far from a traditional tatami-matted *ryōtei* – its furnishings echoed the latest in chic furniture design from Milan and other European capitals. Shown to our places, still talking among ourselves, we had time to talk and drink while waiting for the luncheon that Yukiko ordered.

The first course, labelled a lemon *nabe* (pot), exemplified the eclecticism and seasonal fit of Japanese cuisine. A medium-sized lemon had been hollowed out and filled with a slightly tart *granité* of Japanese pears (*nashi mizore ae*) which served as a sauce for a colourful melange of shellfish meats, soft seaweed bits, diced cucumber, and red radish.

After this mouth-refreshing sorbet came the appetiser. Each of us received a gleaming black lacquered board, about 20 × 30 cm, on which small objects had been artfully arranged, seemingly haphazardly: small white fish-balls (*tsukimi dango*) representing the (forthcoming) autumn moon; deep golden fried slices of fish (*sanma kenchin-yaki*); slices of tiny purple aubergine, sweet and tender, adorned with a chestnut puree (*kurumi tofu yaki nasu*); small shrimp, parboiled and mounded with roe (*seou ebi*); and seasoned roasted chestnut meats that had been restuffed into fresh green-spined shells.

The arrangement on the black lacquer suggested the scattering of leaves and fruit as summer melds into autumn, to which of course the chestnuts, seasonal fish, fish-balls, as well as the *nabe* (stewing pot) of the previous dish also hinted.

Some of the qualities of taste and texture were surprising, as were the numerous allusions to autumn interwoven with those to the season we both thought we were still very definitely in. Our seasonal savvy was out of synch obviously: the occasional comforting breezes signalled the cusp of autumn, which we had ignored. Or rather, we had not been attuned to the subtlety of the season's turning. Our attention had been directed by the reiteration of autumnal offerings in the menu.

The crisp-looking *tsukimi dango* were surprisingly quite frothy on the tongue. The chestnuts, far from being mealy as expected, were crunchy. And above all, the visual qualities of the ingredients, the blazing colours of autumn in shiny browns, mellow yellows, and dark reds, set against the background of black lacquer, which itself was on a polished white pine table, heightened our sensory experience.

The next course was labelled *o-wan*: bowl. A bowl can contain rice, of course, or soup, but in this case, as expected (and greatly appreciated) it contained a steamed soup-custard: *matsutake dobin mushi*. The chef was being doubly playful. *Chawan mushi* is a steamed savoury custard, much appreciated in the colder months. It is normally served in a tea bowl hence the name (*cha* = tea; *wan* = bowl), but here the custard had been made and steamed in individual small teapots, evoking the original name without actually mentioning it, and, by inserting the highly valued (and priced) autumnal *matsutake* pine mushrooms, the chef unequivocally set the meal more solidly into its seasonal context (if by chance the previous elements had failed to convince us). One of the great charms of *chawan mushi* is that the custard hides various treasures, much like raisins in an English custard, to add interest to its fairly bland texture. In this case slices of fragrant brown *matsutake* were the main attraction. There were chunks of savoury grilled *hamo* (pike conger, or pike eel), old ivory-coloured gingko nuts and, for visual, textural and taste contrast, mandarin segments, peeled and lightly marinated in rice vinegar.

It being autumn also meant the start of the *shun* or proper season for *katsuo*, a small relative of the tuna that swarms through the Black Current that kisses the Pacific coast of Japan at that time. In November, particularly, its flesh is considered at its peak. The next dish – *katsuo tataki* – featured succulent triangles of flash-seared and then ice-dipped *katsuo* fillet, the smoky flavour of its charred outer surfaces a foil to the tenderness of the garnet-coloured, glistening rare centre. Accompaniments were chopped green onions and a sauce of mildly sour *ponzu* (citron) and soy sauce.

This piscean steak tartare was contrasted with a *yakimono* ("cooked thing") – a morsel of sea bass wrapped in filo pastry to form a Japanese flavoured Western-style "pie" (*suzuki hōsho pai tsutsumi*), a marvelous blend of Japanese and Western techniques. This was served with two minuscule mounds of lightly cooked vegetables – aromatic *gobō* (burdock root, a characteristic element in stews and other cold-weather dishes) and juicy sweet Japanese spinach leaves, stems and pink-tinged root tops.

A stew – *nimono* – followed. In a rich stock, *yuba* (dried sheets of tofu, that most versatile of foods) had been gently simmered and now floated like folded scrolls of creamy velum. Some soft, spongy *Daitokuji-fu* (Daitoku-temple style fried gluten) had been added, as a French chef would croutons. In the broth as well were hand-rolled noodles of newly-harvested *soba* (buckwheat). These dark-flecked noodles with their robust wholemeal-like colour and taste and *al dente* texture were ideally partnered with the mountain vegetables (*sansai*) – lily bulbs and wild greens – in Yoshino-style, that is battered and stewed in *kuzu* (arrowroot) flour. The stew, perhaps more than anything else, reflected Japanese preferences for a subtle variety of textures – crisp, soft, slick, smooth – within the same dish. The mainstays of frugal stews and ascetic diets – dried tofu, gluten, wild vegetables, coarse buckwheat – embody the warmth, flavour, and comfort of the countryside (*inaka*) and home cooking (*haha no aji*, "mother's taste"), and serve as reminders of simpler, albeit harsher, times when wild vegetables and fungi, painstakingly harvested in the mountains throughout the milder seasons, as well as persimmons, sweet potatoes, radishes, pounded rice cakes (*mochi*), and tofu were dried (the latter, "freeze-dried" in the Snow Country) and stored for the colder months. Here in a sophisticated setting and more refined method of cooking and serving, these simple ingredients merely serve as harbingers of the forthcoming cold.

The contrast of the stew in texture, provenance, and freshness with the next dish could not have been sharper: *shun no tempura*, a selection of seasonal vegetables and small pieces of fish tempura-style. Small portions of the freshest ingredients dipped in a chilled, light batter, and immediately fried in sesame-scented oil. The result – unsurprising, since Tsunohazu's origins were in a *tempura* shop – were golden clouds, crunchy on the outside, preserving the perfect fresh flavour of the seasonal offerings. Miniature aubergines, sweet and soft, a slice of orange-fleshed sweet potato, another of Japanese squash, its malachite-green peel peeking through its crisp batter gilding, were served with a traditional sauce of soy, fish stock, grated ginger and radish. With its broad visual and textural similarity to beignets, fritto misto, camarron rebozado and other Western batter-fried dishes, *tempura* is one dish which non-Japanese take to with great ease. It is sociolinguistically amusing that while the origin of the word *tempura* is ascribed by Japanese lexicography to Spanish *tempora* ("fasting day meals") or Portuguese *tempero* ("cooking, preparation"), modern Portuguese or Spanish cookbooks call batter-fried dishes "rebozado" or "frito".

No Japanese meal would be complete without cooked rice, which for many Asian cultures defines a proper meal. Here the chef teases the customer: the next dish was labelled *oshokuji* (meal) on the menu. A meal within a meal, as it were, the defining moment of the event and a witticism on *gohan* – cooked rice – which is the common word for food. In this case rice, in the form of mushroom gruel (*kinoko zōsui*), was simmered till soft but not mushy in light stock and garnished with half-opened parasols of beige-grey *shimeji* mushrooms, aromatic trefoil leaves (*mitsuba*) and a minuscule mound of the restaurant's original salt pickles. Called by the courtly word *kōno-mono* (perfumed things), these homely salt-cured vegetables almost inevitably accompany rice. Steaming hot, glistening white rice, home-cured pickles, and miso soup (*miso shiru*) constitute the most basic yet complete module of a Japanese meal (*ichijū issai*, "one soup, one vegetable" [rice is tacit]), and are evocative of rurality, home foods, and personal comfort.

Finally, we had *mizugashi* ("water sweets"), a classic reference to fresh fruits and nuts, and now used for a final sweet course. Doubtless in concession to the old and new waves of culinary imports, we had cream cheesecake with arrowroot sauce (*kurīmu chīzu honkatsu yose*), a delicate cube

> of exquisite melting creaminess, lapped with a translucent slightly tart sauce, and teamed with a mini-scoop of freshly made white peach sherbet. The plate was scattered with a few ruby-red grains of pomegranate, and three enormous Kyōhō grapes, each the size of a small plum, the peel half-bared to reveal and contrast with the juicy translucent flesh. Coffee, which by now has become one of *the* national drinks of Japan, concluded the meal, which, though considerably hastened at our request, still lasted almost three hours.

It was a most exquisite repast, a veritable feast of the senses. It was a multi-layered experience that involved the seasons, manifold textures and tastes, novel combinations of ingredients and cooking techniques, and aroused aesthetic enjoyment in the colours, presentation, and choice eating and serving implements used throughout. Moreover the service was neither obsequious nor lacking in attention. To say that we were euphoric at the end would not seem an exaggeration of how the three of us felt. However, had we not had some knowledge and previous experience of similar feasts, our appreciation would not have been as keen. Looking back on it and trying to objectify the experience highlights several stark issues. How does one translate the personal, intensely individual experience of this meal to another? What is the relationship between what anthropologists call the "emic" – the realm of personal experience, personal evaluation, personal emotional response – and the "etic" – those parts that can be described "objectively" or at least materially?

Clearly we could describe this late summer-early autumn meal in one of several ways. We could simply give the menu, provide a list of recipes, describe what we saw, or, with some difficulty, what we tasted and felt. But it is very clear that none of those would encompass the totality of the experience, nor, perhaps, would it make clear to any reader, how these discrete elements came together to make a memorable meal, nor why. To make sense of this, or any other meal, we therefore decide, in a sense, to start at the beginning: to introduce the reader to Japanese food as we ourselves were introduced, and to unfold, in clear stages inasmuch as is possible, how this meal, as a sort of prototype for any Japanese meal, comes about. In a way, what we are about to embark upon is something like unfolding a complicated *origami* paper folding: taking a miniaturised whole, and disassembling it, unfolding it to see the marvellous structure it enfolds.

The discovery of any food system starts with the shock of the unknown as it crosses one's sensory faculties. Until the point at which 'strangeness' is recognised by one's palate or nose or eye, the diner is still in the land of the familiar. Attempting to characterise the strangeness is something that is often hard to do because the experience is totally subjective. "This is salty' or "that is sweet' are statements that are, at best, rough approximations of sensations that have, at their base, levels of individual memory and experience tagged on to them. It is when you want to identify a specific "taste point", as it were, along the continuum of sweetness or saltiness – 'not salty enough' or 'too sweet' – that you get into the complexity of individually and culturally learned thresholds of acceptable or appropriate taste or balance of tastes. The elaborate devices invented by oenologists to describe the taste of wine are at best poor analogies (what, after all, does 'flinty' mean to most of us?) and at worse appear to be a source of disbelief and amusement to the layperson.

All this is to say that trying to interpret a food system to those unfamiliar with it is fraught with some unusual difficulties. To start with, therefore, we look at a plain Japanese meal from the vantage point of the outsider, the newcomer, the novice:

> The first Japanese meal I ate was a *teishoku* (set-menu) of *yakiniku*, rice, *miso shiru*, and pickles. It was memorable not because good – on thinking back, it was eaten in a dingy and cheap students' eatery – but because of its strange sensory qualities.
>
> *Yakiniku* consists of thin slices of meat (usually pork) sautéed with soy sauce and salt and slices of onion. Served on a plate decorated with parsley, it was familiar enough not to invite comment (by my unconscious mind or my taste buds). As with all *teishoku*, or complete meals, it came with a bowl of white steamed rice (which I expected) and a bowl of unfamiliar soup.
>
> The physical properties of *miso shiru* soup are such that the clear broth (the *dashi*) is obscured by a cloud of *miso* bean paste. There are characteristic tiny "whirlpools": wells of clear stock that penetrate through the tiny clouds so that you can see the lacquered bottom of the bowl. On that occasion, the *miso shiru* was garnished by pure white cubes of what I was to later learn was tofu bean curd.
>
> In contrast to the meat and rice, this was unknown territory indeed. What were the white cubes, and why were they virtually tasteless? And why did the liquid separate into two layers? Should these be stirred together, or, as in Turkish coffee (which I was familiar with), left to separate? And what was the soup made of in any case? Fortunately there was a group of us present, some more knowledgeable with Japanese food. Someone matter-of-factly picked up the soup bowl, gave it a brisk stir with a pair of chopsticks, and sipped some of the contents straight from the bowl.
>
> The pickles too caused a dilemma of a different sort. They crunched. Loudly. Was that appropriate? Did one accept the domain of noise into polite company? Apparently one did. I crunched loudly.
>
> The utensils provided some difficulty as well. Chopsticks were familiar, but these were *waribashi*, cheap wooden chopsticks that consisted of a thin slip of wood almost, but not quite, bisected lengthwise by a cut. In separating them, I ended up with two uneven pieces of wood, which did not make the meal any easier.

Now, the meal described here was, on any scale of events, a very simple one. Given the place Michael was eating in (and the state of his student finances), it was far from *haute cuisine* in any sense of the word. Its very newness was intriguing, fascinating. It evoked new sensations, as well as triggering new ideas about taste, about relationships between foods: things that every individual carries about since childhood. That simple student meal is difficult to forget *not* because it was great cooking, but because, simple as it was, it cast new light – sensory experiences, taste, sight, texture, handedness – on what he had perceived as food. Michael ate it soon after arriving in Japan as a graduate student, and the questions it has raised came to be answered now, more than twenty years later.

1.1 *AN ANALYTICAL DIMENSION*

THE DIFFICULTIES WE faced on those early occasions with Japanese meals illustrate some of the issues that are significant for understanding the domain of food and of eating. More perhaps than in other domains, the domain of food involves sets of arrayed rules in many dimensions. Aesthetics of sight and of taste compete with those of social consequence and usage. Different modes of service are determined by place, time, and company. These rules are inherent in the foods one eats, and one ignores them at peril.

Some of the dimensions that played a part in the initial meal can be highlighted. These are objective dimensions of any food act. Taste, utensils and presentation, texture, social circumstances, foodstuffs used are some things that can and ought to be considered when examining this "food event".

The idea of an "event" is crucial for the discussion throughout this book. There is nothing more personal, and thus more subjective, than eating. And even an understanding of the physical properties involved, what anthropologists call an "etic" description, does little to change the intersubjectivity.

The apparent groping about the subject above is done to good purpose. Not to confuse the reader, but to emphasise the idea that the basis for understanding a food system *must* be founded on some form of description and analysis that attempts (as much as is possible) to be objective and replicable in clearly defined units, so that the indefinable, unquantifiable elements of the analysis can at least be circumscribed and dealt with. These elements are such that they are not only unquantifiable (and can thus only be explained by allusion and analogy) but they also raise strong feelings, sensory and emotional, as Jeanne remembers:

> A round lacquered tray of sushi was set in front of me on a visit to a friend's house, not long after I'd arrived in Japan. Although I could appreciate the beauty of the arrangement, the colours, and shapes against the shiny lacquer, I couldn't get over the gagging sensation I felt at the thought of eating fish raw. I had always loved fish and seafood and had been tempted by the colourful display counter of the sushi bar near my school in Fuchu. Why I, who relished raw oysters, couldn't enjoy sushi or *sashimi* was beyond me. I couldn't leave the food untouched obviously. I started with the

> cooked ones first – prawns, grilled eel, octopus. Then feeling very brave, I progressed to the raw ones, choking them down, the feel of the raw fish barely overcome by the comforting taste of rice. I gulped tea hurriedly to wash down the uncomfortable sensation of raw gobbets. Then I observed a bright yellow-orange piece more closely. It looked familiar, and took me back to childhood summers by the sea with memories of picnics under coconut trees. It was sea-urchin roe, a delicacy that often featured on those feasts, either grilled in their spiny shells over coals or raw, and much loved by my mother. The sweet creaminess of the familiar delicacy was intoxicating. The sensation carried over to the other less familiar pieces, and this time I could chew more slowly, linger over the complex tastes and textures in my mouth, and truly savour what I was eating. Sushi became one of my favourites.

Taste is inherently a matter of both objective factors *and* the stimulus and contextualisation of memory. The aesthetics of food are dominated by previous experience, perhaps to a greater degree than other senses. Whatever the reason, food changes are difficult to analyse precisely because taste is subject to memory, perhaps greatly to memories of childhood comfort, and because the emitter of the sensation – the food itself – is destroyed in the process of sensory appreciation.

The anecdotes above illustrate some of the principles we are to explore here. First is the interplay between subjective emotion and experience, and objective phenomena that are a part of the food act. Each of these meals evoked individual feelings and emotions based on experience and past history. Second, each of the meals described was a social event bound by rules which, initially at least, may be unknown to the outside observer, and certainly unknown to Jeanne and Michael in their first Japanese meals. These rules determine things we take for granted, unconsciously, about a range of issues: which foods go with which, what sensory feelings are appropriate, who is eating, and so forth. These are rules that each of us, a member of a particular society, "knows" and accepts without thought, much less introspection. Third, there is also a further, objective dimension inherent in, though not exemplified by, the descriptions above: the dimension of social action. Of the three meal descriptions, two occurred in public places. Different observations would have been made under other conditions. The relationship between domestic and public food events, between the different sorts of "public" events, and between foods and behaviours appropriate to each, must be explored as well.

Our view is therefore structured by the attempt to understand what the rules of Japanese cuisine are, and the need to do so without, insofar as it is possible, alienating the reader from the very personal experience that is implicit in any food system. This book is, then, among other things, an attempt to come to grips with the contrast between individually felt experience and objectively viewed reality.

1.2 *OBJECTIVES AND METHODOLOGY*

We aim in this book to provide a reasoned overview of the relationship between Japan's culture and its cuisine, and in particular, to highlight how changes occur in this cuisine. In doing so, we also accomplish two subsidiary objectives. We introduce the reader to the world of Japanese food, which, to most non-Japanese, is a strange and opaque field, known more by its difference from the norms with which the European reader is familiar, than for its own qualities. We also bolster some of the theoretical ideas relating cuisine to culture which have been suggested in relation to Western cultures, and show how they apply to Japan as well.

The book is not aimed solely at a target audience of our fellow Japanese specialists. Much of what we say here about Japanese society has been said elsewhere in greater detail and with greater scope. The reader who is not familiar with Japan will find here a brief introduction to Japanese society, which, if it arouses interest, is best pursued by additional reading. What this book does offer, for both the specialist and the non-specialist, is an overview of the relationship between Japan's elaborate and complex cultural choices, and the no-less elaborate culinary ones. We focus, not unnaturally, on issues that have relevance to the realm of food culture. It is these that we are interested in highlighting, dealing in passing, as we do, with other cultural and social features. In practice, what we have done is used issues that arise in the realm of food to tie them to other cultural and historical issues that can be seen in Japanese society today.

The method we used to describe the data on which this book is based is a direct result of the sort of goal we were trying to achieve. An understanding of the subjective experience – ours or anyone's – of food, poses a serious problem of reliability. To put it simply, are our personal observations generalisable to the general public? This is a particular problem given that any individual's taste and memory change over time, and that the chemistry of the senses is affected by personal health, emotional state, and previous experiences.[1] This has meant that the methodological strategy had to answer to sometimes contradictory requirements. On the one hand, it had to deal with individual experience, on the other, the results had to apply to the Japanese population as a whole, or at least, we had to be able to claim, to apply to a significant proportion of it. Thus this book is a quintessentially personal account bolstered by reference to other research. There were two of us involved, so there is some check on flights of fancy and purely individual experience, but given that we are dealing here with the realm of the senses above all, and with a realm that is particularly evanescent, we

1 Not to mention the quantities of alcohol consumed, a problem that bedevils all anthropologists, and particularly those working in societies such as Japan in which alcohol is considered a necessary accompaniment to almost all social interactions, especially food. As a general rule of thumb, the higher the alcohol intake, the better and more copious the data, the worse the ability to record it in comprehensible form.

have intruded more, as persons into the matter of this book, than we would in a drier, more "objectifiable" subject. We agree too, that had others written this book, the results might have been different at the experiential and sensory level, though, we maintain, that the theoretical conclusions would likely have been much the same. Whatever the case, and as a challenge to the reader, we can only suggest one thing: try the cuisine we are about to examine further along. Come to your own conclusions. Happily, they will approximate, in general if not in detail, our own.

In practice, the data derive from a number of sources. Our diaries and letters over a period of some twenty years are one source. In an unsystematic manner, both of us have collected recipes and food anecdotes since our (individual) arrivals in Japan – Jeanne in 1971, Michael in 1975 – and through subsequent years of residence there, as well as occasional visits.

Systematic data were collected initially as part of Michael's study of *matsuri* (festivals) and Jeanne's study of folk craftsmen. Later, a comparative collection of data through interviews and questionnaires was conducted in 1990/91. More data was collected during an extensive field trip in 1996. In addition, we have secured verbal, printed and electronic data from a variety of sources including questioning friends and acquaintances about their experiences, collections of food wrappers, brochures, magazines, flyers, and other food-related items, accessing discussion groups on the Internet, and so on. We spoke to ("interviewed" is too structured a term here, given the circumstances) people in restaurants, bars, shoppers at food shops and supermarkets, vendors, and any one else who crossed our path.

It has taken many years for anthropologists, among others, to come to the realisation that their attempt to write "science" has a great many flaws. Partly these are attributable to a general problem in the "soft" social and human sciences, as opposed to the "hard" ones: molecules don't talk back; humans do. Nuclear physicists, faced with Heisenberg's problem (where the very act of observation corrupts the "purity" of the observed subject), have learned to live with uncertainty. The same is gradually becoming true of social scientists. One consequence of this (gradual) realisation has been to experiment with the end product: the academic monograph. This has taken too many forms to explore here. But we were both dissatisfied with the dry, "objective" tone that has been commonly used. Particularly because, as we argue throughout, food is an inherently intimate and personal experience. As an intentional result, we, the authors, appear far more often, and are present to a much greater degree, than academic readers, at least, may feel appropriate. By and large, we were the only tools we had. Our own impressions of what we saw and heard, and no less importantly, what we tasted and smelled, form the basis of much of what is said here. We recognise that this "subjectivises" many of the issues, and to the best of our ability, we have provided signposts allowing the reader, wherever possible, to experiment on the same subjects, and to experience the same, or, given the nature of food, similar, experiences.

To follow onto the immediacy of the experience, we have also experimented with the ways in which we have referenced this book. Rather than interpolating references throughout the text, we have provided a short list of the main readings for each chapter at the chapter's end. The references section at the end of the book includes all references we have consulted. Only when we are responding directly to some statement have we made references in the body. Hopefully this will make for smoother reading, and be less intimidating to those readers without academic axes to grind.

1.3 *THE QUESTIONS*

EXOTIC THOUGH IT may seem in some ways to an outsider, Japanese cuisine must, as all cuisines do, have a logic of its own. All cultural institutions are a derivative of numerous factors which can roughly be subsumed under social responses to natural phenomena, mechanical solutions to energetic problems, and the effects of historical processes and accidents. That is to say that people arrange their lives in pragmatic ways to deal with their surroundings, and the solutions they come up with are conditioned, but not absolutely determined, by their past individual and mutual histories.

It is perhaps trite, but nonetheless important to reiterate that food has been more closely bound to nature than many other human institutions. The emergence of modernity, from the point of view of cuisine, is the gradual detachment of a cuisine from its natural ecological surroundings, whether from the climatic dictates of certain kinds of crops, the seasonal dictates of the annual cycle, the bondage to ephemerality and rot, or the need to supply local fuels. Where food has been so "modernised" it has both benefited (in the form of greater flexibility and more variety) and suffered (in the form of lowering standards of taste and the creation of low common denominators).

We cannot therefore ignore modernisation factors if we are to speak of any cuisine, not the least of Japan. Japanese society, and its cuisine, have undergone a radical transformation over the past century that has been far more radical than many other cultures, because most Japanese have wholeheartedly embraced these changes, and, in the past thirty years or so, been the initiators of many of them. Changes in Japanese cuisine can only be understood if we also understand the recent historical changes that have overtaken individual and domestic life, technologies ranging from the railway (which turned the Edo period's taste for mass pilgrimage into the twentieth century's mass tourism) to refrigeration (which made possible the consumption of *sashimi* to all, not just seaside dwellers), and the nation as a whole. So a primary issue here is to ask ourselves about the relationship between Japanese culture as a whole, and its cuisine. Mennel's (1985) discussion of the relationship between class and culinary movement, and Goody's (1982) argument that cuisines essentially *depend* on class point the way here. As Japanese society has mutated from an overtly vertically segmented society into something more fluid, we can and should expect changes in the process of food consumption, the adoption of new and varied foods, and the preferences for particular food forms. And this is only the social aspect of cuisine. So, in broad strokes, we want to understand how Japanese culture and Japanese cuisine are related, how they mutually affect one another, if at all. Superficially, this might seem to be a superfluous question: don't culture and cuisine affect one another? And yet, in the context of contemporary life, economy, and modern communications, we feel this question has to be made overt.

It is also necessary to address questions about specific items in Japanese cuisine, how they come about, their interrelationship, and how they and not others, are chosen to become a part of the "national cuisine." Related to that, of course, is the question of what *is* the national cuisine in Japan? Is there such a thing at all, or has Japan's constant and consistent preference for foreign and new things brought about an excision of its own nature?

To put these questions in some sort of structured form, so as not to be overwhelmed, we addressed ourselves to several questions. What do the Japanese eat (and we recognise that "the Japanese" in this context, as in any other generalisation, is a crude, perhaps misleading abstract)? Why (as a historical question, and as a question of the interaction of various social and cultural forces) do they eat those things? In other words, what mechanisms of choice are in operation to cause some things, rather than others, to be eaten. And finally, we can ask what sorts of effects these choices have on other aspects of Japanese lives, how does cuisine in its various aspects, affect other areas of Japanese life?

1.4 *THE ORGANISATION OF THE BOOK*

In this chapter we started by providing several anecdotes illustrating different food events in Japan. Following this, the chapter elaborates on the sorts of problems that the book raises. In Chapter 2 we discuss the theoretical problems that will be dealt with, both in the context of other writings about food in general, and in the specific Japanese context. Chapter 3 introduces the reader to the parallel histories of Japanese culture and society, and its food history and current food sources. We have not attempted a historian's survey of Japanese history, partly because we are not professional historians, but more importantly, because we are only interested in those aspects of Japanese history which have a bearing on food. Chapter 4 provides an analytical description of a Japanese meal. It shows not only *how* meals are structured but also why, and discusses the elements that allow (or restrict) internal variation. We also connect the structure of Japanese meals with a Japanese cultural and aesthetic preference for modularity, and show how this is utilised in meals as well as other domestic and social arrangements. Where Chapter 4 deals with how Japanese meals are constructed, Chapter 5 deals with how foodstuffs are dealt with, that is, with methods of food preparation. It is these cooking methods, or "styles" that determine and define food "loci": places where food is prepared and consumed, which are dealt with in Chapter 6. The different food styles (e.g. sushi and *tempura*) determine the "positioning" (in a marketing as well as geographical and cultural sense) of Japanese food loci, including the home (where certain foods, but not others are likely to be found), restaurants, bars, and other places. We also discuss how these different places affect one another, and are interrelated through the media, marketing networks, and the different types of meals. In Chapter 7 we start our discussion of the mutual effects of Japanese aesthetics and food. We examine the aesthetic principles of Japanese food and its presentation, as well as showing where these originate from. Chapter 8 tackles the issue from a different viewpoint, as we look at Japanese food culture as a system of rules that is learned by members of the culture. We see how these rules are formed, and how they contribute to retention of practices, as well as to changes in Japanese culture. In Chapter 9 we discuss the art of dining by returning once again to the "meal" as a focus of discussion. We show how various principles discussed earlier can illuminate these food events, by describing and analysing several such events. Here we look at the act of eating as a performative and multi-dimensional act in its own. That is, as a form of artwork in which producers and consumers participate together. We conclude the book by detailing in Chapter 10 some of the lessons that can be learned from the Japanese experience with food, and from our own study of Japanese food culture. We discuss several issues which have broad implications in, as well as, outside Japanese cuisine.

1.5 *TECHNICAL NOTE: WORDS, PRONUNCIATION, AND GLOSSES*

INEVITABLY, IN A work such as this, a great many unfamiliar terms are going to creep in. In fact, given the nature of the subject, they are inevitable. We have tried to be parsimonious in their use. However, to clarify things for the reader unfamiliar with the terminology and the conventions of writing Japanese, we have provided a number of aids.

In the text, the first instance of a new term is followed by a brief gloss in brackets, which may suffice for many readers. The Japanese language has a number of double vowels: ō, ū, ē, whose "long" sounds we have indicated by the use of a macron. Japanese terms used in the text are also explained briefly in a glossary at the back of the book. Where possible and necessary we have also included scientific names, such as for the names of fish and plants, in the glossary.

We have also based many of our opinions, and some of our data, on those of others. Particularly influential have been authors such as Jean Anthelme Brillat-Savarin, Jack Goody, Mary Douglas, Ishige Naomichi, Marvin Harris, and Stephen Mennel.

Japanese names have been written in the Japanese style, that is, surname first. Where we have used someone's name in a personal context, we have usually added the honorific "-san."

READINGS FOR CHAPTER 1

Goody, Jack 1982 *Cooking, Cuisine, and Class.*
Harris, Marvin 1988 *Good to Eat: Riddles of Food and Culture.*
Khare, R.S. 1980 "Food as nutrition and culture: Notes towards an anthropological methodology".
Mennell, Stephen 1985 *All Manners of Food.*

2 A Framework for Discussion

"FOOD," IN CONTRAST to raw material or "foodstuffs" that are the basis of prepared dishes, consists of any given unit of edibles that is accepted in a particular culture. An apple, a bowl of soup, or a steak are equally "foods." "Cooking" refers to ways in which foods are prepared, whether by the mechanical processing of a foodstuff (peeling an apple), or the chemical process of applying one material or another to a foodstuff (extracting nutriments from vegetable and protein into hot water to produce soup). Cooking methods are varied, but fall into several well-defined classes that *most* cultures use to one degree or another. Cutting, pickling, drying, simmering or boiling, baking, roasting, etc. are ways of cooking foodstuffs either to make them palatable or nutritious, or to make them more attractive or interesting. When cooking particular foods becomes elaborated into a set of fixed requirements, that are also associated with rules regarding presentation and participation or exclusion from particular food events, we have a *cuisine.* The choice of foodstuffs, their preparation, the rules of the cuisine, aesthetic rules regarding food appreciation, and ancillary issues such as food loci, are a "food culture" which generally differ in line with overall cultural and sometimes national differences.

To look at it in another way, particular foodstuffs are the domain of a species: all those things the species can physiologically ingest. The domain of *cooking* is that of the human species, which alone (with some very minor exceptions) actually prepares its food artificially. *Cuisines* can be found in those human cultures in which surpluses are great enough to permit the emergence of differentiated social classes, and their consequent attempts to separate themselves from others, as well as to benefit from the new and exotic. A "food event" is any occasion in which food or drink are ingested. Many such involve imposed rules and processes which are culturally valued. A "meal" is a major food event, usually one that is scheduled on a daily basis, and which, in any society, forces the eater or "diner" to engage in a complex of such culturally valued behaviours. The food culture of a society encompasses all those issues relating to food: not only its consumption, but its production, trade, effects, and sources as well.

Food is thus at one and the same time an intensely personal activity and one of the most highly socialised activities humans engage in (Clark 1975). It is, ultimately, a cultural product which must be examined using tools that are her aspects of culture. Before we enter the world of Japanese food, is necessary to provide a framework for the discussion. This heavily based on the works of others: the theoretical discussion of ı ongoing for close to three thousand years.

Necessarily, we cannot, nor should we, provide complete details of the ins and outs of the discussion, some of which is highly abstruse and contentious. Nonetheless, in order to frame what will be said subsequently, we will briefly describe some of the ideas linking human culture and human food.

2.1 *FOOD IN HISTORICAL THEORY*

THROUGHOUT HISTORY, A number of thinkers have devoted some of their attention to the humble issue of food. Some of these considerations have been focused on issues relating either to nutrition (which we touch on here only lightly) or as an element in human morality, relationship with the gods, or propriety.

Philosophical thinking about food in the West can be traced at least to Epicurus, in whose philosophical system food played a major part as a source of satisfaction and pleasure. In contrast, for gloomy St. Augustine, food was a distraction, and gluttony a positive sin. It was not until the rise of the Enlightenment that food began to be viewed (at least among philosophers) as more than a distraction: Brillat-Savarin, a former aristocrat of the *ancièn regime* in France, exile, and cook, emerged as a major proponent of considering food in its cultural and aesthetic dimensions, something taken up by later luminaries, among them Alexander Dumas.

In the philosophical and theoretical thinking of East Asia, food was discussed both as an example of the points the philosopher was trying to make, such as Chuang-Tzu's description of proper butchery, and was the object of regulations and rules to curb gluttony and pleasure, which emerged from Buddhist writings. For Dōgen, who introduced Japan to Zen, food and its preparation were an element in the attainment of enlightenment through meditation. At a later date, Motoori Norinaga, one of the major Shintō and nationalist thinkers of Japan, claimed a mystical connection between Japan and the deities as evident by the aesthetic quality of Japanese rice.

Examination of the main thrust of these ideas displays three prominent themes: food and its social aspects, and food and health, and, much later thoughts about food and individual experience.

Brillat-Savarin, in Europe, placed great importance not only on the pleasure of food, but also on its healthfulness. In this of course he was following common beliefs that held certain foods to be good and healthful, others to be less so, even dangerous: sets of belief that varied from one European culture to another.

In Chinese folk beliefs, a shadow of which has come down to Japanese popular practice, foods are hot, cold, or neutral, and a proper balancing of them is necessary for longevity and health. This relates directly to ideas of balance between the opposite polarities of *yin* and *yang* that permeate Chinese society (and to an extent, Japanese as well). These concepts were at the foundation of much of East Asian philosophical thinking, and ultimately underlie people's beliefs about the healthfulness of the foods they eat.

Some of the earliest writing in Japan on the subject of food emerged from what was to become a major cooking tradition in Japan: that of the Zen monasteries. Dōgen (1200–1253), the founder of the Sōtō Zen school, and the man who introduced Zen to Japan, was also the writer of a manual on cookery, the *Tenzō Kyōkun*. His objective, however, was not so much cookery in the modern sense, as a manual on the spiritual relationship between food and religious practice. Later, cookbooks and monographs on the appreciation of food emerged, particularly during the period of urban expansion in the Edo era.

The other stream of thinking about food had to do with the relationship between food and society. Feasts and proper sacrifices of foods underlie much of China's Confucian thinking about social relations with humans as well as with the divine. Food was recognised as a social force par excellence, both for its production – particularly, in East Asia, of the rice, which was the preferred staple – and for its consumption.

Modern writing about food and society has followed two paths. On the one hand have been the numerous writers who have documented changes and the historical development of food patterns such as Tannahil and Mennel, writing on European food history, and Yanagita, in Japan, who, among his other writings on traditional folk customs, also collected data on disappearing food usages and history. More recently, also in Japan, at the National Ethnology Museum, scholars led by Ishige have been tracing the evolution of Japanese and other foods in recent centuries.

Looking at food in broader, world perspective, anthropologists such as Mintz have traced the historical effects of the European addiction to sugar, and Farb and Armelagos, among others, have tried to make sense of the vast material on food customs world-wide.

The social sciences – roughly sociology and anthropology – entered the food arena somewhat late. Moreover, less concerned with food itself, and more with using data from food studies to make points in (rather esoteric) intellectual and theoretical arguments raging in these disciplines, analyses of food have tended to verge on personal vendettas.

One of the first social scientists to seriously consider the issue of food in this century, and certainly the most famous such discussant, was Claude Levi-Strauss. In *Le cru et le cuit* Levi-Strauss combined two perennial French intellectual concerns – how people think, and what people eat – into an argument that reinforced his "structuralist' view of human society. The structuralist view (put briefly, and possibly inaccurately) is that human mental life is based on a binary inclusion/exclusion principle. All human behaviour and culture is a reflection of that dichotomy. That is, human groups, religions, architecture and all other artefacts and sociofacts, reflect that fundamental opposition. Based on this initial (and still unproved, at least to the cold-hearted and empiricism-prone non-French intellectual world) assumption, Levi-Strauss has argued forcefully that food preferences have much to do with a set of principles – the culinary triangle – that derives from his structuralist theory. Put as simply as we can, the "culinary triangle" theory argues that people's foods all fall into roughly three criteria: fresh/natural/wild, cooked/artefactual/civilised, and rotted/dead/uncivilised. Food choices, the use of cooking utensils, and choices of whom to eat with (and whom to eat!) are all based on this simple structure, within which oppositions can be constructed on structured binary lines. Satisfying intellectually as such an approach might be to some, it does little to help understand the empirical and theoretical questions we raise throughout this book.

British and North American social science came on the scene of food studies slightly later. At first, with the exception of nutrition studies which took off in the fifties, much of the work was anecdotal and unfocussed, a minor part of overall social and cultural studies. Such is the case with Farb and Armelagos's attempt to lay the foundations for a discussion in their *Anthropology of Food*, which is less an analysis than a compendium of strange culinary practices, nonetheless at least introduced the issue to these disciplines, steering the study of food away from the study of nutritional practices, which had predominated until then.

Two major views emerged in social science, theoretical corollaries of ongoing debates that initially had nothing to do with food. In one corner, the symbolists, largely headed by Mary Douglas, with which others such as Fischler and Moulin can be included, argue that much of human food culture can be viewed (and, to a degree, explained) by the ways in which individuals and groups organised and elaborated on their intellectual and symbolic worlds. The need for psychic and intellectual order, the desire for separating types of behaviour one from another, all of these made the issue of food an ongoing intellectual concern in all societies. This intellectual concern expressed itself in using food in complex and elaborate *symbolic* ways, to represent, refine, project social realities on the field of social experience.

Douglas's approach, and that of the many who have followed in her footsteps, leads to more complex analysis than would seem at first sight. Within the realm of all food systems (regularised ways of preparing and serving food characteristic of a specific culture), people assign psychological and emotional values – they think of their food symbolically – to their food. This is obvious from the most elementary observation. As Douglas (1982) notes, some food events tend to be highly structured by close and *necessary* (at least for the people involved) association between particular foodstuffs: consider the intimate and necessary relationship between meat and potatoes in North American and British cultures, or the implications of the term "fish-and-chips" or "Christmas dinner." This association between foods in a food event can be extended to the relationship – necessary, permitted, or forbidden – between food events or parts of them, and other aspects of life. For example, food has an important temporal dimension in most cultures. We eat morning, midday, and evening meals, and in some societies such as the Chinese (*dim-sum*), Philippine (*merienda*) and British ("elevenses"), "in-between meals": a temporal cycle that is rarely modified, and which has emerged as a function of economic and social processes. There are also cycles of lower frequency, such as weekly (Sunday dinner in the UK), or yearly (Christmas dinner). This relationship between food and other social events must also be explored in terms of autonomy and unity: how dependent are foods and food events on other social and cultural features, such as seasons or places? Is it proper to eat a dinner in a public place such as a bank, and (at the level of discrete food events) is it a social solecism to drink green tea with red meat? And for the foodstuffs themselves as Douglas notes, we must take account of textures, tastes, how they interrelate, whether they can be prepared in public or must be dealt with in private, and whether these decisions are left open to individuals, whether they have sanctions attached to them, or whether they are socially confined to a class or group.

Douglas and her followers' major intellectual critics were Harris and his students. In a series of essays they argue that human food practices, even those that seemed highly illogical, such as the Hindu ban on meat, the American preference for beef (which some such as Sahlins argued was symbolic) could better be understood from a material viewpoint. That is, Harris and his students argue convincingly, Hindus do not eat their cows not because cows have symbolic value: they do not eat them because the products of living cows – milk, and particularly dung – are of greater value to the poor Indian farmer, than the small amount of meat the cows would yield if slaughtered. Similarly, Americans eat more beef than pork (by a large factor), not because beef is associated with the frontier and the wild days of the West, but because the rise of the railways, on the one hand, and the use of arable land for corn (maize) on the other, made the use of the West's prairies for cattle more profitable, and cheaper, than would have been the case with pigs.

These two viewpoints, which we have presented in rather stark contrast, are in our view not necessarily antithetical. As we shall see subsequently from the Japanese material, people very clearly use their foods in symbolic ways, Yet, at the same time there are often very good identifiable material reasons for food choices and food usages. Both the "materialist" and the "symbolist" views, therefore, can contribute to our understanding of Japanese food culture.

Jack Goody has approached the issue of food from another angle. In *Cooking, Cuisine, and Class*, he argued convincingly that the elaboration of food we call cooking is universal to all human societies. But this universal practice is directly related, and receives an additional twist, by the introduction of social features which essentially divide human societies into two types. On the one hand are those many societies (or parts thereof) in which the energy and other resources in supply are sufficient, or barely more than that, to subsist on. Though a smattering of individuals may have more resources at their command, these are generally dissipated in striving after political gain, the acquisition of force, raising more offspring, or whatever. Such societies are generally labelled "subsistence societies" and most societies in human history have been of this sort. On the other hand, some societies produce surpluses which go well above that needed for the subsistence of its members. As is usual in human societies, someone – having more strength, greater organisational abilities, more force, more brains, or is better situated – comes along and skims off the surplus. These societies tend to be able to afford *specialists*, individuals who do not provide food for themselves or their immediate families, but subsist, as it were, at one remove from subsistence. Rulers (of all stripes and political persuasions) and tax officials are of this kidney. So are professional artists – painters, sculptors, musicians, and cooks – and their assorted hangers on – critics, publishers, cookbook writers, anthropologists. Such societies are *differentiated* societies, and they tend, with time and the multiplication of specialist roles, to become *complex*: roles multiply, become dependent on one another, resources are transmuted into various material and symbolic goods.

Simple societies, says Goody, practice "cooking" – preparing food for consumption usually by heating. Materials are simple, and most are of local derivation, rates of food change are low, and dependent, ultimately, on local climatic and environmental conditions. There is no or little specialisation, no or little differences between members of the society in terms of foods eaten, preparation methods, and so on, even if a section of the populace benefits from greater qualities of food. Complex societies, on the other hand, have a "cuisine" – a complex, rule-bound social systems of food preparation and consumption related inextricably to complex social matrixes in those societies. Among their specialists are some who deal in supplying foods from afar, foods that are rare, or foods that need special costly preparation. There are specialists in food preparation, and others who specialise in food presentation.

There are tensions associated with such class distinctions. Such is the case in both European society (modern or early) as in the dominant East Asian societies, as K.C. Chang (1977) points out. In the modern context, one needs to add that societies which practice a cuisine also have extensive and intensive contacts with other cultures which supply them both with raw materials and with new ideas for their cuisine (among other things).

The relationship between cuisine and its social matrix is complex and derives from the complexity of the internal relationships of such "differentiated" societies. Several of these issues are particularly relevant to the Japanese case. First, there is an increased range of ingredients and menus resulting from contacts with other societies, and from the continuous interplay between food habits of different classes. Second, cuisines which otherwise might become locally specialised, or, as in the case of the Japanese, have become so, become universalised with universal literary access. Simply put, among things people read are cookbooks and cooking magazines. And there is often a link between eating and health, and a public assessment of consumables as bad or good (Goody 1982: 192). Our focus here is therefore on a *cuisine* and how it develops, and not on the rather more restricted realm of "cooking."

2.2 *SOME POINTS OF AGREEMENT*

NOTWITHSTANDING THE (SOMETIMES thunderous) disagreements, some of which have been briefly addressed above, there are some points which, all social scientists interested in food agree, are worth pursuing intellectually.

One point of agreement is that the understanding of any particular food culture must take into account the historical and environmental factors that have brought the elements of that culture into being. This does not imply historical determinism. There is no argument that particular historical or geographical features *necessarily* yield particular cultural features. But there must be a recognition that environments determine agricultural possibilities, and by doing so, limit particular societies from pursuing particular cultural paths. So too, historical factors – political, social, technical, and other processes and developments – must be kept in mind when discussing particular features.

Sociologists spend a great deal of their time trying to understand the norms that drive and direct human activities. To simplify, a norm is a socially expected behaviour in a particular set of circumstances. That norms are "expected" merely means that they are not always received, and to say that they are socially expected, means that different actors, under different circumstances may be expected to behave differently.

In all societies there are sets of enduring "clusters" as it were of norms, which are associated together, and which demand particular behaviours. Some of these "social institutions" have strong immediate effects on individual behaviour and crop up persistently when we talk about food.

Families are clearly a central "locus" – an arena of activity – of food behaviours, as well as a universal social institution. A family is where most humans are first fed, first learn – by example and then by word – about food, proper behaviour in the presence of food, and the ideologies and beliefs associated with food. The household – roughly, the family acting as an economic unit – is the basis for food practices in later life, as well as for food practices, ranging from cooking and eating to changes in food culture.

Other social institutions are important for food culture as well. Two of these are particularly prominent, certainly in the Japanese context. One is school, where a large proportion of youngsters in the twentieth century, receive their socialisation into behaviours outside the home. This includes their exposure to new food patterns, which they learn as part of the school system, as well as from their peers.

Work constitutes another channel of influence on food practices. Where people's lives are highly integrated with their work, and where one's workplace is a major centre of one's daily activities, food inevitably enters into the activities of the organisation in some form.

There is also a clear association between food and class. Those who are more wealthy are likely to have access to better food, more variety, and in greater amounts than others in the same society. As we know from Veblen, such differences are not only substantive, but also expressive: individuals who have wealth wish not only to enjoy it. They also want to demonstrate that they have the wealth, and to separate themselves in overt ways from their social "inferiors." This proves to be the case in food consumption, which, in all societies, simple as well as complex, comes to symbolise and represent differences between classes and between individuals.

The ideological dimension of human life, whether religious belief or social philosophy, affects the consumption of food, its presentation, and its importance. Certainly, in almost all societies, foods have a religious dimension of some sort. Religion almost always is at the basis of justifications of particular food cycles, particularly annual ones, of festivity and restraint. Moreover, the ways in which foods are presented, the ways in which specific foods are consumed, come to assume ritual importance. They come to define, in varied and complex ways, who "we" are, as well as separating "us" from "them."

Foods are universally consumed in cycles: one day replicates another, repeated days are part of annual cycles. These might arise from material needs, such as human physiology and the agricultural environment. However, certainly in modern industrial societies, these cycles are matters of choice, matters of representations of self and of society. Thus, paradoxically, the *symbolic* importance of choice grows as the *material* basis of food choice become less important: we choose foods not because that is what is available, but because particular foods we choose from a large variety say something about what and how we are.

Many authors have pointed out that food is not solely, or even largely, a social and collective issue. It goes, not unnaturally, deeply into the process of being and of becoming an individual. Physiological need, and bodily senses determine, in concert with social learning, what foods are desirable, eaten, enjoyed. Socialisation into enjoying and eating, from the recipient's – that is the individual's – point of view needs to be considered as well.

Part of the experiences individuals undergo in modern food cultures is the search for variety, paradoxically intertwined with a desire for standardisation of experience. The latter, following a well-known phenomenon most people in developed societies have come into contact with, can be labelled "McDonaldisation" (Ritzer 1993), and it affects individual experience and forms it as well. The search for variety of experience is also apparently related to the "keep up with the Joneses" phenomenon, in which individual drives for variety, or for display of wealth, are fuelled by intra-social competition.

Finally, an individual element that must not be forgotten derives from the aesthetic and artistic element in food. The individual artist-chef is under social pressure, as well as her own internal drives, to innovate, to create new art works, to find different channels for aesthetic expression.

The above summary does only scant justice to the width of theoretical insights that have emerged in the study of food. We shall be utilising these ideas as we proceed to make sense of the Japanese data. Certainly, we do not find ourselves agreeing with all that has been said, nor do we intend to settle theoretical debates and conflicts that have been raging for some time. Nonetheless, the overarching theoretical presentation above frames the entirety of this work.

2.3 *THE UTILITY OF THE CONCEPT OF "RULES"*

THROUGHOUT THIS BOOK we make repeated reference to a concept of social and cultural "rules." It is an anthropological conceit (well, of some anthropologists, at any rate) that societies can be viewed *as if* they are composed of consciously and unconsciously known rules, that the "natives" follow. While it is doubtful whether this view does justice to the ways in which people think (Dreyfus [1997] a philosopher and cyberneticist in particular has been scathing about this view and its implications), it is a convenient shorthand for an outside observer to describe what it is the natives (or what the anthropologist *thinks* the natives) are doing. Some of these perceived rules are carried out consciously – individuals know, in any culture, at a conscious level, that, to take a simple example, one uses different tones of voice to children and to adults. Other rules are known unconsciously – who are "adults" and who are "children" – but can be retrieved into conscious knowledge, as for example, when a nosy social scientist ask 'Why?" Of course, knowledge of these "rules" is not fully congruent between individuals, differs in interpretation, and is subject to debate, manipulation, chicanery, and other individual vagaries. Food can be subject to this sort of rendering as well, and it is a useful way to conceptualise how this very complex system we have been describing comes into being at an individual and collective level.

It makes sense to consider food culture in the context of rules for a number of reasons. First, it allows us to more clearly highlight elements of a given food culture, whether for comparative purposes, or so that we can see where such rules lead. Moreover, rules, as we all know, are often enough breached in actual execution, otherwise, of course, we would need neither police nor critics. Rules, for the social scientist, are an outsider's attempt to reach the essence of the actor's norms. Quite often, actors are unconscious of abstracted rule(s): they know, somehow, that things are either wrong or right. One of the experiments we did during the progress of this study illustrates this nicely: asked to place items on a plate or table, Japanese respondents always had a clear idea of right or wrong placement, but could rarely explain why or how they reached that intuitive conclusion.

There are rules for all elements of a food culture. In some areas of life, or for some instances, in some societies, they may be formally stated – "the soup spoon goes outwards of the knife on the right side" – or informally known – "cooked savoury vegetables go with meat." And as such, they are not innate. They must be learned, consciously or unconsciously. How we learn these rules, from whom, and when, therefore, become issues of concern if we try to understand them. Clearly, too, these rules differ, in small details or large, depending on who is doing the teaching, and whom the learning. This is another way of saying that subsets of food rules apply to different parts of the population. And, where we find that many, or most of the rules are followed in the same way throughout a society, we can argue that the society itself is relatively homogenous: something we see in Japanese food culture, and which reflects a great degree of uniformity within Japanese culture as a whole.[1]

That rules are a way to achieve what Elias calls "the civilisation of appetite," arises because certain segments of the population have more power, have more access to the media, and are able to impose their wills to a greater degree on others: their rules prevail. Thus it is in Japan, where local standards of taste remain as cultural codicils, whereas the culture as a whole has accepted the aesthetic and taste canons of a relatively small elite – samurai and merchants – and of the relatively restricted Tokyo area, albeit influenced by more "refined" Kyoto taste and Osaka lavishness. This, the rules of three great cities, and particularly of their wealthier inhabitants, are what is familiar overseas as Japanese cuisine.

2.4 *THE FOOD EVENT AS AN ANALYTICAL PHENOMENON*

Food can be conceptualised in terms of several conceptual issues. The basic phenomenon is that of food itself. The nature of consumed foodstuffs in any society raises a series of interrelated questions: What foodstuffs (that is, edible material) are chosen to make food in any particular society? How is it handled or prepared, a question which raises issues of available technology and manpower.

Food consumption is not haphazard. Food is usually consumed in ritualised settings, with certain people in attendance, and specific rules regarding the event. The issue of events, different for each society, raises a number of questions as well, which we should be able to answer: we should know which foods are associated (or forbidden) with which other foods and why, who participates in which events, who prepares and serves, what determines event timing and repetition, what ideas are associated with foods or arrangements of foods. Closely related, and serving as a bridge to larger issues such as religion and ideology, are questions of timing. When do food events occur? What triggers them? Under what circumstances are they repeated, and by whom, for what reasons?

1 This is not to be taken too far. Though Japanese and foreign scholars have for many years extolled the homogeneity of Japanese society, studies in the past couple of decades have increasingly shown the fissures in Japanese society, and differences due to gender, age, background, place of birth and education. Nonetheless, at least at some levels, Japanese society is far more homogenous than most other nation states.

The foregoing issues also raise questions of broader scope, such as the autonomy of the foods and events, their association with other cultural features, and so on. And at a more complex, and abstract level, we should ask questions of general cultural significance, two of which are particularly important: how is the food system related to the corpus of other arts in the society concerned? And, how does change come about, if at all, and what are its implications, both for the cuisine in question, and, reciprocally, for the culture it is a part of?

To deal with this complex series of questions in an orderly way, we choose, throughout, to focus on what Douglas has called the "food event." Any occasion in which an individual human ingests something orally (to be pedantic) is a *food event.* Using this definition can of course lead into strange byways, ranging from the simplistic bovine-like event of chewing a stick of chewing gum, or more elaborately, a piece of betel nut, to a multiple-course multi-day Chinese Imperial dinner. But within any human food culture, there is to be found a central food event, one which, for the native members themselves, represents the essence of good, appropriate, filling and fulfilling dining. This will usually be defined in terms of the constituents of the food event – a staple, such as rice, a combination of foods, such as the Sunday dinner in Britain – or the presence of a particular set of diners, such as the family. These central, or major food events we shall call "meals" which is more a bow to familiarity than a proper definition. Meals are useful heuristic devices because, at least in all those societies that possess a cuisine (and, we would venture, in all societies) there is such an event. Moreover, methodologically and empirically meals are a useful focus for examination because individuals in societies that have (or "do") meals, can identify them as such (however called). A meal is a central food event, one that, normally, involves a household (if eaten domestically), and one that has a number of qualities associated with it. Meals generally include a central carbohydrate, they have a normative (for the society concerned) structure, they are consumed most often in the domestic sphere, with people who are part of the household. True, each of these terms requires some elaboration and qualification to be useful analytically, but significantly, almost every normal human being can identify such a food event for his culture.

Meals are composed of many elements besides the ingestion of food. And just as the cuisine as a whole is subject to change, so too are its identifiable elements such as meals. Even in France, where meals and mealtimes approach sanctity, there is evidence that meals are losing their structure and centrality. Such changes, as Herpin (1988) and others have shown, affect different social classes to different degrees.

Nonetheless, what characterises meals *overall* is that they are highly structured, very rule-bound events. These rules determine food choice, order of the menu, diners and diner behaviour. And when one speaks of meals, or of a cuisine "changing" one must keep in mind that such changes may affect one, but not others, of the set of rules. In practice, of course, changes in one set of rules, say in the number and order of dishes for a Sunday dinner, will also affect others.

After all, if one is serving fewer dishes in a modern family, the server might need less help, and thus rules about who serves at the table may be changed as well. Moreover, with changes in the realms of work, of relations between sexes and between generations, there are bound to occur changes in such a way that the original format of the meal appears (from a conservative point of view) to be losing its structure. From another point of view, however, participants and potential participants are simply rearranging the rules: they are, in other words, bringing about change.

2.5 *CHANGE IN FOODS*

CLEARLY, AS ALMOST anyone in the latter half of the century has experienced, foods (as well as other cultural features) undergo change. Of course, we are living in a period in human civilisation in which change is particularly noticeable, sharp, and fast. It affects everyone, not always for the better. This is, in a sense, a direct correlate of the idea of cuisine. If food culture did not change, how could members of the elite maintain their supposed separation from the herd? As they reach for different and exotic foodstuffs, as they make their dining arrangements and rituals more complex, in order to highlight their differences, so too do they draw those with less resources into adopting these new fashions. Essentially this implies that change is constantly being generated within the system, whether it relies on exotica imported from abroad, or on elaborating whatever items (material, social, or behavioural) are already in the system. As Clark (1975a, b) observes of 19th century France, the ideas diffuse through participation in restaurant meals, publications, criticism, artistic presentation, literature, and every other media imaginable. In the twentieth century, films, TV, standardisation, international travel, and global marketing can be added. Significantly, this diffusive process which precipitates and carries change, can and does bring about two diametrically opposed results (and Japan experiences both). It brings about a diffusion of elite gastronomy to a wider audience (provided that audience is enjoying other benefits of a complex society, particularly economic ones), yet, at the same time, the standardisation we have spoken of above may also bring about a *reduction* in choice and in sensitivity to choices.

Food, as one of a large number of inter-related cultural elements that make up our society, changes according to general rules that affect everything else, though Mary Douglas has suggested the opposite view, that "pressure of the social system upon the food system will always tend to destroy the autonomy of the latter when a social system is undergoing rapid social change. This has the reactionary implication that social stability is favourable to the development of food as an art form and social change inimical to it." (Douglas 1982: 111–112). As we shall see, at least in the Japanese case, this is not true.

Given too that Japanese society has changed even more radically than most (as the past 150 years of its history demonstrate) one can, and should expect

Japanese food to have changed radically as well. This is indeed the case, as we show throughout the book. Moreover, these changes are still in the process of happening even as this book is read.

Change in food systems, as in any other human area of human culture, is often brought about by endogenous means (or triggered from without, e.g., Chinese migrations overseas have resulted in cross-borrowings between ethnic Chinese and indigenous food systems in Asia). That is, by the innovations proposed and carried out by persons in a society, who, for whatever reason, consciously or unconsciously create a new method, product, social process, in coming to terms with changes in their environment. Such persons may be individuals, or even collectives: several people working on a project, without knowing who was the specific individual innovator.

Much change takes place in the individual exposure to cultural institutions. People learn about change, demand change, because of their experiences as diners, whether at home or in public. If the restaurant is where change is bitten off and swallowed, the domestic kitchen is where changes in food are digested and absorbed. It is here that individuals take their first steps in infancy into the food culture of their society, and it is here where the decision is made – paraphrasing Lenin, people vote with their palates – whether a particular food is acceptable or not. The contrast between restaurants – public eating places – and the home kitchen or dining room is not just the difference between two spheres of activity. It is manifestly a dynamic relationship which, taken as a whole, is a core part of what constitutes any culture's cuisine.

Individual cooks are under contradictory pressures to both maintain norms and standards, and to provide new meals, new taste sensations, whether for their clients, or for their families. The housewife expected to rustle up "something interesting" is, in the micro, expected to be no less ingenious than the three-star chef. Both of them also must operate under the same rules: invent, but with comprehensible and acceptable limits, or your production will not be accepted.

Nonetheless, initiative and innovation, sometimes at very detailed levels, are the order of the day. Many cooks are also *artists*, and like artists in other fields, they are drawn to experiment, to create new things, to push their actions to the limit. This is not restricted to the professionals. Housewives in Japan (and to a far, far lesser though growing degree, househusbands) try new things. New foodstuffs, new foods, new arrangements of the table and of menus. These are all in the realm of individual artistic effort: a response, individual or collective, to the aesthetic drive.

Another source of change derives from pressures generated within a culture, but which do not concern food directly. We deal with this case when we detail changes that have come about in, for example, convenience foods in Japan, due to social factors such as marketing, which are not necessarily food related.

Japanese culture is, and has been for the past century, a society in which change is the norm, rather than the exception. In this, it exemplifies modernity, to an even greater degree than Western societies such as the US (whose fundamental social realities have hardly changed as much) in the past century. These changes – in the size and composition of the family, in the position of women and children in society, in the work regime, in access to means of production, in leisure – drag changes in food along with them. This can be seen everywhere and anywhere in Japan. Some of these changes, and their effects on food, though by no means all, are detailed throughout the book. Many of those are brought as illustrative examples, and more detailed work is needed to uncover even a fair fraction of them.

A third source of change is that from exogenous sources. Whether these are the discovery of a new trade route, as Vasco de Gama did when he started the Portuguese trade with the Spice Islands, or whether it is the introduction of the microwave, curry, or meat eating from abroad, such changes have differing impacts, speeds of absorption and acceptability. As we shall see, Japanese acceptance of new foods is high, but there are definite parameters which determine how and what foods are accepted.

The importance to Japan of overseas trade ties, and of overseas ideas in technology can hardly be overestimated. Japan has also, in parallel, imported foreign ideas in the realms of aesthetics generally, and food specifically. Many of these, as we shall see, have been incorporated to a greater or lesser degree in the corpus of Japanese food culture. Not all of these new items or their sources can be documented, since they tend to derive from multiple sources, and to have been incorporated at different rates and times.

Japan has excelled, for the past thousand years at least, and even before that, in its ability to import and incorporate. Importation of new ideas, Ivan Morris has noted, is almost always followed by a period of closure, during which Japan has incorporated those new ideas and turned them into something that is peculiarly, and undeniably, Japanese. This elegant ability to incorporate outside ideas perhaps is the basis of Japan's strength and cultural viability. A large number of ideas and of technological gadgets have been imported, then given that particular Japanese twist. The realm of technology is easier to identify. From writing and ceramics, which the Japanese imported from their close neighbours and gave particular Japanese flavours to, through guns,[2] to VCRs, micro-chips, and microwave ovens. All of these have been accepted by the Japanese, and adapted to their individual, domestic, or industrial needs. Japanese imported Chinese forms of government, Korean and Chinese religious concepts, European industrial patterns, American management ideas, changed them, and made them uniquely their own. Often these ideas – Quality Circles, Just In Time production – were then re-exported to their places of origin.

2 Japanese first learned about firearms from the Portuguese in 1502. By 1550 there were more guns in Japan (all of local manufacture) than in the whole of Europe at the same time.

2.6 *FOOD AS AN AESTHETIC AND AS ART*

Aesthetics are an important element in any description of food. Aesthetic elements are deeply associated with socially-learned preferences. In the following discussion we intend to try and show how the Japanese view their food culture in its aesthetic terms, and how these terms can be understood by someone from outside Japanese culture. Clearly, aesthetic choices, aesthetic descriptions, and aesthetic ideas are not easy to translate from one culture to another. No less clearly, trying to *interpret* the aesthetics of one culture to others is important. To do so, however, we must first try to describe the phenomenon of aesthetics in an analytical manner.

The origins of food aesthetic must be found in the human physiology. As Brillat-Savarin and later writers have indicated, food must be understood, if it is to be understood at all, from the palate, the tongue, the nasal membranes. Food links the biological characteristics of humanity, and its social impulses. Humans are addicted to sugar (which, as Mintz's [1985] wonderful monograph shows, has had a tremendous impact on human history and demography), salt, and a variety of other flavouring and aromatic additives. By presenting these in varied combinations they indicate both states of being ("I am rich enough to afford this," "Eating this will give strength") and are able to make aesthetic – sensually pleasing – statements. Historically, as more and more flavours were added to the palette, as it were, different statements could be made, and laws of aesthetic presentation could be formulated, whether expressly or as covert rules known only to the cognoscenti. "Good" flavours can of course be learned. Curry (that is, highly spiced Indian food) and the appreciation of curry were *learned* by the British populace over several centuries, first as a result of trading with India, then as result of returned expatriates, and finally, by the waves of immigrants who brought their much hotter cuisine with them. The "dangerous" (as Rozin and Rozin would have it) flavour of hot chillies soon became a desirable aesthetic experience. While this learning was done on a social level, there is evidence to suggest that physiological reactions which are initially inherent in the human organism from birth, are soon modified by learning from parents' reactions, actual experiences, and surrounding environmental pressures. Inevitably, therefore, an individual's appreciation of aesthetic elements in food is tied directly to two factors: human physiology and human society. At the same time, however, an "aesthetic" food probably must also be a *pleasing* food, one that includes elements derived from birth, and possibly even from early human origins.

Moreover, as Barlosius and Manz (1988) argue, an aesthetic is developed not only from the satisfaction of a physiological need, but also from the process of elaborating on that need, providing alternatives and differentiation, all of which are, ultimately, supplied socially rather than individually. The refinement of taste, Barlosius (1987) argues, emerges as a society provides subtle and individual alterations to the sensory stimulation offered to members of a culture. These "alterations-within-rules" provide a number of things. At the physiological level, one would imagine that constant *positive* stimulation is engendered, since the nerve endings are allowed to switch from one sensation to another, which maintains interest. At the individual level, this elaboration is accompanied and also expressed in the form of elaboration on various senses: sight, smell, sound and so on, which are brought together in what appear to humans to be pleasing patterns. At the social level, these different sensual stimuli are accompanied by complex rules: the social persona, no less than the physical one, requires new stimuli to provide interest. Thus the connection between class status and the emergence of both major aestheticism and cuisines is not surprising: it is the wealthy and powerful who, partly to dissociate themselves from their lessers, and partly because they have the means, elaborate on both the foods they eat *and* on the rules of service, presentation, and dining.

Modern industrialised and fast food show another aspect of that pattern: by providing standardised food, they eliminate the subtle variations that hand-made, artistically-oriented foods provide, and by doing so, limit the ability of those who eat those foods to discriminate. In effect, it "de-aestheticises" aspects of life. One has to be *trained* to detect subtleties, it is never inherent, and the standardisation which is an effect of marketing, industrialisation and "rationalisation" of food, is inherently opposed to its aesthetic quality. Though food industrialisation does mean greater accessibility and more gross variety available to all classes, it also, effectively, isolates those who consume food from their aesthetic and culinary heritage, a heritage and culture that is often extremely rich, as Grignon and Grignon's detailed survey of 12,000 French households shows: a process we shall see is occurring in Japan as well.

Aesthetics, in any sphere of life, goes beyond the individual consumer. It may well be an inherent part of our phylogenetic makeup (since there is evidence of aesthetic sense in many hominid species, including *sapiens*, *neanderthalis*, and *habilis*), but the expression and appreciation of aesthetic arts are clearly forged in a social crucible. For the aesthetic purist art is art, immutable (and this, indeed is the position one of the authors here, trained in the arts, takes); for the more sociologically inclined, art is a function of/embedded in a social matrix (and this is the position the other one of us, trained in the social sciences, takes).

An "aesthetic" then, can be viewed as a shared taste, one in which more than one individual participates, and which evokes and involves rules of sensory reception and transmission. Not everyone, perhaps, enjoys oil-heated ova, burned grain, and fermented muscle, but most people can learn to appreciate fried eggs, toast, and ham: one is an "objective" or "etic" biological description, the other a "cultural" or "emic" one. One might evoke equal distaste in a member of any culture, the other would be highly attractive to members of some cultures. So we share, in our smaller or larger islands of common taste, a preference for certain foodstuffs prepared in certain ways. And we are able to judge, based partly on our physiology, but definitely mutated by experience whether the food has been prepared according to the canons we have come to expect.

We find the aesthetic impulse – elaborated to greater or lesser degrees – in all societies. But from a sociological point of view, there is a difference between an aesthetic and an art, which is analogous to the difference between cooking and cuisine. An aesthetic often gives rise to an art, and art – not the appreciation of aesthetic experience, but its codification – is thus a quintessential social phenomenon. In complex societies, where surpluses allow the specialist to exist, we can find artistic expression not as an individual or group expression of aesthetic preferences and sense, but as a social institution, one in which non-artists as well as artists are involved, one in which the economics of the system are complex, and one in which there is an interaction of roles, which inevitably affect the aesthetic. It is particularly important to note that in such a social setting – one of high differentiation and specialisation, and great complexity – the aesthetic is *modified* by social positioning (that is to say, the Delia Smiths and James Beards have more ability to enforce their views than the Joe Bloggses and John Smiths), and, no less importantly, several different aesthetics, of different social classes, sub-cultures, and groups, can happily (more or less) coexist, and, indeed, as Mennel elaborately shows (1982), exchange aesthetic and technical ideas.

This effect is clearly observable in Japan. Economic distribution in Japan before and well into the mid-twentieth century left much of the population in the realm of a subsistence economy. While individuals could, and did, exercise aesthetic taste, expressed often in daily items, the appreciation of art and activities associated with art – specialist producers, critics and professional aesthetes, collections – was limited to the small percentage (circa 15%) of the population who were wealthy, and thus, by internal definition, members (potential or actual) of the art world. Since about the nineteen sixties, however, things have changed. Japan has become wealthy and powerful. No less importantly, income has been better distributed, to the point that over 80% of the Japanese population have been reported to consider themselves part of the middle-classes: an extraordinary achievement in what was a feudal-like country 150 years ago. With this process has occurred a process of "samuraisation" in which members of much of the society have adopted the aesthetic preferences of what used to be the politico-military elite. Flower arranging, Tea-ceremony, scroll-collecting, pottery collecting have become common achievements, indeed, prerequisites for any normal social and cultural life. Art, in short, has become popular. This of course has not skipped food: the desires and demands of the upper classes that Mennel documents so well, have been experienced, and indeed are craved by all. The aesthetic judgements of food and other aesthetic experiences are available to virtually everyone. A similar process has occurred elsewhere. The French bourgeoisie enhanced their cultural position partly, at least, by adopting the *grande cuisine* of the *ancièn regime*. By associating themselves with a (suitably modified) grand tradition, the French bourgeois shared in the grand tradition, became, in effect, owners of it, just as the modern Japanese middle-classes have.

Inasmuch as the aesthetic experience is an individual one, how can it be characterised and examined? After all, "*chacun à son goût*" and "*de coloribus et gustibus non est disputandum*" and yet, individuals are trained towards (and away from) certain aesthetic evaluations. Food is, particularly but not solely in complex societies, an aesthetic experience. In differentiated and complex societies, where a preserved and philosophical aesthetic can emerge (since only differentiated societies, with their excess resources, can produce the necessary social specialisation) the cooking aesthetic can also become an "art." This does not mean that complex societies, whether the Aztec, the Chinese, modern Europeans or Japanese, are the only ones equipped to understand and appreciate art, nor that they are the only ones to enjoy good cooking. It *does* mean that they have the resources to devote to producing specialists who do nothing but art (if only as art critic). When we address the question of food as art, we need to ask then "How does the sensory experience translate itself into an aesthetic?" and "How does the aesthetic become art?"

One of the first to think actively on the issue of the relationship between the individual as an animal appetite, and as a thinking (and thus "enjoying") being, and as a member of a society was Brillat-Savarin. His writing is notably devoid of most *answers* (except, perhaps, for his marvellous recipe for a cure for sexual exhaustion: Viagra addicts take note!) but full of important questions. The most significant of which is embodied in the French title of his magnum opus: La *physiologie* du goût (emphasis ours). We are unable to divorce social experience from sensory-personal experience, says Brillat-Savarin, and nowhere is this more obvious than in the realm of food. This does, however, pose a problem for a form of analysis that is quintessentially social. How does one deal with the realm of the personal *and then* translate it into the general? While this problem is an endemic methodological one – the issue of reliability – it is most strongly highlighted here, where every experience, every food event *at the sensory level* is a transitory one. There is no way to record a food event. And since these events are so personal, so intimate, so tied, as any psychologist will tell one, to primary feelings and infant emotions and satisfactions, they must be crucial for understanding how people function and why.

In the event, the solution to that problem is not one we can deal with fully. The only way that it *can* be dealt with, is by comparing personal experiences, and trying to translate them into some sort of common denominator, in the hope that the reader has similar physiological equipment and understanding. Inevitably, therefore, part of the method employed here is to expose the authors to a very great degree. This is not narcissism nor exhibitionism. It assumes, as a methodological device, that human beings share some inner sensory stimuli, and that, by analogy if by no other means, such experiences can be transferred from one to another. This can lead, as in the case of oenology to an over-proliferation of technical terminology which become in-group and initiate mysteries. The Japanese language does that as well. It has numerous words for textures which Europeans have no linguistic equivalents for. These Japanese terms differ from the oenological ones in that they tend to be onomatopoeic, rather than used as analogies, e.g. "flinty" as a oenological term for harsh, and in contrast *pari-pari* for substances that yield crunchily to the teeth.

2.7 *FOOD CULTURE AND TOTAL CULTURE*

WHEN CONSIDERING CULTURE, particularly public culture which crosses class lines and yet is mutated by this crossing, we should make a distinction, one pioneered by Alfred Kroeber, between *culture,* and *fashion.* Roughly, for our purposes these are graduated "shallower" instances of the same thing: of the ways in which individuals and their social surroundings interact to make a collective whole. The distinction is particularly significant, because it points out that people make *choices* about their cultural being. They do not necessarily think of it as "culture" (though many Japanese do) but by making these choices they are creating culture. Within this culture, fashion moves at a quicker pace, picking up and dropping items and behaviours through some of the mechanisms that have been discussed above. And even fashion has its internal waves – its modes – which add both coherence and instability to the whole.

What is particularly important here is that these expressive and visible aspects of a culture are intimately related to aspects of the total society. They can, of course, be divorced from a society, particularly where artefacts are concerned. We do, after all, enjoy Greek sculpture, Inca weaving, and T'ang pottery, even though the societies that produced these are long gone. But the living, changing movement of these artefacts and their creation are intimately linked to features in those particular societies. To add a level of enjoyment, we must have at least a minimal understanding of the social and environmental backgrounds which brought these – expressions of aesthetic impulse moulded by social factors – to life.

In the realm of food, most particularly in the exploration we are going to make of a contemporary food culture, we inevitably must try to understand something of the surroundings of the food culture described. Very roughly speaking, food in this book will be related to two kinds of social factors. At the micro level are the influence of institutions that impinge in an immediate fashion on individuals in Japanese society (as they do, in their local forms, on everyone anywhere) such as shops, families, and the media. At the macro level are features that affect individuals at second hand, and that derive from more overarching institutions.

At the level of individual exposure to specific institutions, individuals experience food in three broad settings: at home, at school, and at public eating places which, for the time being, we'll call restaurants. All of these institutions are, sometimes simultaneously, sometimes alternately, conservative and radical. That is, they retain food practices, but also serve as a channel for food changes.

There are two institutions directly concerned with food with which we deal extensively here. One of these is the household – the domestic and private realm and the other is the public realm of the "restaurant," that is, the public eating house. It is these two institutions in which most *individual* experience of food is located for the average member of Japanese society. True, other institutions may, and do have a major effect. Notable are the school system, where, particularly in the early years of education, students receive school lunches from the state, and by doing so, learn a "standard" (and also changing) Japanese food culture, for good or ill. Marketing – shops, wholesalers, producers, importers – also play a part, even a major part, in the making of Japan's food culture. But individuals come into contact with food there more indirectly. Nonetheless, the household and "restaurant" are *the* major loci where food, in its immediately edible form, is consumed, dealt with, prepared, for most individuals. Thus, though we make extensive reference to other institutions, those mentioned here and others, we focus primarily on the two major food foci.

Choices in food culture are clearly related to, sometimes (as we shall see in food fads) a direct result of, macro-factors in the society. Industrial needs, sometimes dictated by a combination of financial, and political concerns, determine what foods are available, what not. Meat is expensive in Japan *partly* because, though demand and supply are both high, supply from overseas is restricted.

Major trends in the society also play a role and must be accounted for. Ideological considerations such as nationalism, more individual ones such as fear of pollution, particular fashions and fads in other realms of activity that sweep society, all of these affect what people eat, what they think about what they eat, and how they deal with their food and its ancillary issues. To add to all this, technological changes, their distribution affected by economic issues which are *not* always related to food, also determine, sometimes very strongly, how a food culture develops, and what it chooses to consume, what raw materials are available, even, sometimes, how people feel about particular foods or foodstuffs.

2.8 *A STRUCTURED VIEW OF JAPANESE FOOD*

A MAJOR ELEMENT in this book has to do with changes in Japanese cuisine. Many of the foods and food-related issues we describe revolve around issues of change. Our own view of changes in Japanese food is strongly stimulated by the works of Mennel, Goody, and Clark. Broadly speaking, Mennel and Goody separately argue that upper classes, eager to distance themselves from the lower, elaborate on their food culture by the introduction of expensive new substances and processes, by the elaboration of dining rules, and by social exclusion practices in their food events. Lower classes retaliate, when they can, by becoming wealthier, and adopting the customs of the elite, which then tries to re-invent their exclusivity. Clark's detailed model shows how French cuisine, as an aspect of

French culture, evolved originally from the aristocratic culture before the Revolution, became a means for upwardly mobile bourgeoisie to emulate the elite, and was codified and elaborated by chefs in public eating houses, and then brought to the public through the growing influence of the media: journalists, feullitonists, and even fiction authors.

And what happens when, as in the Japanese case, an entire society "moves up in the world" as it were? Then we find that, with the intrusion of modern media and communication, an abundance of resources, and a willingness to learn and adapt. The entire society emulates the behaviour of the elites, and, specifically, of former, no longer extant elites: a solution which keeps a certain balance, and lowers the tension between the classes as well. This process, one we have called "samuraisation" after the class which, though no longer extant, is still emulated to some degree, is what has happened in Japanese society.

A mechanism similar to that in the French case operates within Japanese society to create, structure, and ultimately change Japanese cuisine as well. Moreover, the model of change that we posit here, assumes the intervening stages inherent in a number of modern institutions. Media are one important element, since journals, magazine, books, TV, all contribute to awareness of new things, and to their domestic adoption. Some social institutions that are peculiar to Japanese society play a part as well. This is the case, for instance, with the high incidence of *gaishoku* (eating out) that all Japanese are exposed to. Thus restaurants and bars become agents of change in the food realm.

Exogenous change (at least in food, and probably in other areas of life in Japan as well) involves a process whereby an item or cultural idea enters Japanese society – through returning Japanese, exposure to media, meeting foreigners – and then may be picked up as a curiosity by a limited segment of the population. As the item is interpreted and reinterpreted by Japanese users, more and more *Japanese* content is added on: social usage, decoration and presentation, associated social practices, and even substantial changes in taste, texture, size, and so on. Once such an object is "Japanised" it is ready to be broadcast to the population at large, who are able to integrate it into the vast array of cultural items at their disposal because it has acceptable hallmarks of Japanese use. The dispersion agents, in the case of food, are primarily eating places and the media, who, particularly if sufficiently stimulated by commercial interests (such as importers) find themselves leading a spurt of popularity for that dish or cultural item. This is the case, in recent years, with items ranging through Italian desserts (tiramisu), Southeast Asian sweets (*nata de coco*), and Middle Eastern vegetables (*morohēya*).

Throughout this process of change, however, whether from indigenous or exogenous sources, Japanese cuisine has managed to maintain and protect its own inherent, basic characteristics. These do not consist in the usage of particular foods or preparation methods, but in an underlying philosophy on the one hand, and a particular *cluster* of features on the other.

READINGS FOR CHAPTER 2

Clark, Priscilla P. 1975a, b "Thoughts for food: French cuisine and French culture".
Douglas, Mary 1982 "Food as a system of communication".
Farb, Peter and George Armelagos 1980 *Consuming Passions: The Anthropology of Eating.*
Fischler, Claude 1988 "Food, self and identity".
Goody, Jack 1982 *Cooking, Cuisine, and Class.*
Grignon, Claude and Christiane Grignon, 1980 "Styles d'alimentation et gouts populaires".
Harris, Marvin 1988 *Good to eat: Riddles of Food and Culture.*
Mennell, Stephen 1987 "On the civilizing of appetite".
Elias, Norbert 1982 *The Civilizing Process.*
Ritzer, George 1993 *The McDonaldization of Society: An Investigation into the Changing Character of Contemporary Social Life.*

3 Japanese Food in its Background

No cuisine or food culture can be understood unless the historical, geographical, social, and intellectual bases are understood as well. This does not deny the importance of symbolic and cognitive issues. To the contrary, we want to show here how concrete situations affect and interact with symbolic ones. Not only is a brief historical overview necessary, but socio-historical aspects of Japan are an important element in understanding how cultural change – in food as well as other aspects of Japan – is generated and maintained. We have restricted the discussion in this chapter to issues that have direct bearing on the main theme. This includes not only historical issues, but some discussion of prominent institutions in Japanese society: the matrix, as it were, within which Japanese cuisine exists.

3.1 *GEOGRAPHY AND HISTORY*

Two geographical features dominate the history (including the culinary history) of Japan. First is the topographical and climatic nature of the Japanese islands, second is the enormous cultural influence from the mainland, specifically from China and Korea, and later from Europe and America. Both of these issues feature prominently not only factually, but also in Japanese thinking. Better- and less-educated Japanese are prone to discussing geographical and historical hypotheses, particularly over cups of saké or glasses of beer, once they have captured a willing foreign ear. Clearly therefore, these issues are both "etic" (objectively identifiable) and "emic" (conscious or unconscious expressions of cultural concern).

The Japanese archipelago comprises four major islands (from largest to smallest: Honshu, Kyushu, Hokkaido, Shikoku) and thousands of smaller ones, many of them populated. At the closest distance it is only about 100 km from Korea on the Asian mainland. To the south, a chain of islands extends through the Ryukyus (Okinawa) and Taiwan to the Philippines and Indonesia. To the north, the island of Hokkaido is separated from its nearest major neighbour, the island of Sakhalin by a narrow straight, and Sakhalin is in turn separated from the Asian mainland north of Manchuria by another narrow body of water.

Thus, anyone with even the simplest technological means at his disposal can easily visit Japan (and the reverse) from the mainland, and many came to settle. This has had a profound influence on the Japanese and their culture. People migrated to Japan in prehistoric times across each of the three narrow straits, bringing with them crops and ways of life that blended over the millennia into the Japan of history. In historical times most of the influence has been across the straits from Korea, sometimes from China via Korea, and sometimes directly from China. Writing, pottery, metal work, and, inevitably, cooking methods and preferences were introduced in that way, assimilated, and made "Japanese."

The climate in Japan varies from the subtropical in southern Kyushu[1] to the sub-polar in northern Hokkaido. Rice is today grown almost as far north as Asahikawa in mid-Hokkaido. Tropical fruit and sugar-cane are grown in southern Kyushu and the Ryukyus. Nonetheless, the combination of natural resources, common topography, and lengthy human usage make of the island chain a relatively homogenous area for our purposes, something particularly true since the homogenisation of the Japanese countryside after World War II. Characterised by hot and humid summers and cool winters, the climate is strongly affected by heavy monsoon downpours during the early summer months. There is an abundance of flowing water (though few navigable waters, and the existence of difficult mountain ranges and seas has meant some local isolation) and rich arable land has historically been the basis of the economy.

The influence of the Asian land mass has expressed itself in both natural and cultivated flora, the most important of which, in cultural terms, is the rice plant (*Oryza sativa*). Rice has been the mainstay of the Japanese diet, at least nominally, since its prehistoric introduction (even if many poor peasants had no access to it as food for political reasons during some historical periods such as the Edo era). Other grains such as millet and buckwheat, and more recent crops such as sweet potatoes and wheat have come a poor second in terms of cultural preference.

Cultivated paddy rice requires a great deal of effort and social co-operation, which has led many writers to conclude that its cultivation has formed the basis for Japanese norms of co-operative organisation originating in the village. Certainly rice has penetrated the culinary culture to such an extent that, in common with other Asian cultures, the word for a proper meal is "boiled rice." Rice cultivation was encouraged by the authorities since the emergence of the Japanese state in the eighth century AD, and increasing rice yield and rice area was the objective of any well-meaning, serious government until very recently.

1 We ignore Okinawa (the Ryukyu Islands) for two reasons. First, because its culture differs in some important respects from that of mainland Japan. Second, because the culinary history of Okinawa, and other relevant data were not accessible to us during the research for this volume.

3.2 *HISTORICAL MATRIX*

The japanese state which emerged in the Yamato plain during the seventh century spread its aegis through the islands, completing its domination of the northernmost island, Hokkaido, only in the eighteenth century. Rice culture and the sinified aspects of metropolitan culture, including the cultivation of vegetables, fruits, and flowers from local and mainland origins, were spread by this integration. Local crops and specialities continued to be raised and consumed, some of them finding their way into the national cuisine, others having a more local distribution.

The rise of a large aristocratic-bureaucratic state from the eighth to the twelfth centuries brought about refinements in arts and aesthetic ideas. Some of these were heavily influenced by Chinese ideas in religion and writing. Others had native origins. The aristocratic state crumbled under its own inconsistencies, and was succeeded by a military-bureaucratic form of government, the *bakufu*. Run by military men from the provinces, removed from the luxuries of the court in Heian-Kyo (later Kyoto), the *bakufu* began as an austere attempt to foster warrior virtues of simplicity and restraint. Very soon, however, the military caste developed its own aesthetic, different from and rivalling that of the imperial court. In the fifteenth century large merchant-populated cities began emerging in Japan. These – Osaka, Nagasaki, and Edo – became the cradles of a third aesthetic, that of the townsman and merchant. Edo, the capital of the *bakufu* under the Tokugawa *shoguns*, was a meeting point exemplifying the crossing of austere samurai living with ostentatious, sumptuous merchant extravagances. The mingling of these different ideas and social classes brought forth a mix of restraint and opulence, a demand for perfection in small details, and a solid, well-established set of social, cultural, and aesthetic behaviours in all areas of life. During this latter period, Japanese society was organised into a formal system of four classes: at the top, the scholar-warriors (*bushi*) from whom came the "retainer" officials (*samurai*), below them the farmers (about 80% of the population), then craftsmen, with merchants at the bottom. These divisions reflected formal Confucian ideology, rather than actual power or wealth in the society. The four strata were formally distinct and impermeable, though in practice marriages and economic alliances were contracted between them, and the distinctions were not as sharp as the government pretended to believe. Two other classes existed as well in practice: the *kuge*, a tiny group of aristocrats around the Imperial court in Kyoto, and a much larger group, *hinin*, the outcasts. These included workers in leather and dead animals (*Eta*), nomadic foresters, and others. Each of these classes has had an impact on Japanese cuisine. This impact derived both from their economic and political situation, and, in some cases, from the ideology that maintained them.

Bushi ideology (whether they actually lived up to it is a different matter) was one of frugality and what we today would call minimalism. A samurai was supposed to be content with his lot, be it a ball of rice or a feast. Moreover, a samurai had to hold himself ready at all times to protect himself and his lord, and to be on constant alert. One of Michael's teachers recalled that *his* teacher, who had grown up in this ethos, would leap up in the middle of a meal and jam a student's rice bowl into his mouth, if the student's vigilance lapsed for a second, or if the rim of the bowl covered his eyes and obscured his vision. Samurai had, by reasons of this ideology, to develop practices in terms of the foods they ate (small quantities, no elaboration) and in the ways in which they ate.[2]

The merchant and craftsman ethos was pre-eminently (particularly during the Edo period) that of townsmen, urbanites who delighted in the pleasures and enjoyment of their urban surroundings,. The merchants, being richer, had the wherewithal to show off their wealth, to display ostentatiously what they had won, against the odds and the official state ideology. Craftsmen delighted, in their turn, in displaying their skills, and in putting those skills to uses that the powers-that-be, "puritanical" (in that they considered it inappropriate and morally wrong for commoners to enjoy privileges that heretofore had been those of their 'betters') and serious as they could be, would have frowned on. The result was an explosion of ingenuity and ostentation in foods as in everything else.

Farmers subsisted largely on what rice the taxman left, on millet or, after the introduction by Europeans in the sixteenth century, sweet potatoes. Farmer diet included anything edible, and required the application of skill and forethought to preservation and preparation of foods, to low use of expensive fuel, and to frugality. Food sources for farmers and rural people included primarily the crops they raised in paddy, dry fields, and orchards, but also the product of streams, sea, and mountain. In other words, there was a balance between cultivated foods and wild ones. Overall, however, the diet of farmers was a poor one, consisting largely of some form of grain (not necessarily rice), and vegetables, which in the winter were pickled, more often than not.

For well over five hundred years, Japan had been divided into large feudal fiefs – *han* – which were often isolated from one another by geography and the works of men. The barriers between the *han* were patrolled ferociously. People lacking a pass signed by their neighbourhood Buddhist temple and countersigned by the *han* officials, were turned away from the barriers, liable to arrest and questioning. The result was the emergence of several distinct cuisines in different areas of the country. Much of the difference was the result of different *han* ecologies. For example, the predominance of sweet potato in the menus of the warm Kyushu areas, or of specific fish dishes such as stews in those of the colder north. Some, however, was due to the intentional socio-political isolation of the *han* by their rulers: the governments were, quite often and for good reasons,

2 One example is the requirement of *bushi* that they sit in *seiza*, that is, on their knees. This, explained one contemporary teacher, was because rising to one's feet to defend oneself *even when eating* was easier than doing so when sitting tailor-fashion, with one's feet crossed.

afraid of forces uniting against it, whether peasants or *bushi* of different areas. The local *daimyō* were as anxious to ensure isolation as a means of maintaining their independence from the central government.

From the seventeenth century a great leveller and exchanger of cuisines and cooking techniques emerged in the form of the city of Edo. The Tokugawa family assumed control of Japan in the early seventeenth century, continuing and elaborating on the system of isolating *han* from one another. However, to ensure compliance with its rule, the Tokugawa *bakufu*, or military government, required each *daimyō* to spend stipulated amounts of time each year at the capital, Edo. With their hungry retainers, they provided demand for non-Edo foods, which found outlet in speciality foods restaurants: the regional cookeries of their day, and the precursor of specialist regional restaurants today.

3.3 *RELIGION*

ANOTHER FACTOR – RELIGION – was also influential in determining the shape of Japanese cuisine. Unusually to Western eyes, two great religions – Shintō and Buddhism – coexist in Japan, to the point that most Japanese adhere to both. Shintō, the original religion of the Japanese people is a belief that centres around ideas of naturalism and purity. Deities – *kami* – being purer than humans, humans must strive to emulate them. Shintō also lays great emphasis on natural purity and natural offerings to the gods, so that offerings were expected to come from the traditional sources, and represent the essence of purity. This is not to say that a practical side was missing, as can be seen from the following event witnessed during the preparation for a festival:

> The priest, Mr. Asano, came out of his house, walked to the small shrine, and considered the offerings. On high-footed wooden trays lay a series of gifts. A mound of raw rice on one. On another a luscious pyramid of crisp local Star King apples. Several Chinese cabbages on a third. A large moon-shaped *mochi* rice cake on another. Pride of place was given to a large fresh *katsuo* (bonito), its eyes gleaming, its fins still slightly moving as its paler underbelly pulsed.
>
> "Wonderful, wonderful," sighed the priest, his face aglow.
>
> "So you think the *kami* (deities) will be pleased?" asked one of the men from the neighbourhood association, who had arranged the offerings.
>
> Mr. Asano smiled. "No, I was just thinking that this is exactly the *shun* (peak season) for *katsuo*, and that this marvellous fish will be absolutely delicious at the *naorai* (ritual feast)."

The *kami* did, indeed get the essence, but the more material part of the offerings went for a feast for the organisers and worshippers. Unsurprisingly, the modes of presentation, and the types of food required in these services, percolate through the population and create a structure of demand for certain types of produce and arrangements.

Buddhism, an import from India via China and Korea, has been thriving in Japan since the seventh century. It complements Shintō in that its major concerns are the afterlife, and like Shintō, Buddhism requires elaborate offerings of food. Buddhism has contributed to Japanese food both directly and indirectly. Directly, because the requirement for flower offerings, as well as for sweet foods, has brought about a passion for flowers among most Japanese, and a thriving confectionary industry about which more later. Most prominently, however, Buddhism's preference for vegetarian products has meant that Japan has evolved one of the most complex and elaborate vegetarian cuisines in the world. This has reached its apex in *kaiseki ryōri*, the food presented during lengthy Tea ceremonies, which owes its existence and aesthetic background directly to Zen, one of the many forms of Japanese Buddhism.

In sum, Japanese religions have contributed two important things to Japanese cuisine. On the one hand they have formed the ideational and aesthetic basis for many of the preparation and presentation ideas implicit in, and part of, Japanese cuisine: freshness, balance, restraint, all owe a great deal to this tradition. On the other hand, due to their ideas and practices, these religions have also been the foundry in which many prominent dishes have been created, from purely vegetarian tofu dishes, to rich lengthy feasts.

3.4 *GAIJIN AT THE GATES: EXTERNAL INFLUENCES*

JAPAN HAS HISTORICALLY been a borrower. This is no less true in the realm of food than it is in the realms of electronics, law, or entertainment. At the same time, Japan has always been an *innovator* in the sense that the Japanese have absorbed, then modified their imports. Here too, the same is true of Japanese food, which contains elements from the cultures with which the Japanese have come into contact. This is to say that two treasured popular beliefs, one foreign the other Japanese, must be closely examined. It has been a commonplace among many commentators on modern Japan, that Japanese culture is not "innovative." It has been argued that the Japanese have borrowed every element of their culture and merely modified it: something that is particularly galling (during the days of Japan's almost miraculous industrial growth) to Japan's commercial competitors. On the other hand, some Japanese ideologists and social scientists have argued that Japan is a unique case, a unique cultural entity. Both of these viewpoints are both right and wrong: in the absolute sense, *every* culture is both unique (the cluster of traits it displays are not replicated in other cultures) and a borrower (it builds on ideas from elsewhere). But the borrower-innovator debate is important because of what it tells us about the people, or views, conducting it. For a great many Westerners, Japan has been perceived as a (might one say, convenient) threat. From its successful resistance to European colonialism in the sixteenth century, through its rapid industrialisation and rise to a world power in the twentieth, it has been portrayed as a predator: industrial, political, military, and cultural. And as an outsider, it has never been forgiven (at least by European cultures, which include, of course the US) for being the first, and most presumptuous upstart.[3]

The other side of the ideological barrier is somewhat similar. The idea that Japanese cultural institutions are unique not only as individual instances, but are in a class all their own is undoubtedly linked to the *uncertainty* and sense of discomfort Japanese intellectuals feel about Japan's success. Japan *has* borrowed, continually and incessantly, and it *has* been overshadowed, politically, intellectually and militarily, by China, by Europe, and more recently the US. It is not particularly surprising that a view which espouses Japan's uniqueness – and therefore, overtly and covertly, the idea that Japan must be judged by unique standards – has become prevalent in *some* intellectual circles.

The most pervasive influence over Japanese culture for well over a thousand years, however, has been China. The influence, starting in the sixth century and progressively growing stronger, was brought about largely by Japanese fascination with the giant complex culture to their west. Japanese political systems were borrowed wholeheartedly from China in much the same way as British jurisprudence still owes much to its several-times-removed Roman predecessor. Political ideas, as pervasive as mutual responsibility, hierarchy and the sacredness of order, derived, ultimately, from Chinese conceptions. These conceptions spun over to material issues, whether the architecture of palaces, city planning (the old city of Kyoto is based to this day on the north-south grid pattern of the ideal Chinese city), porcelain, writing, and the arts. Significantly, in each case, Japanese inventiveness produced localised variants of the Chinese originals, which, at the very least, were far better adapted to Japan, whether to its weather and climate, its language, or its political life.[4]

In the realm of food, the methods of rice cultivation adopted by the Japanese probably had their origins in China, as do some of the other foodstuffs, notably the soy bean, which, in its various guises, as curd (tofu), or condiment (*shoyu* [soy sauce] or *miso* [bean paste]) is another of the staples of the Japanese kitchen. The use of the common Japanese eating utensils – chopsticks and bowl – derive ultimately from China as well.

---

3 A case in point is the tremendous anti-Japanese feeling still current in the UK, as compared to anti-German feeling. It is insufficient to explain that on the basis of the treatment of prisoners-of-war during World War II: prisoners of war were treated badly by the Japanese (among others) but certainly not only the Japanese, and yet that is constantly brought up. It is quite likely that the attitude of the British *public* (that is, not of the prisoners themselves, or their families, who have good cause) has to do with the fact that the rise of Japanese imperial aggression coincided with the decline and fall of British imperial aggression and pretensions. Not only were the Japanese rivals, but they were *Asian* rivals, beating the British at their own game.

4 And, in some cases such as the Tea ceremony, ensured its survival when, due to political upheavals, the Chinese original disappeared or became moribund.

Here is the place to underline the fact that the Japanese did not copy blindly. Compare for instance Chinese and Japanese chopsticks. The former are longer, commonly have a rounded cross-section, and the better makes are of ivory or expensive woods. Japanese chopsticks are shorter, often of a square cross-section, and made preferably, even in the most expensive eating places, of materials that can be disposed of: wooden *waribashi* in which a piece of wood is sawn almost in two lengthwise, to be finally split by the diner,[5] or green bamboo in more expensive places.

Korea came into contact with Japan even before China, and the Japanese debt to Korean culture is inestimable. Certainly, many of the Chinese influences we deal with were filtered first through Korea, before reaching Japan. The argument about who produced which idea first is here immaterial. The two countries share foodstuffs such as forms of sushi (Kor.: *kimpap* [*makizushi*] or *chupap* [*nigirizushi*]), types of cooking, and some modes of cooking. They differ in many large and small things, ranging from the composition of utensils (metal and ceramic in Korea, wood and ceramic in Japan), to the spiciness of the food. The influence extends to the aesthetic, in that misshapen, ordinary Korean rice bowls became collectibles for Tea ceremony devotees, and, by extension, helped set the aesthetic values for pottery in general.

Much of this influence is owed to the sad circumstances of the repeated attempts by Japanese warlords – the Meiji government was the most successful of these, though far from the only one – to occupy Korea. In doing so, they plundered not only objects of value, but also brought back with them Korean craftsmen, who contributed immeasurably to Japanese technical and aesthetic knowledge.

Since the early sixteenth century, Japan has been exposed to the West. Roughly speaking, the food influences came about in three great waves. In each case, Western foods were adopted by the Japanese, modified, and eventually became Japanese foods in their own right. The first wave was during the Aizu-Momoyama period of civil war. The influences then (culinarily speaking) were mainly from the Portuguese and Spanish. Foodstuffs include the humble sweet-potato, maize, and peppers. In the realm of cooked foods we find baked cakes – *kasutera* – and the by-now completely Japanised *tempura* (deep batter frying) introduced by the Portuguese. The second wave occurred after Japan was opened to the rest of the world at the end of the Edo period. At that time, the Japanese started a wide-sweeping series of changes in their food habits, as they tried to accommodate themselves to the West. Meat in a variety of forms, and some "Japanese" dishes – *karē-raisu* and *tonkatsu* – come down from that period. The third period occurred after World War II. Characterised at first by austerity, by the seventies, the Japanese were experimenting with major changes in their diet, ranging from the introduction of haute cuisine to convenience foods, and trying

5 The sexual implications – of "splitting" a virginity – are not lost on the Japanese, and the subject of much nudge-nudge wink-wink in male drinking circles and hostess bars.

virtually everything in between. What characterises almost all those changes, is not that they were introduced into Japan, but that in almost each case, once sufficient time had past, these foods became quintessentially Japanese, and this came about because the Japanese were able to modify those foods to their own taste.

Kasutera is one such example. It is, in practice, a sponge cake. But what a sponge cake! High, deep yellow, and sumptuous, it has been the pride and joy of Nagasaki, where the Spanish, Portuguese and Dutch influence was strongest in the sixteenth and later centuries. Bakeries specialising in nothing more than *kasutera* abound, and the sheer artistry imposed on something so apparently mundane is probably unique to Japanese culture. The same is true of another Western dish with a peculiar history: *karē-raisu*. British colonial rulers and traders developed a taste for spicy Indian foods, ones they often generically called *curry*, a word deriving from a Southern Indian vegetarian "stew." Transplanted to Japan when that country opened its doors for exploitation in the mid-eighteenth century, some of the British traders and diplomats instructed their Japanese domestic staff in the preparation of the food. Transferred by cooks who had worked in the Yokohama foreign colony, it soon became modified, and very popular food indeed, to the point that an early Japanese food critic (circa 1890) extolled it as the food of the future, one that would bring Japan from an age of culinary barbarism to culinary and healthful heights of modernity. In the same vein, the ability of the average Japanese to consume Western foods in Western ways has brought about an innovative dairy industry in Japan, in which delights such as slices of butter studded with raisins, and strawberry-flavoured cheeses, as well as more conventional excellent Camembert-type cheeses are a consumer staple.

By far the most ubiquitous introduction in post-war affluent Japan were Western fast-food corporations. McDonald's, Kentucky Fried Chicken, and their various competitors and emulators flourished, as Japanese youth flocked to the adapted familiarity of these forms of food and eating. Some changes were of course inevitable, in advertising, presentation, and even the flavour and make-up of the product.[6] The degree to which these introductions have affected the *cuisine* of Japan is difficult to assess. It has, however, affected the *food culture* inasmuch as in terms of volume such fast-food places provide competition for the traditional take-away and snack foods, which have enjoyed large followings for centuries.

The desire for Western food has often been a phenomenon associated with the desire to be modern, to be become "internationalised" in Japanese society. In the days of Japan's (perceived) political and economic inferiority to the West, such food choices were, in a sense, political statements. Being "internationalist" meant associating oneself with European culture, partly because European

6 For an excellent film of the process by which a large food franchise adapts itself to Japan, see "The Colonel Comes to Japan."

culture was a model to be emulated. In recent decades, however, "internationalism" has an added dimension. In the world of food culture, "Whatever is not Japanese, Korean, Chinese, Indian, American, French, Italian cooking, is ethnic," as a Japanese informant pronounced. In nineties Japan, ethnic food is as common as hamburger. This may range from the exotica of Ethiopian cooking, Egyptian pot-herbs, and Turkish coffee, to the more commonplace Thai soups and relishes. Everything and almost anything can find its place in the Japanese kitchen, or plate. Thus the use of Western, South Asian, and Latin American herbs and spices, which would not normally be found in traditional Japanese cooking, is to be found today in many homes. And individuals will try a variety of new foods suggested by the media, by their neighbourhood shop, by a restaurant or pub they go to.

Families eat outside the home, and their children bring in new ideas for dishes, some Japanese, some not. The older generation, one must remember, grew up in an atmosphere of restraint and deprivation. There was not much to choose from even if you had the money. However, the children are growing up in a very affluent society. As a consequence, there are recognisable differences between children and their parents. Younger people on the one hand tend to not have the ability to appreciate the subtlety of Japanese foods. On the other hand, they demand and have more experience with Western foods and other "exotic" edibles.

3.5 *THE BUSINESS OF FOOD*

The issue of food in the modern world cannot be discussed, let alone understood without some understanding of the commercial and industrial processes that underlie much of modern food habits. The average Japanese household does not raise its own food any more than the average European does. This simple statement, obvious on the face of it, implies a great number of associated issues. If so, where does the food come from? How does the household acquire this food? Does the means of acquisition affect the food eaten, and if so, how?

In 1985 Japanese consumed an average of 2,617 kcal/day (UK average 3,397; US average 3,546 [Kōkawa 1991]). Less than half of that derives from Japanese food sources. The Japanese homemaker is faced with a large choice, but that choice is restricted in many ways. This paradoxical statement has to do less with food, than with the structure of the Japanese economy and legal/political system. This has to do with a combination of three interrelated issues: Japanese farming, food imports, and the food market. All three are characterised by a great degree of politicisation in which the interests of others – the government, farmers, overseas powers – are put before the consumer.

Japanese farmers have had a disproportionate effect on the political system due to the way in which the Japanese constituency voting system works. Thus they have succeeded in two major aims: keeping foreign rice and other agricultural products out (by pricing it out of reach, by demanding intolerably rigorous "health safety" checks) and keeping prices of their own products, notably rice, as high as possible. Moreover, the Japanese government, following some bitter lessons, has tried as much as possible to ensure *strategic* food stocks and expertise, since they see Japan as extremely vulnerable to food blackmail and pressure. As a consequence, legal and non-tariff barriers have been erected to keep the flow of foreign food out of Japan, or at least at a premium with which Japanese farmers can compete. Raising prices still further is the overall "inefficiency" of Japanese farming. Japanese farms tend to be small, and the major crops are generally grown on small paddies or fields, harvested by hand or by small and not-necessarily efficient machinery. There has been a great migration of farmers to city jobs, but this has not resulted in the emergence of large agribusinesses (at least, not the at the rate the government would like to see this happening). The result is that many farmers raise hand-tended (often by wives, while husbands take city jobs) and relatively expensive crops. In a sense the consumer is torn by the desire for cheaper foodstuffs, on the one hand, and the desire to maintain the traditional countryside and its social and material infrastructure – not a minor consideration in a densely populated, yet affluent nation where most people are only one or two generations removed from the farm – on the other. The tension between the two has led, in recent years, to attempts to revive the connection between urbanites and country-farmers, by helping urbanites to invest, financially and directly, in the well-being of rural communities, for which they, in return, receive "natural" and locally grown crops, as well as a set of pseudo social relations.

What has all this meant in terms of food? Three important areas need to be discussed: changes in production, in wholesaling, and in retailing. Each of these changes has an effect on the food the Japanese eat, and consequently on Japanese cuisine as well. A very personal example, one of many, comes from an interview of an elderly manager in Hokkaido:

> My family has engaged in the sale of *surume* (dried squid) for several generations. I took over the business from my father, and together with my sister, we have supplied *surume* from our hometown bay for years. Now? Now the whole business is in disarray. Obviously, our *surume* is first class, from only the best squid, and it takes time and patience to clean and dry it. So what do the large wholesalers do? They go to Korea and Taiwan and get cheap *surume*, and import it. First, they don't know what the good fish are, second, they use artificial drying processes. So we get poor quality *surume*. But do the young people of today care? Not a bit! They simply can't tell real Japanese stuff from cheap foreign imitations. I can eat a piece of *surume* and tell you which waters it comes from, which area of Japan! Do you think any youngster today can do that?

Ignoring for a moment the rhetoric, the *production* process of foodstuffs in Japan has changed since the seventies. Meat is imported from Australia, citrus from the US, mangoes from the Philippines, and fish from Antarctic waters. This is not of course unique to Japan, but Japanese consumers have been forced to adapt to changes in a diet in which they must adopt foreign derived foodstuffs into their own cuisine. For the average cook this has meant, of course, greater choice, and, occasionally, cheaper prices. The issue of price is a cogent one because even though Japanese society today is one of conspicuous consumption, consumers do have preferences for lower prices. And with the internationalisation of Japanese diet has come a lessening of the delicate definition of foods and tastes. Young people, we were constantly informed, have little of the fine palate of their predecessors, and this seems to be borne out, at least insofar as changing tastes can show. Moreover, food production has moved from the many small manufacturers into the realm of the large companies. "I will be the last of my family making *natto* in town," one man said unhappily. "It is not just that the younger generation do not eat *natto*, but that no one in my family is prepared to put in the long hours, the lack of amenities, that the job requires. True, mine tastes better, and there are many townspeople who move to Tokyo who place orders with me, and I will ship anywhere in Japan, but all these hand-crafted foods are a thing of the past." A thing of the past indeed, but one that will be sorely missed. A *miso* manufacturer in the same town has been more successful than the *natto* maker. His production scale is larger (as is the customer base: most Japanese foods require *miso*, not all Japanese like *natto*) and he sells 200 kg of *miso* per month. Like the *natto* maker, a percentage of his product is shipped to expatriates. Townspeople, nostalgic for the taste of home, order a third of his production of *miso* while living in Tokyo. Like the *natto* maker, he is conscious of the changing taste of the Japanese: "People buy more of the sweeter variety of *miso*, and less of the old-fashioned drier-tasting variety." And, there is no question, his product is far better, far tastier, than the industrial variety, full of the aroma of wood and beans, aged and lovingly prepared in traditional vats.

> The *miso* is a dark, almost clumped substance, so unlike the smoothly blended industrial products. The saltiness does not get in the way of a redolent earthy bouquet and demanding taste. The taste lingers on the tongue, and even the *tamari* – the liquid that oozes from the solider *miso* – wafts several blended odours. The pickles, which have been thoroughly mixed and preserved in the *miso*, are crunchy yet soft. They convey an awareness of their origins, in fields and in the earth, that the sanitised versions in supermarkets do not. All one needs, when eating the dark, almost black slices of *nasu* (aubergine) or *kyūri* (cucumber), is a bowl of hot freshly cooked rice to allow the flavours to seep in more gradually.

The large companies, on the other hand, for reasons that range from health concerns to bulk shipping, make a standardised, rather bland product of whatever they make. Younger people, as many informants noted sadly, have acquired a homogenised palate, no longer able to distinguish between the products of different areas but for the labels or the generic and stereotypical differences ("black *miso* from Kyūshū, white *miso* from Tōhoku, red *miso* from Chūgoku") they expect.

Though Japan is, in terms of arable land, farming techniques, and population devoted to farming, *technically* able to supply its own food *needs*, it does not supply its own food *wants*. Quite simply, the demand for imported foods is very high. Japanese meals are composed of a large, and growing, amount of imports. Much of these, particularly meat and fruit, are imported from developed countries such as the US and Australia. This includes both luxury goods (there is a lovely store near Tsukiji, the wholesale fish market, which imports and sells only malt whiskey) and industrial foodstuffs: Japan imports some £700 million worth of soy beans and sorghum, largely from the USA and China.

For reasons of domestic food security, as well as a means of saving foreign exchange, the Japanese government resisted food imports for many years. This resistance was aided and abetted by Japanese nationalist feelings, which we shall discuss subsequently. On the government side, customs and, later, non-tariff barriers were erected to keep foreign foods out. Citrus fruit and meat from overseas were subjected to lengthy and destructive inspections. Quality of overseas foods was impugned. And even though there was a clear demand for overseas exotic fruit, their import was often delayed until Japanese farmers could start growing them themselves. Moreover, the Japanese mercantile system was, until recently, complex and difficult to master by foreigners, which meant that the ability of a Japanese consumer to enjoy foreign foodstuffs was often conditioned by the complexity of the marketing system in which traditional relationships and small-scales were the norm.

Japanese retail trading has an extremely long history. The house of Mitsui originated as a cash-and-carry department store in the Edo period during the seventeenth century by Mitsui Hachirobei. Under the pressure of development, Japanese retailing developed apace. Soon after World War II the Japanese government was faced with the problem of dealing with hundreds of thousands of returning servicemen. One solution was to encourage – through liberal licensing and small loans – the creation of small shops throughout the nation. While this solved the immediate problem – shops averaged 1.5 employees (usually owner and wife), had a turnover of about 70 customers *a week*, and barely allowed one to earn a living[7] – it created another one down the road. Such a marketing system is hardly "efficient" and restrictive laws and customary procedures (such as, for example, the need to secure permission from all affected shop owners when

7 To put this into perspective, the first five years after the end of World War II (that is, until the Americans obligingly jump-started the Japanese economy by intervening in the Korean War), the major problem for some of the returning Japanese population was *starvation*. A living income of any sort was not to be despised.

building marketing premises over 10,000 sq feet) prohibited the rise of modern department stores. Customers bore the major brunt of the system in limited choice and high prices. It is only in the most recent decade that new and innovative marketing structures have spread to the hinterland, whether in the form of new supermarket chains, convenience stores, or home-delivery systems.

One of the changes that accompanies modernisation in all countries is the rationalisation and distancing of food supplies. "Rationalisation" does not, in this case, mean some abstract value, but specifically refers to the changing of food into a commodity, one that supplies a mass good using capitalist principles to a mass of people, whatever individual preferences may be. In such a system, efficiency, profit, quality, and only lastly, aesthetic (including flavour, taste, smell) are the values entertained. This is accompanied by, and is both a cause and a consequence of, distancing. That is, there are many steps between producer and final consumer of a food product. This has a number of implications, and as we shall see, has also brought about a counter-reaction which expresses itself in Japan in several ways such as the natural food movement, and attempts to tempt urbanites to involve themselves in countryside matters.

In practical terms, the distancing between producer and consumer has expressed itself in a continuing movement towards bigger and more "rationalised" supplies of foodstuffs. Before the modern century, as elsewhere in the world, foodstuffs were largely consumed directly by producers (eighty percent of Japan's population were rural, supplying their own produce, until the twentieth century). With urbanisation, which started in the sixteenth century on a large scale, shops selling food, including rice, started to appear. Until well after the Second World War, the standard marketing pattern was either in street stall markets, or in small grocery stores with less than thirty square meters of space. Though Japan pioneered the world in the creation of department stores (the first, Mitsui department store, was founded in the seventeenth century), large food shops – supermarkets – appeared only well after World War Two as a general phenomenon, and after a hard rear-guard action by small neighbourhood stores, which included the insertion of small food stalls in a modern market phenomenon, into the floors of many large department store chains.

Obviously, changes in wholesaling have also meant that there is less variety in any given foodstuff, though there are more types of foodstuff to choose from. One shop's products are very much like any other's because the wholesalers who supply them are the same, and that is what they offer. Until well into the eighties, Japanese wholesaling was a chaotic affair, with any product passing through numerous intermediate wholesalers and sub-sellers. This has changed as the need for saving expenses has grown, and lines of sales have become more streamlined. While overall from a capitalist point of view (both the consumer's and the producer's) this is probably beneficial, from a culinary point of view this has become a leveler of differences and of potential culinary surprises, both good and bad. Moreover, as current economic waves shake out the many trading companies that have been bringing foods from overseas, there is even more "rationalisation" and uniformity – the curse of innovative and interesting cooking – than there was before.

Shimo-Kitazawa is the eponym of a "youth town" where the young and affluent (in modern Japan, the terms are almost synonymous) come to play. But for well over twenty years we have made it a stopping place because even for the traditional-minded such as ourselves, it provides a wonderful opportunity to enjoy the contrasts of two types of shops, the traditional and the modern. Near the exit to the station stands a medium-sized Daimaru-Peacock supermarket, with two wonderfully complex food floors. Opposite the supermarket, and in marked contrast, stand the stalls of the old Shimo-Kitazawa covered market, with the stallholders still shouting their wares. At first sight, the two domains exhibit a strong, almost ludicrous contrast. Upon reflection, their similarities become more apparent. Peacock contains everything one could want in terms of food. In the greengrocer section are piles of Kyōhō grapes, the giant purple orbs selling in small bunches. Beside them are giant pink and yellow peaches, tiny watermelons, and a host of vegetables, including the by now ubiquitous *morohēya*, one of the most recent food fads.

In contrast to the well-lighted supermarket, the market is a jumble of little stalls built along a series of cross-cutting corridors. The owners are busy dealing with their stock, much of which lies piled in heaps, glistening or dry, according to their natures. One elderly couple sells a variety of pickled goods – plums, radishes in vinegar, in salt, and in saké lees, dried and pickled fish, fresh bamboo shoots, several varieties of local *miso* pickles (they are somewhat taken aback when Michael insists on the strongest smelling, and most unusual pickles he can find). In the meantime Jeanne is inspecting the *senbei* merchant's stock. Still in old-fashioned jars there are honey-coloured salty rice biscuits of varying shapes. Home-made crackers wrapped in *nori*, white ones with sesame, and enormous jars of mixed *senbei* and nuts, which can be bought at the supermarket in elegant plastic envelopes (at twice the price) but are here available by weight from a charming elderly lady who wants to make sure we know they are savoury, and not sweet.

Many of the foods available in the supermarket are available in the covered market as well. Even the conviviality of some of the sellers in the supermarket is an up-market version of the warm curiosity and rather pleased demeanour of the market-people. And where the market has stalls, the supermarket has bays, many of which project an air of "difference" and local produce. Clearly, the market, which is the livelier and the warmer of the two, is losing ground. There are fewer customers than there used to be – people looking for bargains, and older people who prefer either the specialist offerings of the stalls, or are simply habituated to shopping there, with their personal touch, rather than at the impersonal long lines of the supermarket till. For while the supermarket sellers have adopted, as if by rote, the politeness and cries of the market, it is obviously a formula, not something that they feel as they cry out "*irrasshaimase*!! (welcome!)" or "*omataseshimashita*! (sorry to keep you waiting)"

3.6 *THE JAPANESE HOUSEHOLD: WHERE ONE EATS*

As IN ANY society, the locus of most food activity is the household. Anthropologists have long puzzled over the precise nature of the Japanese family, and the household that is associated with it. On the face of it, a Japanese household looks uncomplicated: a couple and two children are the norm. But looking under the surface, one can see the vestiges of a more traditional form, the *ie*. Throughout much of Japanese history, *ie* ("house", as in 'House of') constituted, a corporate, indissoluble unit, which has had statutory existence and rights until the end of World War II. Individuals were recognised solely as members of a particular *ie*, and the head of the *ie*, normally an adult male, had rights to punish and reward as he saw fit. In practice, *ie* were run as capitalist corporate bodies, with much effort devoted to acquiring wealth so that it could be handed down to future members. All this came largely to an end with the enactment of the new family law after World War II, which dissolved the *ie* and established the main domestic forum in Western terms, that is, as dissoluble units lasting the lifetime of a particular marriage, rather than presumptively in perpetuity.

Many rural households, which account for about 15% of the population, still maintain an *ie* form, as do households in other realms – entertainment (kabuki), small merchants, craftsmen, priests – where some productive item must be maintained collectively. But the majority of urban households, having little property to pass on to descendants, are very similar to any modern family in Europe or America. Nonetheless, and notwithstanding the growing number of career women and dual-income families, Japanese households remain very traditional in some ways. Men rarely participate in housework, and women do almost all shopping, cooking, and much of the child-raising chores. Husbands, particularly career *sarariman* (white collar workers) return late from work, and expect to have their meals ready, whether the wife has her own career or not. Women we surveyed noted that they satisfied the food demands of their children and husbands for breakfast and supper, while pleasing themselves and their infants during the daytime.

What had been wider links to related *ie* are also weakening significantly, as more and more Japanese are moving away from the neighbourhood of their natal homes (and, no less importantly in Japanese culture, their family burial grounds) and losing contact with their relatives. Here too, the relationship to rural areas plays a part. Since the demographic mix of rural and urban dwellers has almost completely reversed itself in the past fifty years, many urban households still maintain ties to their rural origins. However, as second and third generation urbanites emerge, these are becoming more and more tenuous.

The relationships within the family have also changed. To Western eyes modern Japanese families are still male-dominated and age-oriented. But much of the traditional formulations are gone or are going. It is rare (and unsurprising, given the small houses and flats in Japan) to find more than two generations living under one roof. Fathers no longer have absolute authority over their offspring, and while many siblings still address one another in terms of their relative seniority, there is far less obedience and authority involved. Above all, Japanese women have achieved a greater degree of independence, exhibiting less subservience to the demands of their male relatives (fathers, husbands, or sons). All of these changes express themselves to some degree in the realm of food, food choices, and food presentation as well.

The first harbinger of change was the issue of population. Between 1870 and 1970, the Japanese population changed its demography in two ways. First, as a result of industrialisation, from a population that was about 80% rural, it became a population that was over 80% urban, and even the "rural" population included many who actually live in substantial towns. No less importantly, the Japanese government was highly successful in a programme intended to reduce population growth. A government-induced programme for use of condoms and induced abortions meant that the Japanese natural increase was held to very low levels, the population increasing from 117 million in 1965 to 125.6 million in 1995, with a population growth rate of 0.2%. This has meant significant reduction in the size of families: the average family size currently being 2.8 persons. A growing affluence, a growing desire by women to be more independent, and a growing consumerism have lead to a phenomenon of working couples. This has expressed itself in the re-organisation of the Japanese kitchen, as well as in its contents. With less time to spend in the kitchen, prepared foods have become a major industrial segment. Virtually all households we know, as well as those appearing in our sample, take some advantage of this trend, whether in the form of ready meals ordered from shops (*demae*), bought portions from supermarkets and department stores, or frozen ready-made foods.

We looked at detailed daily household consumption for over a hundred Japanese households, interviewing about one third of them in depth, after receiving a month of detailed food consumption schedules from them. Overall, there is a clear shift in Japanese food consumption and preferences. For example, our survey as well as others indicate that approximately 50% of all Japanese have bread for breakfast, with the number declining the greater the age. There are a number of reasons for this, which shows how important a broad perspective is. Bread meals are quicker to prepare than rice meals, bread is considered a confectionery, rather than a proper staple, bread is considered modern, and bread goes better with what has become the Japanese national drink:[8] coffee.

8 We are, of course being slightly facetious here, but judging from the number of coffeeshops, this is not really an exaggeration in empirical terms.

For the evening meal, on the other hand, there is a strong preference for Japanese foods. The older one is, the more pronounced this preference. The reasons for the consumption of these foods have to do with a complex array of factors. Japanese foods, as we shall see, are far more labour-intensive than Western foods. They require more plates, greater skills with the knife, and more minutes to put together in a way that is considered culturally proper. On the other hand, with the rise of neighbourhood supermarkets, and particularly the prevalence in these establishments of ready-made foods, life is made easier, and there has been an *increase* in the consumption of traditional Japanese foods.

There are other factors as well. Most domestic foods are prepared by women. In recent decades there has been a rise in the number of women working away from home, which means that the time they can devote to domestic duties, including food preparation, has declined. This in turn has meant a greater appeal for the ready-made or frozen foods, which can be prepared quickly and easily. To add to that, even in "traditional" households, for our purposes here, those in which there is a division of labour between wives and husbands, husbands will often eat their main meals outside the house, including the evening, and sometimes the morning meal. This means that housewives who are mothers are under pressure by their children to provide foods the children prefer: often Western-type foods. So it is not surprising to find that hamburgers are the top choice among 15 to 19 year olds (Gaishoku kenkyū sentā 1997. Table 7–6), with spaghetti a close second. Again, the picture is not so simple: when asked (by us as well as by others) what their preferred comfort food is, most people responded with the desire for Japanese foods: noodles, *hiyayakko* (cold tofu), *omuraisu* (rice omelette) or *nimono* (stews).

A (very) generalised picture of Japanese domestic food is as follows. Three meals and two to three snacks a day are served. On weekdays, breakfast is a punctuated, rather individual affair. Most employed workers must be on their way early, to catch transportation to work, and many urban blue- and white-collar families do not eat breakfasts together. Breakfast may be a Japanese meal of rice, soup, grilled salt fish, vegetables and green tea (or coffee), or a Western-style meal of bread, jam, coffee or tea, ham, cooked eggs.

The midday meal is also separate: men eat in their office, perhaps a *bentō* (lunch box) brought from home, often at a local eatery or the firm's canteen. At home the wife and small children will have a warm meal. Consumption of Western foods, even outside the main urban areas, is high (around 50% of foods consumed), though a mixture of Japanese and Western foods and cooking styles is perhaps a more accurate description. School children eat a school lunch, which is a blend of Japanese and Western foods and cooking methods as well. The evening meal is more likely to consist of Japanese dishes and cooking: about 20% of households have some form of sushi. Preferences range from about 30% of evening meals being Japanese in young households, to over 50% in older ones. About 25% of evening meals in young households are Western, down to about 10% for older (main couple 45 years or older) households. These numbers are subject to different interpretations, and not all findings agree, but they serve as a useful indicator of the sheer variety of food consumption and the importance of foreign foods.

In between main meals, snacks (*oyatsu*) are consumed. Mothers and children, we found, would have a mixture of sweet and savoury, Japanese and Western foods. The emphasis was often on nutrition: young mothers, in particular, were anxious that their children would have balanced diets, according to the conventional wisdom of the time: during our data collection in 1990–1991 all were emphatic that they gave their children milk to drink, whatever the snack. When snacking on their own, women tended to have either Western "teas" (milk tea and a cream cake) or Japanese *okashi* sweets with Japanese tea. Men tended to have noodles or coffee. Households in farming areas, in our experience, tend to have traditional snacks: plates of pickled vegetables or dried fish, pieces of fruit, green tea and *senbei* (rice crackers). Evening snacks differ markedly for people working outside the home and home-makers. For those working outside the house evening snacks generally are *otsumami*: drinking foods, ranging from peanuts and *senbei* to a variety of bar foods to full meals. The most popular ones being *yakitori* (grilled skewered chicken bits), which accounted for 36.4% of all *otsumami* served, *tori no kara-age* (Chinese style deep-fried chicken) 23.7%, tofu-based dishes 21.2%, vegetable salads 18.6%, and grilled fish 16.1%. What characterises most of these evening snacks is that they are quintessentially drinking foods: heavy on flavours, easy to consume while devoting one's attention to other things such as talk. In the home, women will provide snacks – cakes, fruit, noodles are common – for themselves and the children, notably for children studying for their exams.

During weekends and special events such as the New Year, the pattern described roughly above changes. Families tend to eat meals together, and these meals tend to be more elaborate. Many families go out to eat at Western, Chinese, Japanese, or *esunikku* (ethnic) restaurants, depending on the internal family dynamics and preferences. Food is also more often ordered in during weekends than during the week, preferred foods being sushi and noodles: a traditional, often-utilised convenience.

Ready-made, "convenience" foods have a long history in Japan. Tofu bean curd is difficult and time-consuming to make at home, and there is evidence for commercial manufacture in small lots from the Edo period. The same is true of soy sauce and other condiments, which are still made by farm households today in some cases, but which have been manufactured extensively by factory methods for centuries. The trend continues today to its logical conclusion, one in which virtually *all* foods, including cooked white rice, can be bought, ready to eat, at most supermarket and department store food section counters.

The changes in food preparation and purchasing cannot be seen in isolation from domestic food technology. One of the first modern appliances used in the Japanese kitchen was the electrical rice cooker, which ensures, as one of our friends put it, "that even the newest bride from the most pampered household will be able to cook rice properly." Modern rice cookers allow for settings of different rice types, and different resultant textures, for timed cooking, and so on. But the first ones that we used as students were simply of the "Put in the rice, add water, plug in, push the 'start' button, wait till done" variety. And they worked! Perhaps well enough to ensure a young bride a few more minutes of sleep, and less disapproval from her fearsome mother-in-law, always ready to criticise, and less ready to forgive burnt or undercooked rice than any other sin. Later on, the microwave oven became an almost overnight hit in the early eighties, as, some time later, did the electronic water kettle that not only boiled water but kept it warm and had a convenient pump server to boot.

Some less common machines include counter-top automatic bread machines and *mochi* makers. *Mochi* – pounded glutinous rice – is a perennial favourite. It is eaten at festivals and weddings, serves as offering for Shintō and Buddhist deities, and provides lots of energy (it is a must in stews for sumo wrestlers [*chanko nabe*]). As one huckster was heard to remark "... it gives wonderful results with your husband, lady, try it tonight and you'll see." The process of making *mochi* is arduous. Special high-starch sticky rice is steamed. The hot cooked rice is then placed in a large mortar, usually made of a hollowed log, and pounded with a massive mallet. The doughy mixture must be turned from time to time. Of course, every once in a while the pounder or the turner misses, and smashed fingers are the result. And of course, as is usually the case, the showy role of pounder is reserved for males, and the less prestigious (and more dangerous) role of turner, for females. In some villages this is evened out: a pounder who hits a turner's fingers is required to strap the heavy mortar to his back and climb over the roof of the house! Most modern housewives would not have the time nor the equipment, nor a willing helper (nor the knowledge, sniffed one elderly farm-wife of our acquaintance) to prepare *mochi*. The *mochi* machine cooks the rice and then pounds it to the proper sticky life-threatening[9] consistency. One of the more recent technological improvements has been in the realm of refrigeration, and the change reflects the changes in domestic choices. To elaborate on that, however, it is necessary first to have a brief look at the Japanese home in its physical "machine for living" aspect.

In the present century most Japanese houses have been so small as to be labelled "rabbit-hutches" by a Japanese commentator. We have already referred to the Japanese cultural preference for "modularity" in life. This finds its way into construction, that is, people's lifestyles as well. Traditionally (and this holds to this day) rooms were designed to accommodate various arrangements of standard *tatami* mats. *Tatami* mats are made by compressing rice straw (a 60 cm pile of straw is compressed into a mat ten cm thick) onto a wooden frame, then covering it by a surface of woven grass. *Tatami* are of standard size – 90 × 180 cm – and

9 Every year, several people, usually the elderly who have trouble chewing, die of suffocation as *mochi* cakes are greedily swallowed, usually during New Year celebrations. For an amusing, and true-to life example of the issue, one can see Itami Juzo's *Tampopo*.

traditional Japanese rooms are measured by the number of *tatami* they enclose. Each such mat is traditionally sufficient for the sleeping space of one individual. The mats' modularity means that certain placements of these mats are most attractive. Thus there are four, four and a half, six mat rooms and so on. In practice this has meant that Japanese rooms might be sized four-and-a-half mats (7.27 metre sq or approximately 74 feet sq), and a flat might consist of two such rooms, or even one, with perhaps a tiny kitchen or kitchen nook half or a quarter that size. Accordingly, most kitchen utensils and furnishings had to be appropriately small. With affluence, and a growth in the size of accommodations, there has been an equivalent change in the sizes of such furnishing items as washing machines, and refrigerators. Modern Japanese refrigerators, as a friend pointed out, have become so efficient that the latest models have freezer compartments with drawers that accommodate frozen-food packages whose measurements have been standardised throughout the industry. Note that this requires a great deal of agreement and co-ordination on the part of food and utilities manufacturers: frozen dinners (or dinner portions) have the contents clearly printed on one narrow side (the "spine"), they are of the same size, and they can therefore be stacked in the freezer drawers somewhat like a video cassette library (which they resemble in size, and sometimes in flavour, added one male informant).

The overall picture presented here frames our further discussion. What it demonstrates is two major issues. First, the great *variety* of consumed foods in the home. It is undeniably true that many of the "non-Japanese" (and we have already seen how tricky a label that is) foods are prepared using Japanese ideas of cooking, flavouring, and presentation. Nonetheless, there is great variety to which almost every individual is exposed from an early age. Second, there is an overall trend in which more and more "foreign" foods are being incorporated into the repertoire of Japanese foods in the home. The home, in other words, is no longer a bastion of traditional "Japanese-ness," at least in the realm of food.

Both of these trends are related to the reordering of Japanese society in some rather fundamental ways. One crucial reordering is the gradual dissolution of the age-old, Confucian-sanctioned hierarchies. The importance of children – traditionally subservient to parents and elders – has been growing in Japanese postwar society. Special segments of the economy are devoted strictly to children's interests and preferences. The influence of their preferences in domestic arrangements has risen: it is children who often decide what is to be eaten in many households. Parallel to this, but less intense, has been a rise in the acceptance of female autonomy and rights. That is not to say that Japanese women now have equal privileges as men, but rather that industry has recognised that they are an economic segment that must be catered to as well. For a society which, until about twenty years ago, was strictly adult-male oriented, this is a major revolution indeed.

The Japanese eat out a great deal. This is due partly to the business style that emerged in modern Japan, partly to historical circumstances of the presence of a large and sophisticated entertainment and hospitality industry, whose roots go well beyond those in the West. A major element is a material and emotional issue. Until fairly recently, Japanese in the metropolitan areas did not entertain at home. That was because of physical circumstances – most homes were too small to do any entertaining – as well as the emotional and intellectual separation between *uchi* (the inside, and also a euphemism for "my home" and *soto* (the outside). One met others outside, beyond the boundaries of the intimate domestic sphere. Thus locales catering food and drink to patrons have existed in Japan for centuries, and have increased in proportion to Japanese affluence.

In 1982 there were 838,449 food shops (restaurants, bars, coffee-shops, *ryōtei* but excepting food retailers or wholesalers. Food barrows are not mentioned at all) in Japan, in a population of about 113 million people. There were 1,964,880 employees, and the annual turnover was 8,685,774 million yen (about £34 billion). In 1992 there were 591,925 establishments *but* bars, cabarets, beer-halls, and *ryōtei* had been taken off the list. There were 3,037,568 employees (including owner-operators) and an annual turnover of 16,491,362 million yen (approximately £66 billion) in a population of 124 million. The 1992 figures also provide some clues about the dining structure: the largest category (80%) were *shokudō* that is, restaurants. Six percent of the total served noodles, and 7.6% served sushi.

The most common foods eaten out by individuals are hamburgers and other fast foods, *rāmen* noodles, and set menus when eating alone. In company, the preferences shifts: on dates, couples prefer steaks, hamburgers and other Western foods, *otsumami* and other drinking foods, and Italian food. In a larger group, the preference is for *otsumami* (almost double the next category), Chinese food, Western food, and *nabe* (stew-pot) cooking. This data indicates an important point that must be kept in mind. Food preferences are highly susceptible to situational, and particularly social dynamics. This means that an understanding of the social and cultural matrix in which foods are prepared and consumed is absolutely crucial if one is to understand the nature of the food, let alone the food culture.

3.7 GURUME: *THE RISE OF LUXURY AS A LIFESTYLE*

WOULD YOU PAY £120 for a kilo of meat? Yes, in Japan, there are purchasers for such luxuries. Notwithstanding a number of downturns (e.g., the 1973 "oil shock," the 1995 "bubble" bursting, the 1998 economic recession), Japanese economy has been phenomenally successful in bringing prosperity to most of its population. Even though there have been some dissenting voices, surveys consistently show that most Japanese consider themselves to be members of the middle class, and as members of this class, they spend. Conspicuous consumption and display occurs in almost all societies, from the most simple to the most technologically advanced. The Japanese are no exception. Elaborate aristocratic feasts to which commoners were witness are recorded for Heian Japan, and participation in Western feasts indicated breeding and money in the nineteenth century. In recent years a new Japanese term for this sort of consumption has been adopted from French: *gurume*. Fine foods and wine, in addition to exotica and a general knowledge of good food are characterised as *gurume* items. The availability of luxury foods for much of the population at the end of the century is in stark contrast to the privations and even hunger of its middle.

> The tiny shop under the rails at Shibuya where Jeanne used to go to purchase foreign goods then not widely available in supermarkets or department stores – spiced sardines, a particular blend of American instant coffee, Swiss chocolate, Dutch cheeses – has now upgraded itself to real *gurume* status. In addition to its usual stock, it has devoted half the shop to an extensive display of coffee beans, roasted on the premises and ground to order. Everything from the fabulously expensive Blue Mountain coffee (the Japanese buy most of the crop years ahead) through the shop's own special blends of Kilimanjaro with Brazilian. To acquaint novices to these gourmet coffees, the shop owner has worked out a unique marking system. For each intrinsic quality – i.e., acidity, aroma, bitterness, depth/complexity, sweetness – each coffee bean is graded from 0 to 10. On each label, next to the coffee variety's name, is a circular chart with 5 vectors radiating from the centre. The ratings are marked along the vector lines and all the points joined to give a graphic shape that clearly gives at a glance the qualities of each coffee, and at the same time, is a very useful and rapid means of comparing various varieties. It can also serve to point out other varieties that a customer may wish to try, according to their similarity in graphic terms with one that she has been satisfied with.

Luxurious living and consumption in a purposefully understated way have been Japanese traditions since affluence first hit Japan during the days of *sakoku* ("closed country": 1637–1856),[10] when Japan, closing itself off from the world, enjoyed a period of relative peace and prosperity that was unprecedented. Now, however, every possible taste is catered to. Food magazines explore and list the best shops for meat, condiments, cakes of particular varieties (German, French, or Japanese). Specialist shops sell everything from freshly-made sausages flown in from Hokkaido, to malt whiskeys flown in directly from Scotland. Lobsters from Eastern Canada, salmon from Alaska, and French wines can now be ordered by post from Guru-Mail, the national postal service, and other mail order firms. For

10 The Japanese authorities of the late Momoyama and the Edo periods were highly suspicious of the Western powers (Portugal and Spain) and their colonisation and Christianisation policies. When a pro-Christian revolt of poor farmers and samurai broke out in Shimabara in Kyushu in 1637, the *bakufu* (Shogun's government) declared a total foreign exclusion, and all overseas contact, except with the traders of a small Dutch factory in Deshima, and a similar one in Nagasaki, were forbidden. The *sakoku* (exclusion) policy lasted until 1856 when first the Americans, then the British and Russians forced the Japanese to abandon it.

the average Japanese this constant assault is welcome, providing a sense of choice, which is vast, and of prosperity, which is evident. French restaurants in large urban centres, good, bad and indifferent, are packed full at lunch-time. And everyone, of course, can be a gourmet, if only an expert on something as homely as *karē-raisu*.

3.8 *FROM WILD TO NATURAL: THE RISE OF THE NATURAL FOOD MOVEMENT*

JAPAN HAS EXPERIENCED several horrifying abuses of industrial and mercantile power in the food realm. In the fifties and sixties, cases of industrial pollution poisoning affected hundred of people who suffered variously from Minamata and *itai-itai* pollution diseases. One Japanese milk company in the fifties was found guilty of adulterating their milk with arsenic, to make it whiter. As a result, some Japanese now fear the industrialised foods they eat and a strong and growing demand for more "natural" foods is emerging.

Wild natural foods have been a feature of the Japanese diet for millennia. Historically, wild foods were an important supplement. Almost all wild foods were exploited, mainly by the poor. Without the ability to gather wild harvests in summer and autumn, fewer households would have survived than actually did. Even in the modern century, for many rural households such wild foods are still a common item of diet. Our friends and neighbours in Akita would collect *fuki* (sweet coltsfoot), fiddlehead ferns, and mushrooms as a matter of course for eating immediately as well as preserving. The town we lived in had set aside wild stands of sweet chestnuts for residents to harvest come autumn.

This preference for wild foods combines with and is related to the reaction to heavily industrialised foodstuffs. Since the affluent seventies, however, collecting, consuming, and preserving wild vegetables and fruit have become expressions of modernity and civilisation, rather than the opposite. A recent volume (Asquith and Kalland 1996) shows the manifold aspects of the Japanese desire to reduce nature to its essentials, and to encompass it within the daily activities of their lives. The use of wild foods is a part of the struggle of Japanese to ensure some form of cultural continuity between the (often idealised) past, and the highly mechanised, often impersonal present, as it shades into an even more alienating future. A group of Tokyo women we interviewed, who had formed a co-operative natural food bakery exemplify the feeling that is growing within the Japanese populace:

> Many people are tired of not knowing where their food comes from. But Japanese nowadays are woefully uneducated when it comes to their own food. As a result, many of us suffer from poor nutrition and illness. When we started the bakery some two years ago, we were simply a group of housewives who were interested in giving our children some pure, good

> food. We got together, went and learned from a professional how to bake commercially, and started the business. Our customers are mainly local people, people who are concerned with their health and want decent, edible bread. True, it costs a bit more, but it is much more nutritious and tasty, and most people recognise this and appreciate it. Even small kids come by to get a small bun or cake.

The natural food movement in Japan is still a small affair, numbering some 20,000 people formally, but having a wider influence as more shops and food outlets convert to the idea of natural foods. It is a small minority of the Japanese populace, and yet its presence demonstrates several points. Beyond the fact of a growing awareness of the risks associated with industrial foods, the growing number of natural food shops and outlets of various sorts, individual as well as collective efforts, underlines the sheer variety of modern Japanese food culture. The natural food movement and its formal offshoots and chains represents a significant, albeit small, economic niche. It also descends from a respectable East Asian tradition, which associated particular foods with health, longevity, and so on. In some ways, it also lays to rest the myth of Japanese uniformity. Among the "natural food enthusiasts" we observed and interviewed, there was an enormous variety of opinion, participation, and practise. These ranged from one-man commercial operations for a new, healthy tofu as a cure for cancer and source of longevity, individuals who try to grow their own produce, groups manufacturing a food from organically grown produce, to large commercial companies anxious to cash in on this commercial niche.

3.9 *FOOD AS A SYMBOL:* NIHONJIN *AND OTHER* -RON

For many Japanese, particularly older ones, the essential nature of Japan is an almost mystical, unique spiritual identity. *Nihonjin-ron* refers to the almost ineffable sense of Japanese things, ways of doing things, beliefs, uniqueness, that many Japanese feel exists. Whether this uniqueness exists objectively or not is not the issue, the sense of uniqueness undoubtedly is. *Nihonjin-ron* philosophy suggests roughly that the Japanese are (racially, culturally, socially, mentally: there is a wide variety of opinion and belief) "different" from other nations and cultures. They are in fact "unique" and their achievements, language, political and social behaviour, must be understood against this supposed uniqueness. This uniqueness is to be preserved, since, in some extreme views, it is also superior, and inherently and morally more "valuable" than others. Philosophies such as this are, alas, neither new nor unique to the Japanese. The difference, if any, with other nations' perceptions of their uniqueness is the number of *popular* adherents to some of the milder (and more silly) derivatives of these beliefs. The Japanese-are-unique theme expresses itself in some bizarre ways, as for instance a common fad of identifying individual traits by blood type (many Japanese are type A with which attributes of generosity, hard work, and non-concrete thinking are associated) or basing the uniqueness of Japanese thinking on the supposed deep differences between Japanese and any other language (similarities to Korean are conveniently ignored). Another recent belief is that Japanese guts are longer, since the Japanese historically have eaten little, or almost no meat, and that therefore Japanese are biologically different, to the point of difference in mental processes, than other people. How prevalent such ideas are in Japanese society, whether people really fully accept them or not, and what the implications are, is still being debated. Nonetheless, the emergence of such beliefs is an echo of a persistent strain of thought that does express itself from time to time, including in the realm of food.

Nihonjin-ron expresses itself in many ways, some of them quite unattractive, ranging from ultra-nationalism, through the less blatant manipulations by *Mombushō* (the Japanese Ministry of Education) of the history of World War II to reflect Japanese atrocities in positive light. Foreigners are often ranked after Japanese, and nationalism becomes a powerful force disguising prejudice and outright oppression of "other" groups, whether these are women, *burakumin* outcasts, or guest workers, in everything from housing to entering bars. As Dale has pointed out, for intellectuals Japanese nationalism was a way to measure themselves and their achievements and protect them from Western (the dominant "other" since the middle of the last century) intellectual incursions, for politicians it was a convenient and often deeply felt rallying cry. In the realm of food, *nihonjin-ron* and nationalism express themselves as well.

Perceiving a relationship between Japanese food and the essential nature of Japan is not new. Motoori Norinaga, one of Japan's earliest nationalist ideologues, in the eighteenth century, argued that the evidence that Japan was the country selected by the gods was the exemplary and inimitable quality of its rice. To non-Japanese eyes these ideas seem close to ludicrous (though not of course when viewed against the pronouncement of some of the more rabid historical figures in any country). The mystical nature of rice for the Japanese, which we discuss subsequently, accounts for some of this, but it is the nationalistic and jingoistic echoes that concern us here.

For half a century the Pacific Rim (as it is now known) resounded to the efforts and successes of Japanese nationalism. Much of the price for that was paid by common people: the Japanese themselves, then the Koreans, the Chinese, and Southeast Asians, notably Filipinos. The attractions of the nationalist position still beckon to the average Japanese. And they are strongly associated, in the common eye, with food. "If Western businessmen ate Japanese rice, they would learn to be as successful" called one pre-recession ad in a Japanese train. To Japanese, certainly for the Japanese government, which has the historical example of avoidable famine before it, food security does equate with national security. And for many Japanese, the evidence of their eyes and ears *is* that Japan – its language, its customs, its successes – are unique, special, incomparable. This is true, at an observable level of food as well. "What is the *shushoku* (staple) in your country [read 'it is of course different from ours {rice} because you are different from us"] and "Do you eat sushi"? are standard questions for almost any foreigner who sets foot in Japan for any length of time. And the distance from "unique" to "superior" is often a very small one in anyone's mind. Rice, or rather, "Japanese rice" is clearly, to some degree, an issue of *nihonjin-ron*. As Ohnuki-Tierney (1993) notes, "Japanese rice" is a modern invention. Like most sensible peasants, traditional Japanese rice farmers raised a great many kinds of rice (a study of traditional Iban farmers has shown that they raise some *two-hundred* different varieties of rice). It is only with the rise of a modern central government and its economic and media organs that rice was "homogenised" as it were. Japanese rice tends to be sweeter, moister, and with a slightly fragrant flavour. It differs in many subjective aspects from rice eaten in many other countries (Thailand, Philippines, China, Korea, Italy, US), but whether it is "the best" as Motoori Norinaga would have it, is not really a debatable issue. It *is* however, a basis by which Japanese judge themselves and others, a standard, however reached, that needs to be upheld. Besides the obvious economic issues relating to it, there is another, more basic psychological and emotional reason. Nor is it particularly important that *historically*, as some experts argue, quite a few Japanese did not eat rice as a staple. For modern Japanese (as well as for foreigners), Japanese are, at least partly, defined by the rice they eat. And, nominally, at least, this rice is *Japanese* rice.

This sense of uniqueness and national support can translate into a certain amount of underlying contempt for other countries – notably the low-valued Southeast Asian ones[11] – and their products, which in turn often helps translate into either dismissing their products, industrial or agricultural, as valueless, or to wholesale exploitation and ecological rapine, as the 1997/8 Indonesian fires have demonstrated. It is not, of course, that this feeling of superiority *drives* the exploitation, but that it hinders the provision of any brakes on the processes undertaken overseas, and by doing so, exports misery elsewhere than Japan.

This finds expression, peculiarly, in the natural food movement which is burgeoning in Japan. One of the elements that is repeated in many of the natural foods advertised is a nationalistic slant, something along the lines of "we have been eating this foreign muck, now let us try true, proper, natural Japanese food – Japanese produced and Japanese grown." Admittedly, this is a minor element in a complex and long-standing issue, involving as it does, Japanese experiences with rampant capitalism in the food area and its concomitant food pollution and adulteration.

11 That highly useful institution (for scholars interested in surveys of Japanese life, at least), the Japanese Government, runs annual surveys on every aspect of Japanese life. One perennially popular one examines Japanese attitudes to other countries and their citizens. America, China, and until recently, Russia, score consistently highly in popular appreciation. South East Asian countries score low, and correspondingly high in questions relating to degree of distaste or disapproval.

The symbolic nature of food means that food usage and its meaning can be manipulated in other ways as well, some of them to the untutored eye at least, very puzzling, certainly rather odd, and in distinct contrast to the *nihonjin-ron* model. Meat, for example, and foreign foods in general, have been viewed as catalysts for Westernisation in the most physical of senses. Starting with the Meiji period, when Japanese writers could write that the consumption of curry rice, or more specifically, milk and meat after WWII, could make the Japanese smarter and more "Western"[12] and to the late twentieth when a slick marketer could claim that eating hamburgers would make the Japanese more blond (Fujita 1992).

What is important about all these statements is not the credulity of writers or readers, but the salience of food as a means to structure social facts. Whatever the physical realities of food, the *meaning* of food, as these examples show, is a complex and deep one for Japanese culture. This is not of course unique, and all the evidence from several different cultures demonstrates that, to paraphrase an important anthropology paper on another subject, food is not just good to eat, it is good to think. The Japanese, like other cultures, think deeply on their food. The results they have come to are indeed unique, even if the process itself is a common one.

3.10 *SUMMARY*

WHAT THIS BRIEF overview of the processes that have directed Japanese food does not, of course, do justice to all the elements of this complex story. It shows, however, that the development of Japanese food depends on a number of factors external to issues strictly related to food. Japan's geographical features (that is, its climate and topography, as well as its location in relation to major features) are of primary importance. However, on that stage, human beings have created their own landscape, one of countries, agricultural practices, laws and regulations, exclusions and human ideas. These have had a major effect on the sorts of "choices" Japanese culture has made insofar as its food is concerned.

The end result of the process can be defined, in very gross terms in the following way:

Japanese cuisine is characterised by being nominally centred on cooked rice, introduced from mainland Asia. Side dishes and cooking methods from a number of different sources accompany this central staple. These foods and food processes have been modified extensively by the Japanese, along with virtually all other cultural items acquired. Japanese inventions have been blended in with innovations from abroad in such a way as to hide the seams between the two sources. This process continues today in a two-stream fashion: on the one hand, the pace of introductions from abroad has accelerated, not the least because of

12 To be fair, some Japanese writers, such as Kanagaki Robun (Keene 1956) made fun of these tendencies as well.

Japan's recent prosperity, and, at the same time, a variety of cultural and legal barriers have made this process, to some extent, a controlled and relatively non-disruptive one.

As we said, this characterisation is gross, and we will now turn our attention to trying to refine it, and to discussing and demonstrating the mechanisms and processes by which this marvellous set of human activities maintains itself and is maintained. To do so, we must start with a minute description of what a Japanese meal is, which is what we address in the next chapter.

READINGS FOR CHAPTER 3

Asquith, Pamela J. and Arne Kalland (eds) 1997 *Japanese Images of Nature: Cultural Perspectives.*

Cobbi, Jane 1978 *Le Vegetal dans la Vie Japonaise: L'utilisation Alimentaire de Plantes Sauvages dans un Village de Montagne, Kaidamura.*

Dale, Peter N. 1986 *The Myth of Japanese Uniqueness.*

Ishida, Eichiro 1974 *Japanese Culture: A Study of Origins and Characteristics.*

Ishige, Naomichi, et al. 1989 *The Food of the Showa era.*

Kagawa, Aya 1991 *Standard Tables of Food Composition in Japan, 1991.*

Knight, John 1999 "Sharing Suzuki's rice: Commodity narratives in the rural revitalization movement".

Nakane, Chie 1970 *Japanese Society.*

Ohnuki-Tierney, Emiko 1993 *Rice as Self: Japanese Identities through Time.*

Woronoff, Jon 1981 *Japan's Wasted Workers.*

4 Food Events and Their Meaning

It is useful to proceed by looking at a central food event – a meal – from which we can expand the discussion to other food events as well. Every food event, like all evanescent art forms, differs from any other, but, notwithstanding this difference, there are categorical similarities which can be pursued. There are a number of types of food event within Japanese society. That is an acceptable scholarly way to say that Japanese, as anyone else, eat in different contexts and on different occasions. We can however identify at least one *core* event – a meal – defined as a food event that has a regular appearance (or is expected to) in the life of any average individual, and which is both expected and necessary. In modern Japan, most people eat three main meals a day, though this has only fairly recently in this century become a norm, and in practical terms is true for almost all Japanese only since the post-war period.

A breakfast we had in the summer of 1996 exemplifies some of the issues.

> Jeanne had a Western breakfast, Michael, Japanese. Both were served on lacquered trays while we looked out over the hotel's small garden. Jeanne's breakfast consisted of coffee, orange juice, two thick toast slices, two fried eggs that had been liberally peppered, two slices of grilled ham resting on slices of lettuce. A quarter of a grapefruit rested on a small round plate with two grapes on top. Each grape had been sliced so that it had a flat base, and the top had been peeled into a flower shape, exposing the pulp. There were two pats of butter, and three containers of jam. The waiter served the coffee from a coffee-pot. Talking it over later, we noted that the waiter was careful to pour the coffee deliberately with a flourish, and to pour no more than two thirds of a cup
>
> Michael's Japanese breakfast was in effect standard. A teapot held green tea for a ceramic handle-less tea-cup. A slice of grilled salted salmon rested on a small bamboo leaf on one side of a lacquered black plate. A covered lacquered container held steamed white rice, the slotted top of the container supporting a plastic rice paddle for moving the rice to the small, plain, *tenmoku* ware *chawan* (rice bowl). A black, punt-shaped container bore a transparent plastic-wrapped oblong of several sheets of *nori*. A larger round plate, garnished with a green bamboo leaf held *takuan* (radish bran

pickle), two slices of *kamaboko* (fish paste), and two small pieces of sweet omelette.

It is immediately apparent that the meal is intended to be eaten simultaneously, that is, unlike the European meal in which one course follows another, all the food to be consumed appears on the table at once. True,. this may be a feature of the fact that this is a hotel meal, and breakfast at that, but as we shall see presently, it is in general often true of Japanese meals that they are consumed as single tray meals or a variation thereof.

Another thing worth considering is that in both the Western and the Japanese version of the meal, great care is taken over presentation. The proper placement of food, the right way to move the material, the proper way to serve are classified as part of appropriate manners in many societies. *How* a food is served is often as important as what the food is.

Food events (Douglas and Gross 1981) – any event in which food is consumed – are structured and affected by several features of life. They are subject to time: different sorts of food events take place at different times of the day, month, and year. They are subject to social conditions: a food event in which only one individual participates in the food is likely to be manifestly different from one in which twenty, or even two, participate. Food events are subject to alterations due to economic and political conditions, social and ideological strictures, and other human effects.

The differences between different kinds of food events express themselves in visible and observable dimensions: foodstuffs, setting, service, timing, which are dependent on social features. In this chapter we shall try to illuminate the differences between different kinds of Japanese food events, and relate them to the social features that structure them.

4.1 *THE SCHEMATIC STRUCTURE OF THE JAPANESE MEAL*

To START, LET us consider a Japanese meal as a schematic model. A model *for* – to cite Geertz (1966) – which individuals may or may not follow, but which most will recognise and acknowledge as a representation of the ways things "should be."

A "schematic" Japanese meal consists of three elements: a carbohydrate, a soup (*suimono*), and a side dish (*okazu*). The preferred normal carbohydrate is plain cooked rice – *gohan* – though as we shall see other carbohydrates are quite common. The soup is generally a fish-stock based broth. Side dishes come in many forms, but in the most basic form it is usually a vegetable, traditionally quite often pickled. This basic module is called one-soup one-vegetable, *ichijū issai*, the presence of rice (or a substitute if rice is not available) is taken for granted. For younger Japanese, in their teens and twenties, *okazu* always implies some form of protein – meat, poultry, or fish – though this was not always the case. In the simplest possible meal, each one of these elements will be served in a dish of its own, eaten with chopsticks. It would be washed down with a beverage, normally tea, boiled water, or barley water.

An important, albeit covert feature of Japanese society must be considered here: modularity. For generations many aspects of Japanese life have been based on the construction of larger, complex domains by bringing together smaller, more basic elements, analogous perhaps to the "primitives" of some computer languages: basic building blocks, which, by inspired combination can yield complex structures. This can be seen in the structuring of social organisations, architectural elements, and manufacture. It is also visible in the construction of food events. It is as if the Japanese *consciously* construct elaborate social constructs of "empty" vessels which can be filled at leisure. An effect that derives from that is a principle of internal autonomy, which allows any element to change, mutate, enlarge or shrink so long as its "topological" relations with other elements remain the same. We can see this effect, and how these principles operate, in the case of Japanese meals.

These elements and the way we conceive of them pull the entire "corpus" of meal types into focus. To do so, let's consider each element in terms of its composing features.

We start, as is proper, with boiled rice. *Gohan* or *meshi*, as the name implies, is the central item of our schematic meal. Ignoring for the moment some specific permitted variations, it is simply that: a bowl of white cooked rice. People do put flavourings on the cooked rice – *furikake* (flakes of *nori*, salted salmon, and other flavourings), curry sauce,[1] may be added to white rice, and there are risotto-like versions of rice (*takikomi gohan*) featuring seasonal delicacies such as bamboo shoots or gingko nuts added during cooking, beans to colour the rice (*sekihan*) and even a form of sushi (*chirashi-zushi*). Nonetheless, the standard is white rice served as is. Cooked rice is judged by a number of sensory criteria. It must have the right flavour, of course, but it must also have an appropriate stickiness (*nebari*) dictated by the use of chopsticks, but which has become, by now, an issue of aesthetics as well, and a visible lustre when cooked.

The serving utensil is a *chawan*, (lit. 'tea-bowl'), most often (or normatively) of ceramic, sometimes of wood. With the exception of Korean restaurants or food, it is never served in metal bowls, and we have never seen it served in glass.

Food, as we have noted, is a social marker, a way by which people express various social sentiments without having to iterate them aloud. One way of doing this is by way of the quality of materials used. And Japanese diners are not loath

1 There are exceptions to this. The simplest is celebratory red rice (*sekihan*), actually red wine-coloured from the azuki beans cooked with it. Rice with more elaborate flavourings or more than one addition are "scattered" sushi rice (*chirashi*) and a wide range of all-in-one dish *donburi* which feature meat, fish or poultry and vegetables cooked separately but served on top of rice in a large ceramic bowl or lacquered container, often with a lid. But in such cases, they constitute a dish, or even a meal on their own.

to play the "Best rice ..." game. "The best rice comes from certain rice fields near Uji," one informant told us, describing the precise location of the field. "I can tell not only which field the rice I eat is from, but when it has been cut." Whether true or not (and such a boast rivals the efforts of the most finicky of wine-lovers), the concern with the quality of rice is a paramount cultural concern. Special parties go out to be near the fields where *shinmai* ('new' rice: the first of the season) is harvested so that the sugar in the rice will not become starch in the time between cutting and selling at the rice shop. Special bags of *shinmai* can be bought or ordered from many rice merchants. In actual terms, Japanese today eat about 70 kg of rice per person per year. This is less than half the 180 litres of rice which were the standard rice ration in Edo period Japan. This measure, a *koku*, also served as an economic measure, since stipends to retainers were paid in *koku* of rice. But the emotional and symbolic importance of rice continues to overshadow all others in the realm of food.

Most individuals, however, would not be capable of identifying the product of one field from another, any more than a blindfolded layman can distinguish between several wines at a tasting.[2] An expensive *chawan* (rice bowl) in addition, serves notice that the owner is wealthy, a cultural connoisseur, has a family history of importance, knows proper etiquette and so on. The production, use, and (rarely ostentatious) display of proper ceramic utensils has been an ongoing feature of Japanese society for generations, and has become widespread as a result of the Tea ceremony.[3] Ceramics were valued and treasured even before Sen-no-Rikyu, who codified the Tea ceremony in the sixteenth century, made a business of certifying tea utensils. The value of certain utensils has incremented with use from generation to generation. In the 1950s with the rise of the folkcraft movement, pottery began to obsess the average middle-class Japanese more than ever. For our point of view, this opens a large field in which the meal can be played, using only the ceramic utensils. Even without changing the parameters of the shape – a rice bowl must fit the hand, must be of rounded shape, cannot contain too much – there are innumerable variations on the theme. The external high valuation placed on certain objects means that there is also an extreme range of value (in cash terms) of utensils used. And finally (perhaps no less importantly) all of these differences – rice provenance included – are in the form of extremely subtle clues which only the cognoscenti know and are able to fully appreciate.

2 There are, of course, varietal rice types whose popularity waxes and wanes with fashion. Koshihikari noted for its quality and corresponding price is one, and is in great demand. Akita friends swear by Akitakomachi, perhaps because the name evokes a classical beauty and poet who resided near Yuzawa. A third well-known rice variety, Sasanishiki, also commands high prices. All of these illustrate the intersections of issues such as the rise of the *gurume*, marketing, and conspicuous consumption in modern Japan, all of which will be discussed subsequently.

3 Specialist journals on fine cooking, such as Shiki no Aji, cite the provenance (maker, type of glaze, kiln, source, etc.) of implements – ceramic, lacquer, wood or even glass – on which foods are photographed.

The use of a particular rice bowl is thus in itself a signal of wealth, erudition, and quality. It can convey seasonality by extremely delicate hints (not to mention convoluted ones: a bowl made in emulation of a famous tea bowl indicating a season by reference to the season in which the original tea-bowl came to light, for example), the event, or anything else by a covert, sometimes acknowledged, game of hidden witticisms and classical literary or historical references. The association with the Tea ceremony gives the rice bowl a hidden potential: it is associated with the most refined, the most expensive of all culturally valued activities. Meat is the centrepiece in the British Sunday dinner, and its quality and presentation are central to the definition of the meal. The situation is far more complex in our schematic Japanese meal. The centrepiece is rice, without which the event could not be defined a proper meal. Its intrinsic quality, the care taken in its presentation, its lustre, the serving bowl – are, without question, significant, and yet, because of its constant presence at most meals, and because of the unchanging nature of the rice itself, whose methods of preparation and (lack of) seasoning are restricted intentionally to preserve its pristine nature and flavour, it is an element that, no matter how significant, does not call attention to itself in the same way as a hunk of roast does. It is also worth noting that whereas second helpings of accompanying dishes are not provided for in formal meals outside the home, the same does not hold true for rice, and men usually have two or more helpings.[4]

Shirumono, the "soup" element of a Japanese meal, suggest greater complexity, and more dimensions than the rice element. Where rice has an on-off quality commensurate with its great importance – one either eats rice and has a "meal" or does not, and has a "snack" – *shirumono* allows the cook to make several distinct kinds of statements. The generic term *shirumono* refers to both clear light soups called *suimono* and thick soups (*shiru*). *Suimono* are more usually served in restaurants, and include three elements: a piece of fish, seafood or poultry; a vegetable which complements the fish; and an aromatic garnish, such as a sprig of trefoil (*mitsuba)* greens or citron slivers. More often, however, in the modern world, *shirumono* means *miso shiru*: a broth to which fermented soy bean paste (*miso)* has been added.

The making of *suimono* is a complex process. The foremost source of flavouring for *suimono* is prime fish stock (*ichiban dashi*). It is actually incorrect to call *ichiban dashi* "stock" because neither boiling or long simmering of the stock ingredients is involved, and if so, would be likely to ruin its characteristic delicacy of flavour and aroma. *Ichiban dashi* is more properly a tea based on processed fish flakes (*katsuobushi*) and seaweed. However it has no hint of fish or seaweed, and ignorant first-time sippers may be forgiven for mistaking it for very refined, fat-free chicken stock. In contrast to French classic stocks that are simmered as long

4 When saké is drunk throughout a meal, whether at home or outside, no plain rice is served until the drinking is done. Our neighbours in Akita explained this as, "out or respect for the rice, which, being the same major ingredient in saké, should not have to share the limelight."

as possible for maximum flavour, *dashi* is almost instanteous stock. The time required is no more than it takes to let the required amount of water to come to the boil.

First, to prepare the *katsuo bushi.* A fillet of dried, fermented, and aged bonito *(katsuo),* closely resembling an extremely hard chunk of driftwood,[5] is shaved (with an implement called *katsuobushi kezuriki,* somewhat like a reversed carpenter's plane set in a box) into thin flakes. The resulting shavings will look as if you had been playing rather extensively with a pencil sharpener. Set the shavings aside. Lately, instant *dashi* powder (*dashi no moto*) has superseded this procedure, and very few home cooks make stock from scratch.

Giant kelp (*konbu*) strips are placed in cold water in a pot and brought slowly to the boil at medium heat. Just before the water boils, the kelp is taken out. Cold water is added to lower the temperature of the water and the *katsuo* flakes are added. Just before the water comes to the boil, the heat is turned off. Once the flakes have settled at the bottom of the pot, the surface is skimmed of foam and other floating impurities. The used kelp and flakes can be simmered further for use in secondary stock (*niban dashi*) suitable for stews and *miso* soup.

It is the *ichiban dashi* which forms the basis for *suimono,* by the addition of one, or a combination of two garnishes. These garnishes, particularly when the soup remains clear, exhibit a great deal of variety, from vegetables, through elaborate "knots" of vegetable jellies, to cheeks of *tai* (bream). The transparency of the soup demands and accepts only the visually attractive, and thus constitutes a challenge to the cook, as well as to the diner.

The most common (in both senses of the term: wide-spread and non-elite) soup, however, is based on *miso,* particularly in home cooking. *Miso,* an essential flavouring in Japanese cooking, is a paste made by fermenting soy-beans with salt. It varies regionally, from a pale creamy yellow to almost black. The colour, saltiness, and overall flavour are determined by the amount of salt, the kind of fermenting agent used (rice-based, wheat-based, or barley-based), and the coarseness of the grinding. *Miso* making used to be a cottage industry in some places, and was, until the advent of modern industrial methods and marketing, a strictly local product. The numbers of *miso* types have declined in the present century, but are still quite large. Each household has a distinctive flavour for its *miso* soup, and restaurants strive to emulate this individuality by blending several *miso* types.

The *miso* is blended into the stock, and the pot immediately removed from the heat. The result is a cloudy, warm mixture which provides the stock with depth and body. Sometimes the stock is made more robust by adding *niboshi,* dried small fish. Additions and garnishes are legion: green-onions, tofu cubes, small clams, radish slices.

5 Somewhat similar to Bombay duck, which is not a duck but a rock-hard dried fillet of fish. Heating is required to enable the cutting off of pieces, which are then crumbled for use in cooking or as a garnish.

In the choice of the garnishes the cook/server is making a series of statements about position, wealth and perspicacity at a covert level, and statements about the season, the rest of the meal, the ambience, at an overt level. There are also historical and political issues to be considered. *Miso shiru* originated as a Kantō (Eastern Japan) food, and its spread throughout the islands is an indication of the penetration of metropolitan fashions, the homogenisation of Japanese culture and life since the start of the century.

In serving *suimono* as in serving rice, the utensils play a part. The normative ideal is to serve it in lidded lacquered wooden bowls. The quality of the lacquer, its decoration, the shape of the bowl (usually, but not always, a footed flattened hemisphere, lacquered red inside and black or red without) allows for a great deal of innovation, decoration, and overt statements. There is a pull factor, a correlation between the wealth and connoiseurship of contents and container. A clear *suimono must* be served in a quality bowl. Not only would a poor, badly lacquered[6] bowl be immediately obvious through the clear liquid, but it would also be ludicrous, making mock of the attempt to preserve a high-level ambience. Of course, as in most prescriptions of that sort, there are many exceptions. The shape of the bowl may be different, middle-range establishments may use cheaper lacquer or even plastic, the quality of which improves constantly. But these exceptions serve to prove the rule: they are attempts to *emulate* for good or for ill, statements of quality and richness.

Okazu (the accompanying side dishes) help define the food event. The most basic module is one soup, one dish, usually a vegetable (*ichijū issai*), though nowadays, one soup, three dishes (*ichijū sansai*) is more common (rather like the British meat and two veg): an "upgrading" coming about through the gradual rise of affluence in Japanese society. One soup, three dishes is also the traditional basic module for *kaiseki*,[7] the meal preceding a "thick tea" *(koicha)* ceremony, and its prevalence in daily family meals illustrates the percolation of formerly-elite practices into the mass of the population.

Most cooks are guided by certain basic principles in assembling a menu. Foremost is to judiciously combine the flavours of the mountain and the flavours of the sea – *yama no sachi, umi no sachi* – and those of (cultivated) field and river. Next is to consider the harmony of all the accompanying dishes in terms of colour, their intrinsic texture, and the added texture imparted by the five methods of cooking – deep and shallow frying, stewing, steaming, grilling – as

6 The quality of lacquer is generally judged by the number of layers of material deposited on the wooden base. It does not require too much perspicacity to distinguish a one- or two-layered lacquer from a multi-layered one.

7 Although in general, *kaiseki* refers to the Tea ceremony meal, there is another *kaiseki*, written using a different Chinese character, which is used to denote a multi-course banquet held in a *ryōtei* for a group of people belonging to an organisation or who share a hobby, e.g., flower arrangement, traditional singing, etc. This would normally feature games or some other group entertainment, on special occasions such as New Year. At fancier restaurants, the term could also appear on the menu and denotes a multi-course Japanese meal.

well as the combination of the five flavours – salty, sweet, sour, bitter, and sharp. The contrast of cool or chilled dishes with hot is also considered.

The principles underlying the basic module of one soup three dishes is the result of various influences on endogenous frugal foodstuffs culled from nature. Prominent among those influences were some we have discussed broadly above: aristocratic and samurai practices of eating from low footed lacquered trays, each tray holding one "course"; Chinese chronological celebrations and the accompanying ritual foods, seasonings (soy sauce) and cooking styles (use of oil); Buddhist vegetarian preferences brought from China by Japanese scholar-monks; the all-encompassing aesthetic desiderata of the Tea ceremony; Western – *namban* (Portuguese and Spanish), Dutch, British – and other foreign ingredients (meat) and styles of cooking (baking); and the exuberant lifestyle of Edo and Osaka townspeople that made them very receptive to novelty and stimulated creativity in food, as well as other matters.

The combining and arrangement of foods (the two are inseparable) in the normal household or restaurant are supported by an aesthetic and ideological structure. This has been elaborated, as many other aesthetic endeavors in Japan, by schools of aesthetic thought or cooking styles. The Shijoryu style of cooking, for example, assembles its menu on the basis of the "three taste peaks" embodied in traditional *sankaishiki* (decorative or aesthetic) principles. That is, it believes that tastiness (*oishisa*) and quality alone are not sufficiently valid criteria for putting foods together. Much as music has its low notes and high notes, and mountain landscapes have valleys and deep gorges, so a menu must display similar high and low contrasts to create a rhythmic pattern while dining. The three peaks are – from highest to lowest – stewed dishes (*kuchitorizakana*), grilled fish (*yakizakana*), and raw fish (*ikezukuri*). *Kuchitorizakana* or *kumizakana* (*zakana* in this term derives from "saké" (wine) and not the more usual "*sakana*": fish), literally "take to the mouth" or "grouped" dish, consisted of seven or nine mixed delicacies, such as steamed fish paste (*kamaboko*), sweetened chestnut puree (*kuri kinton*), or omelette-wrapped shrimp (*tamago-maki ebi*). *Yakizakana* was usually salt-grilled red bream (*tai*) served on a big platter or lacquer tray. *Ikezukuri* (lit. "raw preparation") was *sashimi* of bream, bonito, prawn or other seasonal fish and seafood. All of these were enhanced by decorative garnishes keyed to the season and mood. The peaks represent not only figurative taste constructs but also more concrete ones expressed in the heights of serving implements used. Whether served in a large platter for a group or smaller individual portions, the serving dishes used must likewise have correspondingly varied heights and depths.

The cooking and food styles have a reciprocal influence on the major aesthetic icon in Japanese culture: the Tea ceremony. The principles of *ichijū sansai* are codified within the structure of *kaiseki* (Tea ceremony cuisine). It is this ritualisation which is partially responsible for the preservation of the aesthetic principles of Japanese cuisine as coherent standards. Though individuals and households can engage in changing, manipulating, and elaborating (or simplifying) these forms, they remain as known standards for comparison. That a great many people participate in the Tea ceremony in one way or another, ensures that these principles are, at the very least, known in some measure to a large swathe of the population.

Tea ceremony cuisine (*kaiseki*) has codified this "one soup three dishes" module as: soup, a raw (usually fish or seafood) dish, pickles, and stew. In *kaiseki* terminology, these are *shiru*, *mukō zuke*, *kōnomono*, and *nimono*. Of these, only *mukō zuke* is not common usage, although it has entered food specialists' jargon and regularly appears in *ryōtei* (traditional exclusive restaurant) and *ryōri-ya* (traditional restaurant) menus, as well as food journals. The simmered stew (*nimono*) is the centrepiece in *kaiseki* and represents the acme of the host's or hostess's skill in choice of seasonal ingredients, textural harmony, and flavouring. Two sub-courses follow, a light almost flavourless consommé to clean off the eating implements, literally called "chopstick wash" (*hashi arai*) and a tray or rectangular container (*hassun*)[8] of mountain and sea (or field and river) delicacies to accompany the saké[9] that is offered again at this time. Other saké accompaniments, called *shiizakana*, *azukebachi* or *susume zakana*, may be added if the courses are deemed insufficient. While up to 17 courses may have been offered in the past, the aim in *kaiseki* is for the host or hostess to give a simple yet well-thought out repast as a background to tea-drinking, and any more than the standard one soup three dishes (plus *hashi arai* and *hassun*) would prove too burdensome and probably require professional help, thus negating the essence of *kaiseki*.

We can see that when additional dishes are added to the basic structure, there is a definite progression of preferences. Raw fish or other seafood is at the top of the list. Next comes grilled fish. Then a stewed dish. What happens beyond the one soup three dishes structure? Traditionally, hors d'oeuvres called *saké no sakana* (also called *tsuki dashi*, *sakitsuke* or *kozuke*) are served before the raw fish. After the stewed dish, a vinegar or citrus-juice marinaded *sunomono* is served. Beyond this, a further structure called *nijū nanasai* (two soups seven dishes) exists. It comprises saké hors d'ouevres, clear soup (*suimono*), *sashimi*, grilled dish, *kuchikawari* (with 7 or 9 assorted tidbits), stewed dish, vinegared dish, *miso* soup, sweet and green tea. Modern complex menus are structured quite differently from this, and will include a deep-fried dish (*agemono*) and steamed dish (*mushimono*) in addition to the above, though a nod to tradition is indicated, as for example when another item is substituted for a stewed dish, it is called "stewed dish substitute" (*nimono kawari*).

Beyond the choices determined by the traditional menu structure and methods of cooking, are influencing factors such as the season, the occasion, the ages and gender of the diners, as well as elements of the cook's and diners' individuality including class, wealth, pretensions, and regional origin. References

8 The course's name is literally "eight (Japanese) inches", the standard measure for the wooden (normally cedar) flat trays used to serve the tidbits.

9 Which, in contrast to other non-Tea ceremony events and saké-drinking banquets, is offered at the same time as rice. This is in recognition of the role of saké in enhancing the flavours of the various dishes that accompany rice, as well as to denote that the saké is not the main attraction in the meal.

to the season are not only in the seasonal ingredients used, but also in the edible decorations used called *tsuma*, ranging from aromatic Japanese pepper sprigs to *shiso* flower buds and bamboo leaves. The references can often be obscure, and, given the multiple and manifold usage of signs in Japanese society, sometimes misleading. One such example is the slip of jagged green plastic that often accompanies dishes in cheaper restaurants and picnic boxes, sometimes serving as a separator between different items. Originally the green was a slip of aspidistra leaf, whose greenness was an indicator of the freshness of the contents. As an indicator of freshness, the plastic leaf fails miserably, as a *sign* indicating freshness, if unconsciously, to the Japanese diner, it performs its duty admirably well.

Japanese meal arrangements, notably but not only the *okazu*, also make explicit references to nature that go beyond the immediate. Proper food presentation, particularly in the upper (that is, more expensive and elaborate) levels of dining, includes an indication of the seasons, whether by use of conventional (and inedible) signs, such as appropriate leaves or seeds, or by the provision of foods that are in *shun*: the peak of perfection. As foods enter their individual *shun*, discerning Japanese and their suppliers – wholesalers, retailers, restaurateurs – are under pressure to supply the appropriate item. And up-market restaurants will take great pains in their presentations, to ensure that the menu is kept up to date, or, more properly, up to season. Plum blossoms might decorate a food in the winter or early spring,[10] chestnuts in the fall, whether in symbolic form – for example, vegetables cut in the appropriate shapes – or the actual products. By doing so the environment of most Japanese is suffused with *some* form of association and communication with nature (artificially engendered or not, is not the point)[11] and, by so doing, with their conceptions of what Japanese culture is, or is supposed to be: sensitive to the natural world, aware of the tiniest hint, the most restrained statement.

To translate menu structures derived from *kaiseki* and the formal cooking schools to home cooked dishes (*sōzai*) and everyday occasions, requires simplification: one soup two dishes would comprise *miso* soup, a cooked vegetable, and *sashimi* or other raw fish/seafood dish, such as *namasu* (vinegar or citrus marinaded seafood similar to seviche). Another dish might be added to make one soup three dishes: the standard addition is a grilled or dry-cooked dish (*yakimono*), usually fish. A stewed dish may be substituted for the grilled dish. In the modern world, the formal structures, even abbreviated as they are, would be hard to follow

---

10 Traditional and modern calendar reckoning are in conflict. Thus though plum blooms in February in the Kantō region, it is regarded a "spring" flower by some, and a "winter" one by other sources.

11 One of our friends, as a student, carried out a study of street decorations put up by merchant associations in small Japanese neighbourhoods. These, which, it must be emphasised, are made of plastic and other artificial materials, are changed with the seasons. This means that street-posts are decorated in the spring with sprigs of artificial cherry-blossoms, in summer with green leaves, autumn with red maple leaves, and winter with pine needles draped with tinsel to represent snow. No one seems to feel it incongruous to represent the changes of *natural* seasons by using *artificial* materials.

but for the emergence and rising importance of convenience foods, modern marketing and transportation methods, and the supermarket. For women who also work outside the home, ensuring one soup three dishes for dinner everyday is not an easy task. Here the vast range of ready-to-eat dishes sold at supermarkets and department stores is a godsend. "On my way home from work, I already have a mental image of what I want to serve, based on what I have in the house. But if I don't have the main dish thought out, either *yakimono* or *nimono*, then I first see what looks freshest and most interesting and then buy that, and plan to cook that from scratch. After that, I just look around some more and choose two or three other items to round it out, perhaps a tray of good-looking *sashimi* and some seasoned vegetables. Having all those cooked dishes to choose from is so convenient, and I don't have the trouble of buying too much. A few hundred grams is sufficient for each," said one informant, a career woman and experienced housewife.

Allied with the variance in ingredients and cooking method is the variety of utensils and their constituent materials, ranging from ceramic, stoneware, glass, through wood, leaves, and stones. Because the plate on which a dish is served is as much a part of it, and in fact each item in a Japanese meal is intended to be a piece of art in itself, great care is taken in selecting the proper setting for the food. The average household would thus have a variety of utensils – bowls, plates, dishes – in a wide range of colours – red, black, green, yellow, brown – and made of a variety of materials and finishes: lacquerware (plain or with gold motifs), pottery (ceramicware and stoneware) from kilns throughout Japan in rough, crazed, cracked, and smooth glazes. Fanciful shapes – triangles, fans, shells, squares, octagons, pentagons, cylinders, crescents – would also be present, representing both the taste of the owner and the necessities imposed by the form, colour, taste, and evocative nature of the food to be served: "Plates are the clothes for food," Rōsanjin, the noted ceramicist and cook has noted.

Having briefly discussed the elements of a Japanese meal it is possible to see how putting these elements together in different ways, creates different types of food events. These different types correlate with significant social features, and link meals to other elements of Japanese society, ranging from religion to modern industry. Just manipulating the three elements we have discussed, generates three distinct types of Japanese food events. Each of these will be discussed in turn.

4.2 *CENTRAL RICE MEALS*

THE MEAL WHICH is most commonly eaten, the one for which the word "*gohan*" stands emotionally and practically, is a meal in which rice is the centrepiece. In other words, the type model described above. In a normal household, this may well be the main meal of the day, where all the household members gather:

> In the family setting, meals are relatively informal, so while we set the table, with willing if obstructive help of the baby, Mitsuko moves the rice

> from the automatic rice cooker to the serving tub, and covers it. In the meantime we place a setting before the five of us. Excluding the baby, each of us receives a bowl for *miso shiru*, another for rice, and a flat plate for *okazu*. On the flat plate we put a mound of shredded cabbage topped with a dab of mayonnaise, and beside it several pieces of *chorogi* (Chinese artichoke) pickle, of which Michael is extremely fond. Mitsuko quickly moves a slice of salted grilled herring onto each plate, after putting the rice container, its paddle poking up, in the centre of the table. *Miso shiru* is quickly ladled out to each bowl. She serves rice to each diner in turn. We sit down, each of the adults helping themselves to a pair of chopsticks from the container in the centre of the table, the baby playing with his plastic utensils. We drink cold *mugi-cha* (barley tea) to cool us in the hot day.

The description is of a simple meal in which rice predominates. It is, in essence, the "type-case" of the Japanese meal. Our friend Mitsuko made sure that everyone's rice bowl was kept full, each diner had a set amount of *okazu*, and anyone could ask for more soup. Though times have changed, and meals are neither gulped down, nor do people try to cram as much rice into their bellies in a sitting as they can, the centrality of rice is quite clear. No one is upset, nor expects, all the foods to be consumed, but avoiding eating rice would be a solecism.

These "central rice meals" as we label them here, characterise most of the family meals in a survey we conducted in 1991. Middle-class families tended to have fewer of these meals than they would have had twenty or more years before. Breakfast, for instance, was often a Western meal, particularly for children and younger adults. But a family meal (excepting eating-out) was indicated by the presence of a rice bowl, a flow of rice, and, because the families we surveyed were (as most of Japan) able to afford it, a variety of enticing and tasty *okazu*. But – most housewives, young and old, we interviewed were at pains to state – rice is central to a *proper* meal. It, more than anything else, defines the meal. The importance of rice was brought home to us more than once. In one memorable occasion being hosted by a young family in a mountain village in Niigata prefecture, we had several courses ranging from *teppanyaki* to sliced corned beef and bananas. It ended, however, with a bowl of curry rice which, perforce, we were expected to finish.

4.3 *PERIPHERAL RICE MEALS*

Rice is not always at the centre of the proceedings. In fact, a "*gohan*" can include rice only peripherally, a sop to "proper" food, as well as a psychological necessity. For the modern European or American, the importance of a single carbohydrate staple is not so evident. We can, and do eat a variety of staple starches: potatoes, rice, noodles, polenta. We tend to forget that in recent history, as Murcott notes, and indeed even today for many families in the UK, potatoes are a "must have" for any truly satisfying meal. In Japan, as throughout most of East, Southeast, and South Asia, rice is that staple.

In modern Japanese society, however, this staple – *shushoku* – is not necessarily the centrepiece of meals. This has of course been true of all societies throughout time, in which staples have been peripheralised during specific food events such as feasts. Feasts are not everyday experiences, but, nonetheless, people are familiar with feasts partly, at least, because they structurally replicate daily meals. In Japan, a "peripheral rice meal" emulates a "central rice meal" in the presence and quantity of rice. The same amount of rice is there, but the *okazu* is expanded enormously and the rice is pushed to the periphery at the end. Most feasts, which are always peripheral-rice meals, are also undertaken with a set of formal rules in operation, such as exhibited, in abbreviated form, at the dinner we describe here:

> The party was a celebration of the completion of a complicated piece of collective work. The host, the most senior man present, was from Kyushu. The venue was not a restaurant, but a *ryōtei* (traditional exclusive restaurant) famed for its Kyushu cuisine. The *ryōtei* itself occupied several floors furnished in traditional settings, an oasis of traditional fittings amidst the skyscrapers and modernity of city life. We entered through a small and very narrow "cat's lap" garden, with raked gravel and a small pond, into a wide *genkan* (entryway) where we deposited outdoor gear (shoes, summer hats) with kimono-dressed receptionists, one of whom led us upstairs. Conveyed to the second floor along polished wood floors, we entered a 24–*tatami* room. The halls were panelled in polished wood, decorated with traditional objets-d'art and discreet flower arrangements (a decor that persisted, as we later discovered, in the washrooms as well).
>
> We entered the room to find most of the guests already seated around an open-sided square. They were sitting formally, mostly on their knees, on cushions around the external side of the hollow square. Our proper bowing and formal introduction elicited a certain amount of laughter, Noda-san (our host) saying quite loudly that "modern Japanese no longer know how to do that sort of thing." Much practised in formal bowing – Jeanne in the etiquette of flower arranging, Michael in that of *iaido* – we laughed too. There were twelve of us. It was a hot mid-summer evening, and everyone (except one friend, the irrepressible Ito, who wore a gaudy silk shirt in deference to the formality of the occasion) wore dark business suits.
>
> A toast, drunk in beer, though saké was available, started the proceedings. Then the waitresses arrived, in elegant kimono, and first ensuring that everyone had a drink of their choosing, brought in the food. Since it was the middle of an extremely hot summer, the menu was labelled appropriately *Natsu hoyuru* (summer blaze).

The first course was individual servings of *tori goma hitashi* (chilled boiled chicken with sesame), which, our genial host informed us, was a speciality of his home town in Kyushu, of which he was particularly fond. Small chunks of chicken flesh had been quickly scalded in a light stock thickened with sesame oil, giving the dish an almost Chinese aura. This, served in rustic ceramic jars, was accompanied by green, crisp asparagus that had been cut to be handled with chopsticks, and which cut the heavier smell and taste of the sesame with a hint of the fresh sharpness of newly cut grass.

A *mori awase* ("mixed mound") followed: a collection of titbits arranged on individual rough ceramic plates. The delicacies included *Yanagawa maki* (loach [a small riverine fish] cooked in egg), salted *ayu* (sweetfish) intestines, Arima style sculpin [a spiny river fish] stewed with powdered *sansho* spice. Arima, in Central Japan, is traditionally the source of the best *sansho*, a spice evocative of summer since it is used frequently on such summer delicacies as grilled eel. There was a small mound of glistening dark red candied arbutus, appropriately called *yamamomo* (mountain peach). The fruit, a small, nubbly red sphere with a cherry-like stone has a vague strawberry-like flavour, and matures in mid-summer. A few small pieces of fresh corn on the cob, roasted and lightly dabbed with light soy sauce, and *miso*-glazed taro completed the ensemble, which was decorated with fresh bamboo leaves for effect.

The main course was introduced by a *tsukuri* (a "food word" for *sashimi*) of *ishigarei usutzukuri*. Thin slices of rock turbot, a small delicate flatfish that is greatly prized in Japan as elsewhere, had been lightly marinated in *ponzu* sauce. *Ponzu* is the juice of a small bitter orange, with a remarkably refreshing taste. The fish, pale pink shading to darker flesh, was served with a small "nest" of young green shoots, which had just come into season.

The main course was divided into three elements: *nimono* (simmered or stewed things), *yakimono* (roasted, or grilled foods), and *sunomono* (vinegared, or pickled things). The *nimono* was served cold: slices of grilled eggplant, cubes of *umedofu* (tofu flavoured with plums), a small *saimaki* roll, soft-cooked kidney beans, green shoots, and yellow sweet bean paste cubes accompanied the centrepiece: *tori jibuni*. Chicken sections had been stewed in a pot in a thick broth of freshly harvested *soba* (buckwheat flour), plain flour, *mirin*, soy sauce, and stock, then allowed to cool. The end result, balanced against the garnishing, was a surprisingly refreshing, light summery dish.

The *yakimono* was *tachiuo kenchinyaki* (cutlass fish: a long, vertically flattened fish looking somewhat like an eel). Slices of the silvery fish had been cooked in a style of cooking imported from China, with tofu, carrots, *shiitake* mushrooms, bamboo sprouts, and *gobō* (burdock root). This was accompanied by pickled *myōga* (Japanese ginger) buds. The same word *myōga*, written with different characters, means divine blessing, or

> protection, though our host refused to be drawn into a discussion of what he was protecting us *from*. Finally the course was completed with Chinese-style vegetables
>
> The final element of the main course was a *sunomono* collection: pickles intended to see the rice through and to refresh the palate. Pickled slices of *saba* (mackerel), cucumbers, young shoots, and red peppers, were pickled in *nanban* ("Southern barbarian" [i.e., Spanish or Portuguese]) style, a delicate escabeche. These were served with small containers of freshly cooked rice: the necessary "centre" of any meal.
>
> As is not unusual, the alcohol, the good food, and the fact that most of the participants knew one another for some time meant that the party got louder as the evening wore on. Eventually, staggering somewhat from the weight of food and drink, we made our way back to the hot streets.

As can be seen, there are several differences between the family meal described earlier, and the formal feast. First, in the same manner as a classical European (= French) meal, there were several "covers." Each cover – we called them "courses" above – consists of several foods arrayed in some manner, on a tray, in dishes, and so on. Each cover is cleared, and another is brought in. Rice only features peripherally, at the end. Saké drinking party etiquette requires rice to be served after saké is no longer drunk: the tastes of rice and rice-derived saké clash, say purists.

There is also a great deal of "fit" between the occasion, the foods, and the utensils used. The latter are elaborate, fine pottery, good lacquer, hand-blown glass dishes appropriate to the summer. Not a piece of plastic in sight. Moreover, the fit extends throughout the event. With the exception of one iconoclastic guest for whom allowances were made, most people were dressed formally. The *ryōtei* was a formal place in which polished wood, fine decoration, and traditional craftsmanship extended itself to the confines of the equally impressive toilets with cedarwood sinks and fresh floral arrangement, lacquered fittings, and handcrafted (unrolled) tissue paper. The idea that there must be a "fit" between events is not, of course, unique to Japanese thinking. It underlies, as Irvine says, many formal human activities. This fit helps us explore the entire structure of peripheral rice meals. They occur quite often as markers and signifiers of important events, they formalise and publicise issues of importance to the participants, whether these be a couple being married, criminal gangs cementing an alliance, or seasonal changes. This is not surprising: feasts normally require a great investment and many resources. And they afford their participants with a great deal of sensory satisfaction and pleasure, in addition to an opportunity to display valued social facts and sentiments.

Nor is it surprising that white rice, which defines a proper meal and the expected modular accompaniment of pickles, is here pushed into the periphery. Rice, after all, is designed to satisfy one's *food* needs: to fill one up. Feasts, and rice-peripheral meals are undoubtedly feasts, are intended to do many other things: demonstrate prestige, define sociability and social togetherness, display wealth. The plastic, autonomous structure of the elements of Japanese meals allows this sort of display and ostentation. Rice, the indicator of togetherness, remains much the same, but the *okazu* element of the meal is infinitely expandable in theory. Wealth without refinement would be ludicrous and incongruous, given Japanese self-view as a refined culture, one that appreciates and understands elaboration and good taste, and thus the sheer number and variety of courses must be accompanied by elaboration and refinement of utensils, service, setting, and the demeanour and presentation of the participants.

4.4 OYATSU: *NON-RICE FOOD EVENTS*

THERE IS A third type of food event commonly found in Japan, essentially, a residual category which includes the various food events that occur practically in all societies that can afford them. In the European context these are snacks, nibbles, light meals, or whatever. In the Japanese case, these too operate under rules which can be identified from observation:

> We had been sitting and discussing the construction of kites. Mr. Saito, now in his nineties, is an expert, and Jeanne has been following his work for several years. Old Mrs. Saito, hobbling slightly (she is over eighty, and rather overweight) brings a tray to the table. There are small glass plates for each of us. Each one has two slices of crisp juicy, almost ice-white *nashi* pears. Each has been peeled with deft strokes, then cut to the same size. On the plate one slightly occludes the other. There is a toothpick for picking up the pieces.

In our sample of household eating habits, the variety of foods eaten during *oyatsu* tilted significantly to the ready-made, the Western, and the sweet. But this is not necessarily a fair representation: most of our respondents were women and housewives. Gobbling a quick noodle bowl at a *tachi-soba* stand qualifies as *oyatsu*, as does a hamburger from a well-known American chain. As in many other cultures, Japanese like to snack on the run, and the scale of such snacks is huge.

In no-rice food events, white-cooked rice (in a bowl on its own) is dispensed with completely.[12] This is not a proper "meal." It is intended to stave off hunger, not satisfy it. And because no specific rules obtain, there is a huge choice and a huge variety. Walking down the street in Shibuya, which used to be one of our favourite places, we try to count the snacks available, only to give up after half an hour. There are *tako-yaki*, fried dough balls, the batter larded with small bits of octopus and pickle. These stalls compete with *tai-yaki*, fish-shaped (a *tai* is a sea-

12 In sushi, the rice is not strictly speaking "white", because it has been flavoured, and moreover is very intimately linked with the fish and seafood.

bream, hence the name) waffles stuffed with bean paste. Or one could try *dango*: balls of pounded glutinous rice coated with black sweet bean paste. There are of course Western foods as well. Sandwiches of every description (one dubious pleasure from student days, which has since lost ground, is filled with spaghetti), madeleine cakes. Sweet and savoury crépes. Grilled squid. Many of these dishes, particularly the traditional Japanese ones, are found mainly at fairs and festivals, but even on a busy shopping street there is a great deal of choice.

Unlike rice-centred meals, snacks are less a matter of display[13] and messages, more a matter of individual choice. Mothers with small babies will indulge their own taste, and teach their babies, when choosing *oyatsu*, while they must cater to the rest of the family in rice meals. And because these are a convenience, they often consist of ready-made foods. This of course has immense implications for the food industry, where the culture of wrapping leads to a whole industry devoted to wrapping little bits of food in attractive and interesting ways.

Oyatsu also cross boundaries quickly between savoury and sweet flavours. A common snack offered to guests in rural areas is pickles, which more frequently twenty or more years ago than now, were home-made, and reflected specific household tastes. In Yuzawa, where we did much research, housewives would bring out glorious pickles: gourds stuffed with wild mushrooms, stuffed with chrysanthemum leaves further stuffed with bits of eggplant, the whole pickled in saké lees or bran. Sliced across, these morsels yielded surprising concentric circles of appetising contrasting colours, textures and flavours, which were eaten with toothpicks (which, a friend of ours noted, drily, are a sign of rusticity). In other cases such snacks might be Western cakes, or a bag of dried snacks, according to age, gender, and personal preference. On the street one could snack on simple items such as grilled squid, or more complicated meals such as *oden*, a meal in itself, albeit without rice, either sitting at wooden stools or standing in front of the mobile kiosk.

4.5 *SUMMARY*

To SUMMARISE, JAPANESE meals are highly structured events, and the different versions of a Japanese "meal" are defined by the relative position of the major carbohydrate – rice – whose presence is culturally very important. The structure of these meals correlates with a number of other features of meals that we have not yet discussed.

The relationship between various aspects of Japanese meals is "governed" by a rule of consistency and appropriateness. Certain types of meals are associated

13 A particularly interesting snack may be provided for an important guest or occasion, the individually wrapped item prominently displaying a prestigious local or national brand. In the case of fresh Western or Japanese delicacies, the shop name would be displayed on the accompanying napkin, plastic fork and clear cellophane covering.

with certain types of foods (they are more likely to feature than others) with certain types of utensils, with certain types of social gatherings, and with certain types of calendrical and temporal events. To give an example, a rice-centred meal is likely to have *miso shiru* and a small (less than three) number of side dishes, is likely to have less-expensive utensils and a smaller number of them, is likely to take place in a family home or cheap restaurant, and is likely to occur on a work day as midday or evening meal. Now this example is purposely trite: it reflects common knowledge about "fit" that we all have, whatever our culture of origin. This is precisely where a great difficulty lies, since we may assume that this makes *all* instances, and all elements, similar to ones we know. Japanese meals differ in a marked manner from Western ones in that they are componential. That is, each of the three elements can enlarge or shrink, changing its significance in the overall order of food events, and by doing so, both define the event (as a rice-centred meal, as a rice-peripheral meal, or as a no-rice meal). And this variation in one element is not necessarily contingent on changes in others. Neither rice nor its bowl would seem (on quick visual examination) to change much from one meal to another. The *okazu* change quite markedly, indicating a feast, and the *suimono* contents, which might change, are far more affected by regional variations and preferences.

READINGS FOR CHAPTER 4

Douglas, Mary 1982 "Food as a system of communication".
Ashkenazi, Michael 1993 *Matsuri: Festivals of a Japanese Town.*
McMillan, Charles 1989 *The Japanese Industrial System.*
Murcott, Anne (ed.) 1983 *The Sociology of Food and Eating.*
Yanagi, Soetsu 1926 [1955] *The Way of the Potter.*
Irvine, Judith T. 1979 "Formality and informality in communicative events".
Brillat-Savarin, Jean Anthelme 1978 *The Physiology of Taste.*

5 Food Preparation Styles

THE BALANCE OF two basic overarching techniques determines the "Japaneseness" of foods more than any other: cutting and heating. Not unnaturally, of course, these lie at the foundation of *any* cuisine, but in the Japanese context, the specific application of those two techniques in particular ways are crucial. The two techniques are related directly to two important concepts that are inherent in the cuisine: visual presentation and flavour. Though a number of writers, including celebrated chefs such as Tsuji (1974) have emphasised presentation, flavours – particularly those that derive directly from nature – are as important.

The techniques of both cutting and heating that are employed are direct derivatives of this cultural imperative to allow foods to be shown – visually and palatally – to their best advantage. The various techniques used have both technological and social prerequisites and consequences. None of these techniques is unique to Japan. What *is* unique is the constellation, and, to a great degree, the way the techniques structure styles: institutional complexes, clusters of behavioural rules relating to a highly specified technique, which are found in households and public food loci. Styles incorporate not only a medium of *preparing* a food, but also the associated form of presenting it, and rules about consuming it. When considering the various cooking styles, one must take into consideration a number of factors. First, the styles of cooking emerged as an initial result of specific ecological and technological realities, which are intertwined. Of these, the use of low-cost fuels (and consequent energy-saving devices), the social implications of housing size, and the historical access to "exotic" foods and food preparation methods are probably the most significant. Second, the cooking "styles" come about as a cooking *technique* is refined, and becomes, in a sense, autonomous, with specific rules of preparation and presentation. What this means, and what we shall see in greater detail later, is that this has led to the emergence of eating establishments – restaurants and others – that deal exclusively in one of these styles.

The different techniques can be summarised under a number of headings which are "native" categories, that is, defined by Japanese canons of practice: *yakimono* – foods that have been subjected directly to fire or heat, whether grilled over charcoal or seared on some kind of skillet, and any liquid or seasoning used reduced to a glaze; *nimono* – simmered dishes, conceptually similar to Western stews; *namasumono* – foods based on raw foodstuffs, such as *sashimi*; *agemono* – deep fried foods; *mushimono* – steamed foods. Each or any of these might appear in a standard meal as part of the *okazu*, as we noted in the previous chapter. Individually, each of these techniques has also brought about specific styles, some of which we shall discuss here.

5.1 *RAW FOODS:* NAMASUMONO

Sashimi consists of raw (as well as barely cooked or steamed) fish that has been cut into thin slices, and is eaten alone or with a garnish. "I went out with a fisherman I met in Kyushu," recounted one friend gleefully. "He took along nothing but a bottle of saké. We caught some squid, which he quickly peeled and sliced while they were still writhing, then we popped them into our mouths, washing it down with the saké. It was the best *sashimi* I have ever tasted. The fish was pale white, translucent. It tasted just of the sea, with none of the rubbery mustiness in even day-old squid. The texture yielded to the teeth, and the flavour of the squid was sweetly delicate, like eating flower petals."

As mentioned, not all *sashimi* is completely raw. In November, one of Japan's favourite fish, the bonito, reaches its peak.

> After purchasing a perfect *katsuo* (bonito) fillet (we could only afford one, the prices going to several thousand yen a piece) we lit the charcoal grill and blew it to a white heat. The dark brown flesh sizzled quickly on one side until it charred and flaked slightly, then we repeated it on the other until the entire piece of meat was covered with a black, ashy crust. Removed from the griddle it cracked, showing the red brown meat inside. The air was redolent of the scent of the meat, a scent reminiscent of the driftwood fires of childhood, of seaweed in a cold breeze, even of the sound of the sea. Sliced quickly into half-centimetre thick slices, we barely waited to sit down, taking slices of the fish, dipping them into a sauce of *yuzu* (Japanese citron), soy sauce, chopped green onion, some *dashi*, and ginger. Each slice tasted richly like a combination of fresh beef and red fish. The texture of the slices varied from soft in the middle, to almost crisp at the charred edges. Barely seen highlights of colour flashed on the surface of each slice. To a confirmed fish eater such as Jeanne, the slices are redolent of the sea at its most lush. The dark slices are enhanced by the slightly tart flavour of the dipping sauce, and nothing stands between one's palate and the natural memory-taste of the sea. To a confirmed carnivore, the slices are initially welcome because they resemble, in their texture as well as taste, the best underdone slices of beef.[1] It is only with the second or third

1 *Katsuo tataki* is a speciality of the Tosa district in Shikoku. It is said that Sakamoto Ryoma, one of Tosa's distinguished politician/samurai, introduced this flash-seared style of cooking to the region, applied to its most popular fish, after a long sojourn in Nagasaki, where he had learned to

taste, as the fresh fish is still on the tongue, that the more subtle aromas and flavours of seafood permeate into consciousness. Overall, whatever one's persuasion, seared fresh raw bonito is the epitome of sensuousness.

The inherent nature of these foods is that they are as close as possible to the natural state of the foodstuff. Rawness embodies *the* natural flavour of any foodstuff. Thus raw fish is the true essence of fish. Paradoxically, to get to this "natural" flavour, one must exercise the highest possible *human* discrimination and skill. This paradox exemplifies an apparent paradox in Japanese thinking: the conflation of natural and human. The "true" or "natural" flavour of a fish (or meat, or fruit) becomes evident only through human intervention. And yet the human intervention must be as "natural", that is, as minimal as possible, and yet conversely, the final effects are artistically elaborate, and must be so.[2] It must flow, in some mystical way, "with" the demands of the natural object. Like the butcher described in the Daoist classic *Chuang-tzu*, it is only by complete study of natural processes that human intervention can be minimised, become non-intrusive. The art of wielding a knife, as we shall see later on, becomes the paramount chef's art, because it is by cutting appropriately that both visual, tactile, and oral needs are satisfied.

The central idiom of cutting is necessarily the cutting of fish, but other items have to be cut as well. Though traditional Japanese cooking does not resort to as much fancy imagery cutting as Chinese cuisine does, preferring simpler, cleaner, less elaborate lines, there is plenty of that too. Most good cookbooks illustrate up to ten or so different basic cuts, ranging from roundels of carrots in the shape of cherry blossoms, to elaborate cuts made in pieces of *kamaboko* (fish paste) for the creation of red-and-white chequerboard effects or complicated knots. This is of course a cultural skill: one that is taught, by example, precept, literature, and the surrounding environment, rather than just one source. Japanese hand-tool usage differs in a number of ways from that seen in Europe: planes and saws are drawn rather than pushed, and their cutting surfaces are formed accordingly. But more

---

appreciate such Western delicacies as smoked salmon and rare beefsteak. True or not, this story makes for interesting food history.

Before the *tataki* style of searing became prevalent, many aficionados of *katsuo* were known to have died of food poisoning, and the addition of hot or spicy condiments such as garlic, ginger and green onions, together with citron, to the soy sauce seasoning is to further ensure that any harmful bacteria are neutralised.

The same effect is ascribed to *wasabi*. Before its widespread use in sushi, ptomaine poisoning was said to be common. *Wasabi*'s (as well as the pickled ginger's no doubt) bactericidal properties are not widely recognised by most sushi lovers, who are more than sufficiently impressed by its appetite-stimulating pepperiness and the nose-clearing (and sometimes mind- and skull-blowing) sensation it generates.

2 A "minimalist", natural presentation of raw fish, in the form of an entire creature, with its head, tail, and fins still intact, and occasionally quivering, but its body flesh carved into bite-size portions, is a macabre spectacle that appears in drinking banquets at sea- and riverside restaurants, but would rarely be considered appropriate for Tea ceremony cuisine, which defines itself primarily as presenting the seasons of nature, and thus nature itself, on a plate.

significantly, the capabilities of such tools are taken to the ultimate degree. If a blade does not split a hair by gravity, that is resting on its own weight alone, it is not deemed sufficiently keen. Thus knives and chisels are used not only to shape but as well to apply the final finish on wooden surfaces where a European craftsman would use sandpaper or a file. These differences, derived initially from different metallurgical and materials knowledge, but now a part of everyday material culture, extend into knife shapes and cutting forms used in cooking as well. In that sense, at least, Japanese cooking differs significantly *at a fundamental, basic level* from that of other cultures. Of course, such details can be learned, but as a comprehensive system they are to be experienced: one problem with trying to instil them in non-Japanese.[3]

5.2 NIMONO: NABEMONO *AND ENTERTAINMENT*

Rice is obviously the pot-cooked food par-excellence. But many Japanese dishes excluding rice are cooked in a pot, or pot-like utensil as well. Perhaps the best known in the West is *sukiyaki*. Excluding the various forms of soup – *shirumono* – pot-cooked foods tend to fall into two classes: table-top one-pot preparations and "stews." The former *tend* to be of "foreign" provenance, the latter Japanese.

The idea of cooking foods before the eyes of the diners is said to have originated in China. Indeed, "Mongolian" hot pot is a common and beloved dish in northern China and it is offered in many small roadside stands throughout China today. In Japan the idea has many different forms. *Sukiyaki*, which is supposed to have originated from the custom of quickly grilling meat on a hoe blade, is served with a dip consisting of raw egg and soy sauce. It is generally sweetened with sugar and *mirin* (sweet rice liquor). Its defining characteristic is the final use of the rich stock to cook *shirataki* noodles made of *konnyaku* (devil's tongue root jelly). In all the different variations of table-top pots, meat or fish slices are used to flavour a stock in which vegetables are later cooked, the broth with the remainder of the vegetables is then used to flavour a carbohydrate-surrogate (noodles made of root vegetables such as devil's tongue root or beans). The quality of the cuts, their arrangement on the platter in which they are

3 Recently sushi and *sashimi* restaurants outside Japan have been employing non-Japanese chefs. While the end-results may often be acceptable, it is disconcerting to see, for one used to the composed yet relaxed demeanor and erect posture of a professional Japanese sushi chef, a sushi "chef" crouched gauchely over a cutting board, glancing from the side at the emerging slices. While this scene was not meant for display, the fact that it was on view to customers at all, characterises the restaurant's offerings, food and otherwise, as not truly Japanese. Not because the chefs were not Japanese, nor even because they had not been trained in Japan, but because the attention to *all* the aspects of a dining experience which characterises a superlative "Japanese" meal (which was being signalled by the restaurant's elegant decor, attentive service, and high prices) was not present. In such a meal, it is not only the "seen" parts that are significant – i.e., the food itself and its physical locus, the serving of it to the diner. The "unseen" parts are just as important – the methods, attitudes of its preparers during its preparation; the physical characteristics of the kitchen.

brought to the table, are what define the quality of the dish. Significantly, though these are quite often formal dishes, served in peripheral-rice meals, they are intended to promote conviviality, rather than formality.

Shabu-shabu, meaning "swish-swish", is the eponymous table-top stew. It is a very amiable, sociable way to eat, and it exemplifies some of the principles we are concerned with here. Table-top pots are *intended* to produce conviviality. Even the stiffest of social functions tends to break down under the need to communally fish for titbits in a boiling pot. The idea that food is a social glue is of course common to all societies. Japanese cuisine excels, however, in reserving a special niche for the final preparation of food by the diners themselves as a participatory entertainment in itself.[4]

With the growing affluence of Japanese society, Japanese have had the resources to spend on a great many forms of entertainment. In the early 70s, Fukutake was already commenting that the Japanese need "wholesome" entertainment, whatever that would have meant to a writer of his age and class. Indeed, a great many forms of social entertainment in Japan are "wholesome", or depending on perspective, lively and even childish. Visitors to geisha parties have commented how, even when the subtext of the event is a serious or a sexually charged one, the overt behaviours and practices are childish. In the context of entertainment, people are actively *encouraged* to show their child-like sides in public, to make fools of themselves, sing songs together, or play finger games. There are numerous instances of that sort of behaviour in Japanese society, and numerous occasions in which the average (usually male) adult is actively encouraged to put aside the trappings of adulthood and power and indulge in the childish. Japanese generally recognise the social benefit of being able to do so, whatever others may say. It relieves some of the tension of living in a highly restrictive society, it allows people who are usually separated by minute nuances of precedence – age, position, schooling – to shed some of that burden. By doing so these behaviours introduce a looseness into Japanese social relations which might otherwise be unbearable: a social safety valve if you wish.

The process of consuming a table-top *nabe* together, with the mess it entails (as in American lobster restaurants, one is often offered a bib before eating to catch the splatter from food), the informal eating and drinking in which precedence is rarely adhered to – all of these contribute to social cohesion by breaking down the rules that normally constrain eating and other behaviour. These cook-and-feed-yourself modes of eating are even *graphically* different. In a formal dining situation, the diners will be arranged in the shape of an open rectangle, seated by rank, with the most important person at the outside of the head, lesser luminaries trailing around the outside, and the lowest social standings sitting inside the square, if necessary. That is of course impossible in

4 Other forms of food as entertainment centre on the professional chef's performance skills. The preparation of sushi and *sashimi*, as well as *tempura*, and in recent times, *teppanyaki*, have always been spectator-oriented.

self-cook forms of dining. In most cases, the diners have to sit at a round table, where a proper hierarchy is hard to establish. For a society which prides itself on its hierarchic nature (the Japanese rendition of an influential book on Japanese culture and society is *Vertical Society* [Nakane 1970]), the ability to relax stiff social rules in socially sanctioned ways is perhaps a necessity: the flip side of hierarchy and order.

Japanese cuisine, to a greater degree perhaps than classical European cuisine, is also characterised by a vertical replication of dishes, which, depending on circumstances, can appear at either the upper or lower parts of the spectrum, depending on their cost and elaboration. A common stew called *oden* is an example of that.

Clustered around many urban train stations in Japan it is common to find a jumble of bars, night-spots, and *pachinko* parlours. Generically, such places are crucial to Japanese social relations, since they constitute an intermediary zone between the work environment and the domestic sphere. As night falls, barrows are wheeled out which sell items such as roast chestnuts, magazines (not all pornographic), fruit (often delicious, and at lower prices than those in the shops), and other street foods. One of the most noticeable types, and certainly the ones that stay open the longest, are those serving *oden*, a sovereign cure both for over-drinking and for the late night hungries. While there are restaurants which specialise in high-quality *oden*, their best flavour is at the right ambience: the lantern or bare-bulb lit barrow.

> In the dark, the barrow is peculiarly inviting. The square stew pot simmers gently. One seats oneself on the bench, perhaps apologising to those already seated. In the brownish stock float a variety of pieces. There are translucent triangles of devil's tongue root jelly, black specks decorating the surface. *Konbu* seaweed is tied into thick knots, shining like green parchment rolls. Pieces of *kamaboko* (fish paste) in duller colours than the more familiar red-dyed crescents. Crunchy-looking hockey-puck shaped disks of *daikon* radish. Tubes of *hanpen* (a fish-paste cake). Boiled eggs. Small potatoes. Octopus.
>
> The counterman, after the usual "*Irasshaimase*" selects those pieces one wants, slipping them into a Western-type (shallow) soup bowl, adds a dab of hot Chinese mustard on the side, and offers the chopstick container. There is usually a choice of saké, beer, and for the adventurous, or those on the wrong side of drunkenness, there is fiery *shochu*, a sort of junior vodka distilled from sweet potatoes. The broth is based on a *niban-dashi*. The pieces have simmered at a very low heat, so that the flavour of each and every piece, and no less importantly, its texture, remain intact. The *konnyaku* (devil's tongue root) is jelly-like. The *daikon* falls apart in the mouth into sweetish bitter strands. This is complemented by the strong iodiny flavour of the seaweed. For those with simpler (or more Western tastes) there are rounds of boiled potato and hard-boiled eggs. When it starts raining, as is

often the case in spring and summer, the barrow-man will shelter the bench with a tarpaulin, and, lit by the gas lamp, the raindrops thrumming on the overhead, late night passers-by satisfy the midnight munchies.

5.3 AGEMONO: *FRYING AND THE ART OF BORROWING*

CRISP, DEEP-FRIED FOODS need no real introduction. They are a staple of almost all street cuisines on all continents. Whether they are South American buñuelos, Middle Eastern/South Asian jalebis, or fish and chips, foods fried in deep fat are almost synonymous with street (and thus fast) foods. Roughly speaking, there are three distinct styles of fried foods in Japanese cuisine. *Tempura*, which may be of Portuguese origin, is deep-fried batter-coated nuggets of seafood and vegetables. Stir-frying over very high heat in a little oil is an art that Japanese cuisine has borrowed from China. Finally, *teppan yaki* – the art of fry-grilling foods, often meat, on little or no fat – actually preceded sushi to the West as a popular dish, and following Japanese native categories, will be discussed under *yakimono*. The significance of each of these styles of cooking is related less to their importance in Japanese cuisine or daily life, and more to the important issue of cultural borrowing and transfer, since in each of these cases, we can see cultural transfer from a slightly different perspective.

Like many Japanese cooking styles, good *tempura* is a specialist's art. Partly this is a function of the need for very good (and thus expensive, used only-once) oil. Restaurants of less than superior quality, as well as the average housewife, can get around this by filtering and storing *tempura* oil after use. This, not unnaturally, creates a technically-derived hierarchy of *tempura* restaurants. Some such restaurants, blending their own oils, using only the freshest fish and vegetables, can pick and choose their customers, remaining open for brief hours each evening, closed except by invitation. Michael's father, on an official visit to Japan, found it incomprehensible that a small restaurant serving only five people at a time, could make a profit. Yet the serving of high quality *tempura* illustrates one of the theses of this book: that the Japanese cultural preference is for the effortless and restrained presentation ("display" would be too strong a word) of the results of pains-taking as a mark of social and cultural esteem.

Properly speaking, every *tempura* meal *should* be, as one cook interviewed implied, a "feast". Most *tempura* dishes are a series of small servings served directly by the cook to the diner's plate as soon as they are lifted out of the oil. Sizes are small, which means that a large number of servings are necessary, which, in turn, means that even more than sushi, good quality *tempura* is labour-intensive, because meticulous attention is required to ensure that each item of food reaches the diner still piping hot.

> We sat down to eat at the counter, the better to observe the cook, as well as to savour the food's freshness to the utmost by eliminating any instance of

delay in its delivery to us from its source (as if there could even be more than a few imperceptible parts of a second). The cook was a young man, one of his hands slightly scarred by an oil burn, his white cap and wraparound apron immaculate. We chose the *teishoku* (set menu), so that we could compare it to other places. Another couple came in and sat at one of the small tables, and the waitress, an elderly woman, approached to take their order. We watched carefully as the chef rapidly dipped two large prawns in the thin batter. From experience, we knew how tricky this is: the first time we tried it at home, the kitchen was spattered. The dripping pieces were slipped gently into the sizzling oil. The chef watched intently. As the pieces took on a slightly gilded colour, they were deftly removed with metal-tipped cooking chopsticks, and allowed to drain, then swiftly slipped onto a pristine folded sheet of white paper laid on a rimless basketwork tray.

We each had a small bowl of *miso shiru* garnished with tiny clams, a bowl of steaming rice, a small round plate of pickles, and a bowl of dip. The dip was made of *dashi* strengthened with soy sauce, in which we dissolved a small white cone of grated *daikon* radish tipped with grated ginger. The cook laid a basket with a prawn on the counter before each of us. Not a single drop of oil marred the dazzling white surface of the paper. I dip the prawn quickly into the sauce: to let it get soggy would be sacrilege. As my teeth cut into the crisp, light coating, the aroma of fresh prawn steams into my mouth, alternating with delicate tingles from the radish and the sharpish nip of ginger. The characteristic aroma of tempura emanates from the sesame oil added to the frying oil. Each shop keeps the proportions of its oil mix a secret. Unlike fish and chips, the batter is delicate, so flavourful on its own account, that bits of separated batter are scooped out assiduously (so as to leave the oil as clear as possible) and used as a garnish called *tenkasu* for other dishes. The batter is so light, delicate, and brittle that it is more like gilding that yields effortlessly to the teeth. Most importantly, it preserves so thoroughly the individual freshness of each item – prawn, green pepper, sweet potato, fish, *shiitake* mushroom, squid. By enclosing each ingredient and shielding it from direct contact with hot oil, the tempura batter seals in each ingredient's essences which would have evaporated and escaped into the oil or volatilised into the surrounding air. Thus each ingredient's fresh taste is crystallised within the crisp crust, waiting for the diner to release it, undiminished by its rapid cooking.

While we are enjoying the first morsel, the cook is getting ready for the second serving: pieces of vegetables – a slice each of tiny aubergine, sweet potato, squash, a whole sweet green pepper the size of a little finger – and fish. Again, each piece has its natural flavour and consistency intact: the aubergine is sweet and moist, the pepper is aromatic, the sweet potato is still crunchy and not at all mealy or even sweet (those who envision fried gooey sickly sweet yams are in for a surprise), and the aroma of *shiitake* mushroom is enhanced.

> After several courses of different items, the end is signified by *kakiage* – a fritter of small shrimp and chopped aromatic trefoil (*mitsuba*). As a fitting dessert, and since this is Japan of the late twentieth century, we try one of the shop's innovations: *tempura* ice cream. The chef extricates a small ball of sponge cake wrapped around some hard frozen ice cream from a freezer. This is rapidly dipped into batter, swiftly fried, and served, the ice cream still solid under the steaming crackly crust. It is a wonderful contrast of textures and temperatures. Appropriate to Japanese taste and modern wit, the ice cream is of green tea flavour.

Tempura was a popular street food already in the Edo period, cooked and served on bamboo skewers, and sold from small mobile stalls (*yatai*). During the middle of this century, a process of upscaling began. It was a food that, when prepared "wastefully" (that is, involving several cooks to prepare relatively few dishes, sure of fresh oil and very fresh ingredients), maintained the canons of taste for high quality Japanese food in a flamboyant way: freshness in *tempura*, as in sushi is readily apparent because of the sealing qualities of batter and hot oil. Textures are clear, crisply identifiable, and any deviation from the standard of freshness and quality is unmistakably and immediately apparent.

The material nature of *tempura* is of course germane to its success. Everything from fish through fresh vegetables to ice-cream can be "tempura-ed." The flavour of *tempura*, while being both characteristic and delicate, can be enhanced in many ways by judicious use of spices. Most shops will offer a dipping sauce of soy, *mirin*, and *dashi*, into which one stirs a cone of freshly grated radish and ginger. For proper aficionados, the flavour of choice, particularly with the more delicate foods are dipping salts in a variety of flavours (the most recent addition, to our amusement, being curry).[5]

Yet, for the true connoisseur, it is not just the food itself, but the ambience, the attention of the individual counterman to the individual guest. This of course is a mainstay of the Japanese food industry: the individual attention of a counterman, whether in a *tempura-ya*, or a cheap bar, is one of the major sources of social reinforcement that Japanese have. There is strong evidence to suggest, for instance, that much of the time spent with bar hostesses is less sexual than communicative: the counter-person (or the bar-girl) serving as surrogate friend/confidant/companion. The counter in *tempura* in this instance (and even more so, in *sushi-ya*) and the easy-going exchange of commentary revolving around the food being prepared, being a different version of the solicited and purchased companionship from drinking bars.

5 This was not a widespread innovation during the summer of 1996. The innovator replied that he just had a brainwave. With curry rice being a popular dish, the young cook believed that mild curry flavoured salt might catch on. It put an interesting spin on *tempura*, and we would not at all be surprised if this further developed into various permutations of curry *tempura*.

5.4 YAKIMONO: TEPPAN

The farmhouse was extensive – perched on the top of a mountain surrounded by fields – it was far too large for Mr. Haneda and his family. He had been married for only a few years and as yet had no children. His mother still lived on the farm. and the two women took care of the farming while Haneda, an engineer by training, worked for a construction firm. The farm supplied many of their needs, but obviously not all. Even the cash-crop – silkworms – was a mere supplement to the family income.

After we had a luxurious bath, Mr. Haneda showed us around the farmhouse, a structure much larger than most modern Japanese can ever hope to live in. Then, dressed in summer *yukata* loaned us for the occasion, we sat down to dinner. Mrs. Haneda (the elder) apologised for the poor offering. The subsequent dinner would belie her words. A large electric *teppan*, a flat metal griddle, was placed in the centre of the table. While it was warming up, we were offered beer and nibbled at one of our favourite summer drinking foods: boiled green soy beans (*eda mame*). Served in their pods, the beans are eaten by pressing the pods between the teeth to release the jade-coloured beans. They are quite addictive – the salt on the pods seasoning the beans as they are released into the mouth.

When the griddle was hot enough, Mrs. Haneda rubbed the surface with a piece of beef fat. Then she brought out a large platter of thinly sliced beef, another of pork, and a third of cut vegetables: carrots, bean sprouts, bamboo shoots, white cabbage, snow peas. These were placed on the griddle and allowed to brown slightly, whereupon we were urged to eat. Helping ourselves from the hot griddle, we dipped the morsels into a *ponzu* sauce, made of soy sauce and citron juice, and ate. We asked whether the vegetables were from their own garden, and Mr. Haneda admitted that no, most were bought at the supermarket. After the "traditional" foods (and after our stomachs were near bursting), Mrs. Haneda brought out a special treat – a plate of sliced tinned corned beef – which, for politeness sake, we had to taste as well.

And of course, no meal can possibly be complete without rice. In this case, full bowls of *karē-raisu*, loaded to the gunwales with the smooth yellow-brown sauce, afloat with vegetables and meat – something which, in normal circumstances, we would have enjoyed thoroughly – but here was gilding the lily.

The meal was not, of course, a standard one. "Cooked-at-the-table" meals, of which there are many styles, are generally not daily occurrences. It is important to note, within that context, that the *pièce de résistance* as it were, was the foreign food: the corned beef. It can only be presumed to be due to a mistaken idea that foreigners like to see their meat in one block. In other areas of Asia preserved canned meat is considered a delicacy. Significantly, though it is made in Japan by Japanese companies, it is still considered a "foreign food."

The problems of Japan's farming population are a direct result of the demographic changes that overcame Japan in the past one hundred years. Within that time, essentially within the span of memory of Haneda's mother, the population has changed from an overwhelmingly rural to an overwhelmingly urban one. This is coupled with the growing demand for imported luxuries, which have, in effect, become staples. Moreover, to add to the problem, farm mechanisation has not been either a priority or a major success in Japan. There are several reasons for this. In common with many rice-growing countries, Japanese farm plots tend to be small. Tiny paddies, some no larger than four square meters, dot the country side. The American occupation-engendered land reform was beneficial in providing Japan with enough food for its needs after World War II, but fifty years later it also causes problems for agricultural "rationalisation."[6] A second problem has been the resistance of many farmers to the introduction of farming technology. The reason too, is apparently partly demographic: younger people, who might adopt newer farming methods in an adventurous spirit, are leaving the countryside in search of more exciting lives in the cities. As one teenage informant told us many years ago, in the cities "*asobi ga ii* (There's good fun [to be had])." The country-city divide is less a matter of greater economic opportunities, or the availability of the good things in life – Japan has succeeded in distributing the benefits of modernisation far more than any other newly-industrialised country – as in the different lifestyles available. Moreover, small plots have meant that many farmers, such as the Hanedas, need to have one member of the family, normally the male, take a non-farming job.

Teppan-yaki is, possibly, an offshoot of one of the earliest forms of cookery. In some ultra-expensive restaurants it is still possible to enjoy it in the traditional style: fish, vegetables, and meat cooked on a pre-heated stone, perhaps scattered with salt crystals. The advent of technology, which has made the resulting electrically heated iron sheet (which is what a *teppan* literally is) cheaply available to any household, has brought that form of cooking back. In the West, of course, *teppan*-style restaurants have been stereotyped as "Japanese restaurants" since well before sushi became an item in the fashion circuit, and is usually the first (if not the only) type of Japanese restaurant that will be established in a community abroad that does not have a substantial Japanese population. The *teppan* (or "Japanese-grill") chef will attend, with his sharpened knives and guttural cries, to each diner sitting over a *teppan*. The meal is a show, and a far cry from either the calm attentions of a *tempura* chef, or the raucous *irasshaimase* that every Japanese expects when he enters a service establishment. In practice, it is a Japanese

6 This is not to say that we are in favour of so-called "rationalisation" in which large agribusinesses, usually with the aid of a government, expel farmers and farming communities from the land. But we do recognise that there is a serious issue here, in that small farmers simply cannot compete with large agribusinesses.

cultural translation *for Western eyes* of a set of Japanese traditions. In the Japanese context, to a member of Japanese culture, these behaviours do not stand out – they are, in fact, a seamless part of everyday life – admittedly not to the same exaggerated degree of performance. In the Western setting, where the personal attention expected of good service comes (if it does) in a different idiom, this is either comical, or weird and wonderful.

Teppan-yaki foods vary from the extremely expensive, when they include luxury foodstuffs and luxurious settings, such as "Japanese steak houses" in the West, to the poorest of all foods. Like table-top pots, they tend to be foods that generate conviviality. Foods cooked on teppan in everyday life are usually fast foods, e.g., *konomiyaki*, whole cuttlefish on a skewer, dry-fried noodles (*yakisoba*), meant to be eaten while standing in front of the shop or, most likely, a mobile kiosk (*yatai*). *Teppan* cooking of fast food has been popular since the Edo period. They can and do carry multiple cultural messages as well, as the example of *monjya-yaki* shows.

In the midst of food scarcity throughout World War II, a new dish was born, called *monjya-yaki*. One explanation of the term is that it derives from "*Nanimonja?*" ("What is this?") indicating the poverty, both conceptual and material, from which this street food sprang. *Monjya-yaki* was originally a hodge-podge of assorted vegetables, whatever one could lay one's hands on that was edible essentially, mixed in a thin batter (water and wheat flour) and dry-fried on a griddle (*teppan*). Nowadays, it still consists of a thin batter, but mixed with more palatable and luxurious ingredients – *hakusai* cabbage, mushrooms of various kinds, green peppers, and shrimp, meat, or poultry. The resulting crust is scraped off using a metal griddle scraper (a miniature version of the utensil hamburger cooks use for clearing burnt bits off griddles) and eaten, sometimes dipped in sauce, either soy or Worcestershire. With the rise of prosperity, this quintessential Tokyo food of austerity has become a *gurume* item.

> Kanagaki-san showed us how to make the *monjya*. First she lit the gas to heat the *teppan* and allowed it to warm up, as in *okonomiyaki*. She then poured a ring of chopped vegetables, octopus, and meat on the sizzling teppan. In the ring she carefully poured a very thin batter made of flour and water. Using a small scraper, each diner scraped off some of the slightly burned, almost caramelised crust, together with some of the vegetables, dipped in sauce, and ate. The process is laborious, albeit very sociable. One sometimes has to chase the runlets of batter around the griddle, and the heat is intense. Around us, other diners were doing the same thing, intensely occupied with one another and with the food before them in a sort of shared race – will the dough burn? Am I taking my fair share or more? – apparently highly enjoyable to all.

Now, in practice, the taste of *monjya-yaki* is a meagre version of *okonomiyaki*, a food that is usually associated with student life, and hardly haute-cuisine. The association is made more powerful simply by the fact that *okonomiyaki* places may *also* serve *monjya-yaki*, partly to indicate their roots in Tokyo (lower class) *shitamachi* culture. It helps that both foods are relatively cheap, and have been a staple of student life for many decades. Neither of these foods is particularly delicate. But, by the gradual addition of new, enriching elements, what has been the food of the poor becomes a gourmet item for the rich, or more precisely, the novelty-chasing rich. Unlike Mennel's model, what has happened in Japan is that the entire nation has become rich: the enrichment and elitisation of the food is not a transfer between *classes* but a transfer between *generations*.

As we have seen from other examples, the generation gap in Japan, is, in some ways, far greater than in other post World War II societies. The generation of Japanese who now control the country – those who grew up during the hungry two decades after the war – have a different perspective than their children. Growing up after the war meant deprivation, and a sense of national solidarity in facing adversity. The domestic market was small, and a great deal of energy was spent in trying to make the country work, to export, to save. This is not the case now in two major respects. First, the children of those who grew up during the years of austerity are greatly indulged, at least in material things. Second, they are far more exposed, than their parents were, to influences that are "strange": from abroad and from Japan's own home-grown fringe cultures. In the realm of food this expresses itself, in a nutshell, in the taste choices that are made in *monjya-yaki*. For the parents, *monjya-yaki* represents the food of hardship. People ate it because there was little else to eat, certainly little else to eat as a treat. The modern elaboration of *monjya-yaki* is, to many elderly Tokyoites, an easy return to nostalgia. The food is elaborated as a tribute to the fact that they – their generation – had succeeded by hard work in pulling themselves and their nation from the depths of destructive defeat. Younger people see *monjya-yaki* in a completely different light. For them it is one of the choices available, among many, to try new taste experiences. And, as such, it must compete with other experiences, and *therefore* there must be a richness, a variety, and elaboration of the foods and therefore of the experience.

Like many other cuisines, Japanese cuisine also includes a style of grilled meats, something common in many Southeast and Southwest Asian cuisines. It is possible, though no serious evidence has been provided, that the style derives from prehistoric Southeast Asian immigrants. Of the three most common styles, one is a clear, and recognised, "ethnic" variant: Korean barbecue and its derivatives (e.g. *jingizu-kan*, Genghis Khan cooking), these were probably imported into Japan during the period of the Japanese occupation of Korea (1910–1945). Unlike *robata-yaki* (hearth-side cooking) and *yakitori* (grilled skewered chicken bits), Korean barbecue is occasionally prepared at home, perhaps because the technique, which is that of cooking-at-the-table, lends itself more easily to home cooking.

A Korean barbecue is prepared over a small gas-fired burner on the table top. In Korea, in the early eighties, it was still done over a pot of coals sunk into the table, though even in Korea that is rapidly disappearing. In Japan virtually all

Korean barbecue cooking, and all home barbecuing, is done on gas burners, which, topped by a grille, and having a small water tray at the bottom beneath the flame, provide adequate heat for quick grilling of meat and vegetables. This is usually a self-cook style affair: diners place strips of meat and vegetables on the grill, and help themselves. All diners take turns replenishing the grill. However, in contrast to Japanese methods, the meat is pre-marinated and highly spiced (usually with a sauce of soy, wine, green onion, garlic, and sesame seeds), and cut in long thick chunks or strips, rather than in the paper-thin slices of most Japanese dishes. Moreover, the names used for the cuts (e.g. *karubi*, Korean: *kalbi*) give clear evidence of the "foreign-ness" of the food.

One interesting variant on the theme is *jingizu-kan*, named for Genghis Khan, the Mongol emperor. In this style, the heat source is capped by a wide, low-domed cast-iron plate, on which the meat is grilled (or, more properly grill-fried, since there is no exposure to the flame), while the juices collect in the rim. The resemblance to a Mongol soldier's helmet is the source for the name.

One aspect of this style of cooking that cannot be ignored is the "foreign-ness" of the dish, which is maintained as such despite the fact that *karubi* – cut beef (brisket) – is available in many supermarkets. In practice, Korean food, including *kimchi* (spicy pickles) and grilled meats, has been thoroughly absorbed into Japanese cuisine. Unlike *karē-raisu,* another Japanised food however, the boundaries with Korean barbecue seem to be far more rigid. This should not be surprising, considering the differential sources of these two foods. Where *karē-raisu* is the product of what was (at the time) considered a superior culture worth emulating, Korean barbecue is the product of a culture the Japanese, since their nationalistic days, have looked down upon. The Korean minority in Japan – some of whom are the descendants of potters and other craftsmen brought over by Hideyoshi, others servants and workmen brought by force into Japan during the Japanese occupation of Korea before World War II (and whose current descendants are third- and fourth-generation Japanese residents, but not accepted as Japanese nationals) – is greatly looked down upon, socially, economically, and politically. Thus Korean food, too, is not something that many Japanese are anxious to admit as a Japanese, or even Japanised food.[7]

Japanese attitudes towards other nationalities have varied somewhat over the past fifty years. An occasional survey of public opinion, run every few years, assesses popular attitudes to various countries and cultures. Several things remain constant. Africans persistently came in at the bottom of the appeal and admiration ladder. Koreans and Southeast Asians slightly higher. Various European countries, the United States, Russia, and China fought it out at the top, changes in the top slots generally reflecting changes in the politics of the day. In many ways, this is of course a reflection of what, in many circumstances, could

7 As for the Korean claim that they invented sushi, and particularly *maki* rolls, well .... Most Japanese we suggested the idea too were outraged at the possibility. Sort of like reacting to the suggestion that fish-and-chips was a British adaptation of French fried frog-legs and pommes frites.

only be called racism. Whether this is the same racism as in the West, and whether it arises from the same sources is doubtful. Nonetheless, this undoubtedly reflects on Japanese food culture as well. The prevalence of Korean restaurants owes much to the presence of Japanese of Korean descent, who, willingly or not, are forced to maintain their roots simply because Japanese society refuses to allow them to intermingle and submerge their identity in the Japanese mass. Influence on Japanese cuisine is not necessarily reflected, therefore, in popularity of the donor of a new method or food.

The other two styles of grilling, *robata-yaki* and *yakitori* are a different kettle of fish. Because of the associations they evoke, they fit the rather large and fuzzy bordered world of *mizu-shobai* (water business, that is, the night entertainment and hospitality business) than merely being restaurant food. By far the most ubiquitous form of grilling in Japanese cuisine is *yakitori* (literally, "grilled bird"). *Yakitori* is a subset of a form of grilling that can be found from the Middle East (in the form of *kebab* or *sikh*), through Northern Indian and central Asian cooking, to the *satays* of Southeast Asia. Small chunks of meat are dipped in a sauce or spiced, threaded on a skewer, and grilled over charcoal. In Japan this style of cooking has become an autonomous style. *Yakitori* are conceptually and physically different from metal skewered Western shish kebabs. The skewers are generally small, made of bamboo, and about 10 cm long. Vegetables are used in addition to chicken: neatly arrayed *shiitake* mushrooms, whole small *piman* (Japanese sweet green peppers), green onions. However, chicken bits are rarely alternated on the same skewer with several kinds of vegetables, e.g., Japanese *yakitori* would never feature tomatoes, mushrooms and onions all in one skewer. In fact, tomatoes hardly ever. However, pieces of boneless chicken may be alternated with green onions in one skewer.

Michael, who has a taste for low-class eating places (the result of impoverished studenthood which he has not shaken off) went to have a drink and a bite to eat in a working-class commercial/entertainment zone (*sakariba)*, around a major railway station in Tokyo. Crowds of merrymakers – the normal crowd to be found any night of the week – swirled around, tempted by the sights and sounds of the various styles of eating and drinking on offer:

> It was a small drinking bar, and the three customers included one who was obviously a construction worker, in split-toed cotton and rubber boots *(jika-tabi)* and jodhpur-shaped work trousers, and two nondescript, somewhat drunk men arguing about travel abroad. There was a man behind the counter, and a woman helper, or perhaps the owner, offered me a chilled towel (*shibori)*, and a glass of water. For some moments I was ignored, the customers and operators alike wondering how to deal with this blond, strange, anomaly. At the first word of my purposely broadly accented, Akita-tinged speech, there was a perceptible brightening of outlook. I ordered *tsukune* (small balls of minced chicken meat grilled on a skewer), and choose to have the meat dipped in sauce, rather than just lightly salted.

> After a long pull at a beer (the summer had been almost inhumanly hot) the counterwoman felt comfortable enough to ask what I was doing, where I had learned Japanese, where I was from.
>
> The place was dingy and small. Tattered notices – printed advertisements, as well as hand-written notices of prices of specialities – adorned the walls. As with many Japanese establishments, cartons labelled with the trademarks of food, printing, or supply companies were sequestered in every corner, hiding mysterious contents. The *tsukune* were good, and I ordered *shiitake* mushrooms and *piman* peppers with a flask of saké, at which point the two middle-aged gentlemen beside me (there were a total of five seats in the bar) involved me in a discussion of why foreigners (carefully using the polite "*gaikoku no kata*" rather than the colloquial "*gaijin*" they had been using before among themselves) ate peppery foods. We moved on to discussing travel in foreign lands, and the quality of food to be had there. In the meantime I had some grilled livers, chunks of breast meat, and then *tsukune* again.
>
> Each of the orders is threaded onto small wooden skewers, and depending on the order, there may be one (the *tsukune*), and others two or three skewers. As in any style of eating, there is an etiquette, which is probably more pronounced in an all-male, cheap bar such as this one. The skewer is stripped using the side of the mouth, often while the diner is still talking. Containers of sauce and salt are passed from one diner to another without the help of the server or of the cook behind his counter.

While the example provided above was of a lower-class establishment, *yakitori* can be found at all price ranges. And, of course, since it is a time-consuming job to prepare, all supermarkets have ready-to-eat skewers for the housewife to buy (heat) and serve. *Yakitori*, like many other foods, is primarily a drinking food. That is, it is more likely to be eaten by males, and less likely to be served as part of a domestic meal.

Yakitori is one of the vast repertoire of charcoal-grilled foods that are prevalent worldwide. A more homely and emphatically "rural" variation is the repertoire of hearthside (*irori*) cooking. In its more ambitious, more refined, and more varied restaurant variation, it is known as *robata-yaki* (hearth grill).

Traditional Japanese houses, such as our much loved rented nineteenth-century house in Yuzawa, generally had one source of warmth for cold days. A square, wood-framed and metal-sheet lined hearth is sunk in the middle of the matted floor. It is filled with fine sand, and a kettle hook with a fish-shaped toggle suspended from the roof beams. The sand provides both a base for a small charcoal fire, and a medium into which skewers and stands may be placed to prepare foods.

> Okuyama-san arrived in the midst of a snowstorm in late November to provide us with our first taste of *kiritampo*, an Akita speciality. He eyed the *irori* (hearth) with approval. "They don't make them like this anymore," he

declared. Sadly, we agreed. The roof outside was piled with a meter of snow (it had been snowing for a fortnight, and would snow for an additional month). The vast room with its high black beams was in shadow, and the only heat was provided by the hearth, in which we had built a charcoal fire that was glowing happily. Around it we had arranged flat *zabuton* cushions, a couple of bottles of saké, and a very non-Japanese dessert of apricot mousse.

We had lit the fire half an hour before, and it now glowed, a red and black pile, in the middle of the sand, the large iron pot suspended above it, the water steaming, as per earlier instructions. Okuyama-san arranged the foodstuffs. First, the *kiritampo*, made of briefly pounded newly harvested *mochi* rice which had been shaped generously around thick, flat wooden skewers, somewhat like corn-dogs. The skewers were stuck into the sand so that the *kiritampo* leaned over the glowing coals. He added some *hata hata* fish, which had been previously marinated in salt and mild vinegar, skewers protruding from their mouths. Several flasks of saké were set to warm in the kettle which steamed gently over the coals. Looking up into the heavy beams of the high roof, feeling the mat-covered boards beneath me, the gloom made me think of the sheer antiquity of the house and the custom, as generations of Akita people sat and chatted (and drank. How they drank!!) through the long snowfalls, huddled around the cheery warmth. The smell of the grilling fish soon began to circulate through the icy cold of the room, away from the glow. It was joined by the roast-corn smell of the *kiritampo*, and, when Okuyama-san opened a container of smoked pickles, by the heady scents of fermentation from the pickles and the saké alike.

Charred on the outside, the fish has a curious texture, somewhat tough and grainy, almost like *bacalao*. The *kiritampo* too was unusual, as the grains popped and charred slightly in the heat. Munched off the skewers, they seemed like the essence of Akita. The light of the fire, and the glow from behind the paper *shoji* in the room where the baby slept provided most of the illumination.

The changes in modern Japanese houses have not skipped over the sunked *irori* hearth. Very few modern houses, unless they have a room expressly made for the Tea ceremony (*chashitsu*), provide one. The modernisation of living arrangements has also meant the disappearance of many conveniences that would have graced a Japanese house until fifty years ago. These disappearances include ceiling-height niches for household altars, charcoal *kotatsu* warming tables, and the *irori* hearth. For many people in modern Japan, these *do* however represent symbols of past home comfort. Their absence is felt as a matter of nostalgia, which opens the way for such elements of Japanese cuisine as the natural food movement, as well as the various commercial forms of maintaining ties with "traditional" Japan, which are exemplified by everything from rural home-stay programmes, to elaborate and sophisticated attempts to tie the country to the town.

In Japan today, almost the only way an average Japanese can experience the feeling of the traditional *irori* is by going to a restaurant specialising in *robata-yaki*, where the customers sit around sand-pit hearths, on either sunken *irori* or raised daises. Fish, meat, vegetables are grilled and served before the customer. Like *yakitori*, *robata-yaki* is often largely a male-dominated, drinking-type establishment. It evokes, to some degree, the rustic, idyllic feeling of nostalgia highly prized in modern Japan.

5.5 NIMONO: MEN-RUI

THE PREFERENCE FOR rice does not inhibit Japanese cuisine from providing a large number of other carbohydrates. Historically, in fact, up to the end of World War II, many peasants did not consume rice at all, the grain which they raised going totally on taxes and rents. Other, less prestigious grains were consumed, including wheat, barley (*mugi*), millet (*kibi*), buckwheat (*soba*), as well as root crops such as sweet potatoes (*satsuma imo*). In modern Japan, root crops are consumed largely as vegetable dishes (part of the *okazu*). Wheat and buckwheat, on the other hand, have widely been accepted as a carbohydrate base in the form of *men-rui* (noodles). Noodles fall into several categories both in terms of the noodles (materials and technique) and in the terms of the dish and its constituents and cooking method. Very broadly speaking there are four categories: buckwheat noodles (*soba*), wheat noodles (*udon*), Chinese style noodles (*chūka soba* or *rāmen*), and a loose category of noodles made of other substances such as beans (*harusame*) or devil's tongue root (*shirataki*). *Soba* noodles are generally thin cut noodles, bought either dried, or handmade. *Udon*, which are generally thick (4 mm diameter) in Eastern and Northern Japan, and thin in Shikoku and Western Japan, are generally cut, but may be extruded (like spaghetti). Chinese-style hand-pulled noodles are traditionally made by swinging the strands between the cook's fingers (considered a luxury) or cut.

> We watched in fascination through the window as the master prepared the *soba*. First he mixed the greyish-brown dough with strong kneading motions, like those of a potter preparing clay. Unlike wheat flour, buckwheat flour is much stiffer, and the master had to use real effort in his kneading. When the consistency was to his satisfaction, he took a long rolling pin and started rolling the dough out on the wooden counter. Once the layer was about two millimetres thick, he folded the layer of dough over several times, using the rolling pin. Then with a special heavy sharp chopper, he cut the noodles neatly, suspending each cut bunch from a line beside him.

All types of noodles are generally industrially made. Like Japanese-style noodles, Chinese-style noodles too come in several varieties. There is, however, a peculiar linguistic and conceptual ambiguity here, with several kinds of noodles, generically called *rāmen,* fitting into the same category, though they are socially and sensorily rather distinct. Colloquially, "*rāmen*" encompasses both "*chūka-soba*" ("Chinese buckwheat," actually wheat noodles) and "Sapporo rāmen." To add to the confusion, specialist Chinese restaurants make Chinese noodles which are identified by the term *reimen.*

The distinguishing characteristics of all these noodle types constitute "native knowledge" in the sense that the average Japanese has no difficulty distinguishing between these different products. This has to do with several experiential and visual cues that the different dishes provide. All of these noodles are most often served in bowls of stock, garnished with vegetables, meat or fish, *mochi* and so on, which give the name to the dish. The stock of Japanese-style noodles (*udon* and *soba*) is always based on *dashi,* whereas the stock for Chinese noodles (as viewers of the film *Tampopo* can ascertain) are more like Western pork and chicken stocks. It is true, as the noodle professor in Itami's *Tampopo* says, that the soup is the soul of the noodle dish, but it is the "garnishes", essential elements of the dish, that name and create the specific dish eaten.

Japanese noodle dishes tend to have poetic or rather iconic names. *Tsukimi* (moon viewing) for a bowl in which a raw egg and sheets of *nori* evoke a moon hidden by clouds, *chikara* (power) for a dish containing a large cake of *mochi* (pounded rice cake) which evokes the reputedly favourite food of sumo wrestlers and people seeking strength in the winter, and *tanuki* (racoon dog) containing tofu and other items that that animal is reputed to fancy, *kamo nanban* ("Southern Barbarian duck") is cooked according to historical Japanese notions of European meat cooking. In contrast, Chinese noodle dishes names tend to be pragmatically descriptive ("with roast pork and pickled gourd"). The garnishes for all these dishes serve to make the centre of the dish – the noodles and stock – more interesting and more varied.

> This was the first time Jeanne had ever eaten at a *tachi-soba* shop. Like all of its ilk, it was designed to provide a quick, cheap lunch for businessmen and office workers on the go. Smaller *tachi-soba* stands can be seen around railway stations where they offer quick snacks to men heading home, or out of their offices. It was a long room, deep rather than wide, with a counter running the length. A machine dispensed coloured tickets, one for each of the four noodle types on offer. The cooking area is steamy, hot, with four people working at a dizzying pace. One receives the order, among multiple others loudly conveyed at a staccato pace. We watched as, with practised motions, a ladleful of soup is poured into a bowl. A knot of brown *soba* noodles is fished from the boiling pot with a wire ladle, briskly shaken to drain excess water, then folded into the bowl. Chopped green onions and a *tempura* fried prawn are popped on top, and the bowls are handed over –

the whole operation taking less time than it would to receive a burger in a fast food chain.

The counterman indicated a cold water dispenser near a stack of glasses. There were large plastic jars of pickled plums (*umeboshi)* scattered along the narrow counter which ran along all sides of the room, and jars of chopsticks. Helping ourselves, we watched our fellow diners as we ate. The noodles were chewy, though it seems that in recent years the proportion of buckwheat has diminished, and they lack the depth of flavour and slight aftertaste of bitterness imparted by a full measure of buckwheat. The stock is a dark, somewhat sweet *dashi.* Properly it should be flavoured with soy sauce and *mirin.* The green flavour of the onions contrasts nicely with the sweetness of the stock. Small bites of the prawn add to the variety, and by the time it is gone, one is still wanting a bit more.

Men (Jeanne was the only woman) strode in in a hurry, perused the menu briefly, then put coins into the machine. Receiving their lunch, they leaned against the counter, one or two reading newspapers or racing forms as they stood and ate, slurping their noodles quickly. After finishing, they hurriedly drank a quick glass of cold water or two, some not even bothering to do so, and hurried out. We timed the average diner. Five minutes. Ronald McDonald, eat your heart out.

Each type of named noodle dish is normally (always, in a restaurant) served in a specific bowl, whose shape and glaze varies from any others. There are, of course, pragmatic reasons for that: helping the order cook stick to the dish ordered. But beyond that, there is another element worth considering.

We have noted the importance of the utensils as a dimension of Japanese foods. Nowhere is this more demonstrable than in the serving of noodles. The use of different utensils here reinforces the distinctiveness of each dish. In *rāmen* dishes, in contrast, almost all the noodle dishes (and there are a great variety here too) are served in the same style and glaze of bowl: most often "Chinese" (Greek key motif around the rim in red, and a polychrome flower design in the middle). One possible clue to this difference is that many of the Japanese-style noodle dishes are named iconically, whereas the Chinese-style dishes are named descriptively: "*miso rāmen*" (noodles in soup thickened with *miso* paste), or "*chashūmen*" (noodles with roast pork slices). Whatever the historical reasoning and causes behind this difference, one aspect to this is separating the "traditionally" Japanese from the invasive outside. Considering the tension in Japan between "internationalism" – the desire to emulate and to be considered a part of a larger world order – and nationalism, it is not surprising to find this tension being exhibited within the framework of Japanese cuisine as well. It is not to say that "nationalist" Japanese eat *soba*, whereas internationalists eat *rāmen*, but that the field of cuisine allows for a reflection, however hidden, of a debate that has prodded Japanese society for decades and more.

Since its prehistory, Japan has been subject to tides and influences from the outside. Being an island culture, it has also been fortunate in its ability to insulate itself, at least from time to time, and to some degree, from such influences. This in itself is neither novel nor surprising. What is interesting, however, is the degree of energy Japanese, lay-people and scholars alike, have devoted to arguing, on philosophical as well as ideological grounds, the desirability and degree of "purity" (that is, "Japanese-ness") or of "internationalism" of Japan's varied and rich cultural matrix.

We have already made reference to the idea of *nihonjin-ron*: broadly speaking, the idea of Japanese uniqueness, which is often coupled with the idea of Japanese superiority. The idea is also closely related with the idea of Japanese *purity*, a term which, in itself, has strong emotional and religious connotations. In Japan's autochthonous religion, Shintō, the main conceptual structure is the opposition between *hare* (purity, associated with light and brightness) and *ke* (pollution, associated with darkness). These are not absolute, since all being is permeated with different degrees of each of these qualities. The moral thrust of Shintō is to ensure purity, so that humans may associate with the divine. Shintō rituals always include elements of purification, using a variety of symbolic items (salt, fire, water) and actions.

The leap thus from purity of actions and surroundings, to purity of culture, nation, or race, is a slight one. Foreign foods, whether *kare-raisu* or *chūka-soba* must undergo a lengthy period of what can only be termed "purification" before they can be subsumed within the corpus of proper Japanese foods. This is of course only one element of the adoption of foreign foods and their incorporation, something we shall discuss in detail. But it is well to remember that foods are not incorporated so much *physically* (in any culture! Note the British supposed reluctance to try "foreign muck": a staple of comedy shows) so much as emotionally and spiritually.

While the direct connection between nationalism and the incorporation of new foreign foods is on the whole, tenuous, there is nonetheless a thread that connects them via this concept of purity. This, as studies in several areas have demonstrated, is central to Japanese beliefs, and, what is more important, to their unquestioned, even unconscious assumptions about themselves and their world. Hendry (1986) has shown how important these concepts are in the education of children to proper Japanese footwear practices (keeping the *ke* outside from the *hare* inside by changing footwear). It is just as important, as a concept put into practice, in the incorporation of "outside" brides into "inside" the house: brides, being outsiders, must be ritually purified before they can be incorporated into a household as wives. So it is not terribly surprising to find that foreign foods are, within the context of Japanese food culture, "kept in their place" until such time as they can be incorporated by a series of means. Eventually, some will make the grade and cross the divide as many have already done, shedding not only their marked "garb" – foreign name, foreign crockery, place in the meal order – but their foreign-ness as a whole.

5.6 MALE AND FEMALE IN THE FOOD GAME

Bar foods tend to include a category which spans alcohol-related and other food styles. *Getemono* ("exotic foods" or "rough foods") are all related on the one hand to male potency, and on the other to Chinese ideas of health and yin-yang medicine. These include cheaper and more ubiquitous kinds of meat such as *horumon* (offal, innards) through expensive and rare delicacies – *mamushi* (a small native viper), *fugu* testicles, bear meat – which, generally speaking, consist of meat that is supposed to confer either vigour or potency, or both.

As in the food traditions of many other cultures, there is a preference for such male foods to be of animal origin. Thus simple cultures, such as the Murngin described by Rappaport (1967) to more complex ones such as the British and French, tend to view meat as a masculine domain. The Japanese are no exception, and *horumon* tend to be served at low-cost bars where men can drink and eat mounds of boiled innards, and exchange "masculine", slightly salacious talk.

Other *getemono* are far more expensive. Restaurants specialising in bear meat, monkey, snake and insects, are to be found here and there. They cater to those who are, in their own minds, jaded, or, more often, to individuals, particularly men, for whom the particular food has associations of power and virility. Conspicuous consumption is of course an issue here as well: the sheer rarity of some foods, such as bear meat, is what makes them expensive: a variation on acquiring the steady services of a *geisha*, and a way of showing off. Suspicion of farm-raised food has also contributed to the popularity of wild meat such as boar, which has led to farm-reared boar appearing on the market as well. But many Japanese do indeed believe in the efficacy of the foods they eat, and particularly of those with sexual or medicinal connotations. Some of these beliefs can be traced to Chinese food and health systems, and others to local Japanese beliefs that have survived, and then been revived or renewed by the migration of people to the cities as well as by the media, anxious to latch on to anything odd or exotic.

In contrast to the male domain of meats, sweets, in Japanese cuisine as elsewhere, tend to be the domain of women. Native cakes and confectionery have benefited from influences from abroad, notably China, but have developed most strongly under the influence of *kaiseki*, the dishes and cuisine that accompany the Tea ceremony. As the following illustrates, however, there are also more homey aspects which appeal to the more muscular:

> It was so cold, that runnels of ice had formed along the sidewalks, and the runners' feet slipped occasionally on the pavement. It was also dark and gloomy, the sky overcast, threatening rain or snow that never seemed quite to materialise that winter. The line of white clad figures could be described as ghosts in the dimness, but for the regular shouts of *washoi washoi* and the

> occasional yell by a senior to *ganbare* ("Keep up!"). And then, surprisingly, came the tinkle of a small bell. Crossing the path of the long straggling line of figures came another one, this one naked but for a loincloth and *haramaki*, a towel around his head, sports shoes incongruously on his feet. The sound came from a tiny bell stuck into the back of the loincloth. He waved at the line of runners cheerfully, on his way to his own *kangeiko* or mid-winter austerity. This was our last day of the full week early morning practice. We ran into the courtyard of the practice hall, and tiredly climbed the stairs to the clubhouse, where, glory of glories, there was the smell of something warm and appetising on the hob. One of the seniors, running ahead of us, had provided a warm bowl of *oshiruko*. The sweetness was terrifying, even for someone with a sweet tooth. Yet the flavour of the small red beans came through clearly, enhanced when one bit into one of the crunchy bits of bean in the otherwise thick and smooth soup. In the purple broth floated islands of white, like warm icebergs in a hot sea: squares of *mochi* little more than one bite each, which stuck to teeth and palate. The pot was large, but a group of hungry twenty-year olds (and one slightly older) can go through an enormous amount of food in a short time. So by the time eight o'clock and the first classes rolled by, there was a happy set of replete faces on their way to face the day.

The emergence of sugar as desired commodity has had one of the greatest impacts on human society that can be envisaged. In Africa and the Americas it was sugar that led to the human tragedy of enslavement on the one hand, and decimation of the native Indians on the other. In Europe it led to massive changes in diet, to the accumulation of wealth, and to other changes even harder to chart.

The use of sugar in Japan which was mainly of vegetable origin (recovered from cooked beans and some fruit) received a boost with trade of raw sugar from China, indirectly from India (from where the Chinese learned the process of sugar manufacture). By the end of the Muromachi period, sugar had joined soy sauce, saké, salt, vinegar, honey, *ame* syrup, and *miso* in regular use as seasoning. While some sweet foods became widely accepted into the cuisine – beans, for example, as a separate food, are always cooked with sugar – the idea of a separate sweet course, so common in European cooking, has gained widespread currency only fairly recently.[8] The *use* of sweeteners is also different, following the Japanese preference for blending and softening, as well as contrasting taste experiences. Sweet foods in Japanese cuisine tend to be found under specific conditions. For example, almost all cooked beans – that is, where beans are served as a separate dish (rather than comprising basic ingredients in some other dish, such as *miso*) during a meal, or in a boxed lunch (*bentō*) – are sweetened.

---

8 The increased consumption of coffee and tea and the proliferation of specialist coffee- and tea-houses offering selections of patisserie do indicate, however, that sugar has become a more conspicuous element in contemporary Japanese meals.

Prior to the Chinese importations, the word *kashi* or, politely, *okashi,* (sweets) referred mainly to fruits and nuts. The development of Japanese confectionery and sweets – *wagashi* – which came into its own during the Edo period was greatly aided by the introduction of tea, and heavily influenced by Chinese confectionery and snack foods (*dim sum*) brought in at the same time as Buddhism, as well as Portuguese confections such as *kasutera*. Indeed, Ego (in Suzuki 1995) argues that some of the forms of *okashi* are Japanese developments of Portuguese and Spanish originals. A seminal influence on the entire tradition of *wagashi* is ascribed to Southeast Asian sweets. Such dishes as *buchi* and *halohalo* from the Philippines display clear similarities, in the form of ingredients (*an*, *mochi*) even if the expression, that is the dishes constructed, emerge with a different feel and taste. Whether or not, as scholars such as Ishida Eichirō have argued, this proves a cultural continuity between South East Asia and Japan, is a moot point.

Wagashi are classed as "fresh" or "raw" – *nama gashi*, in which the moisture content ranges from 30–40% and thus does not keep well and most are meant to be eaten as soon as made – and *hoshi gashi*, "dry". Extremely dry sweets, moulded into complex shapes, and made mainly of toasted flour (e.g., wheat, soy) and sugar, are a type of *hoshi gashi.* Kyoto-made dry sweets, moulded into flower, bird, and fruit shapes, are more like opaque, pastel coloured candy, and are called *kyogashi.* They are said to have originated from similar dry confections brought over from Tang China called *karakudamono* (Chinese sweets).[9] These are usually taken with green tea or an abbreviated Tea ceremony. Between these two main categories, there is another called "half-raw", *hannama.*

The ingredients that characterise fresh *wagashi* are sweetened beans, *an*, in paste form or whole, and rice in the form of *mochi* (pounded glutinous rice cake) or flour (*jōshinkō*). The range of *wagashi* is enormous – they can be steamed, grilled, pureed, fried or jelled. While most are eaten at room temperature, there are those, such as *oshiruko,* that are eaten hot and served in lacquerware bowls, rather like sweet soups, and served with a savoury pickle on the side. Likewise, there are those that are served with fine-shaved ice and are a summer-time treat. While both these ingredients – sweetened beans and rice – appear elsewhere in confectionery (notably Southeast Asia), it is in Japan that they have evolved into intricately executed sweets that look almost too beautiful to eat. This aesthetic perfection and the allusions to the seasons embodied in the shapes of these sweets are owed largely to the influence of Tea. (We use this common abbreviated form of "Tea ceremony" to reflect everyday Japanese usage, i.e., *ocha.*)

Among the prerequisites of food that is partaken during Tea are that it reflect the season and that it be fresh. The basic materials of Japanese sweets, white rice, dark bean paste, are, as their counterparts in French confectionery – marzipan and fondant, egg white and chocolate – extremely malleable. They are

9 *Kara* is written with the character for Tang (China) and *kudamono* written with the character for "sweet(s)". Normally, *kudamono* means "fruit(s)".

thus extremely suited to artistic manipulation, and to visual representation of a variety of symbolic elements. Some of these may be extremely subtle, such as the use of a fresh cherry-leaf wrapping around a finished "cake" to represent spring. Others are more blatant reproductions of fruits and nuts – peach, chestnut (including burrs), depending on the season. Certainly, like marzipan, *mochi* too can be used to represent purity. Indeed, the pounding of *mochi* traditionally signified (and still does) protection against evil, the start of new things, and great felicity.

Specialist shops may produce anything from three items to hundreds. A famous shop in Tokyo, which has been in operation since the eighteenth century at the same location, sells nothing but *mochi dango*: (three balls of *mochi*, threaded on a skewer and grilled over a charcoal fire), and in only three flavours: slightly sweetened soy-sauce, tea, and millet flour. In other places one can purchase concoctions in the shape of flowers, seasonal fruit, or abstract geometric shapes echoing contemporary design.

Historically, many of the finest examples of *wagashi* have originated in Kyoto, always the centre of Japanese High Culture. Kyoto tradition laid the groundwork for the Tea ceremony principle of seasonal "appropriateness". Shape, colour, flavour, or some associated material (such as, for example, the pickled young cherry-leaves in *sakura-mochi*, a spring speciality) was expected to indicate the seasons. Some *wagashi* such as *chimaki* made reference to Kyoto's Gion festival. In the festival, ten-meter-spired carts, all heavily decorated, are dragged through the streets. The *chimaki*, flavoured rice wrapped in bamboo leaves and bound in a long spiral, refer to the shape of the carts. Some such references may be extremely obvious: there are many *wagashi* that imitate, in shape and colour if not flavour, the fruit of a particular season. To indicate autumn, for example, there are *konerigaki* representing persimmons, or chestnut-flavoured and shaped *sasaguri*. Some references may be obscure, arising from the classical cultural history of Japan, the reign of a particular emperor, or a local or regional incident.

The quintessential *wagashi* are to be found in the reverse images of *daifuku* and *ohagi*. These two foods epitomise the contradictory impulses in Japanese culture. *Daifuku*, in which soft *mochi* surrounds a centre of purple sweet bean-jam, and *hagi* in which a generous dollop of bean-jam covers a slice of *mochi*. *Daifuku* look rather like small marzipan balls. *Ohagi*, which come in a number of minor variations, look often like small elongated meatballs, or, if one exercises some imagination, chocolate balls. Though the tastes are quite similar, it is the difference in *texture* that is at issue. One is bland, sticky to the bite; the other sweet and porridgy, and, paradoxically, each of these changes over: *ohagi* is, in the final analysis, far less sweet to the palate, than its opposite. The emotional appeal of the *mochi* base is a powerful element in the attraction of these two foods. *Mochi* represents warmth, family, appetite satisfaction. A close analogy is the American concept of apple pie. Beyond that immediate emotional impact, however, it is the juxtaposition of the two elements of these remarkably simple sweets: bland/sweet ; white/dark ; chewy/soft and crunchy. It epitomises, in some way, the mental game that Japanese culture foists on its members, as well as on outsiders: the concepts of "in" and "out" exemplified in the game of *honne* and *tatemae.*

In Japanese culture, external actions – *tatemae* – are contrasted with *honne* – internal feelings. Either of those may be personal or that of a group. Individuals, families, organisations, all practise *honne* and *tatemae.* The one implies one's real feelings, the other implies public acceptance, public behaviour, "face". Because these are very imprecise and vague notions, and yet crucially important, they are also easily, and ceaselessly, manipulated, changed, and presented in many forms and ways. An individual has his own *tatemae* which might form a part of the group *honne,* and that same individual must, if he is to preserve his standing as a member of the group, present the group's *tatemae* which might be different from his own within the group: a game of boxes within boxes, but one that has social and cultural sanction. It is also a game that is endlessly and persistently difficult for foreigners to cope with and adapt to (and, perhaps, that is one of its purposes) as many a foreign businessman can report. The contrasts between *ohagi* and *daifuku* in a way exemplify this difference: which is inside, which is out, the *mochi* or the *an*? And does it make a difference? Well, it does (a subtle one, but nonetheless real) to be sure, but also, as one Japanese informant said, it doesn't: it boils down to an issue of which style you prefer, and that, in itself, can change from moment to moment, situation to situation.

Wagashi fulfil a role not asimilar, at least in concept, to snacks accompanying liquor (*otsumami*). But *otsumami* are consciously robust, and often finger foods, since they need to accompany drinking. *Otsumami* also are quintessential male foods, since it is males, and male taste that prevail in styles of drinking and drink-associated matters. In *wagashi,* in contrast, it is feminine elements that prevail, and the ideas of small size, regular placement on a dish, and representations of nature, are all important.

The Japanese male preserve of *getemono* is not exclusive to Japan. For most cultures in which masculinity is an expressive and jealously guarded value (and which is not?) there are "male preserves" which quite often are expressed in foods. In societies such as the Chinese and Indian, where foods are classified in a coherent (more or less) system, of "cold" and "hot" foods, there is both an ideological justification, and a proper (culturally speaking) place for "male" foods, as well, of course, for "female" foods. These domains are part of the entire ideological domain of meaning for a culture, related to religious and spiritual beliefs, to structures of inter-gender relations, and often to very deep and culturally significant psychological imperative elements of a culture.

The preserves of "female" and of "male" foods in Japan are far less coherent than in Chinese or other systems. Men will and do usually eat *okashi* (Michael was introduced to *oshiruko* [sweet bean soup] at his martial arts club), and women, quite often those in the water trades, will eat male foods such as *horumon.* So too, the domains of male and female in Japan tend to be, if not obscured, then not as hard and fast as they might seem to be from a superficial examination of the facts. Cross-gender activity is not only ignored often enough, but in some circumstances accepted and even sanctioned. There are of course famous examples, such as *onnagata* (kabuki female-impersonator actors), who act (in their roles) with such quintessential femininity that they can even serve (and do) as role models for proper female deportment. The obverse are male-dressers in female revues such as Takarazuka, who carry on their male roles to everyday public life. The strict separation of genders and their coupling with specific sexes is very much blurred in Japan, and individuals can and will switch from one role to another – male to female, female to male – as circumstances and their own nature dictate (see for example Lunsing 1999). Notwithstanding the inroads of both European morality, and the Japanese government's distaste down through the ages, Japanese have always been suspicious of, and avoided, hard and fast sexual distinctions. This view of gender differences carries over into the realm of food as well: how can one have exclusively "male" and "female" foods, when the very categories themselves are, at one and the same time, rigid, and yet fuzzy-bordered?

Part of the solution to this puzzle lies in Japanese attitudes towards symbolic things in general. Sexual attributions and attributes are, in the final analysis, symbolic constructions. They are what people believe is a reality, rather than a reality which is of course, extremely complex and fluid. Ohnuki-Tierney (1988) among others, argues that the Japanese attitude towards the multiplicity of signifying elements (to use a term encompassing signs, symbols and icons) is a form of activity, verbal and material, that simulates play rather than deep emotional or symbolic intent. Play, says Huitzinga, is serious business: it is where humans enrich their lives, practice obscure activities that may be useful in daily life, refresh themselves from stress, enhance in-group feeling. This is true, as well, of Japanese use of the manifold and varied signifying elements in their culture. Thus it would seem that the term "symbol" to Japanese is a fluid and very flexible thing. Symbols "mean" with different intensity, depending on use and context. Eating a *getemono*, or for that matter, an *okashi*, as well as *avoiding* those particular foods, can be symbolic statements about masculinity and femininity in Japanese society. Thus, where symbols are playful, and can be played with, so too can one's preference for this or another kind of food, or, for that matter, this or another kind of sex, entertainment, or reading matter. At the time of eating that food, it might be a statement of a particular gender position. But, the Japanese are ready to concede, perhaps it is not. Ambiguity and indirection, playfulness rather than seriousness, is the name of the game.

Anyone who has spent any time in Japan is struck by the ability of the Japanese to fall so naturally into a role they have found themselves in. And the adoption of the duties incumbent on a particular role is total, committed, *and that is precisely what is valued.* A company managing director clowning at a party, a respected professor dressed only in loincloth and carrying a standard in a festival procession, or, to take an extreme, the cringe-making behaviour of participants at humiliating game shows – these are not, in the Japanese cultural context, unusual or surprising. Japanese recognise that this is only a part of an individual's complete set of behaviours, and more opprobrium would be attached to half-hearted participation than to participating in something that might be personally embarrassing. As a general rule, *roles* are not to be taken "seriously", that is, as the be-all and end-all of a person. There are plenty of roles one is expected to play in one's lifetime, in a large variety of circumstances. But, according to the Japanese ethos, whatever the role, it is to be entered into wholeheartedly. The male-female gender distinctions are, therefore, far more fuzzy and ambiguous in Japanese behaviour than they would be elsewhere.

5.7 *SUMMARY*

THERE ARE A number of points worth emphasising that arise from this chapter. First is that, as noted, cooking methods, like any other cultural process, do not exist in vacuum. They have historical roots, though that reason alone is insufficient to explain them. They also "connect" to other features of people's lives, whether economic, social or political. A second point worth remembering is that many of these processes are shared by Japanese cuisine with other cuisines. The difference is in the emphases on particular foods, as well as on the clusters of practices that we find. Another element is also important: the vast array of techniques, some formally codified, others at the level, essentially, of "folk practice" that both the Japanese *cook* and the Japanese *diner* have at their command. For the cook this offers a vast repertoire to choose from. This has important implications. The professional chef, in competition with others, cannot specialise in *all* the cooking styles available. This means that the professional world of cooking in Japan, as we shall see in the following chapter, is *forced* into specialised niches. For the domestic cook it means something similar, but with different consequences. So long as the cook (or, in practice, her family) is prepared to stay with a repertoire of the tried-and-true, there is no problem. But what happens when family members bring in experiences from outside the home? Specialising (effectively competing) with all the possibilities is impossible, and thus, in modern, affluent Japan, we find *industrial* changes, in the form of fast foods, cook's helpers, take-outs, and so on, which structure daily lives just as they are structured themselves, by domestic demand.

The Japanese diner, as well, is faced with a wealth of cooking styles. As individuals, any one is free to choose what he or she (purse permitting) wishes to eat. But people exist in a social matrix, one that forces them to participate in group activities, whether in the family group, the workplace, or with friends. Normal human processes mean that an individual must display a certain amount of knowledge, of familiarity with foods and techniques as an aspect of the presentation of self that all humans *must* do as social animals. This, in turn, forces the individual to start making assessments and judgements, trials of new techniques. Willing or not, the individual-in-society is drawn into, and participates in, the practices of his society. This means, in practice, that encounters with social divisions and groupings, both expressed by food and implied by particular forms of dining (a derivative of particular forms of cooking) become daily occurrences, drawing the individual more firmly into the social web. One might prefer eating *hanbāga* (or fish and chips), but one, as a social being in Japan, *must* know the implications of eating *okonomiyaki* versus those of eating *kaiseki*. Locations where such particular foods are served imply particular rules of behaviour, even of enjoyment and experience.

READINGS FOR CHAPTER 5

Anderson, Eugene. N. 1988 *The Food of China.*

Dalby, Liza C. 1983 *Geisha.*

Embree, John F. 1939 *Suye Mura: A Japanese Village.*

Kawabata 1990 *Confectionery Kyoto.*

Lunsing, Wim 1999 "Prostitution, dating, mating and marriage: Love, sex and materialism in Japan".

Masuda, K. 1975 "Bride's progress: How a *yome* becomes a *shutome*".

Mintz, Sidney 1996 *Tasting Food, Tasting Freedom: Excursions into Eating, Culture, and the Past.*

Nakane, Chie 1970 *Japanese Society.*

Suzuki Soukou, Shiraishi Kazuko, Ego Michiko and Yamaguchi Takashi 1995 *Well-made Japanese Confections.*

Tsuji, Kaichi 1974 *Kaiseki: Zen Tastes in Japanese Cooking.*

1 *Odemae bento* with *tai*. Gift to guests at a roof-raising party.

2 Meal at a Buddhist temple.

3 *Kombu* drying racks.

4 A small offering at a Shinto shrine. Trays include a watermelon and vegetables.

5 *Ichijū sansai.*

6 Tea-kettle on *irori* at Tea ceremony.

7 New Year offering at a shrine: *mochi* cake, cooked rice.

8 Sushi close up. Back row from left: *hamachi*, *saké*, *ika*, *akagai*. Front row from left: *ebi*, *ikura*.

9 Outdoors *robata yaki.*

10 Sushi shop in Tsukiji.

11 *Daikon* drying on racks before pickling.

6 Food Loci

FOOD PREPARATION AND consumption take place at a specific place – a locus – in Japan as elsewhere. The loci are divided, in Japan as elsewhere, between domestic and public loci. The distinctions between these go much farther than an assumption of plain/homey and fancy. To understand the loci, one must also understand some of the social background which forms them in modern Japanese society.

Moreover, unusually, the domestic and public spheres (in cuisine) are much more highly segregated, for reasons that will become clear below, than in many other countries. In fact, we can see the operation of the principle of compartmentalisation, so important throughout Japanese culture.

European food history, while it cannot serve as a template or analogy for Japanese cuisine, offers some interesting parallels. The emergence of modern European food styles was a consequence of three factors. The native foods of the post medieval period were largely of local origin. There were few "public" places to eat, with the exception of taverns. The meals of commoners and of aristocracy were different largely in terms of the amounts of foods served and in the relative scarcity of some of the food items. This changed rapidly in the period encompassing the Enlightenment and the Industrial Revolution.

First, the growing trade with spice- and exotic-food producing areas radically changed European food. Spices such as pepper and nutmeg filtered down to the lower classes as European colonial ambitions, to a large part fuelled by a hunger for those spices, continued to spread. Non-spice staples such as chocolate, tea, sugar, and coffee created major changes in preference, and the staple foods changed as well.

Second, the singular events of the French revolution, whatever deleterious effects they may have had on parts of the European population, were highly beneficial to European cuisine. French aristocrats, deprived of their estates, migrated to England and the US. Separated from their wealth yet hungering for the comforts of home, they opened restaurants and served as domestic cooks, necessarily modifying the heavy canons of aristocratic cuisine for the lighter, more accessible dishes and meals they were forced to partake of. By doing so, they created the standard of European meals – the course dinner – which still exists today, whether as the British family's Sunday roast or the French family's main meal.

Finally, by the nineteenth century, technological and social innovations began to affect the kitchen. Technology brought about better means of preserving (and thus marketing) food, better and smaller kitchen furnishings and utensils. Social innovations brought a rise in the number of literate women, and thus, correspondingly a market for cookery books in Britain. The process of culinary innovations filtering downwards was accelerated by these processes because *technically*, the domestic food locus could try to emulate the kitchens of great houses, and the products of great chefs. It still takes an entire bullock to provide a potful of "proper" stock, but few restaurants or kitchens, let alone households, will go to those lengths. Chefs also adapted their menus to changing taste, and when they entered the burgeoning cookbook market, had to further simplify their recipes.

Norbert Elias argues (1982) that much of the change derived from the philosophical desire that became prevalent in Europe to "tame" the concept of appetite. That is, that part and parcel of the intellectual revolution of the Enlightenment and its Renaissance predecessor, was also the concept that appetites, including those for food, should be refined, controlled, and distanced from the need to stuff oneself. Whatever the merit of this argument in detail, it would seem far more reasonable to assume that the material conditions, largely deriving from technical and social innovations (such as international trade) lay at the source of the intellectual traditions. This argument is peripheral to what we are dealing with here, but it is worth keeping in mind, since the evolution of "civilised" eating in Japan, and particularly its extension in the nineteenth and twentieth centuries, differed from that in Europe, and yet can be seen as parallel to it.

Japanese urban households were not suited for entertaining guests, particularly with the mass building of the late nineteenth and twentieth centuries. In contrast the institutions of catering and of dining entertainment were well established in Japan, and gained impetus from the rise of the merchant classes during the time of Tokugawa-enforced peace. A variety of eating establishments were operating in Japan from at least the sixteenth century, encouraged perhaps by the flourishing pilgrimage industry. Many dishes of Japanese cuisine are labour-intensive, and, moreover, require a great deal of learned skill, so that a niche for specialist cooks was a very varied one. Technology, in the form, of specialist pots, pans, and so on, was a relatively minor aspect of cooking, well answered by Japanese technological prowess. Preserved foods were already well incorporated into the Japanese cuisine, and many such as sushi were refined further, but in the context of public, rather than domestic cookery. Finally, the emergence of a middle class, able to mediate between the cuisines of the upper class and that of the lower, was late in coming in Japan. When it finally emerged as a major force after World War II, the segmentation of food loci was already well established.

The interaction of ecological/technological necessity and social/cultural institutions and preferences is always a two-way street. Ecological bases create frameworks, or limits, which structure social institutions such as food distribution. Viewed from the other side, social institutions create ecological and technological conditions, such as the import of new crops, or the creation of new means of preparing familiar foods. Here it is useful to look at this relationship through the technological viewpoint. In other words, we want to see what styles of cooking are available in the Japanese canon of food preparation, and then see how this has structured food loci and contributed to the food compartmentalisation we have discussed earlier.

The food styles the Japanese public enjoys become translated, in the realm of the public consumption of foods, into specialist food-loci. These specialist eating places complement, and must be viewed in complement to the household, where most food is consumed for most people. Each of these loci provides slightly different implications for service, for social grouping, for presentation, and for infra-food issues such as economics. The loci of food consumption, in Japan as elsewhere, tend to cluster around two poles. On the one hand are private, or closed loci: the home, private parties or rituals, groups of people related socially in some way. The other pole is that of public consumption which is accessible, or at least visible, to people not of the group. Of course, to some degree there is a mixing of these two poles, with one or another locus belonging to both, or shifting for a given instance, towards the other pole. Public restaurants may close their door for the owner's private party, or families may join a neighbourhood picnic. Nonetheless, there are significant differences in style and meaning, for different loci.

6.1 *THE HOME*

In the morning we looked out through the wide panoramic window of the Okuyamas' house. Far in the distance, past the busy town, the green checks of the rice fields, the wooded slopes of the other side of the Omono river valley, towered the white, almost perfect cone of "Ugo Fuji" – Mount Chōkai – in solitary glory. Directly below the window came the susurrus of the wind passing through a small cedar grove. From the mountain at our backs came the slight scent of pines and cedars, tinged with wood smoke.

Near the house, Shunzō was preparing *fuki* (sweet coltsfoot) which he had picked that morning. He had built a small fire outside in the yard on which he was boiling a large can of water. Stripping away the broad leaves, he had left the stalks, which after blanching, were peeled and put to one side. In the house, Miyako was preparing breakfast, which we soon went in to eat.

"But, first," said Shunzō in his usual impish, slightly shy, but definitely inarguable manner, "we need something to drink. Have a beer." Jeanne could refuse gracefully, but Michael had to sit through a couple of cans of Heineken while breakfast was being served. At each setting were a set of dishes. A flat rectangular plate held two slices of roast beef. A smaller bowl held intensely flavoured *tsukudani* (vegetables boiled down in soy-sauce), and a grilled fillet of small mackerel with the skin and head (but no tail). In the middle of the table Miyako had placed two bowls, one of the *fuki* that had been prepared earlier by Shunzō, the other of large soft *umeboshi*. The pickled plums and the cooked vegetables were salty, awakening, and added flavour to the fresh rice, which Miyako brought along with bowls of *miso shiru*.

The breakfast we ate that day was exceptional, *not* because of our friend's particular preferences in drink (very *few* households, in our experience, have beer as a morning drink) but because it epitomised a "proper" Japanese breakfast. The elements were all there: the rice staple and *miso shiru*, *okazu* of fish and pickles. In truth however, even in that small scene, there are some additional data that ought to be considered.

Breakfast the following day was different. Miyako admitted that she likes coffee and drinks it every day. For breakfast we had two slices of ham folded over and resting on some sliced cabbage with two slices of cucumber as garnish. With it came rice, and a *miso shiru* with a tofu piece and some radish. Several central plates contained the *okazu*: soft *umeboshi*, *matsutake* (pine mushroom) and radish pickle, and a *tsukudani*. All of these were in square nested plates with a patterned blue glaze. A large blue bowl in the centre of the table cradled a mound of rice-bran pickled mini aubergines. Beside it stood a Western-style plate of oranges. Each had been quartered, the middle pith cut off, and each slice cut half way along the peel to release the flesh.

The ladies enjoyed a morning cup of coffee in Western cups of a brownish rough glaze, whereas the men drank beer in glazed Japanese teacups. A large glass plate of morning glory flowers on the vine was in the middle of the table.

The beer here comes into its own as a highlight of the attitude Japanese have for meals in general, and breakfast in particular: it is highly amenable to experimentation. Shunzō is by no means an alcoholic, and is, in fact, one of the most abstemious Japanese we know. The beer was drunk not for its alcoholic high, but because it served to mark him as "modern" and, more importantly, because it was an experiment in aesthetics and taste: was it, or was it not appropriate for such a meal? This sort of question has been repeated in our acquaintance many times: on other occasions he has tried butter (served in slices, to be eaten with a fork, both standard butter, and that peculiarly Japanese invention, raisin-embedded butter), cheesecake (both *reya*, that is gelatine, and baked cheesecakes), and more recently, flavoured processed cheeses (natural, smoked, and strawberry). Miyako's rather shy admission that she loves coffee is of a piece as well. In terms of amount drunk, variety, number of places where one can drink, and quality of the drink, coffee certainly ranks today as Japan's national drink, far eclipsing tea, and even possibly beer. Certainly the Japanese economy, in its best years, has ensured a steady supply of such gourmet delicacies as Blue Mountain coffee, which is available (notwithstanding its small production area in Jamaica) throughout Japan. Shunzō's experiments with food, odd as they may be to a prejudiced European eye, are completely orthodox in two senses. First, they exemplify the fascination Japanese culture has with the exotic and the foreign. And, second, because the *context* of these new and foreign foods (and other items as well) has not necessarily been conveyed along with the item, Japanese feel free to experiment, to break what to an observer from the donating culture concerned, would be a terrible mis-alliance: *strawberry* flavoured cheese? Well why not?

For the "average" Japanese household the food consumed is a compromise between a number of pressures. Finances obviously play a major part, with the availability of particular foods determined in the first instance by the amount of the household budget, which is determined by the income-generating activities of the household. In the second instance, the income of the household also determines the arrangement, furnishing, and equipping of the food preparation areas. Until the end of the nineteen-eighties, almost all Japanese kitchens were small and, by comparable European standards, poorly equipped. The average size of the kitchen *plus* the attached dining room was often no larger than two *jō*. Four was about the norm. This strictly limited the number and sizes of kitchen equipment. Refrigerators were small (.5 cu. meter). Two burner gas ranges were the norm, and ovens, including microwave ranges, a rarity. The only category of items that was highly varied was serving utensils, with many households keeping ceremonial and special sets of dishes in closets hidden beneath the eaves.

Several factors have brought about a change. First and foremost has been the move of Japanese society into a consumer-oriented economy and society. Secondarily has been a rise in the expectations not only of men, but also of women. This complex phenomenon has been brought about partly by the rise of two-career, or at least, two income-households, which in turn has fed into the consumer economy by making more disposable income available. The prioritisation of women's needs has been a slow one in Japan. For reasons of economics – higher rate of return on electronic, versus electrical goods, and the difficulties Japanese domestic appliance makers had to meet American standards – Japanese appliance makers had lagged behind in the export race. Nonetheless, several kitchen appliances were added with growing frequency to the venerable and successful rice-cooker. Smaller appliances – mixers, toaster ovens – were followed by mid-sized appliances such as ovens and microwaves in the early eighties. Large refrigerators started catching on in the early nineties with 452 litre-capacity not unusual, and more significantly, with a larger freezer section than in 1970 or 1980 models.

All this has meant that the Japanese kitchen has changed fundamentally over the past few decades, in line with changes in other aspects of the culture. With more women at work, the use of convenience foods has increased. This has taken two forms. One has been an extension of traditional services such as *demae* (delivered foods) and *mochikaeri* (take-away). These services have been provided by Japanese restaurants and cook shops since the Edo period. Second, there has been a rise in the various forms of convenience foods that require little preparation. Dried soup packets were pioneered by the Imperial Army before and during World War II. These techniques were extended to the civilian market, and became necessities with large numbers of Japanese businessmen, who, travelling abroad, felt the need for some home comfort foods. One business acquaintance of ours never left on a business trip in the seventies without a kilo or so of dried food packets to supplement his diet. Frozen ready-made dinners which required heating in a conventional or microwave oven obviously had to await the emergence of two complementary appliances: large freezers and ovens, which were not to be found in most households before the early nineties.

The availability of pre-packed and ready-made foods was also stimulated by another social factor. Throughout the post war years, Japan has seen a rise in the number of single-person households. This was brought about by the gradual rise in the age of marriage (from about 22 years old for women and 25 for men in the sixties, to about 27 and 29 in the nineties), by the decision of many women not to marry, and, peculiarly, by the requirements of the Japanese work environment. Many middle-aged businessmen, rotated throughout the organisation they were working for, must need relocate to a different part of Japan or overseas. This creates a tension with the education system under which their families live, in which any disruption of a child's study is likely to make him or her fall behind in the race to enter a prestigious university, which, in turn, is the key to a successful career. As a result, many Japanese families split at this stage, with the wife and (school-bound) children remaining in the family home while the father/husband/main earner is forced to relocate to another city and establish a single-person household, returning to the main household several times a year, if possible.

A consequence of the availability of individual portions of ready-to-eat and processed foods has been a broadening and greater variation not only of the Japanese diet, but also of the menus of specific households. As we have noted elsewhere in this volume, Japanese tastes have changed, but they have changed most radically for the young. Preferences for foreign foods, for meat over fish, and for the kinds of fish which, in the words of one food wholesaler "do not require them [young people] to make any effort about their food" abound. As a result, in many households certain meals, notably breakfast but also other meals, have become individual affairs, with different generations, and even individuals, eating different things from the choice of frozen individual portions.

The household menu, as we have seen, reflects the evolution of the Japanese household over time. From being a centralised, unitary cell, it is becoming far more varied and heterogeneous, with households having to make adaptations to changes in their composition and environment. This of course is true in many fields other than food as well, and we can see how these changes parallel changes in food loci outside the home.

6.2 *EATING OUT*

Numerous studies of restaurants demonstrate the complexity of the restaurant as a mediation locus between the public and the private. It is where people come to see and be seen, come to learn about their own and foreign culture (however sanitised and domesticated), and where the realms of domestic cooking are contrasted (in flattering or unflattering ways) with the realms of public life. The emergence of public eating places, where *cuisine* and not only *food* are served differed in scope and in time of emergence from one society to another. In European restaurants – establishments specialising in serving food on the premises, rather than as a service to travellers (inns), addenda to drinking (wine shops and taverns), or household supplements (roast shops and bake shops) – emerged as common phenomena after the French revolution. Both rich and poor generally dined at home (their own and their friends). In East Asia such establishments emerged much earlier. The increasing spread of urban living in China during the T'ang dynasty (617–907 AD) and in Japan during the Edo era (1600–1868) brought about the establishment of restaurants some of which, in the Japanese case, are still extant today.

Restaurants in Europe mediated between the food of the wealthy and the aristocracy, and that of the lesser orders. They were, in short, both communication channels and nurseries for the development of cuisines. This function, unintentional and market driven as it is, and different in the context of modern Japanese society from nineteenth century Europe, continues today, as we shall see when we examine Japanese cooking. French cuisine benefited immeasurably from the emergence of the public restaurant, and the diffusion of aristocratic gastronomy to the general public via restaurants and the media structured the French fascination with, and adherence to, its national gastronomy. A similar process occurred in Japan, though with particular twists that are quintessentially Japanese.

The historical antecedents of public eating houses in Japan, like those in Europe, are in the development of food stalls in the streets, for which there is evidence from the Muromachi period (1338–1573), through the evolution of specialist tea houses (some real tea-houses, some brothels) which also catered food, particularly to travellers, through the evolution of speciality *ryōriya* or cookshops during the Edo period. Illustrations from the Momoyama and early Edo periods (1573–1600 and 1600–1868) show people eating in public houses. Other illustrations show peddlers selling tea and cakes or other street foods along the bridges in the capital. Another illustration, which may or may not be of a public eating place shows a group of fishermen who have set up a horizontal weir through a waterfall. The weir projects out over the river. Fish falling from the waterfall are caught in this ingenious trap, immediately cooked and served to a group of hungry diners seated further from the waterfall: fish at their absolute freshest.

Many public eating houses emerged with the rise of the urban life-style during the days of closed-country and relative economic peace in the Edo period. Most of these catered to the entertainment trade: brothels and theatres, in both of which patrons enjoyed take-away meals delivered to them while they partook of the main entertainment. Notable among those were "dining" boats, in which young bloods, accompanied by musicians, favourite courtesans, and cooks, floated on the rivers and waterways of Edo and other cities. The less fortunate (and, less wealthy) could still go out to enjoy public fireworks shows, and had their stomachs catered to by enterprising fishermen, greengrocers, and food stalls, all waterborne, which came to the customers as required.

Western-style restaurants emerged during Meiji, whether as fashionable emulation of Western dining places which Japanese experts travelling abroad had experienced, or to cater to the foreign concessions in places such as Yokohama. A small number of places started the trend of bringing foreign food to the masses. Rengatei in the Ginza pioneered *hayashi raisu* (beef hash and rice) in 1868, the first year of the Meiji period. Manjo Fruit Parlor, by Tokyo University's main gate, introduced curry rice in 1915 in its most common version, that is, a roux-based very mild sauce simmered, it is claimed, for a minimum of two hours.

Within Japan, as elsewhere in the world, "Japanese" restaurants are a new phenomenon. This may sound odd, but it is a consequence of the evolution of the cooking styles we discussed in the previous chapter: each restaurant should fit itself into one of the food styles we have discussed, and, by doing so, fit into a social and economic framework. Japanese restaurants – *wafu ryōriya* – started appearing in large numbers in Japan as a consequence of the 1964 Olympics, when certain restaurants wanted to distance themselves from the wave of foreign (usually Western)-style restaurants that the government had encouraged to cater to the Olympic visitors. Restaurants before that time were almost entirely specialised, with the exception of a few "Western" restaurants, featuring French-style menus which catered either to the foreign population, or to Japanese with a hankering for the exotic. Some of these, such as Futabatei, in Shibuya took their cuisine very seriously indeed, and swore by their demi-glace sauce (simmered for a month at least). Another very exclusive restaurant in Tokyo's Suginami-ward, specialising in roast beef and steak, will only take a couple at lunch or dinner. By reservation only, of course, and a car is sent for pick up at the train station.

A number of different types of establishment exist. *Ryōtei* are traditional fixed-menu establishments, usually expensive, in which the food served is pure "Japanese" cuisine (in practice, with foreign inclusions), and the cook has focused the menu on the best ingredients of the season. "*Resutoran*" are, generally speaking, establishments that offer some variation, Japanised or not, of Western, and some Indian and Chinese dishes (e.g. steak, curry, spaghetti, pilaff would be equally likely to be on the menu). Included in this terminology are drinking places, which also indicate, by usage, differences between the types of drinks and service offered, e.g. *izakaya* (Japanese drinking places, serving Japanese drinks such as saké, and whiskey) and *bā* (Western drinking place, serving in addition, cocktails and wine). *Ryōriya* is a generic term for cook shops, but in practice it refers to establishments at the middle of the price range and below. Most places serving Japanese food will be termed according to the cooking style they offer: *tempura-ya* and *soba-ya*[1] for example.

Unsurprisingly, most public eating places are fairly small. Some are even tiny, barely allowing room for the cook to work. There are three reasons for this. First is the high price of land in Japan, which makes the creation of a large cook shop quite prohibitive. As a result of this size squeeze, one quite often finds entire floors of buildings packed with restaurants. One which we have frequented for years is only reached by a lift that also serves offices and businesses on lower floors. The lift opens onto a widish, twisting corridor. It is lined on either side by restaurant fronts, maintaining an illusion that the corridor is a busy street, not the inside of a building. A *tempura-ya, sushi-ya, nabemono-ya* (stews and pot-cooked foods), a Chinese (authentic) restaurant and a *chūka ryōriya* (that is, Japanised Chinese cooking), sit cheek by jowl. Each shop front has a large glass display of wax models of its offerings, labelled as to name and price. Customers – many are regulars, or denizens of local shops or offices – crowd the corridors, lingering at the wax displays, waiting for their fancy to be tempted. Shop fronts, complete with pseudo-roofs, are as distinctive as the owners can make them – clean geometric lines of paper and wood for traditional Japanese, or Greek-key pattern borders for Japanese-style Chinese (*chūka*).

Asecond reason for the small size of most (at least, urban) eating places in Japan is the high cost of labour, which in practice means that many start-up businesses do not want, and cannot afford the extra help they would need for running a larger place.

Finally, however, there is a third issue: the nature of the Japanese service relationship. Japanese marketing is, at least in normative terms, seen as an intimate service. It is often characterised by a close, ritualised dependency. In practice this means that the Japanese customer expects a high intensity of personal service at all levels. Eating is a quintessentially *individual* process, and Japanese norms fully recognise that. The diner expects, as a guest, to be "a jewel on the cushion of hospitality" as Nero Wolfe so succinctly puts it. The small, intimate feel of many luxury Japanese eating places emphasise all that. Intimacy, in Japanese culture, is recognised as a *construct*, like many other social features that European society fails to understand and acknowledge. Behind the false, formal intimacy created by place, by the personal attention of the counter-man or the personal waiter, there may or not be real intimacy and empathy. That is not as important, at least in the Japanese context, as providing the appearance –

1 The *ya* suffix indicates a shop, as in e.g. *yao-ya* (greens-shop, or greengrocer).

the *tatemae* – of intimacy. Real intimacy and warmth may or may not flow from its pretence, but in the civilised pretences lie at least the seeds of reality. This also helps explain the reverse: the mass and anonymity of many Japanese cultural settings, ranging from public baths to Shinjuku station. The recognition that intimacy is a social construct means that its reverse – mass participation and anonymity – are constructs as well, something that is not overshadowing, but rather temporary, as ephemeral as Japanese buildings.

Public eating places (bars, restaurants) in Japan have an enormous repertoire of presentations to choose from. They range from the provision of meals in small *ryōtei* run in their homes by retired chefs, through large *beerstübe* style *jingizu-kan* places, where hundreds of eaters quaff beer and grill their own meat on iron griddles, and the ends of the hall are barely visible through the tangy smoke. Not all eating places cluster in the *sakariba* where employees can rush from work to grab a quick bite, or where people can stop on their way back home for a round of convivial eating and drinking. More expensive and exclusive places cater for upper management and the wealthy, others the less affluent. Prices of food vary quite dramatically: one can eat a *gyūdon* (stir-fried beef and onions over a rice bowl), with pickles and *miso shiru* at a chain for about 300 yen, or one can indulge in several hundred thousand yen per person in an exclusive specialist restaurant. And both these establishments might be side by side.

To characterise all such establishments is therefore extremely difficult, even impossible task. What we set out to do here is to provide a summary account of *types* rather than of all the possible variations. This categorisation follows roughly an informed "native" schema, that is, we are trying to illustrate what *Japanese* diners consider when looking at an eating place.

To make the terminology simpler, we refer to all public eating places in which the client sits down on the premises as a restaurant. This of course covers a multitude of types. Here we cover only those typical aspects which help in illuminating some of the general aspects of Japanese cuisine. As elsewhere throughout the world they do not purvey [only] food. They purvey an atmosphere, an idea of who-you-are to the diner as well. Shelton (1990) has noted how different types of restaurant in the US establish moods which tell the customer, essentially what the customer wants to hear: "you are young and in a hurry" at a fast-food chain, "you are sophisticated" at an up-market Euro-food place. This is of course not surprising: restaurants are places of display par excellence, on a level with the daily evening *paseo* in every Latin American town, where men and women go to see *and be seen.*

The mood setting (in advertisements it is called "ambience") starts at the entrance to a restaurant, where subtle or not-so-subtle hints tell of what can be expected inside. Here, restaurants in Japan have an advantage over others. In most restaurants, a glass case at the foyer exhibits wax models of the delights to be found inside. These wax models are full-sized and (reasonably) true to life. Painted appropriately they represent a statement of the kind of restaurant, and the value of its foods. Cheaper places have the models alone, more expensive places will place some evocative item to indicate the ambience, from a plastic bream caught in a net before a restaurant specialising in Shikoku cuisine, to a *matroushka* doll in the front of a Russian restaurant. Truly expensive places – *ryōtei*, small specialist restaurants – have no wax displays, and often no sign (a commonplace in Kyoto). These establishments are reluctant to provide any evidence of a restaurant behind the facade. Such restaurants tend to be so exclusive that they will rarely accept people walking in from the street: dining is by referral or by reservation only. Clusters of such restaurants can be seen in affluent parts of Japanese cities: in Akasaka in Tokyo (convenient to both government offices and large corporate headquarters) and in the elegant enclaves of Kyoto.

The interior of restaurants reflects the exterior (or, more properly, the reverse). Traditional Japanese *ryōriya* were constructed according to Japanese native architectural canons. This interior is retained in those places that attempt to convey a traditional air. Seating (particularly in places that do *not* cater to a lunchtime business crowd) are quite often on *tatami* with separate cubicles for different groups of diners:

> The taxi ride from the station to Ukai Toriyama, the most beautiful restaurant in the world (Michael's characterisation), takes about ten minutes. For large parties, the restaurant will send their minibus, but we were hungry and impatient. The road wound through clay hills, past a medieval fantasy "love hotel" where couples could come for illicit (and licit) sexual adventure, into a deep pine forest between two hills. The valley is deep and narrow. Pine trees and small groves of bamboo whisper with the wind, and a small clear stream chuckles over rocks. In the valley the owners have assembled an incongruous but peculiarly pleasing assembly of old Meiji and Edo-period houses from all over Japan. There is a mill, several peasant houses, and a number of more prosperous looking buildings. Most are thatched, traditional wattle-and-daub half-timbered structures. The wood is brown, offset by mustard yellow clay walls, and by the pristine white *shoji* sliding doors. An attendant greets us at the lobby. The usual indistinguishable furnishings. A *maneki neko* (a small figurine of a white cat one paw raised beckoning to customers) is on one wall, as well as a collage representing the Treasure Ship with its seven lucky gods of good fortune. An attendant conveys us to one of the smaller houses: what might have been a farmer's storehouse, or even a little *yama-goya* (mountain hut) where he lived while working in distant mountain groves. The entrance is a small hallway, pebble floored, where one removes shoes and climbs onto a small ledge floored with polished wood. A sliding door opens into a *tatami* floored room, in the middle of which is a sand-filed *irori*. There is a *tokonoma* niche, where a scroll depicting a bamboo grove is hung, and before it a simple flower arrangement: irises in a brown ceramic pot. The attendant opens the sliding door at the other side of the room.

> The garden in all its glory becomes a part of the dining room. We are rendered quite breathless by this sight, and sit down in silence regarding the stream which has been crossed by a series of pools and channels. Golden *koi* swim leisurely about, and we have to restrain the four year-old, who wants to paddle his hands in the water. Beyond the garden the hill rises, dark and green, almost sheer, to a clear blue sky.
>
> Aside from the cushions, the *tokonoma* with its scroll and flower arrangement, and a telephone, the room is bare, but then, it hardly needs any kind of decoration with the outside pouring in through the open wall. Attendants bring a shovel-full of coals: the speciality of the place is grilled foods, which we order from a menu written in ornate (and difficult to read) "grass script" characters. A small metal bracket is placed in the sand of the *irori*, and, undisturbed by attendants, we grill the food slowly, washing it down with beer, chatting, stretching on the *tatami*, and, occasionally, forgetting the food in favour of the outside. Finally the waiter returns with the rice, adding a topping – *tororo* (grated yam), a gelatinous, slightly salty sauce – and a pot of *miso shiru.*

Of course, not every restaurant, even in Japanese style, is as luscious as the one described. But restaurants in Japan generally fall into one or another of the "Japanese" or "Western" categories. In the former, furnishings are in "Japanese style": half-timbered walls, low-backed wooden chairs, sometimes *tatami* rooms, where parties can sit in isolation, "Japanese" bric-a-brac decorating the walls. Other restaurants will start with a Western premise, in which tables, chairs with high backs, and Western style decorations predominate. As a general rule, "pristine" decor – Western or Japanese – correlates positively with high prices and more expensive, perhaps authentic food. As one goes down the style the decor becomes what can be termed pragmatic: whatever will suit, and whatever will attract the customers that are the target audience. Cheaper places will also make greater use of obvious technology, whether it is machines to buy meal tickets (very common in those places that serve a rush crowd at lunch-time), or automatic chopsticks dispensers. Places that cater to the young – usually chains such as McDonalds or Dunkin' Donuts – are also less likely to have items such as *maneki neko* or the Seven Lucky Gods. Interestingly enough, and an indication that *presentation* is the name of the game, is that such places sometimes have such good luck tokens, but these are concealed in staff areas.

6.3 *BAR FOODS*

WHILE THERE ARE culturally approved bar foods in most drinking cultures (peanuts and pickled eggs in US bars, crisps and scratchings in the UK, a *meze* in Greece) there is a large array of foods in Japan that are almost exclusively linked to drinking, and, by extension, are or can be considered largely "male foods."

Oden, which we have discussed, is a kind of counter food that may also be sold in more "solid" surroundings than a barrow, but there are cooking styles which are virtually confined to drinking places.

For many Japanese working men (and more women as time goes by) the day is divided into three rather different phases and associated locations. There is work and the workplace, where most of life's activities are centred during working age (e.g. from about 22 to about 65 years of age), and which occupies most of the day and week. In the evenings, there is the family and home, where one sleeps, sometimes eats, and has responsibilities (no matter how attenuated) as spouse and parent. Both of these locations are similar in that one must exhibit highly controlled and structured behaviours. They are different in their essence: public versus private life, but not necessarily in the degree of tension and control that is expected in each. Between the two areas of life is a third, a "zone of transition" (Linhardt 1986): the *sakariba*. *Sakariba* are areas of bars, night-clubs, restaurants, pachinko games parlours, and in some areas, sexual businesses. They are most often to be found in the neighbourhood of major train stations. In Tokyo, Kabukichō in Shinjuku, the Ginza, Dōgenzaka in Shibuya, and many other areas fulfil this function. This is where the *sarariman* go to relax, have a drink, chat with a hostess, cry on a friend's shoulder, or merely have a bite to eat without any social obligation, generally unwind. Establishments range from the popular to the exclusive, from the cheap to the hideously expensive. From places that spill out onto the street in garish lights, crying touts and explicit pictures, to places so reclusive that only aficionados know of them. The pace is generally frenetic, with, in some places, crowds of students milling through the streets, while others cater to working classes (both white- and blue-collar).

There is, of course, a vast range of drinking places to be found in any *sakariba*. And the category "drinking place" is not truly exclusive, since it is often difficult to identify a "drinking" place from any other food place. We estimated that there were about 350 drinking places in a town of 16,000 people. The number in any of the *sakariba* in Tokyo such as Shinjuku is inestimable, let alone the total number in the city or in Japan as a whole. Some are necessarily tiny, others are far larger with mass appeal. However, even in the smallest of places, what sometimes may distinguish them from others in the same category is the food rather than drink, which can be quite standard: most places will offer a local saké (if there is a brewery in the area) or a selection preferred by the owner, a selection of domestic whiskeys, several beers and some wine. Some other drinks such as *shochu* may also be available, but bars, generally speaking, and their "Japanese" counterparts, *izakaya,* are rarely distinctive in terms of drink: it is in food that individual styles have room for expression.

The food served, the atmosphere, the preference of a particular category of customers is what really distinguish drinking places. It is the food that concerns us here. In quite a few cases the food offered may be very restricted. No more than *otsumami* (drinking snacks, finger foods) – crackers, *moromi-miso* with vegetables – may be offered. The range of bar foods, as noted is extremely wide, and we do not intend to catalogue them here. However, it is worthwhile examining some aspects of bars, since they illustrate some useful points about Japanese society.

> It was rather late at night, and we had had no dinner. The blazing heat of the summer in Tokyo meant that we went out rather late at night, needing a walk. Eventually, after walking for about thirty minutes in a residential area, we found a small *nomiya*, the Hanaya. The place is small, seating four people at the counter and two parties of up to 4 people at short-legged tables set on a raised platform floored with *tatami*. Mr. Konno, the owner and chef, asked us to sit at the counter since there were only two of us. The small kitchen (1 × 4 m) runs the width of the shop. As is common in many small places, hand-written vertical signs, tacked to the walls and above the bar, indicate what is available. In addition to the food, Hanaya is unusual in that it offers about twenty kinds of local saké (that is, what might be called a micro-brewery in the beer world: almost unknown outside their area of manufacture), several cocktails including home-made *ume-shu* (a liqueur made by soaking large Japanese green plums in 60% alcohol, with a modicum of sugar [surprisingly powerful stuff, it improves with age]) and 59 food items. Those marked in red are the specials of the day.
>
> We order beer. With the drink we each get a glass plate on which rests a blue glass cup the size of an egg-cup. On the plate rests a single *shisō* leaf (perilla, an aromatic plant). Several small clams cooked in lemon juice and a bit of soy sauce rests on the leaf. Beside the leaf is a slice of lemon on which are two pieces (2 × 4 cm) of devil's tongue root jelly (*konnyaku*), sliced and arranged just like *sashimi*. The *konnyaku*, normally a translucent jelly with black flecks, had been flavoured and coloured by *nori* seaweed within it. It exuded a faint, refreshing smell of the sea, emphasised by its ice green colour. A dab of mustard yellow sea urchin roe (*uni*), sits jauntily on the *konnyaku*. In the cup are small cubes of tuna *maguro sashimi* in *tororo* sauce, garnished with *wasabi* and sesame seeds. The *tororo*, whipped to a froth, is slippery and drips off the chopsticks like a light syrup. Its slight astringency is a counterpoint to the smoothness of the raw tuna, its white foam shows to perfection the pink freshness of the fish.
>
> We then order a summer speciality – salt-grilled sweetfish (*ayu*). It comes curled into swimming shape on a fan-shaped plate glazed a pale celadon. The fish head rests on a *shisō* leaf. Adorning the fish, on its belly, rests a long ginger shoot (not the root) – a fleshy pink and white spear – probably grown without sunlight to blanch like white asparagus, cut lengthwise and a slice of lemon. The ginger shoot has been lightly pickled in rice vinergar. The fish, though small, is absolutely fresh, and completely delicious. The delicate sweet taste of its flesh shines through the slightly salty and smokey crispness of the charred skin.

This sharpens our appetite, and we then order some fresh fried octopus. It arrives on a footed pale brown-glazed plate: six pieces of tentacle, fried Spanish style, and slice of lemon. To the side, Konno-san has dabbed some mayonnaise on a *shisō* leaf. When asked why, he shrugs, "a lot of people like mayonnaise, and it seems to go well with fried octopus." A decade or even five years ago, mayonnaise on Japanese food (that is, distinct from Japanised Western foods such as salads) outside the home would have been extraordinary.

Since it is a humid night, and since it has been a favourite of Jeanne's since student days, we have *hiyayakko* next. A block of creamy silk-like tofu, on which are piled curls of *katsuo-bushi*, grated dried salted salmon (an unusual garnish to tofu and one we'd never before encountered), chopped shallots, and grated ginger. On the side are chopped aromatic and colourful *myōga* shoots. *Myōga* is a relative of ginger and has a similar aromatic tang but less pungent, and its smell is also more floral, less sharp. The pink-tinged shoots, as are most of the vegetables served, have come from the fields of Konno-san's friend in Yokohama. They are grown organically.

"Much of the seasonal awareness today has been lost," Konno-san says. "The large shops try to get things that look perfect, but by doing so, they lose much of the flavour. Now you can eat anything in any season. The distance from Kyushu in the south to Hokkaido in the north (about 3,000 km) is tremendous, so the *total* growing season is very long, and younger people want to satisfy their cravings at all times. As a result, they have lost a sense of the changes of the seasons."

The only other customers in the diminutive shop (so small you could not swing a cat in it) – a party of four (2 couples of thirty-somethings) on the nearby table finish their merrily boisterous drinking and leave. Meanwhile we attend to our next delicacy, Japanese aubergines (*nasu)*. The three aubergines have been flame-roasted till meltingly soft, peeled, and pulled apart, not cut, into sections. They are garnished with a pile of *katsuo-bushi*. Japanese aubergines are tiny, tender, and sweet, requiring no pre-salting before cooking, as with European and Mediterranean aubergines, to drain off bitterness. These, perfectly fresh and picked at the height of summer, are very sweet, with the faint charred tang from its roasting adding piquancy to what may otherwise be considered unrelieved sweetness (perhaps by a non-confirmed *nasu* fancier).

The serving plates are distinctive, and Jeanne compliments Konno-san on their variety. Konno-san seems pleased and says that he selects all the crockery himself. He would like to do some pottery but lacks the time. "I don't buy in Kappabashi (a wholesale area in Tokyo for catering supplies) anymore. I opened this place seven years ago, and have found that in Kappabashi, they all offer roughly the same stock, and at prices that are higher than they ought to be for the trade. I now simply buy locally, at

Tokyū in Shibuya, or at Takashimaya [two major department stores]. There are much more interesting shapes and glazes to choose from."

In practice, he does not have many more dishes than the average middle-class housewife would. Nor does he need that much more. Aside from 4 places at the counter, where we are seating, there are two tables seating 4 each, totalling a maximum of 12 customers at one time. Since there is such a great variety in the plates he uses, there is also no great saving to be had from buying from wholesalers: the overall added expense of buying retail is more than offset by the convenience (Kappabashi is that much further) and freedom of choice. (In addition, price reductions at major department stores' seasonal sales are very substantial.)

Next we try one of Konno-san's own creations. He has wrapped slices of *kamaboko* (fish paste) in *shisō* leaf, and then in *nori*. The *kamaboko* has been cut thickly, and in each slice is a dab of roe dotted with sesame seeds. The whole is then grilled over the gas flame on the stove. The mingled aromas of sesame, nori, and *shiso* spark up the blandness of *kamaboko*. *Shiso* is not a usual garnish for *kamaboko*, and for Jeanne, who likes the herbal piquancy of *shiso*, it is an astonishing and satisfying combination.

Konno-san is not a stereotypical jolly Edokko-type bar owner who chats you up as soon as you've sat down. He is more the quiet type, taking his time to think while he's busy cutting and cooking behind the counter, before replying. He is far from reserved. "I used to be a *sarariman*, and after enduring it for ten years, I quit and opened this place. I never learned to cook in a formal school, simply taking over from an acquaintance who owned this place, an old *ba-chan* (auntie), and going on from there. I like cooking, and cook to please myself. I also like saké, so I have a large variety of drink here.

The choice of which food to put on which plate is not dictated by any rules, but by some intuitive sense. For example, the *tako* (octopus) you ate is round, and I mounded it up. It would be silly to put it on a triangular plate, and it looks better on a round one. Since it is mounded, it also adds to the effect if I put it on a footed plate, to give somewhat of an impression of height, perhaps, yes, like the mounds of fruit in temples."

We then try one of his Western-style dishes, partly out of the desire to nibble, partly for academic interest. The baked potato too comes from a friend's field. It has been peeled, cubed, covered with cheese, bits of bacon, and asparagus, and then baked in the oven. The potato is floury, with the distinct sweetish aftertaste of Iwate Prefecture (Northern Honshu, cold-hardy) potatoes. The cheese is unremarkable but the addition of the bacon bits, and, more importantly, the asparagus, makes an interesting combination.

Finally he offers us some noodles, by way of filling in any gaps in our stomachs. In small lacquered wooden bowls Konno-san has placed thin (Shikoku-style) *udon* in a delicate stock. As garnish are green *kaiware daikon*

> (giant-radish sprouts), chopped shallots, *nori* strips, bits of crunchy brown *tempura* drippings, and thin slices of cucumber. Here too the composition is colourfully summery. The *kaiware* is slightly bitter, astringent, the cucumber rather neutrally refreshing, the *tempura* makes a wonderful crunch. The essence of summer.

Eating at bars is of course highly varied, with Japanese bars – *izakaya* – providing, as Hanaya did, a large variety of food. Two other related issues ought to be commented upon. Japanese society has been known as a conformist, rather group-oriented system. Individuals and their preferences are supposed to be subordinate to the wills and demands of the majority, a will that is often extremely conservative. Such reports – and they do represent the majority – do not however pay sufficient attention to the fact that Japanese society is extremely tolerant of individual aberrations. The owner of Hanaya had been a successful white-collar employee, and yet he had given it all up in order to be his own master, and to run a bar. Other individuals whom we interviewed, or whom we were referred to, had done some variation of the same thing. And within the realm of his domain, Konno-san felt it appropriate and legitimate to educate the tastes of his customers, to indulge himself in what he thought was appropriate and right. There are a great many such places throughout Japan, each representing, in effect, the fact that in these aspects – of individual choice and effort – Japanese society can be very tolerant.

A second, historical feature that Konno-san represents must also not be ignored: the mutual effect of food and utensils. Kitaoji Rōsanjin, artist/potter and gastronome, epitomises this idea. A potter of fiercely independent ideas, he should perhaps be remembered for the fact that most of his pottery was constructed for use: to complement the dishes cooked at the restaurant he ran with a partner. Not being satisfied with the choice of pottery available commercially, he set out to make his own. The dishes on which Japanese food is served are a major component of the dining experience. We have already made reference to different kinds of plates associated with different foods. But this association is far deeper than has been discussed, in the framework of utility and mechanics, in Chapter 3. For, with time, and as Japanese pottery became a major item of aesthetic interest (due partly to the Tea ceremony, of which more subsequently), there developed an inextricable bond between Japanese food and the containers it was served in. Konno-san represents merely one aspect of that: the individual food artist who is concerned with the *presentation* and not merely with the taste, of his food.

6.4 *GEOGRAPHICAL CHOICE AND* "ESUNIKKU" *RESTAURANTS*

UNDER MANY CIRCUMSTANCES, "Japanese" cuisine in a restaurant approaches what has become fashionable around the Pacific rim, particularly California and

Australia, as "fusion" cooking. Attempts are made, with greater or lesser success, to blend Japanese and Western cooking and flavours:

> We ate at a new restaurant that had been recently opened. Greeted at the door by a quiet waiter in black suit and bow tie, we were conveyed to a table. The *Irasshaimase* ("Welcome") was subdued. The table was laid Western style.
>
> The special of the day was *karē-raisu* with different variations: seafood, steak, *ise-ebi* (crayfish) and scallop, and something mysteriously called "special." Beer was served in German steins, heavy low-relief pottery mugs with pewter lids. With it we had several plates of *eda-mame*, the boiled and then chilled green pods of soybeans which are a ubiquitous summer beer accompaniment. As a starter we had small river fish, somewhat like an *ayu*. This had been cooked long in *mirin* until caramelised, and the flesh was brown and rather hard. We alternated between chewing the flesh (an odd, sweet flavour) and munching on the salty freshness of the *eda-mame*.
>
> While we waited for the curry, we had a plate of escargot. The snails had been cooked with garlic butter and served with slices of rather limp toast. The utensils were proper for the occasion (chafing dish, tongs, and escargot fork).
>
> The *karē-raisu* finally arrived. It was served in large, deep, boat shaped bowls as *karē-raisu* "ought" to be served. These bowls had been divided in half by a low ridge. White rice on one side and a pool of dark brown curry sauce (mildly hot) on the other. *Karē-raisu* is not complete without a pickle, and these had been brought as well. A plate with three small bowls was placed on the table. One contained a sweet mango chutney, another a Japanese green relish, redolent of *shisō* buds and greens. A third was full of the inevitable bright red pickled gourd that true *karē-raisu* eaters always expect with their meal. Utensils were, of course, Western: large old-fashioned soup spoon and fork. With the *karē-raisu* each diner also received a small salad plate consisting of lettuce leaves, some slices of cucumber, one tomato slice in Italian dressing. We drank a good semi-dry German wine with it all.

The meal we had was not particularly memorable. It is however brought here to show some of the choices that face the diner, and, of course, the restaurant business. To reiterate some of the main points:

The presentation of the restaurant was confused, uncertain. Western ambience and service, but the need for making the Japanese customer feel at home was clear in the *irasshaimase* and in the ambivalence it created: Do we shout out a greeting (unsuitable in a Western restaurant) or not (make our customers unhappy)? The same was true of the food, where Japanese dishes, arranged in Japanese ways, and requiring Japanese plates, were mixed with German and

French utensils and foods. And finally, though an up-market hotel restaurant, they had offered what is one of the most simple, and lower-class of Japanese foods: the common *karē-raisu*, albeit much tarted up. A perfect demonstration of Mennel's thesis about cuisine: lower class foods are appropriated by upper class cooks by adding expensive ingredients (in this case, seafood and steak) to the low-class recipe. Thus the experience here was a demonstration of the process in which foods are "classicised" as they move up from the lower rungs of the taste/ cuisine ladder to the higher ones.

As in most modern societies, Japanese cuisine and food choices are permeated by foreign influences. French and Italian restaurants are of course commonplace, as are Indian and to a lesser degree, Indonesian, but in recent years, the scenery has become more varied – Malaysian, Vietnamese, even Ethiopian. In many of these cases, a particular "ethnic" food is adopted simply because the owner or chef prefers it. One restaurant, which boasted "home-made curry", offered a plethora of Vietnamese dishes, all well-made, spicy, heavily imbued with *nuoc mam* fish sauce. "The owner simply likes Vietnamese food, spent a few months there learning the ropes, and has been cooking it since," one of the waitresses confided.

Most respondents recognise several distinct geographical cuisines under the category of foreign food. Accepted geographical headings are *chūgoku ryōri* (Chinese cooking) which is distinct, one should note, from *chūka ryori* (Japanese-style Chinese]); *fransu ryōri*; *itaria ryōri*; *kankoku-ryōri* (Korean cooking); *indo ryōri*; *supein ryōri*. The representative dishes and distinguishing seasonings or characteristics of each cuisine in this category are widely known, and the terminology is used matter-of-factly, that is, without translation. "Paella", "pilaf", "risotto", "ratatouille", "tantanmen" or "bibinba" are widely used in conversation, journal articles, restaurant advertisements. Beyond this category of mainly Western European and major Asian cuisines, a new category has arisen, that of ethnic and regional cooking. *Esunikku ryōri* subsumes all other geographical bases, ranging from Afghan through Zambian cooking. And the most popular of all is Thai cooking (*tai ryōri*,) echoing its success in the US, Europe and elsewhere. This curiosity about lesser-known foreign cuisines has also extended to native cuisine, and compared to the 70s and 80s, when only major regions such as Kansai or Hokkaido were represented, there is now a very conspicuous proliferation of more localised Japanese cuisines: Nagasaki, Iwate and Kanazawa cuisines are among the best known.

The geographical distinctions underlie, or perhaps express, differences between generations and between classes, and attempts by local communities to claw back their identity. Younger people choose and tend to be more knowledgeable about various foreign foods, with particular fads rising and falling precipitously, as with all other fads, in youth culture. Older people may avoid certain "foreign" foods ("Indian [i.e., authentic] curries are too hot for me, I prefer our Japanese *bon-karē*") or even regard them with suspicion, but will delight in extolling and experiencing native regional specialities. So pervasive is the need among many people to express their geographical preferences, that localised foods can be acquired through the mail, making a profitable economic sector for local communities, who bind city dwellers to their products and interests, and for mail-order entities, such as food producers and the National Postal Service.

The differences in "locality" preferences are also differences between the generations, and between town and country in Japan. Many Japanese rural communities have suffered large demographic losses as younger people emigrate to the metropolis to find jobs, and, more importantly to them perhaps, to find a more interesting and entertaining life. With growing affluence in the countryside, and far better communications (high-speed bullet trains now reach much of the length of Honshu, cutting down travelling times by as much as three or five hours), local communities are fighting back. One way of doing so (and boosting their marketing to boot) is to create the atmosphere of a *gurume* (gourmet) paradise. Thus one place will heavily extol its fresh tuna cuisine, another the quality of its speciality: salmon roe on rice. Many of these specialities have been created within the last few years, often designed especially to attract Japanese custom which is becoming more and more demanding, and more and more sophisticated.

The "sophisticate" label, essentially means the ability (and the resources: time and money) to appreciate and try new and different experiences. At that point, the population of Japan differs. People who came into adulthood soon after World War II, are more likely to be interested in, and to pursue, local foods and "regional" expertise. Respondents from our survey who were in their forties and above overwhelmingly preferred regional Japanese delicacies. They were willing to, and indeed do, try regional restaurants, ordered regional food by mail-order, and could sometimes cite the specialities of various regions in Japan, and even the *shun* (peak season) of those delicacies. Much of that information reaches them by way of travel advertisements (broadcast mailings, hoardings, on buses and trains, in magazines and newspapers) and even from the Japan postal service's semi-annual catalogue of local delicacies. Overall, this category of the population tended to be somewhat disparaging of younger people and their food choices.

Younger respondents – those in their teens and twenties – were far more knowledgeable about foreign foods, and far preferred *esunikku* foods, a category which includes all foreign foods *except major* Western and *major* Asian (Chinese and Indian). They also far preferred to try new restaurants in those categories, and to cook them at home experimentally, using authentic seasonings such as fish sauce or, when making curry, preferring individual spices over commercially mixed curry powder. Several Japanese publications, and numerous articles are dedicated to the "newest" ethnic restaurants, the "best" ethnic places, and so on. This group tended to be far less attracted to the particular taste sensations of traditional Japanese cuisine, and also tended to disparage traditional Japanese restaurants, with their *tatami* floors and separate dining cubicles. Needless to say, this group has been raised in Western-furnished houses, which means that having been accustomed to sitting on Western chairs, their legs no longer tolerate prolonged traditional sitting on reed-matted floors.

The broad choice of "region" or ethnicity in Japanese restaurants reflects two things. First is the great diversity *within Japanese society* between its different categories. This reflection is of course only made possible by the combination of affluence and good communication. Second, it reflects the ability of Japanese society to encompass a great number of different, even contrasting viewpoints. That is perhaps owed to the componential nature of Japanese social beliefs and structures. Elements of any individual's life – membership in work, study, kinship, or play groups; individual activities; food choices – are, to a certain extent, compartmentalised off from one another. An individual is expected and encouraged to "enter into the spirit of the thing" and to behave under certain rules in circumstance or context A, which would be inappropriate, and which he would eschew, under circumstance or context B. Neither blame nor praise accrues to the individual from his actions: they are consequences of circumstances. Individuals can merely choose to *be* in those circumstances. Or not. If they choose to participate, they are expected to, and encouraged, to behave as circumstances dictate. In fact, they are expected to be *enthusiastic* participants. A change of circumstances means a change of rules of behaviour, to which the individual is expected to adjust. Praise or blame is allocated based on the individual's willingness to participate and enthusiasm in doing so. This may seem extremely odd to outsiders, but makes perfect sense to Japanese.

Evidence of this cultural mind set can easily be seen in the "appropriate" – arrogant, cruel, brutal – behaviour of Japanese soldiery in World War II, for which many Japanese participants still feel little, if any, guilt. Another expression of this close identification with one's circumstances or context is the marked difference in the cleanliness of residential areas with that of commercial ones. And by extension, the seeming disregard for litter in public places versus a meticulous attention to neatness and hygiene in one's home or office. When one is inside the home, or the office, places in which an individual belongs and is strongly and identifiably affiliated to, then one is accountable for one's behaviour. However, beyond this framework or context of affiliation, as in a public place (unless one is an employee of that place, e.g., a policeman, a street cleaner) – the average individual has no connection and senses no identication with the place, thus making him or her relax the usual rules that apply for general cleanliness. If for the French "autres places, autres mores," is a social truism, for the Japanese "autres circonstances, autres règles sociales" is the norm.

For the Japanese diner, there is a wide of choice places available when deciding to eat at a restaurant. The choice breaks down into three dimensions: cooking style (since restaurants mainly specialise in one or another of the styles we discussed earlier), cost (often related to class), and region (which may be within Japan, or without, i.e., foreign). The choice of a cooking style reflects the popularity of specific styles of cooking as well as individual choice. But the choice is also related to the industrial realities of the age. *Tempura* – once a street food – has become largely a restaurant food, whereas at the lower end of the market, *hanbāga* have become street food. The choice of a region may depend on individual history and origins, but it is also, though more weakly, affected by issues of cost and of style.[2] The price range of a chosen restaurant is obviously closely related to class, whether that be one's own financial resources or those of the organisation one is a member of (since many business firms give their employees generous entertainment allowances).

There is clear statistical evidence that certain social categories correlate with certain eating out habits. There are definite patterns of preference, affected by such factors as the individual's social circumstances, age, and gender. Lone individuals do eat out, but a male and a female single would not frequent the same type of establishment. A female single would also eat out at a far lower frequency than when part of a couple or in company with others, and different group structures bring about different choices. Younger people choose food categories different from their elders. All of this is neither surprising nor unique to Japan: it is replicated in one form or other throughout the industrial and industrialising world. Two facts are, however, significant. First, all choices can be accommodated within the Japanese (certainly the metropolitan) environment. A publication devoted to youth life-style (Piamapgurume 1996) lists over 3,000 *restaurants* in Tokyo in categories ranging from *soba* and sushi to grills, coffee bars, and sandwich houses. This does not cover minuscule neighbourhood eateries run by a lone *ba-chan* ("auntie") or man, usually offering non-fancy home-cooking, and catering to single students or workers who live on their own and have no cooking facilities or do not care to cook. Thus, comparing the listing with actual available places, we found that it covers only about 50–60% of all eating-out food locations (excluding supermarkets and shops), and those *only* in *major* Tokyo urban nodes.[3]

This leads to our second point: the sort of cognitive choice any individual in Japan must make while eating out. The wide variety of choices *requires* the emergence of a sophisticated clientele, just as it is an expression of such a clientele. The average Japanese diner is aware of the differing styles and geographical types, and is able to select from among them: otherwise the great variety would be unlikely to exist.

2 Some styles of cooking are intimately related to regions in Japan. Thus *Sapporo rāmen* (Sapporo Chinese-style noodles) which is related, artificially, to Hokkaido. This implication is reinforced by the constant iconic use of Ainu imagery: easily recognisable designs from Ainu weave, images of bearded Ainu men in traditional costume, and the display of wooden bears (a "folk" product of Hokkaido).

3 This can be compared with the estimate of 6,000 restaurants throughout the UK (The Guardian 10 April 1997).

6.5 *SOCIAL CORRELATES OF FOOD LOCI*

One of the crucial questions to be asked when dealing with any particular cuisine, suggest Douglas and Gross (1981) is, "Who eats?" This can be broken down into a number of subsidiary questions the general import of which is to ask who on what occasions regularly eats with whom? And where? To illustrate, it is possible to follow the daily routine of a Japanese housewife. In the morning, she will eat breakfast with her husband as he rushes off to catch his commuter train. This necessitates rising about half-an-hour before to prepare the breakfast. Rice has been put to cook the evening before in the rice cooker which has been timed to prepare the rice by 0600. Salted salmon and *nori* are quickly grilled, and *miso shiru* and coffee are both prepared from dried base. Half-an-hour later it is time to feed the children. Older children will eat a school lunch, though many high-schoolers today will buy a snack from a neighborhood shop, and some will take a packed lunch. Elementary-school children will have a school lunch. Children in pre-school must also be given a rice box for school lunch. The children eat a breakfast of cereal with toast, butter, milk, and small grilled sausages. At 1000 the housewife might buy a cake from the neighbourhood baker, which she will eat with coffee, and milk for the baby. At 1300 she and the baby will eat again, this time a light lunch of *karē-raisu*. At 1600 she and the children will have another snack, and in the evening the entire family will sit together for a joint meal, assuming the husband has not been working late.

The day for a married male will be different. He may well have a breakfast only with his wife, depending on commuting time. At his place of work there are few opportunities for snacking, e.g., if he is hosting a visitor (and even then only the visitor may be offered something to eat besides drink), or if a colleague comes back from a business trip, an edible memento (*omiyage*) in the form of a sweet or savoury snack will be passed around with afternoon tea. Green tea, and sometimes coffee, are drunk in large quantities, beginning with the first cup at 0900, another at 1030, again with lunch, at 1500 and if overtime work continues, a further one or two cups. Lunch time is usually a hurried affair, either alone, or what is more likely, with some office mates of the same rank and seniority, either in a company cafeteria, in a close-by restaurant offering quick set-menu lunches for office-workers, or at his desk from *demae* (delivered food) or home-made *bentō* (lunch box). After work many male workers, and some females, will eat, and largely drink together, either at one place or, if their pockets are deep enough, bar hopping from one favourite bar to another. This after-hours business socialising is an important aspect of Japanese business relations. *Nemawashi,* (literally digging around roots) as this drink-based networking is called, promotes social cohesion and group focus in the Japanese business environment. *Sakariba* activities are more concerned with drink than with food, but they contribute to the totality of food events, and have an important effect on the directions of Japanese cuisine, since so many of the populace participate in them at a very high intensity. On weekends the husband may have meals with his family, and, given the prominence of shopping as a leisure pursuit since the 1970s, some at least of these meals are bound to be outside the home.

For children the picture is once again different. After breakfast with the mother, a breakfast that for more and more young Japanese consists of foods of Western origin (*yō-shoku*) such as toast, milk, cereal, ham and eggs, the child heads for school. At school smaller children will have a snack, provided by the kindergarten, while older children in state schools will have a school lunch. Back at home they will have a snack at around four, and a meal with their mother, and possibly though rarely father, the content of which tends to be balanced between Japanese-, Western-, and other-origin cuisines. Older children studying for their university entrance examinations will probably also have a snack brought in – often *soba* which is supposed to encourage studiousness – late at night by their mother, and may take a packed lunch to the cram school, if they attend one, which most children do.

The structure of school lunches is particularly interesting, since it points out the degree to which issues relating to food can be politicised in subtle ways. Certainly in the lean years after World War II, school-catered lunches provided a sure source of nutrition for some of the populace. It has been, at the same time, a political tool, as it allows the authorities to promote a variety of programmes relating to health, life-style, and so on. The Japanese pre-school system has been organised to reflect some of these realities. Private and public *yōchien* (kindergartens) are monitored by education departments of local authorities. In contrast, *hōikuen* (day-cares) are monitored by the social services department. *Yōchien* provide children below school age with a step up in the educational competition. *Hōikuen* provide working mothers with child care so that they can go to work. Both kindergarten and day-care children are given a daily snack, usually at ten and also sometimes before they go home. Although the kindergarten and day-care provide hot, cooked lunches, the child's home (i.e., mother) is expected to provide a box of cooked rice every day, in a container of fixed size.[4] The daily *okazu* supplied by the institution conforms to local and national nutritional standards. A schedule of the monthly menu is sent to parents in advance, with full details of caloric values of individual food items and the daily total intake. By the 80s, the requirement to bring home-cooked rice was dropped in the Tokyo area for secondary school lunches. By then, general prosperity had ensured that the Tokyo government could supply white cooked rice with school meals.

Though circumstances are changing – more and more women are working outside the home even when their children are small – the ideology often

4 We were told that this was to ensure that we knew exactly how much our child had eaten that day, and by extension, the state of his health.

As well, this ensures that mothers are reminded on a daily basis of their primary function (in the view of elderly male bureaucrats who run the system) to provide nurturing and sustenance to the next generation.

remains. Women are expected – both by their husbands and families, and by the Japanese public at large – to provide most domestic work, even if they also work full time. The prevalence of ready-to-eat foods is a reflection of the reality that many women do not have the time to cook "properly." There is a significant difference here with Western concepts of processed food. Because of the nature of Japanese menus which feature small servings of a variety of dishes, it is time-consuming, labour-intensive, and, often wasteful of ingredients to attempt to provide the standard one soup, three dishes (*ichijū sansai*) from scratch. Moreover, the high quality of freshly cooked, ready-to-eat dishes and the astounding variety of choices[5] available at department store food sections and supermarkets are more than sufficient reasons to convince the busy working person to give up cooking from scratch.

Japanese entertain at home to a far lesser degree than Europeans or Americans. There are a number of reasons for this, but two reasons (which are also consequences) have been the separation of domestic from public, or at least social spheres of life, and the prevalence of alternatives to home entertainment and food. A word of caution is definitely in order. Most of Japan's population is urban, estimated at about 80% or higher, depending on the definition of "rural". In smaller towns, as well as in villages and hamlets, entertaining guests – friends, relatives, neighbours – at home is far more common. Even in those cases, however, the food served is likely to be a mixture of home-cooked and procured from the outside. As a general rule, and farming households may be a vanishing exception, the more formal an event, the more likely it is to be sourced from outside, even when taking place at home.

Meals at home are likely to include parts of the family – a mother and children, particularly younger children – and more rarely the father. Meals in restaurants are more likely to include groups of office-mates, business correspondents, or groups of friends, co-workers, and so on, depending on the economic level of the restaurant. These differences are, in a sense, fundamental to Japanese society and its economy.

Much of Japan's vaunted managerial success has been based upon two principles: an expanding economy which is export-oriented, but which does cater, albeit at a lesser pace, to domestic demand; and an apparently equitable distribution of the national wealth. This latter does not mean that there are neither rich people, nor income differentials, but that these income differentials are relatively low, relatively flat, with few, or at least circumscribed, areas of deprivation and poverty. This economic success is not bought without a price. Women do participate in the economy as producers and workers, but at lower levels, less intensity, and far lower rewards than men. As a general rule until about ten years ago, and still commonly today, women are expected to remove themselves from the working economy once they marry and have children.

5 From regional Japanese to foreign, including ethnic, low-salt, organic, from starters to main dishes to desserts of all kinds – the choices are bewildering and infinite.

They are also paid at far lower rates than men, even when doing the same work.[6]

There are a number of consequences of the particular managerial and industrial pattern the Japanese have adopted. One is that Japanese workers, men and women, married and unmarried, are expected to spend long hours in the office. A second is the practice of cultivating social ties and deepening emotional closeness in the office – *nemawashi* – which means a high frequency of social drinking and eating, a practise the Japanese government has encouraged and abetted by allowing much of this entertainment to be recognised as business expense for tax purposes. It has thus become a way for Japanese companies to reward their personnel through non-taxable "income", and to do so free of tax to themselves.

In food terms, the consequences are less direct, but nonetheless clear. The large number and variety of eating and drinking places is a consequence of this form of business activity, *as well as* the nature and structure of the Japanese home setting that divorces and compartmentalises it absolutely from work.[7] On the days that workers eat at home, they (or their wives or mothers, now occasionally husbands) can choose to cook their meals from scratch, with the aid of labour-saving devices, such as automatic rice cookers with pre-set timer and insulating feature, microwave ovens, or purchase individual portions of frozen, freshly cooked, ready-to-eat, or processed foods. Thus, supermarkets and department stores are flooded with goods, the numbers and sheer variety probably greater, on average, than anywhere else on earth. This staggering choice of goods and foodstuffs – raw, processed, and ready-to-eat (freshly made each day) – is a commonplace in every supermarket and department store, certainly in Tokyo, Osaka, Sendai, Sapporo and other cities, but also in the rural areas.

READINGS FOR CHAPTER 6

Allison, Anne 1991 "Japanese mothers and obentos: The lunchbox as ideological state apparatus".
Befu, Harumi 1974 "An ethnography of dinner entertainment in Japan".
Linhart, Sepp 1986 "Sakariba: Zone of 'evaporation' between work and home?"
Moeran, Brian 1981 "Yanagi Muneyoshi and the Japanese folkcraft movement".
Ohnuki-Tierney, Emiko 1997 "McDonald's in Japan: Changing manners and etiquette".

6 Of course, none of this is peculiar to Japan.

7 For instance, a Japanese employer might show concern that a thirty-something employee is still unmarried, but would never enquire into the quality of any marriage, since marriage and the family belong to another "compartment."

7 Aesthetics in the World of Japanese Food

After finishing Tea with Mrs. Tsuchida, her son-in-law groaned and stretched.

"I've never been to one before," he confessed.
"And how did you like it?"
He hid a grin, and the answer was ambiguous.

Few younger Japanese today would admit to liking *chanoyu* – the Tea ceremony – and many have never experienced it fully in person. Yet, at some level, it has a major effect on their daily lives. To a large measure, the Tea ceremony, by its very rigidity, helps in maintaining a standard for Japanese aesthetics, cuisine included. By 'maintaining a standard' we do not mean Mrs. Beeton's. The term is used here in the sense of a benchmark, and, importantly, one that is widely known and accepted. Consider for a moment the Tea ceremony viewed as a coherent, structured and ordered set of components. There is a *liturgical process* (a series of canonical, detailed, and predetermined actions not created by the actors), elaborate *artefacts* (of particular, predetermined kinds and dimensions), *social setting*, and *sensory impacts*, including taste, vision, and touch. At a further remove, one finds a symbolic layer which intertwines the other elements,[1] representing time and seasons, personal taste, and emotional tense. Each of these, though immutable generally, is flexible enough to accommodate changes and variations internally. There is a set way of performing the ritual, which is sustained and reinforced by a system of schools.[2] There are artefacts which have been treasured, imitated, arranged and formed in particular ways for particular purposes. Specific individuals participate, often restricted to middle and upper classes, or peers at work. And the use of particular foodstuffs, and preparation of foodstuffs, especially in formal, whole day ceremonies, are subject to detailed criteria.

1 There are a number of detailed accounts of the Tea ceremony including manuals for Western readers. For the cultural and social issues a good source is Kondo (1985).
2 The organisation of such schools – *iemoto* and similar structures – and their importance for Japanese culture has been explored by a number of writers. Hsu (1975) describes such structures as foundations of Japanese society. Tea schools have been discussed by Kondo (1985).

Notwithstanding the relatively low attendance in practice at Tea ceremony events, *kaiseki ryōri* is important as a paradigm of good taste for most Japanese. People are exposed to *kaiseki* not only by experiencing the ceremony themselves, but through pictures, through the wax models of foods they see before restaurants, and through many of its terms which have entered Japanese language in one context or another. *Kaiseki* is so penetrative because the Tea ceremony, as a whole, is so multi-vocal. It combines not only an appreciation of the sensory qualities of a non-alcoholic drink, but the need to appreciate (or at least, outwardly present) the correct forms of someone who appreciates painting, flower arrangement, architecture, ceramics, fabrics, poetry, food, formal manners, and even some Chinese history. In other words, it is the eponymous "multi-media event."[3] There are two aspect to this: an aesthetic one, and an industrial/mercantile one.

From the aesthetics point of view, the Tea ceremony centralises and codifies Japanese art. This does not mean that it circumscribes all of Japanese art. It does, however, present a (relatively) invariant set of rules and processes, with ties to most major traditional art forms. One can either agree with them or disagree with them, but at all times the aesthetic principles articulated in the Tea ceremony help serve as a benchmark of what is "Japanese" or at least, what is thought to be so, whether invented or not.

The industrial side is not less important. Few Western consumers realise that the Japanese products they buy have first passed a lengthy process of filtering through the demands of *Japanese* consumers. There is a conventional marketing view that Japanese industry, anxious to garner foreign exchange, first floods external markets, and then satisfies domestic demand. This is untrue, as even the most casual visitor to the great electronics marketing quarter at Akihabara in Tokyo can easily tell. For every model of electronic consumer good sold abroad, there are, in Akihabara shops, between five and ten "for domestic sale-only" models available. The Japanese domestic market is an extremely demanding one, with knowledgeable customers expecting high quality, innovative goods and excellent service. Part of that demand for goods can, no doubt, be traced to the trickle-down influence of the Tea ceremony in most aspects of Japanese life. Participation in the Tea ceremony *requires* a good consumer: one who demands, and is familiar with, a range of high quality goods. With the "samuraisation" of Japanese society, and the universalisation of demand for the pleasures and quality expected formerly only by the governing class, has come a demand for good quality and good services in a global context. Of course, this has not been the only cause for Japanese industrial success, but certainly, the presence of a knowledgeable and discerning customer base, of people ready and willing to spend for *qualitative* conspicuous consumption, is an important element.

Perhaps the area of greatest difficulty in any discussion of food, as in the discussion of most aesthetic experience, is the effect of that evanescent sensation

3 This is a neologism we are not particularly fond of, but, in this case, is appropriate.

called 'taste.' The term here is used, purposely, in its two senses in the English language. The first has the implication of physical sensation. The second the implication of knowledge and appreciation of that sensation. Both of these meanings are particularly subjective and particularly difficult to get at in order to make the issue comprehensible to another, any "other." As Elias (1982) has noted, the idea of "taste" is a social construction, one that *implies* far more than the mere physiological sensation. It also implies the ability to *appreciate* in socially acceptable forms, those taste sensations. To start with, however, we need to examine taste in its physiological guise.

It is useful to keep in mind three things that can lay the basis for communication between individuals (in this case, the authors and the reader). First is the fact that human physiology is probably much the same with some range of variation between individuals. This is a consequence of shared genetic inheritance, overall common ecology. The second is that taste is *learned*. Though the grosser tastes – sweet, salty, sour, bitter, peppery – seem to be obvious biological signs that our physiology has adopted, the precise combination and liking/disliking for them are learned. We can get used to partaking of otherwise "dangerous" flagged substances *if* we are taught to disregard the biological warning. Bitter beer and bitter melon are both what in English is called "acquired tastes." The third has to do with the other meaning of "taste": as a measure of the quality of an individual. This sense of taste is a social device. It indicates to what degree an individual is able to understand, display, and manipulate the rules of his culture in the realm of the aesthetics, whether that be in terms of sartorial choice or choice of food and drink.

7.1 *TASTE: THE PHYSIOLOGICAL ELEMENT*

THE PHYSIOLOGICAL REACTION to a new taste sensation does not necessarily parallel its emotional and internal overtones. Sushi – smooth, cool, sensuous – evokes opposite reactions in Japanese and most Westerners, at least those who have been raised (as for example, most Britons) on a fairly restricted diet. But the *enjoyment* of such a sensation can be learned, and has much to do with the surroundings, the company, the events that precede and are subsequent to the physiological sensation. This seems to be a trite comment, but let us examine it further. Food is multi-dimensional. One does not only eat food, as much as see, taste, and generally experience it. A hint of a familiar "aspect" – taste, smell, sight, texture, sound – in an unfamiliar food can evoke either acceptance or rejection.

To turn this to the discussion of Japanese food, we can see that new foods, means of cooking, and other aspects of dining can be introduced into Japanese cuisine *where there is some familiar element* already in the introduced material. This is very obvious in food because food is so multi-dimensional. A corollary of this statement is that where such familiarity does not exist, or even where it exists in a limited form, as a sort of "entry ticket", Japanese individuals[4] adapt the new by adding familiar trappings to it.

To a large measure, the centrality of rice flavour – subtle, bland, evocative – extends itself to the whole of the Japanese meal. The blandness of the flavour is like the painting of different shades of white. Japanese cooking has been characterised (Sen 1972) as the cuisine of restraint, but it is more than that. The aesthetics of Japanese cuisine, or any other Japanese art for that matter, is based not solely on moderation and control, but on skilful elimination. Where a Western recipe is conceived of as the addition and augmentation of ingredients, Japanese cooking consists of the hiding and concealment of techniques, and even of cooking itself, in order to allow the subtlety of the natural flavours to emerge. The aesthetics of Japanese cuisine are best represented by three principal activities: *kakusu* (hiding), *shinobu* (disguising), and *kezuru* (shaving): as detailed an account of minimalism, in food as in any art, as is conceivable. In the same way that a Japanese garden is perfect when there is nothing more that can be taken out, so it is with Japanese cuisine. When there remains nothing more that can be subtracted from a dish, that is when it is perfect. And this applies as much to the adornment on food, as the food itself. The flavours of the natural food are all there, but they are there to be discovered by the diner, rather than being overt and obvious.

The concept of nature in Japanese society is radically different from European aesthetic ideas. It embraces not the wild and woolly nature of Darwinian enthusiasts, but is more like the Romantic ideal of nature as a simple, uncomplicated version of life. This is combined, paradoxically with the idea that natural and "artificial" are inextricable intertwined, rather than opposed as in the Romantic version. Neither nature nor artifice dictate, in this view, but rather they blend harmonically to produce a whole: the artificial, is, after all, the "natural" province of humanity. Artifice may be so perfect, says Zeami, the founder of Noh theatre (Raz 1976) that it becomes truer to nature than nature itself.

The flavours of nature are thus enhanced by human manipulation, which, in turn, is guided by the need to allow nature to shine through with greater brightness and emphasis. *Sashimi* – a dish of raw fish – may be served in the form of a living fish cut open and served absolutely fresh. It is only in that way that the absolute, unmitigated flavour of the natural may be fully experienced. Accompanying the fish with soy sauce – an essentially artificially created product – is a means of demonstrating *to humans* the real flavour of the fish.

The apparent blandness of Japanese food is therefore, to a greater degree, more intimate, more personal, than it would be if surrounded by rich sauces and strong spices. It requires and demands *more* of the diner than a spiced food would, and, in a sense, at the same time, 'blends" with the essence of the diner. It is thus

4 One could say Japanese culture, but it is really the individual members of it who make the choice.

that the "noodle professor" in the film *Tampopo* can caress the pork in his bowl, and, using a term used between intimates indicate his affection: food is essentially a component of the self, and this emotional closeness is enhanced and strengthened by its bland subtleties.

Colour, in Japanese cultural practice, plays a remarkably contradictory role. On the one hand, colour is restrained, black-and-white or pastel shades. On the other, colour, particularly in fabric produces effects through the clashing and juxtaposition of glowing colours: reds with greens, gold with black and deep blue.

Certain colours are particularly distinctive and are woven deeply into the stylistic and symbolic elements of culture and daily life. Red, white, and green represent the three sacred treasures of the Japanese Emperor and State: sword, mirror, jewel. Each of these colours has manifold references (power, purity and nature; humans, heavens, and earth). And, in many cases, specific colours are used as identifiers of social situations: public hints as to expected behaviour. Gifts wrapped in silver and gold string are wedding gifts. Wrapped in silver and black, they are funereal offerings. In red, gold, and white, offerings to a shrine. Large purple *furoshiki* – carrying kerchiefs for wrapping presents – indicate to all and sundry that the carrier has been, or is going, to a wedding.

In an important sense this knowledge and use of colours is "playful": it allows a breadth of usage and subtle sensory plays on meaning. Here too, the member of Japanese society is distinguished from someone from the outside. Those inside know the multiple referents and messages, can "top" them, and can invent new meanings and presentations.

The idea of playing with such allusions and ideas is deeply embedded in Japanese classical culture. A major poetry form – *renga* – in which a group of poets play around with meanings and symbols around a theme, has produced some of the major poetry works in Japanese. Individually, such poems – *haiku* – are probably familiar to many non-Japanese, but the ability to link such verses in a thematic whole, using images that are classical or mundane, common or elusive, is a major skill. Thus, in a sense, many of the meals we have described here fit a similar format: the foods served should sometimes be seen as notes on a theme, responses, and responses to the responses. Colour, of course plays an important role here, because colour allows subtlety, hints and undertones to be played together with, or in contrast to, the main themes.

The point at which colour is at its most expressive, even glaring, is in the special New Year foods. The distinction of *osechi ryōri* is not so much in the ways of cooking, the ingredients, or the specific recipes, as in the painstaking approach to expressive and lavish visual displays.

Of all holidays, *Oshōgatsu* (New Year) is probably the one that most closely identifies the Japanese, as a whole, with their religion. This, of course, *appears* paradoxical, because most Japanese define themselves as irreligious, and even those who associate themselves with one or other of the manifold religions in Japan, may associate themselves with more than one. The paradox in the previous sentence arises because most Japanese *do* participate in "religious" activities of one sort or another, and the total membership in religions (that is, of recognised members of a religion or sect) far exceed the total Japanese population: there are a total of about 170 *million* "adherents" of religious bodies in a total Japanese population of slightly over 120 million. The reasons for this apparent paradox are complex. It basically boils down to a misdefinition of the term "religion" to fit Western (Christian) prejudices, on the one hand, and the overshadowing of mere religious membership by community membership on the other. Even households or individuals who label themselves as "only" . . . – only Buddhist, only Shintō, only Tenrikyō[5] – will often participate in rituals of other religions in their community because it is a community expectation.

The celebration of New Year – both an intimate family affair and a public display of *nihonjin-ron* sentiment, Japanese culture, and community membership – allows all such shades of religious difference to be subsumed under one overarching emotional and ritual display, much of which is focused around food.

New Year is a public holiday in modern Japan. All economic activity closes down (though in recent years, more and more shops have remained open as late as possible, and open as early as possible after the holiday). Most households prepare cold collations – *osechi ryōri* – to avoid cooking during the holiday. In traditional Japan, fires were put out, to be relit on the new year. People go to visit the shrines and temples, in family or other groups:

> There had been a very slight snowfall the night before, and the streets were slippery. Nonetheless, at about ten o'clock we started to hear the steady tramp and squeak of shoes on the road outside that led to the Shintō shrine. The tock-tock percussion of wooden *geta* sandals was prominent: a somehow haunting sound in the silence. We joined the procession, walking through the clear night air, huddled in our overcoats. The stairs to the shrine were slippery, and there were crowds of people. Women wrapped in colourful kimono and overcoats bordered with false fur, men in suits, and, often enough, in black crested *montsuki* kimono. We waited patiently in line: I had never seen such a crowd at the shrine since I had started visiting it. There were booths lining the entrance path. *Miko* (shrine maidens) in long red culotte-skirts and white tops sold good-luck charms, arrows, and mementoes. We had already received our *ofuda* – a slip of paper indicating we were shrine members – several days before, when we had paid our shrine dues. We met several neighbours and friends and their families, while waiting for our turn. The senior members of the *iaido* (sword play) club, and three of the ladies from the *ikebana* (flower arrangement) school, including the teacher, were there as well. The *iaido* members had their kit with them: they had come directly from a final practice session to honour

5 One of the more successful of the so-called "New Religions." Founded in the middle of the nineteenth century, Tenrikyō has become a burgeoning religio-social movement with headquarters in Tenri-shi near Osaka.

the old year. One of the members, a Buddhist priest, was hurrying back to his temple to conduct the service there by ringing the bell 109 times: banishing all possible human sins.

We edged forward finally, threw our coins into the offertory box, lit our candles, clapped hands and bowed over them, then accepted our portion of *naorai* (shared feast with the deity): a morsel of rice cooked with *azuki* beans to a red colour, and a drink of sanctified saké. After the visit to the shrine we went on to a neighbourhood Buddhist temple, barely in time to hear the huge bronze bell toll out its 109 accounts of human sins. Here we bought hot *amazake*, the milky thick sweet fluid a restorative against the cold, and some *manju* (steamed sweet bean paste-filled buns). We went home to eat *osechi*.

Participation in New Year celebrations is universal in Japan. Families use the holiday as an opportunity to have reunions, visiting together as much as possible. The second and third days of the New Year are devoted to friends and the workplace as individuals pay their respects. In all of those, the hosting household is expected to provide food, and, because of the burden of needing to have food on hand at short notice, *osechi* is often served cold. This means more than sushi which is often a part of *osechi*. Cold grilled and fried foods, preserves, and rice are arranged attractively into lacquered boxes if possible. Special flat drinking goblets, usually sets of three in diminishing sizes, lacquered in red and gold, are used to offer New Year's saké to guests. The dominant colours, in fact, are reds, whites, and golds. One example is *kamaboko*. This is a fish cake made of the protein and collagen extracted from white-fleshed fish. In appearance *kamaboko* usually is shaped into a small (five centimetres in diameter) white loaf shape. For the New Year, the rounded outside is dyed pink or deep red. A common practice is to alternate a dyed slice with an undyed one, or even half a dyed slice with half an undyed one to make a chequerboard-patterned loaf.

Osechi foods are arranged into deep lacquered trays in which the colours are used as irregular block patterns, often divided by green bamboo leaves (today, alas, often represented by green plastic) and pine needles. The colours used commonly reflect items that are, in their use, celebratory. Red grilled bream (whose name "medetai" is a homophone for "congratulations"), golden *ginnan* (gingko nuts), golden sweet omelette, green pine needles. Some of these, and, indeed the colours, are reminiscent, to the European observer, with the colours associated with Christmas, but the implications are quite different. The entrance to Japanese houses is decorated in the New Year with green bamboo staves wrapped with rice straw around pine branches, and decorated with mandarin oranges (*mikan*): implications of growth and the budding new year which are similar in intent, but derive from different traditions and experiences than Yule.

The colours, and no less importantly their cultural and symbolic significance, are reinforced year after year, making them available for other daily uses. That is to say that the emotions aroused by the combination of bold colours – red, green, gold, white – the family feeling and 'Japanese-ness' of New Year events, made the more powerful by the association with both food and company, are available for other cultural items as well. It is no accident that the Japanese flag is based on two simple primary colours, red and white. The emotions the colours, and the combination of colours, arouses in individual Japanese can be very powerful indeed. Interestingly enough, this emotion has led back into the realm of food: the quintessential modern *bentō* – the *hinomaru bentō* – replicates the Japanese flag, whose colours in turn replicate the emotion-raising colours of New Year. A food invented as a patriotic and nationalistic gesture before the Second World War returns as an icon of comfort food and simplicity.

7.2 *COLOUR AND SHAPE IN UTENSILS*

SIMPLICITY AND ITS elaboration can be seen in utensils under circumstances other than the New Year as well. It is useful to keep in mind the dictum that form follows function, and that aesthetics are often justified post-hoc by function as well. The case of the humble rice bowl, the *chawan* is particularly instructive. With the importation of Korean art and culture into Japan, starting roughly with the fifth century, items relating to food came into vogue as well. The high quality of Korean pottery (in comparison to Japanese pottery of the time) meant a gradual switch from the native practice of heavy reliance on wood to ceramics. The use of ceramics was *technically* useful for the service of food, because a ceramic bowl keeps the rice warm, while insulating the user's hand: particularly important for the chopsticks-and-bowl eating favoured in Japan. Thus ceramic came to be material of choice for containing and eating rice, just as the shape was adapted to be comfortable in the hand. Later elaboration of this utensil derived from its technical superiority in the eating mode chosen by the Japanese. Curiously enough, the ceramic bowl has almost disappeared in its place of origin. In Korea, upper classes used metal bowls as a sign of prosperity, and the preference for metal bowls has spread to the average individual as well. Since metal transmits heat, the bowl used for soup or rice can no longer be held in the hand. As a result, Korean cuisine has evolved (back?) from a bowl-and-chopsticks preference, to a bowl-and-chopsticks-and-spoon one, to the point that we were told that holding a bowl in one's hand (as is common in Japan) was a social solecism (not to mention being extremely uncomfortable due to the heat!).

The utensils and service involved in a cuisine are inextricably a part of it. Japanese cuisine has adapted in remarkable ways to the need for different functions, adapting forms to fit. Japanese food can be consumed in the traditional way, sitting on a *tatami* floor, eating from an individual tray placed in front of one. In fact, traditional feasts are often still eaten that way. But they can equally well be eaten from short-legged tables, as they often are in restaurants or meals at the home, or on Western furniture. Each of these requires some adaptation, some adjustment of the meal served, and possibly, of the food as well.

Yet some types of meals – *irori* cooking, sushi bars are examples – require particular ways of serving for them to "work." That is, though sushi can be eaten from a Western table, the quality of the food requires that if one is going to eat the best, it must be eaten in a "traditional" sushi counter: this enables the diner to choose the order of food, to select the dishes, to commune with the chef. And it is this communion, as both informants, and Itami's truck-driver/instructor remind us in the film *Tampopo*, that is at the heart of good Japanese restaurant food.

Communication in the Japanese context relies a great deal on the non-verbal. Indeed, Japanese language usage, in daily life as well as in literature, leaves things unsaid as a matter of course. At the grammatical level, the Japanese language does not require distinctions to indicate singular or plural; first and third person use the same verb form; there are very few variations of tense, or even the subject of a sentence is oftentimes not even mentioned. At the communicative, semantic level, Japanese will omit the subject as being understood. At the complex, interpersonal level, the omission of subject or the use of deictic expressions – that person, that thing, that issue (*ano hito, are, ano koto*) – between intimates or those in the know, results in vague, if not incomprehensible, statements for the outsider listener. While its disadvantages are widely acknowledged, and although it is possible to communicate in an unambiguous manner, the Japanese have elaborated this mechanism into a veritable armoury of ways to confuse, delay, and obfuscate issues in anything from interpersonal and business negotiations, to inter-government dealings. All of this is founded on the idea that there is a separation, mental and emotional, between insiders and outsiders, a distinction that is absolutely crucial for the Japanese. Insiders understand intuitively – without words, by gesture, hint, emotional closeness. Outsiders do not understand.

The communion across a counter between a chef – cooking and preparing his own speciality – and a customer – recognising, by subtle hints, the quality of the food, and interjecting his own personal preferences – exemplifies the essence of interpersonal culture in Japan. To many Japanese, it is the essence of Japanese culture *in toto*. Japanese culture prizes non-verbal, indirect communication. Where the chef understands, in an unmediated way, what the customer "really" wants, and where the customer is able to convey his needs – mood, intentions, preferences – to the chef without explaining them, then real communication is achieved. This perspective does not leave much room for persons who do not have the appropriate keys to enter into such an arrangement. Indeed, foreigners – even, from the perspective of local individuals, those who are Japanese, but outside the group – haven't a chance. Much Japanese communication, including scholastic communication, is at this level. It assumes that the speaker and the listener share an unmediated bond, one that requires neither explanation nor specification.

One can argue – indeed, it is argued, quite vociferously, by business-people and academics alike – that this is a form of mystification and obfuscation, a process by which the Japanese maintain freedom to act economically and politically, to the benefit of those who are on the inside. Against this view, others can argue that given the high homogeneity of Japanese society (less homogeneous than most Japanese seem to think, more homogeneous than many other societies) verbal communication should not be so detailed, since the underlying assumption of any two parties in a communication should be known to both.

This view – that communication is and should be a non-verbal form, of great emotional and lesser informational content – returns us to the question of form. The ability to evoke emotions is, in many ways in Japanese society, a question of form, both in the material and in the behavioural sense. Japanese poetry such as *renga* (linked verse) and *haiku* exploit this process, evoking emotions by rigid application of form and nuance. So too, in daily life, Japanese communication is full of significant pauses that substitute for direct information, but evoke recognisable (to Japanese) emotions in appropriate places.

This concept of concentrating a variety of meanings and emotions into a single object is known as polysemy, and is used by all cultures. It is just that the very formalisation of these expressions in Japanese society, and their reliance on common currencies which have very high circulation, make polysemy very prominent in Japanese usage.

In the realm of food, the arrangement and form of foods on a plate is, quite unconsciously, recognised by most Japanese. Some forms or arrangements are "necessary" to achieve aesthetic configurations that give pleasure, or evoke mood. Others are disruptive and therefore inappropriate. The use of familiar icons – an old rice bowl used as an expensive accoutrement to the Tea ceremony, a fresh green leaf to evoke a season – all contain within themselves, *because there is general "learned" agreement* prevalent in the culture, an expanding "fan" of meanings. The more educated, the more close a person is to the source of the transmission, the richer and more varied is the set of meanings associated, or that can be associated, with that object or form:

> My wife and I decide on the presentation arrangement of dishes. During the slow season in February we look through catalogues of pottery and utensils, decorative items, and sales, and decide what we want to buy, what fits what we intend to offer, and so on. Plates must of course fit the food. We sometimes use new items or materials, but they have to fit the nature of the food they are to contain. I'll give you an example. Until recently, we would not have thought of using glass to hold *sashimi*. It is such a traditional dish. But now, times have changed. Glass has become better, more Japanese. People have become used to using it. And in the summer, which was not traditionally a *sashimi* period, we can now serve *sashimi* because we have refrigeration. Glass is a cool material. So we have taken, recently, to using glass as plates for summer *sashimi* dishes.

Foods in Japan have always been anchored in a material and ideological context. The most immediate of these contexts is the utensils that are used to serve the food. Directly and indirectly, therefore, at least one stream of influence on the making of Japanese ceramics – one of the major ceramic traditions today, which influences potters all over the world – has been the nature of Japanese food.

Pre-modern foods, simpler and less elaborate than those served today for reasons that have been discussed above, necessarily utilised whatever utensils lay at hand. These tended, not unnaturally, to fit together, the materials and intellectual backgrounds which brought forth both the foods and their utensils being of the same source. The use of natural materials was paramount, as, in some cases, it is today: the split bamboo basket frames on which cold noodles are piled, naturally cut chopsticks, plain square wooden cups for cold saké, all remain from this conception.

In the decades after Japan was opened to the world (1856), the Japanese, in their enthusiasm for foreign things and for modernisation, engaged in what was one of the biggest fire sales in history. Art-work and armour, houses and castles, furnishings and fripperies were either sold off or torn down and disposed of, replaced with new Western items or copies of those. Private collectors and museums who had the foresight, enriched themselves during this process, creating magnificent collections of Japanese arts and crafts outside Japan, in far-flung places ranging from Venice to Springfield, Massachusetts, where gem-like museums hold barely known treasures. Some Japanese intellectuals, fearful of the loss of the Japanese aesthetic patrimony, created an inchoate and unsystematic movement, in a variety of fields – folklore and folk craft – to preserve these traditions. Fortunately, they succeeded to a great degree, preserving not only the artefacts, but reviving the processes and technology in various fields – pottery, dyeing, and woodblock printing, house-construction and salt-making – for future generations.

In the crafts and arts this developed into the contemporary *mingei* (folkcraft) movement. Among other things it produced some of Japan's best-known modern craftsmen such as the potter Hamada Shoji as well as the marvellous folk craft museum in Komaba. During the same period, from the early to mid-1900s, the potter, cook, writer, and aesthete Kitaoji Rōsanjin also regenerated interest in traditional kilns and ceramic glazes. An irascible, strong-minded man from a poor family in Kyoto, he eventually rose to fame because of his multiple talents. Whatever the quality of his pottery – some good, some poor, mostly derivative – he is best remembered today in his insistence, as both potter and cook, that pottery utensils must be designed to fit the foods that are to be served in them. By this, Rōsanjin meant far more than merely their shape. Texture and glaze, colour and form, were to agree with the food that was intended for placing on the dish. In effect, Rōsanjin was codifying an unconscious understanding that is embedded in the heart of Japanese philosophy and aesthetics: the need for harmonising disparate elements of experience. For Rōsanjin, the quality of the food and its receptable went hand in hand. The quality of Rōsanjin's food arrangements, as best as can be seen from comments made by and about him, were expressions of the best in Japanese cuisine: naturalism and harmony.

In practice, what this idea does for Japanese cooking is in a sense unique: it broadens the playing field. The cook's ability to create an effect is doubled, once the quality of the utensil is brought into play. It is not just the formal characteristics of the utensil, such as its colour. The idea goes to the heart of the Japanese dining experience, due to the exigencies resulting from the required mode of eating. The Japanese diner is allowed and encouraged to touch and hold the utensils, something that is practised rarely, if ever, in other cuisines. Not just the *chawan* (rice bowl) can be held, but all the little dishes, containing small portions of food, often slippery and difficult to grasp, are there to be handled, weighed in the hand, fondled even, by the diner. This is exemplified in all dining situations, from the most simple to the most formal. In the Tea ceremony, the tea bowl is as much for visual as well as tactile appreciation – it is admired, held reverently in both hands, brought very close to the face during drinking, and then when empty and cleaned, turned over to complete the visual and tactile discovery. The normally unseen and untouched part of the bowl is regarded – to see how the structure of the bowl has been finished and given support, as well as to see the maker's mark and appraise the bowl's value. At a regular meal, the rice bowl is to be brought to the lips, and must fit the hand comfortably. Indeed, when contemplating the purchase of crockery, customers in department stores and utensil shops do not so much *look* at potential purchases (though, naturally, they do so as well) as hold them and weigh them in their hands, assessing their comfort and feel. In essence, the point at which they contemplate buying a rice bowl, feel its heft, and imagine it with steaming rice, is the starting point of their meals.

7.3 *TEXTURE*

TEXTURE FORMS AN important dimension of all Japanese foods. Some foods – *tororo*, *konnyaku*, some fish dishes – are eaten as much for their slippery textures as for their flavour. A common adjective applied by many respondents to good foods is "*yawarakai*" (soft), but this has implications, as one informant said "'Soft' means *ha ni au* (it suits the teeth)."[6] The softness of a food, its similarity to baby-food, arouses powerful emotional reactions (conditioned, without question, by cultural constraints and structures) for every individual. It is not surprising that Itami Juzo's film on food, Tampopo, ends with an apparently irrelevant picture of a mother suckling her baby: good food, soft food, is as intimate, and as comforting, in this cultural view, as a mother's breast milk.

---

6 This may, perhaps, be related to the inherent ideas of *soto* (outside) and *uchi* (inside) which underlie many conceptions of self and other in Japanese society. *Soto*, the outside, is often conceived of as a realm of harsh endeavour, one in which struggle and rigid rules of propriety and strife predominate. It is there that one practices *tatemae*: the presentation of face, or, as Goffman would say, the presentation of self. Acting *tatemae* individuals go against both their personal inclinations – *honne* – and their emotions and human feelings – *ninjō* – which are the proper province of *uchi* (the inside). *Uchi*, in contrast to *soto*, is warm, emotional, "true to oneself." It is the realm of comfort in emotion and in interpersonal, relationships.

The subtle flavours of Japanese foods contribute to enhancing the importance of texture. Though there are a number of food flavouring agents – native herbs and spices – available, the cultural pattern set very early in Japan for freshness and restraint in cooking, means that flavouring agents, when used at all, are kept to a minimum, and only added just before eating, so that the innate flavour of the food is unsullied. One side effect of this restraint is the opening up of another dimension – texture – to the diner. At its most extreme, Japanese food is in direct contrast to some of the highly-flavoured cuisines such as Indian or Mexican. The flavours in Japanese cuisine are so subtle as to make the taste appear bland to the uninitiated. This means that other senses: sight and pressure, must be brought into play to fully appreciate the experience.

The textures of Japanese utensils are clearly related to this issue. The variety of textures in Japanese ceramics, for example, has been a major focus of attention since the art of pottery was introduced. Textural features, whether in the shapes of utensils such as tea bowls, or in their glazes, have played a major part in this aesthetic. This has been transferred to the textures of all food utensils. One of the major reasons for *not* using metal chopsticks, is the different sensation they provide to the diner. The most prized chopsticks are freshly made of cut green bamboo. The feel of the green bamboo, the smoothness of the green outside layer, the warmth imparted by the sweet herbaceous smell of the inner layer, the lightness of the utensil, all of these combine to enhance the diner's pleasure. Individual experience plays a definite part: there is a subtle, yet noticeable difference between drinking soup from a plastic bowl and from a wooden lacquer bowl. The heft of the two is different, the feeling of warmth is absent in the plastic, and the touch of the plastic against one's teeth as the soup is drunk is also, subtly, indefinably, different. The differences that both authors *perceive* between utensils of these two materials is, of course, subjective in the extreme. Yet it is unquestionably reinforced by atmosphere, by the nature of the foods consumed, and by our recognition of unconscious cultural cues. That does not, we argue, obviate the observation: indeed, the subtle cues, the holistic response to all cues in the environment of Japanese food, is what makes it Japanese, far more than the foodstuffs (which may be imported), the cooking methods, or the flavouring. It is the *constellation* of effects, of sensory, social, cultural and other cues that distinguishes a "Japanese" dish from any other kind.

This does have implications for the "importation" of Japanese foods into other cuisines. One can always import a dish or a method of cooking into another cuisine. As we have seen, the Japanese have been doing this for ages. Yet this sort of importation is unlikely to retain its "Japanese-ness" for long, for precisely the same reasons that when foreign cuisine items are brought into Japan, time and practice soon render them Japanese. The essential nature of Japanese food is its conscious multi-dimensionality. Importing foods into Japanese cuisine means the gradual "usurpation" of some of the dimensions in the foreign food by Japanese qualities. The shape, the colour, the utensil's shape or texture, the food's accompaniment, its temperature or spiciness: gradually one, then another, then yet another of these dimensions are subverted to Japanese preferences. At first the food is completely foreign, then it is subtly Japanese, at that point it may be adopted as an "*esunikku ryōri*", and finally, when (if) a critical mass of these dimensions has been Japanised, the food becomes acceptable in the canon of Japanese cuisine. When the reverse happens: when a Japanese food is imported into a foreign cuisine, it may well be imported without all the subtle, multi-dimensional cues that are the essence of Japanese food. The importer rarely knows all these dimensions – given the cultural biases and differences, probably does not consider them important either. This is strongly evident in studies of Japanese restaurants abroad. These studies tend to consider the *gross* elements in Japanese cooking (size of Japanese community, type of food served, when eaten, etc.) in describing the nature of Japanese food overseas. But because it is so inherent in Japanese culture, to the point of not being visible to the Japanese themselves, the multi-dimensional nature of this cuisine is often ignored. A subjective indication is the perceived difference that we (and some of our Japanese friends) have noticed in Japanese restaurants that we favour outside Japan (admittedly, this is a biased and small sample): "It's good, but somehow not Japanese," one friend said after eating at a Northern California Japanese restaurant. "There was something wrong there: the size of the plates? the servings? the light? I can't characterise it, but I can't call it Japanese either." This statement does not, of course, prove our point, but it does indicate that somehow, in some fashion, there is something missing. Or rather, we suggest that there has to be more than one subtle, important dimension, that makes the difference.

7.4 *INFLUENCES OF JAPANESE RELIGION AND PHILOSOPHY*

As WE NOTED in Chapter 2, Japanese religion has been a relatively easygoing mix of two major components, Shintō and Buddhism, each of which has numerous variations, sects, and parts. The two religions in modern Japan are functionally different. Shintō, its rituals and priests, are largely concerned with day-to-day affairs. Buddhism is largely concerned with the afterlife. These are of course generalisations. In addition, both religions have come together in various ways, the most prominent of which are what are technically called New Religious Movements. These include at least several hundred at last count, varying from moderate movements within a sect of Buddhism or Shintō, to active and often dangerously extremist fringe religions. Their numbers also vary considerably, from several tens of believers to several tens of millions.

The major influences on food, however, must be viewed in the very broad brushstroke of "Shintō" and "Buddhism."

The essence of Shintō as a religion, in fact its very name, has to do with the idea of emulating and serving a set of deities – the *kami* – indigenous to the

Japanese islands, who are inherently pure. Historically speaking, the *kami* originated from a number of different locales in Japan, and many were the local *ujigami* (clan gods) in pre-imperial Japan (that is, before the Nara and Heian period conquests of the Yamato state: roughly before the ninth century). The government and the central religious authorities have made great efforts, notably in the modern period, to "rationalise" and unify religious rituals. Many, particularly the important food offerings, echo local and historical food practices.

One distinctive aspect of Shintō, Japan's autochthonous religion, is its great emphasis on purity. Purity – *hare* – is a quality that is associated with certain objects, activities, and people, and pollution – *ke* or *kegare* – is a quality associated with others. As in Judaism, another religion that also emphasises purity, *hare* can be acquired. In other words, individuals and objects can be purified – with running cold water, sea water, salt, fire – and cleansed.

This concept affects the province of food in two ways. First, it puts strictures on the kinds of foodstuffs that can be eaten, and that Japanese feel comfortable with, by characterising certain foods as unclean. Second, certain foods and foodstuffs, by their association with foods served to the *kami* (deities) are deemed inherently clean and edible.

Rice is, of course, the purest and most desirable of foods. A number of Shintō deities are associated with rice in its various forms, most notably Inari, the deity of rice grains and prosperity. Shrines to Inari, with their red asymmetric gateways are instantly recognisable by the statues of foxes that flank them. The fox, Inari's messenger, is propitiated by people who leave offerings of *Inari-zushi*: sweetened rice wrapped in sweetened fried tofu pockets. These are presented to the fox spirit at the small round entrance cut into the base of the shrine.

In most shrines, cooked foods, and anything containing meat are at the very least doubtful, because of possible contamination by blood or other impure substances, and are rarely offered. This of course may be the result of Buddhist influence, since, until 1873, when they were separated by government fiat, shrines (Shintō places of worship) and temples (Buddhist places) incorporated one another to varying degrees. In larger shrines, offerings include millet and other sanctified grains, evidence, presumably, of the pre-rice agriculture which characterised the Japanese islands in prehistoric and historical times. Fresh fruit and vegetables, *wakame* (laver) and *konbu* (kelp) are also offered, and, being of the sea, are inherently pure. Even foreign-derived fruit such as pineapples and bananas are presumably clean, since they are often offered in Shintō rituals:

> While the eerie music of flute (*fue*) and drone (*hichiriki*) plays, three priests solemnly carry offerings to be placed before the altar. Each offering is made of food, properly arrayed on raised trays (*sanbō*) of bare, unadorned cypress wood (*hinoki*). The participants – members of the community, heads of ritual organisations, and other priests – watch from the sidelines as food for the deity (*kami*) is passed hand to hand by the robed priests, until fifteen raised, single-footed *sanbō* trays are laid in ascending rows before the *so-*

> *shintai* (an object representing the *kami*). Each *sanbō* has pyramidal piles of offerings, each meticulously arranged on a folded pristine sheet of white paper. On one, a mound of raw rice grains. On another, two large rounds of *kagami-mochi* (mirror-*mochi* – flattened cakes of *mochi* about twenty centimetres across). There are *sanbō* bearing giant white radishes *(daikon)*, shiny local apples, red and green *wakame* seaweed, and one, incongruously, with a huge pineapple. On one lies a whole live fish.
>
> "The *kami*", later explains one of the priests who is conducting the ritual, "expect to eat only the purest of foodstuffs. The foodstuffs must also come from all the possible sources: ideally, from the sea, the shore, rice-paddies, fields, groves, and mountains. That is, fish, seaweed, rice, fruit, and vegetables. We cook some of the foods in prescribed ways, though, as in the case of the fish, the *kami* prefer to eat most things in their natural state. During the Meiji era, many of these offerings were standardised, as you can see in this book.
>
> The *kami* are the equivalent of very important guests, so we must prepare the freshest and best foods, in as elegant and natural a manner as possible. Later, all of these foods will be offered to members of the community, so that they too will enjoy, if only vicariously, a feast with the *kami*. That is the essence of Shintō."

There are a number of important elements in this brief description.[7] First is an indication of the tremendous *importance* of food. So important that it forms the core of the relationship between individuals and the divine. While the original meal prescriptions are highly elaborated, deriving as they do from court foods of the Heian period, modern offerings, no less solemn, are familiar, to a degree to any Japanese: *mochi*, fruit, vegetables, *sashimi*, dried *konbu* seaweed. Second, these foods, and others, are highlighted and made even more important in the scheme of things by their appearance in the ritual. Third, the ritual requirements neatly define qualities of foods – their association with purity and, as it were, "higher cultural functions" – and the sanctification of their sources, which is made explicit in the ritual. Fourth, though the ritual is quintessentially, indigenously Japanese, a "foreign" element is present. And, finally, the aesthetic forms in which the food is presented, obviously suggest an aesthetic standard to those who participate.

These aesthetic principles underlie much of Japanese daily food. Oppositions between "piles" of food and orderly rows of food trays are one principle. The use of relatively simple blocks of colour (in formal offerings, there are special concoctions of different coloured grains) is another. Purity, expressing itself in simple lines, natural wood of the trays, and the use of plain white paper, is a third.

Daily food might look quiet different from ritual offerings, but it follows the same guiding principles, albeit modified by other pressures. Food offered the

7 A more detailed description of the ritual and religious significance of the elements in such a ritual can be found in Ashkenazi, *Matsuri* (1993).

deities must not only *be* pure, it must also look pure, and the visual spectacle – towers of rice, fruit and vegetables – must be pleasing to the eyes, as well as the noses and palates of the deities. One of our acquaintances, a professional Shintō priest, laughed when asked about the ritual and symbolic significance of some of the colour combinations and food arrangements in offerings. "They simply look better that way. Making an offering *look* good is simply making an offering: there is no difference, because food, for the *kami* or anyone else, is seen as much as tasted."

The nature of food in Japanese cuisine and its presentation is also affected by Buddhist influences. The division of Buddhism into a multi-hued array of sects means that, effectively, there is a flavour of Buddhism for virtually every taste: contemplative, ritualistic, magical, comforting, devotional. Each of these flavours has contributed to the rich Buddhist weft that crosses the warp of Shintō.

As a "foreign" religion, imported from Korea and China, ultimately from India, Buddhism inevitably brought with it culinary demands. Three of these elements are particularly important. The vegetarian cuisine that most (certainly not all) Buddhist sects adhere to, has brought about, notably through the contemplative Zen schools, a strong influence on *kaiseki*. The aesthetic demands that were part of Buddhist rituals – lusher and more elaborate than those of Shintō – had an effect on aesthetic ideas such as flower decorations, which eventually led to the refinement of flower arranging. The ideas from the latter have had a strong influence, as the ritual offerings of Shintō rituals and on *moritsuke* (the placement of foods on a plate). Finally, in the realm of cooking, the Buddhist ritual requirement for sweet foods, used, for example, to celebrate Shakya's (Shakyamuni: the historical Buddha) birthday, have led towards the development of Japanese confectionery (*wagashi*). As mentioned in an earlier discussion of *wagashi*, sweet foods have a restricted niche in Japanese cuisine. Indeed, some of the sweets that are served, have had their origin in foods that were part of Buddhist rituals during the Heian era.

"Zen" is the Japanese rendition of a Chinese translation (*ch'an*) of a Sanskrit word (*Dhyāna*) meaning silent meditation. For our purposes here it can be considered a contemplative "school" (an intellectual orientation) and "sect" (an organisation on the basis of religious affiliation)[8] of Buddhism. The various Zen

8 In the Japanese context both terms are appropriate. Buddhism in Japan, since its inception in the seventh century, has been divided into schools of thought, emphasising one or other of the rich variety of Buddhist thought as it emerged in India, and has been refined in China, Tibet, and Korea. The Japanese, after receiving Buddhism initially from the Koreans, went on to import a number of different such schools from various places, and via various teachers in China. These in turn were elaborated on in Japan.

The Japanese government, ever interested in new forms of control over its populace, soon co-opted many of these schools (which were established initially at an institutional level as monastic-type schools) into formally recognised, government-registered "sects." Membership in Buddhist sects was mutually exclusive (though not with Shintō, since individuals could be members of both religions), and served the purposes of population registry: births and deaths were recorded by Buddhist temples from about the tenth to the nineteenth centuries.

schools emphasise different modes of contemplation and renunciation. They also emphasise unmediated relations between individuals, between humans and the divine, and between humans and their surroundings. The use of repetitive, individual ritual to subdue individuality and "illusion" is heavily emphasised, as is aesthetic contemplation.

The effects of Zen (as well as other schools) on the Tea ceremony are well documented. Performing a Tea ceremony *is* performing a Zen ritual because the principles – concentration, the substitution of unmediated feeling for intellectual consideration, the use of repetitive body movements for enhanced calmness – are shared by both practices.[9] Certainly, ideas of simplicity, and of "naturalness" in Japanese cuisine owe a great deal indirectly to Zen, though, as noted above, it is not easy to disentangle "Zen" notions from "Shintō" notions.[10]

Shōjin ryōri (Buddhist vegetarian cooking) is not unique to Zen institutions, but, perhaps because Zen ideas have been publicised in the West more than other Buddhist traditions, the macrobiotic movement has been strongly affected by these ideas, many of which lie at the aesthetic heart of Japanese cuisine. In Japan, *shōjin ryōri* is still offered at Buddhist temples:

> After the noisy train ride, the quiet of the suburbs was a welcome release. Koganei has little to distinguish it from any other suburb, and coming on the small Sankō-in temple-nunnery is a pleasant surprise. Inside, the halls are dark and sombre, redolent of the smell of incense that immediately evokes "Buddhist temple" once you have smelt it for the first time. The nun showed us to a room with high dark beams, and through the open *shōji* we could see the garden. Some of the maples were turning a deep red, and there was a chrysanthemum in the shade of the trees.
>
> *Zabuton* cushions had been laid for us. We sat and waited in complete and luxurious silence, slowly sipping our green tea, disinclined to talk except in a whisper, as the nun went out to bring back our meal. We had ordered the mid-ranged meal from the three choices offered. Each received a broad, black lacquered tray, on which was a contrast of five plates.
>
> The largest plate, and set furthest away from the diner on the right hand edge of tray, was like a Western shallow soup plate, round with a scalloped rim. It was of white ceramic and round the rim was a border of brilliant red and blue and gold glazed flowers and leaves. On it were six

9 Zen, as an intellectual school which embodies a practice, does not have nor particularly need any reference to a deity. The various concepts of "Buddha-hood" do not exactly correspond to Western (Christian, Muslim, or Jewish) ideas of a deity. Zen *sects* on the other hand are organised religious bodies – churches – which, for all intents and purposes, are organised for the worship of a deity. A wonderful Japanese compromise which allows people to have the cake of religion and dispense with it too.

10 To add to the confusion, both Shintō and Zen intellectual traditions refer to a Chinese tradition, Daoism, whose naturalist tendencies underlie many aspects of Chinese, and thus of Japanese, philosophy.

items, one shaped into a maple leaf, and similarly coloured brilliant red and yellow. This was the most obvious allusion to the season. It was made of simmered gluten (*fu*). Furthest on the plate were two slices of *nori* rolls (*yamato-imo norimaki*). The black line of the *nori* wrapping spiralled into the centre, dotted with light green *wasabi* (horseradish). Instead of rice which usually fills ordinary nori sushi rolls, the filling here was yam (*yamato imo*) that had been mashed, and its translucence made it whiter than a rice roll would have been. In front of the nori rolls were two tiny brick-shaped pieces of freeze-dried (*kōya*) tofu which had been slowly simmered in vegetable stock. Next was a pale yellow chestnut, also simmered in stock till tender. In front were three long slices of burdock, like stacked logs. They had been flavoured with ground *sansho* grains in white miso (*tataki-gōbō*). Finally, sliced green beans simmered in salt provided a centre-point for the arrangement. The taste of the dish was as contrastive as the colours and shapes. Unexpectedly to a tongue expecting the texture and flavour of rice rolls, the mountain yam is bland but with an astringent aftertaste, and the horseradish at its centre gives a welcome burst of vivid flavour. The *gōbō* and beans offered different degrees of crispness, while the *fu* and tofu were soft, spongy, and moist from their flavoured stock.

Soup was a *sumashijiru* (clear soup) through which the black lacquer of the bowl could be seen clearly. A block of tofu had been thinly sliced crosswise to provide long beams of tofu which made the soup appear to be cradling a faceted white crystal. A few leaves of *tsuruna* (a spinach-tasting vine) provided freshness and a bright green contrast. The soup was slightly salty, with only a hint of flavour. Unlike usual *dashi*, the stock in Buddhist temples must adhere to the vegetarian principles of *shōjin ryōri*, which means that it was made without *katsuobushi*, strictly of *konbu*, saké, and mushrooms, a ghostly hint of which permeated the soup.

A small plain white dish held a *sunomono* (vinegared dish) in which *ito-uri* (spaghetti squash) had been simmered lightly until the threads were a translucent yellow, and then lightly seasoned with rice vinegar. A piece of green squash skin had been cut into the shape of a maple leaf and dropped casually onto the noodle-like threads. The sweet-sourness of the dressing was faint enough not to obscure the fresh taste of the squash, and the threads still retained some of the crispness of the raw vegetable.

A shallow saucer, also plain white, with a lacy blue design on the rim, was used for a small mound of *kyuri no furozuke-ni* (old-pickled cucumbers). Usually, pickled cucumbers are lightly salted and lightly pressed for several hours before serving. These, in contrast, had been pickled longer, and were the only strong tasting element in the ensemble, to which the zing from some grated ginger contributed.

The heart of the meal, as always, was rice. Unlike the plain rice of every-day, this was a deep white bowl filled with *mukagogohan*. *Mukago* are the round bulbils that grow along the stems of yams. These had been randomly peeled so that brown bits still adhered to the bean-sized nodules. They had been lightly simmered in saké and salt and some soy sauce had been added to colour the rice a faint brown.

We ate almost in complete silence. The dark room, the almost absolute quiet of the temple around us, even the faint soughing of the wind in the trees outside demanded that the meal be eaten as intended, as it would have been by the proper residents of the temple.

The relationship of *shōjin ryōri* to *kaiseki* is very strong. Offerings, *kaiseki* and *shōjin ryōri* are inherently elements of ritual. Every element must be precise, every detail must accounted for, and thought out well ahead of time. Given the disposition of Zen (and some other religious traditions in Japan) to simplicity and naturalness, it is not surprising that related food offerings are also expected to maintain such simplicity. However, there is a countervailing tendency that must also be accounted for. All humans adorn their rituals, embellishing them with artistry and wealth. Colours, shapes, flavours, are constantly sought for as elaborations on the idea of simplicity. Whatever ideas were espoused of good food in temples, such as Dōgen's,[11] on the moral and spiritual weight required to prepare temple food, it must be remembered that temples were, to some degree, outposts of aristocratic living.[12] Thus simplicity must be counterbalanced with the desire for elaboration, spirituality with the rich texture of experience in the meal. The mutual transmission with the refinements of *kaiseki* on the one hand, and the daily food of the Japanese people on the other, makes of *shōjin* a careful balancing act, and, at the same time, a benchmark of refined food. This refinement is also related to another aspect of Japanese culture, flower arranging.

Flower arrangement (*ikebana* or *ohana*) is one of the better-known Japanese traditional art forms. It involves the selection, preparation, and arrangement of seasonally appropriate plant materials, not only flowers, leaves, and stems, but also tree branches or fruit, in containers appropriate to the materials, the season and occasion, as well as the setting. As in all Japanese arts, the choice of vegetation and display receptacles is dictated by aesthetic considerations that demand a harmony among all the elements. This is essentially the same principle we have seen applied previously to choices of food, particularly in the Tea-ceremony, to which *ikebana* is related both in concept and origin, and because a floral arrangement is also one of the required furnishings in the decorative alcove in a Tea room (*chaseki*).

It is with another principle that we are concerned here – that of the three focal branches in flower arrangement, called *shin* (written with the character

11 The founder of Zen in Japan, who also authored a volume on value, preparation, and consumption of monastic Buddhist food.

12 Most sheltered retired emperors and princesses who wished to withdraw from the world and master Buddhist learning.

"truth"), *soe* (written with the character "support" or "assist"), and *tai* (written with the character "body").[13] These must present the viewer with an ascending and asymmetric order of focus.

These three principal branches are usually rendered in English as Heaven, Human, Earth. The three are expected to be poised in a natural, yet dynamic balance. This triumvirate, which is generally vertically oriented, is a representation of a natural feature: a mountain. The idea of a mountain as a sacred place is prominent in both Buddhism and Shintō. Mountains were the abode of the divine (in Shintō and some schools of Buddhism) and mythical Mt. Meru represents the path to enlightenment in Buddhist thought. The number three (as well as five and seven) has mystical significance as well.

This combination of ideas embodied in the number three (which as well has mystical significance in Buddhism and Shinto) finds its expression throughout the traditional "nature-oriented" arts of Japan: flower-arranging as previously mentioned, *bonkei* (tray landscapes), *bonsai* (miniaturised trees), which share both the idea of the mountain as a centrally important concept, and aesthetic principles such as the triangle we mentioned above, and garden design. It is not surprising to find, therefore, that the principles of Japanese food arrangement (*moritsuke*) replicate these aesthetic principles.

The interrelationship of artistic principles is held together by an underlying, unifying philosophical ideology in which religious and social ideas from Chinese and Japanese sources are combined, and are expressed in some concrete, physically tangible manner. These ideological principles, and no less, their execution are transferable from one realm of activity to another. In a general sense, the individual in Japan, by participating in social and cultural life, is faced with a series of *seemingly* autonomous cultural practices or "models for" behaviours, including artistic behaviour. Because these are expressively *models* they are applicable to other, more-or-less similar areas of behaviour. The individual who experiences flower arrangements, finds similar principles replicated in Tea, or in food. Practices that are common in one area in the realm of social behaviour, are ultimately bound to ideas, and serve as models, in other instances.

This tight weave of cultural and social practice has two effects. First, it unifies Japanese culture with an underlying, tightly delineated set of practices and experiences. Being Japanese is more than a matter of speaking the language or living in the country: it is reinforced and formatted by participation in, and use of, these cultural models, even when one does so unintentionally or under compulsion, as happens to many.[14] Second, it also means that detaching *one* of these "models" and transplanting it to another context is virtually meaningless, because the interconnections and cross-references – metaphors, symbols,

13 This is the terminology used by the Ikenobo School, under which Jeanne was trained. Other schools use different terminology: *shin, so, gyo*.

14 This is naturally applicable to other cultures as well.

signifiers of ideological elements – are simply not there. This tight weave of socio-cultural elements helps explain both why Japanese often feel uncomfortable outside the heavy multi- and self-referential context of their culture (and why some Japanese individuals feel stifled by it!), and why non-Japanese find Japanese culture so difficult to penetrate. It is not that any one element is uniquely strange or inimitable, it is that the weave of the cultural structure, the prevalence of interleaved signifiers and ideas, is so tight.

7.5 *ARTISTIC DIMENSIONS IN JAPANESE FOOD*

ANY CUISINE CAN be viewed as a form of art, and as such, it is an extension of the total artistic system of the culture concerned. For the purposes of this discussion, "art" has a number of characteristics. Normally, one expects an artistic product to be something that has been *manipulated* in some way. This manipulation need not be heavy-handed. A wonderful example is provided by Hendry (1997). The art of Japanese gardening, she shows, is often little more than proper framing. The gardening artist may move a few items in the landscape, providing a frame or reference point, from which a particular effect or view is to be achieved. By doing this often completely inconspicuous manipulation, the artist is able to achieve a desired effect.

Three other related characteristics are also important. All art is based on some sort of sensory effect such as vision, sound, or, in the case of food, taste. It is insufficient to have an intellectual understanding of an art work, one must receive some sensory input as well. Related to that, art exists in a cultural context. Where it is created or presented, on the basis of what ideas, what techniques are used, and what emotional feelings it evokes or denies, are all part of its context. The third characteristic is that art always has a social context as well. Who made the art, whom it was made for, and what is the relationship between maker and audience, what class of people, the economic and political conditions that brought it about, are all crucial both for understanding it, and for enjoying the art as art. Not all of this information – sensory, cultural, or social – is necessary for any individual to enjoy any particular art piece, but certainly a full *understanding* which is a part of the complex relationship of artist and audience (the term here used in the broad sense) is associated with these issues. To examine Japanese food as an art form, therefore, means to have some sort of understanding of these three characteristics.

When considered as an art form, as part of a complex, interrelated artistic tradition, Japanese food is clearly intermeshed into other threads of expressive endeavour. In other words, it is possible to draw associations between other Japanese art forms and food, which illuminate the choices Japanese have made about their food and its presentation.

The same, of course, is true of other cuisines. Some of our Japanese students pointed out the homology between Japanese ink-painting, which leaves large swathes of the canvas (or scroll, in this case) unpainted, and Japanese food, in which small amounts of food are arrayed so as to leave large empty spaces on a plate. In parallel, they noted, British painters such as those of the pre-Raphaelite group felt impelled to fill their canvases, leaving not an inch unpainted, and filling all of the canvas with information. The homology to the British plate – loaded with meat, potatoes, sauce, and heaped with vegetables, none of the plate visible – seems quite clear. It is worthwhile to start our examination here with a consideration of space and framing, and the ways these are dealt with in Japanese food.

7.6 MORITSUKE: *THE USES OF FRAMING AND SPACE*

GIVEN A PLATE of a particular size and shape, and food of a particular coloration, size, and other observable qualities, Japanese individuals will very quickly assemble the food in particular patterns, patterns that are more-or-less the same for the individuals examined during our research.

These bare (and not exhaustively tested) results raise a number of questions. Some of these are clearly methodological: the data are not systematic, may well be biased (we asked friends and acquaintances, without doubt selected on a bias from an entire population), they are not quite reliable, and so on. Given these objections, and basing ourselves on anecdotal evidence, there is nonetheless strong evidence that this patterning arrangement *does* occur.[15]

This patterning-placing of foods is determined by propriety rules, that is, by *moritsuke* – the rules of arranging and placing food on plates. However, the *existence* of such rules does not necessarily dictate their permeation throughout society. Yet, very clearly, in the Japanese case these rules are indeed highly penetrative. To understand why this is so, we have to turn to some of the fundamental characteristics that underlie many other aspects of Japanese culture, principally to the concept of space, or *ma.*

The concept of space is crucial for an understanding of many aspects of Japanese life. A prime example is the Japanese room, bare of all furniture, ready to be turned into whatever the owner desires by the manipulation of a few select elements. It is its emptiness, the space that it encloses, that implies its perfect fit to the protean needs of Japanese life. Similarly, empty space is utilised to maximize possibilities in the arts. Noh theatre, with its bare stage and minimalist stage props (a single pine tree, sometimes merely painted onto the backdrop) is a case in point. Characters on stage are defined as much by their actions and reactions

15 A methodological note. It is clearly of interest to determine, in a properly sampled manner, how deep this pattern recognition *does* go. An interesting research project would be to test a reasonable sample of the Japanese population, factored for age, sex, class, and location, to see (a) if there are observable differences, and (b) how "deep" is the penetration or knowledge of these food arrangement patterns. This, however, is not our main concern in this section.

in emptiness, as they are in their relations to one another. In swordsmanship, *ma* is crucial: it is the distance from your sword to your opponent's that makes the other uncomfortable and you in control, and is a major aspect of all *okuden* ("inner", that is the esoteric teachings) of most sword schools since the Heian period. Japanese painting is composed often of little more than space, with a few strokes of the brush to direct the eye, then the mind. This contrasts strongly with European classical painting traditions in which the whole canvas is charged with paint.

Japanese dishes too, are arranged with due attention to *ma*. As a general rule, a plate is *never* covered, never filled with the food it carries. To the contrary. A large plate, such as the square *hassun* used for one of the courses in a Tea ceremony meal, may contain little more than a few tidbits arranged in two piles at just the appropriate places on the *hassun*'s surface to give due balance between emptiness/space and the occupying food item. "The eye and palate are stimulated by their journey from emptiness to fullness, and vice versa," one of our friends, himself an artist, commented idly. In arranging two piles on a square *hassun,* it is not only the space that is considered, but direction as well. The foods are usually placed on the diagonal relative to the receptacle's frame.

An immediately visible characteristic of Japanese table settings, is the wide range of receptacles used. Where in French (and Chinese – the other great human cuisine) and thus European cuisine, tableware is composed of a set of matched dishes, Japanese tableware is disparate. Rather than uniformity, diversity of glazes, shapes, textures, composition is expected. This of course, as we have noted earlier, presents the Japanese chef with much greater scope, as well as challenges, in how to present the various items of a meal. The functional bases for some of these differences may or may not be immediately obvious – lacquerware's heat-keeping qualities, particularly when lidded, makes it ideal for soups; deep, rather than shallow bowls for soup, because the soup is drunk straight from it. The differentiation can also be attributed to the aesthetic principle of surprise. For the diner this is, physiologically speaking, a more interesting system because the uninterrupted or unvaried application of a stimulus (no matter how exciting initially) tends to dull the senses: one reason for the introduction of *sorbet* between haute cuisine courses. After a while, in a Western dinner, one ceases to be impressed by the plates, however exquisite they may be. Japanese table arrangement, on the other hand, constantly stimulates visual and tactile senses, in addition to palatal ones. The well-set formal Western dinner table impresses with a glittering and harmonious array of crystal, silverware, and uniform chinaware on sumptuous cloth. All the glasses and silverware intended for use during the course of the meal are in place: no surprises there. The chinaware for forthcoming courses will doubtless match the previous ones: again no surprises there either. The surprise comes with the food.

On a tactile dimension, besides the silverware and glassware, Western tableware is not meant to be touched. A Japanese table setting on the other hand is meant to be, the various textures seeming to say, "Touch me". The message is a sybaritic one, perhaps to the untutored diner. To a pottery connoisseur, there are additional messages conveyed by eating off (actually holding) a bowl designed by Kenzan or Ninsei, whose pattern or glaze replicates Ming or Tang pottery (perhaps similar to those conveyed by dining off antique Meissen).

Variations in receptacles and the principle of space both contribute to another principle visible throughout Japanese art: contrast. The unexpected and contrastive are highly valued, which is unsurprising in a society in which conformity and sameness are important for social harmony. Round foods are put on square plates, "wind-blown" arrangement of foods onto straight-sided ones. Preferably, not all the items are visible at all times, some obscuring others, as would happen in a deep dish. Contrast is further expressed in a number of ways. All the plates on a tray, or all the food items on a plate, are rarely arranged in such a way that, from the diner's viewpoint, one straight, predictable line can be drawn through them. Several disparate food items on a plate would never be arranged facing the same direction. The same is true of colour contrasts that are unexpected and seemingly jarring to one accustomed to the predictable ones presented on the Western colour wheel.

Numbers too, contribute to the idea of contrasts. Items are normally served in threes, fives, and sevens: odd numbers all. Japanese explain this by saying that "*shi*" (four) is homophonous with "*shi*" (death). This does not explain the avoidance of two or six. We suspect that there is another, deeper, explanation. In fact, four food items *do* appear on plates, provided they are of different types, and provided they obscure one another. It is not the number that is in point, but symmetry: it is more difficult to avoid symmetry with even numbers than with odd, and symmetry is non-contrastive.

A number of different food arrangement styles, many of them named, are available for the chef to express the principles above. "Mountain" or "cedar" style is piled high, over the shoulder of a deep bowl, to simulate a mountain shouldering above clouds. Fish slices, slightly fanned out, both show the fish off, and convey a sense of the movement of waves. Straight-edged pyramids of round objects like *maki* rolls convey ideas of rurality and piles of saké barrels. It is not any particular arrangement *style* that is important. Nor are there, for all that self-important chefs have tried to do so, any hard and fast rules. It is the expression of principles that underlie much of the working of Japanese food, art, and aesthetics, and even of the subtle psycho-philosophical underpinnings of Japanese society that is important. A specific expression such as a particular arrangement of foods on a plate comes about as a surface expression of deeply embedded principles which the uniformity-making mechanisms of Japanese society bring about. In many cases, these mechanisms – the school system, the economic system, the family – bring about undesirable, even ugly results. In the case of food aesthetics, however, it has yielded a uniformity in *underlying* principles coupled with great freedom of specific expression.

7.7 *JUXTAPOSING THE ARTIFICIAL AND THE NATURAL*

The essence of good Japanese food is food in which the natural qualities of the food are disturbed as little as possible, and the food is served in harmony with its surroundings. Inherent in this definition is the concept that even the artificial nature of a food's surroundings – the utensils which hold it – must be balanced against the particular type of food consumed, and that foods cannot be (one should say, given the "miracles" of refrigeration and rapid transport from different climatic zones "should not be") detached from their surroundings. Most Japanese who consider the issue of food, recognise and accept that the best place to consume any food is in its place of origin. Domestic tourist companies make a living off this very natural assumption, bringing parties to the rice field to taste the newly-harvested rice, to the sea to taste particular fish in the right season, or to the mountains, so that there should be no delay from the picking of *matsutake* mushrooms to the cooking and eating of them.

The issue of the seasons is crucial for understanding this relationship. For the Japanese, the division into four coherent seasons is a definer of the natural environment of Japan. "Do they have four seasons in your country?" foreigners are often asked, a question that is second in frequency only to the "What is the staple in your country?" question. Parenthetically, it must be added that during the Heian period (ninth to eleventh centuries), poets and gourmets recognised some twenty distinct seasons, changing about every two weeks.

Food is clearly related to this concept. Major foods, such as fish species, have particular *shun*. A *shun* is the season at which a particular food is at its peak, normally not more than two weeks in the year. And the proper gourmet and cook take great care to supply such foods with as much ceremony and recognition as possible. Indeed, *shun* have become elements in culturally-based advertising, since, to a degree, they represent an element of aesthetic thinking that is particularly (at least to Japanese eyes) Japanese in nature:

> We sat in a small (six mats) room, overlooking the roofs of the neighbours. There was a *tokonoma* alcove at one side, though the flower arrangement had not been put in place that early in the morning. We had reached the room through a maze of narrow corridors and stairways, from which small, intimate, or larger dining rooms branched out. Throughout the building we could hear the constant sounds of people at work, cleaning, cooking, preparing for the evening when the customers would descend onto the *ryōtei*.
>
> "I am the third generation of my family to run this *ryōtei*," Mr. Ogawa said. "It was founded in 1925 by my grandfather, who had engaged in transportation before that. Our speciality has always been the local foods of the area, its rice, fruit, vegetable, and fish. As the seasons change, we try

to adapt and make use of those products that are in *shun*. In the spring, we offer the fresh young shoots of mountain vegetables. There are, as you know, still elderly grandmas who know the forests, and they go out and collect the good shoots for us. We make them into garnishes for clear soups, or serve them prepared simply with rice. We add the locally grown vegetables as they come onto the market.

In the summer, of course, we make *ayu* (sweetfish) since this fish is particularly good in our cold waters. Sometimes I buy them from fish wholesalers, but I much prefer to deal with the breeders, or even, if at all possible, to have fishermen bring me some of the wild ones they catch. *Ayu* are so delicate that the best way is to simply grill them, and serve immediately.

In the fall, we serve mushrooms. There are so many varieties that grow wild here. The old aunties are invaluable, since it is usually they who know where to find the best ones. One can juxtapose textures – softer and crunchier mushrooms – and colours – white, black, red – and be creative visually as well as in terms of taste. We also serve such things as chestnuts picked from the local groves, cooked as sweets, or used as garnishes to main courses as a savoury dish.

The winter is of course the season for our local delicacy, *kiritampo* (grilled rice dumplings) and of course for *nabemono*. This is necessary because of our cold weather, and when the snow sets in, people eat a lot and are glad of hearty foods.

Today, it being mid summer, we are serving cold soup with bean gluten noodles, a variety of pickles, balanced by some grilled fish and grilled meats, and of course fruits of the season. It is very hot, and people would rather eat these light things: our local peaches, which are so large right now, and also plums which have come into season. But we also serve imported foods, such as papaya and grapefruit: people have become accustomed to them, and perhaps think of them as Japanese fruit! Later in the summer we will also make fruit jellies, which are also very cooling."

The concept of "the natural" requires some elaborating on. The concept is highly context-dependent. Natural, for many Japanese implies the idea of fit, more than of not human-made. In that sense, therefore, even imported foods, the product (in a sense) of a cooler and a transport company are, ultimately, seen as "natural" but *only* when they are fitted into some context, which itself is non-disturbing, thus "natural." Nor is there any particular opprobrium (as is often the case among certain populations in Europe) for the "artificial." Industrial foods, manufactured by utilising biochemistry, can be bought in Japan, proudly declaring themselves to be "artificial food." Thus the fact that a food is, in some way, manipulated, does not make it any less natural *in the Japanese sense.*

READINGS FOR CHAPTER 7

Hayashi, Junichi 1984 "Foreign confectionery transformed into Japanese treats".
Ishige, Naomichi 1981 "Moritsuke … A Japanese garden on the table".
Kondo, Dorinne 1985 "The Way of Tea: A symbolic analysis".
Loveday, Leo and Satomi Chiba 1985 "Partaking with the divine and symbolizing the societal: The semiotics of Japanese food and drink".
Palmer, Elizabeth 1988 *Ikebana: The Art of Japanese Flower Arranging.*
Setagaya Art Museum 1996 *Creative Tradition: The Ceramics of Rosanjin and Masterpieces of the Past Which Influenced Him.*
Suzuki, Daisetz 1959 *Zen and Japanese Culture.*
Tsuji, Kaichi 1974 *Kaiseki: Zen Tastes in Japanese Cooking.*
Varley, H. Paul and George Elison 1981 "The culture of Tea: From its origins to Sen no Rikyu".

8 Learning the Cultural Rules

WHAT DISTINGUISHES A Japanese meal is a set of ordering principles that must be understood because they provide analytical insight into Japanese culture, and because they form, for the diner, a structuring of the dining experience. Ordering principles determine how foods are set before a diner, what is meant to be eaten or presented first, how a meal progresses, and what determines this progression. Ordering principles also mean the progression of food choices over the year, which, as in most cultures, includes some knowledge of a ritual calendar and its bases. Inescapably intertwined in this description are two related issues: the degree and form to which diners' behaviours are determined by the location, the social setting, and the foods eaten, as well as the abstract rules of aesthetic presentation and the degree to which these rules are relative or absolute. These ordering principles are complex and exist on several nested levels. It is also crucial to our understanding that though these ordering principles are overt and firmly connected, they allow, at the same time, a great deal of flexibility and actually encourage, rather than restrict, variation. This variation, however, is channelled along firmly defined lines. To put this latter issue into context, the reader can carry out a simple experiment: set the utensils for your next family meal on the floor of the bedroom, or, alternatively, serve the food in reverse order. That is, in the British household, pudding or dessert, followed by meat, vegetables and carbohydrate, followed by soup (or the reverse of whatever is normal for you). It will quickly become apparent that there are some basic inviolable rules whose disturbance may lead to screams of outrage, if not worse, in all but the most tolerant of households.

The issues surrounding Japanese food come into greater focus when we consider the strange and the abnormal. That is, we must examine extraordinary events, because it is their extra-ordinariness that points out the rules of the ordinary. Mrs. Tagawa's dinner is a case in point. A middle-class housewife, she prepared a dinner for a small group of *gaijin* colleagues of her husband, of whom some had experience with Japanese food, and others did not. Thus she was at pains to utilise foods that were familiar, in order to emphasise and present a Japanese accent that was yet acceptable to non-Japanese.

> The table was set elegantly and with excellent colour sense in an eclectic East-West style. There was a low Western-type flower arrangement in the

middle of the table. There was, however, no tablecloth on the highly polished wood. Instead, each diner had a table mat of richly patterned matte silk. It was a *kara-kusa* (Chinese twining vine) pattern, hand-painted in sombre dyes. There were eight diners, and the mats were randomly varied in turquoise, deep green, and mauve; no two neighbouring diners had the same colour. All however had matching paper napkins, Western silver cutlery, and crystal wine glasses and water goblets. In addition, there were disposable cedar chopsticks encased in white paper, lying horizontally on a chopstick rest, each rest different, immediately in front of each diner. The ceramic ware followed Japanese style in its variety of forms, textures and patterns.

The first course was already arrayed on the table as the diners sat down. It consisted of *sashimi*: two slices of salmon and three of *tai* (sea bream). These were served in low rectangular bowls, the fish resting on one leaf of coriander which substituted for *mitsuba* (trefoil), and garnished with carrots which had been pickle-cooked in garlic (in lieu of *daikon*), and a dab of *wasabi*. A small flat-rimmed plate nearby was provided for soy sauce. The fish had been moistened slightly with soy sauce to hint at its use for some of the guests. A deep bowl containing a cube of sesame tofu, also with a dab of *wasabi*, was to the side. A flat rectangular plate contained caramel-cooked walnuts (of Chinese origin), and two pods of boiled *eda mame* (green soy beans).

With the removal of the first cover, the guests were presented with *osuimono*: a dish of tofu and crab meat balls in a mild clear stock *(dashi)*. This was served in a red lacquered bowl decorated with butterflies. One of the guests, unfamiliar with the lightness and warmth of good lacquerware, asked what kind of plastic the bowls were made of.

The third course consisted of stir-fried chicken bits in a sweet-and-sour sauce, which had been laid on a lettuce leaf – not a Japanese dish, strictly speaking, but certainly part of a repertoire that was as acceptable in Japanese cuisine, as it was familiar to the foreign guests. A cold avocado and mushroom salad, on flat round plates complemented the meat.

The fourth course was quintessentially Japanese: *tororo zaru soba*. Whole wheat-coloured *soba* noodles, chilled, had been lightly mounded on red-lacquered, shallow bowls. The white, frothy, and rather sticky sauce was grated mountain yam. It had a mildly astringent flavour. *Tororo* is a quintessentially "mountain vegetable" dish, associated in many minds with rough, homespun and straw-raincoated farmers. Both the idea of cold noodles and its sauce, whose major interest for the diner is *texture* rather than flavour, were, if truth be told, little appreciated by the non-Japanese guests.

For the fifth course the hostess served *ochazuke*. Traditionally, this dish was a frugal way of disposing of leftover rice and cleaning the bowl. Hot tea was simply sluiced into the bowl, any rice stuck to the sides pried with the chopsticks, and everything consumed,[1] thus avoiding the social solecism of leaving food in one's bowl. As with all cuisine items, *ochazuke* became a dish in its own right, with the addition of garnishes that enhanced the taste of the dish, and its price. Many restaurants in Japan make a speciality of *ochazuke*, or, at least, offer several variants on the menu. One of our friends considers it the acme of Japanese food, something he remembers from childhood, and still prefers today.

Mrs. Tagawa's *ochazuke* was garnished with *wakame* seaweed, sesame seeds, and salmon caviar. A plate of crunchy short-pickled cucumbers, was placed nearby for those who cared to indulge. Finally, the meal ended with slices of persimmon and kiwi served individually to each guest, and coffee and liqueur.

As in most modern cuisines, Mrs. Tagawa's dinner caters to a number of opposing tendencies. There was little emphasis on rice. Though served, it was disguised in the *ochazuke*, which, under normal condition in Japan, would be served to end a meal in which heavy drinking had taken place. The drinks – wine, both red and white with the meal, and coffee and liqueur after – served to emphasise the need to cater to non-Japanese tastes, as was the gradual merging of two traditions, which was handled, overall, in such a skilful manner, that most of the guests were unconscious of the subtlety of the blending. The consumption of a formal dinner follows a number of rules, and this particular one, in which the hosts are Japanese and the guests not, illustrates how these rules are negotiated. The setting, overall, was Western, with the guests in suits, seated at a Western table. This was also set in a country in which Japanese ingredients were not available, even in specialty shops. Thus the challenge for Mrs. Tagawa was how to skillfully blend her limited Japanese provisions with locally available products to result in a dinner presented and prepared in Japanese ways, and yet would not be too much of a cultural shock to the uninitiated. In other words, we see the evolution of a cuisine not only in the process of the passage of foods into upper classes, but also in the passage between one culture and another.

8.1 *LEARNING FOOD AS A CHILD: SCHOOL LUNCH*

THE EDUCATION OF any child in a modern society takes place partly in the home, partly in school, and partly in public areas where the child interacts with peers and others. Learning and teaching about food in the Japanese case since World War II has certainly involved the school lunch. It is here that the Japanese child

1 Isabella Bird, one of the earlier European explorers of Japan in the nineteenth century, was amazed that Japanese porters, carrying large *kago* palanquins (with large Europeans inside them) could survive on what amounts to *ochazuke*.

learns, in her formative years, to adjust to the requirements of others, including the rules of eating and food.

Kindergartens, and, more importantly, the *hōikuen* or day-care centres, to which many children of working mothers go, provide school lunches and snacks. Each child's parents receive a monthly listing of the contents of these meals, as well, sometimes, as their caloric content, exhortations to "Feed me good foods," and ideas about nutrition. Nonetheless, in many cases, each child is *also* required to bring a serving of rice to school. So that "he will eat the rice he is familiar with from home," as one *yōchien* teacher told us. In other words, culturally speaking, they attempt to forge a direct relationship between the food of the home, and publicly shared food. From an early age, therefore, in public as well as private fora, the child is exposed to a particular form of meal: rice+. This in turn, transmutes itself to the later familiarity with, and expectancy of, rice as the definer of a proper meal.

School lunches also present the child with new experiences in foreign foods (if they have not tried them yet) since it is via school lunches that most new usages – meat consumption, milk, whalemeat bacon, Western cakes as snacks – are introduced to the population at large. And while one assumes that the Japanese government makes efforts not to allow the school lunches to be used as platforms for advertising particular food manufacturers and their products, there is no question that tastes are formed for particular types of products through the consumption of new, and foreign foods, in the school lunch.

As in other Asian societies, education is very highly valued. For the past hundred years, since the Meiji Restoration (1868), it has been the ticket to a better life for the individual. Participation in the educational system has meant the success of Japan as a nation, as well as for individuals. Japanese children tend to spend more time, annually, at school, than many others (ranking consistently in the top ten worldwide), and, probably, tend to score extremely high in total hours studying, if homework hours, club hours, and cram school (*juku*) hours are included as well. A Japanese child cramming for the university entrance exams might spend twenty hours a day studying for at least the year before taking the university entrance examinations. *Whatever* is learned in school, is accorded a high value (if only because the school system *says* it is valuable), including food consumption. The process of education does not, however, terminate after childhood. The process of living, in any society, is also a process of learning. How then do Japanese, as adults, learn about their cuisine?

8.2 *LEARNING AS AN ADULT: SOCIAL INTERACTION AND MEDIA*

THE KNOWLEDGE OF Japanese cuisine that the average Japanese possesses is often impressive. When Michael first came to Japan he was offered a lift by a group of road workers in Hokkaido. He spent the day with them, and was treated by this

Japanese equivalent of red-necks or Black Country coal miners to an exhibition and series of informed debates on foods, food preparation, correct seasonings, seasonal foods, where the best wild mushrooms were to be found and what was to be done with them, and whether the weakness of Akita *sashimi* establishments was compensated for by the richness of its winter cookery. It would be quite rare to experience the same breadth and depth of conversation with similar workers elsewhere in the world.

Japanese of many ages and backgrounds are capable of discussing their own food culture with a great degree of knowledge and experience. Some of Michael's Japanese students, resident in the UK for several years, are amazed that they can neither find nor identify local or regional food specialities in the British town where they live. However they could describe, with great detail, desirable qualities of such foods as noodles and soups, and provide information about the "best" (most famous) places to eat these foods in their home-towns in Japan. Some of that, at least, is owed to a genre of popular Japanese literature – *manga.*

One of the means by which information is conveyed in the modern world is by mass publication. Japan is almost unique in the ubiquity and mass of one special type of publication – *manga* comics – which are read by virtually everyone in the population. Certainly, they are a prime source of information for individuals – blue-collar workers, petty tradesmen – who, in other countries, might read to a far lesser degree.

> "The salt that goes with the tempura mushrooms is a natural sea salt. It is made in Australia."
>
> "Australia? Hmm, indeed, using this natural Australian salt brings out the best in the *tempura* mushrooms."
>
> "I never realised that one could make a meal solely out of mushrooms. And these are all grown in Japan, of course. Mushrooms come from Western cuisine, but of course in Japan, we have developed so many ways of making them."
>
> (Oishinbo #45: 22–23)

Manga are ubiquitous. The comic books, usually monochrome (though some, for obscure reasons, are printed on pink paper) can be seen in coffee shops and on trains, read by business types in three-piece suits, students waiting for their friends, and workingmen on their way home. They are truly *books*, soft bound, one to two hundred pages thick. They cover every subject under the sun, from baby raising to scatological sex. Several hundred *manga* are published in Japan every month. They have become a form of folk art, providing new narrative and artistic techniques, and serving as the launch pad for a variety of ideas, fads, and choices.

And they talk about food. The dialogue reproduced above comes about because the protagonist's girlfriend's parents are dissatisfied by a Western meal he invites them to, and so he takes them out to a small Japanese snack bar. These comic books – distinctively drawn by schools of artists with similar styles – are a lively and interesting window into Japanese society. Each book is divided into several episodes, with a curious similarity.

There are two general types of cooking *manga*. In the "lone hero" type, a traditional-minded or modern hero either learns or teaches the virtues of a particular dish or procedure. Thus the lone wandering stranger of *Hōchō Mushuku* ("Vagabond [Cooking] Knife") who fails a challenge – to slice and prepare a particular fish – at a small *fugu* (blowfish) bar, takes lessons in knife sharpening from a recluse and returns to demonstrate his skill. In contrast, the other type, the "double-act", has two protagonists, usually a clown and a straight man, muddling through life and learning about new dishes, procedures, or foods. The bumbling clown of *Ajimonme* learns to keep *fugu* safe after a tramp steals one of the fish and the entire restaurant erupts in an uproar for fear the tramp will die.[2] *Manga* are also physically present in food environments as well:

> Sitting in a small *kabayaki* bar and waiting for the grilled eel to arrive, one reaches for the comic book from a pile set on the side for the patrons. The drawings are in some ways more detailed than Western comics, the characters more human, as they hem and haw, scratch their heads, and the artist bends or twists their expressions or body movements to indicate extreme emotion or stress. And reading through the story, puzzling out the sometimes very folksy terms, one finally comes to "*the picture*": at some point in the story there is always a detailed drawing of some dish that is part of the plot. A series of panels surrounds this "main course", and discuss the dish, the procedure, or the food, in didactic detail.
>
> "There are ten kinds of *fugu* in Japanese seas, of which we eat four kinds: *torafugu*, *mabugu*, *karasufugu*, and *shirafugu*", says one character in a series of panels that illustrate the poisonous yet delicious blowfish.
>
> "We make a Japanese version of mushroom salad by cutting up the mushrooms with *Japanese* (original emphasis in the text) greens, and delicately flavouring with sesame oil, rice vinegar, lemon juice, and salt," details a counterman in the mushroom story quoted above.
>
> Having been drawn to eat *kabayaki* precisely by such an illustrated story, one can now watch the counterman with greater knowledge and sophistication: we know what he is doing and why.

2 The safe preparation of toxic yet exquisitely tasting *fugu* (*Tetraodontidae*, which includes puffers and globefish, all with poisonous viscera) requires, in addition to the standard fish cook's training, a specialised course and practical examination, upon which successful candidates receive a certificate. This certificate is prominently displayed at the entrance to any shop that serves *fugu*. The distinctive taste (and aftertaste) of *fugu* is doubtless due to minute traces of tetradotoxin that remain, despite the most meticulous treatment and which, though harmless, leave a tingly sensation on the tongue and mouth for several hours after eating. Between 1863 and 1963 more than 10,000 cases of *fugu* poisoning were reported in Japan, out of which 6,000 were fatal. Almost all of these were the result of preparation by amateurs. There have been no reported deaths from professionally prepared *fugu* since the 1960s.

Cooking *manga* do not only dispense recipes, but they also drive home two other aspects of Japanese society generally, and of cooking specifically. Most of the comics extol, by demonstration, exhortation, and example, traditional Japanese virtues. The "rōnin"-like sword-for-hire-but-with-principles protagonist of *Hōchō Mushuku* demonstrates persistence, strength, and masculine imperviousness (though one feisty lady mutters "*Baka* [idiot]!" under her breath as he walks away after she has made her favourable inclinations clear to him: modernity is found in strange places!!). The straight man in *Ajimonme* is always cheerful, hardworking, generous, and studious, and even his clowning friend – lazy, untutored, dreaming of wealth – learns a lesson at the end of every episode. And the surrounding characters (there are rarely any out-and-out villains, unlike the one-dimensional rabid villain-brave hero dichotomy of American comics) in the stories are complex, human, salt-of-the-earth types. Thus do we confound modernity and euphorise tradition. In other words, *manga* are and can be part of that ill-defined, broadly understood element of Japanese nationalist sentiment – *nihonjin-ron* – which characterises other aspects of Japanese cuisine.

And yet, paradoxically (and not always in the same panels, but often in the same episodes) we also introduce the influence of the modern world, Westernisation, and of changing Japan. The settings of course are modern – the tall grey buildings and multi-storey offices of modern Japan – but in addition, we also are taken on tours of Western foods, Western restaurants. We are often shown them as inferior unless Japanised, but the stream of foreign influences is definitely not forgotten nor ignored.

Manga are read by virtually everyone, it is to be remembered. And people are *taught* in *manga*. Taught not only about foods which one would not expect working-class people to be adventurous about, but also that *they should be willing and able to try these "fussy" and upper-class activities.* In other words, the *manga* by emphasising common Japanese-ness, and by showing working-class (and other) people as gourmets in their own right, encourages people of all backgrounds to pursue these foods. The *manga* (and other, more dedicated media channels, such as food magazines, home-maker magazines, TV shows, and so on) provide the average Japanese with a sense that these foods – some of them real "gourmet" items, in the sense that small delicate sensations are encouraged and encountered – are the province of everyone, not just of the elite, who may run into things like that in their expensive clubs and big houses.

Certainly one gets the feeling that the strength of Japanese cuisine is in its very permeation into every nook and cranny of society. This is not to say that everyone eats that well, or has access to such foods or such delicacies, but that, when the occasion arises, even the roughest sort of person *could* know how to enjoy the subtleties of such food. An Ethiopian informant of Michael's once said, "Every person should comport himself in such a way that, if the country suddenly decides to crown him king, he should be able to carry it off without embarrassment." In the same way, the message of the cooking *manga* is that every person faced by a dinner of exquisite Japanese delicacies, should know what he is eating, and be able to comment on it intelligently. True, people rarely live up to the image, people eat a variety of bad things, junk food, frozen meals. But the ideological concept is there, is ready for exploitation, because of these popular media channels.

Two of the images evoked by *manga* – epicureanism and "internationalism" – are heavily played in the more specialised food and home journals. It is not surprising, parenthetically, that the third element in the tripod – Japanese virtues, or *nihonjin-ron* – is dropped. For the reason that, primarily, cooking journals are aimed at a different audience, largely young, modern-feeling women. Their concept of Japanese culture and what it implies differs substantially from the male-oriented *manga*.[3] Nonetheless, these too serve as a channel by which the fusion of Japanese and international cooking, and no less, the appreciation of such foods, reaches the mass of Japanese.

One of the most significant channels is the television-journal-book triangle of food media familiar from the BBC. Cooking and, no less, food appreciation programmes are legend. NHK, the Japanese equivalent of the BBC, has of course the lion's share. And several monthly magazines, targeted largely, but not exclusively, at different segments of the female population, accompany many programmes. Here too there is a something of a line drawn between different target populations: traditional food epicures, modern foodies, young/older men, young/older women. Some of these programmes might explore the biochemical characteristics of a particular food element, such as riboflavin, to an (apparently) intent studio audience. Others are spoof or competition shows, in which peculiar or strange foods are explored by volunteers or media stars. In still others, the intricacies of foreign food centres and attractions are explored in greater or lesser depths. And some shows allow the negative side of Japanese gourmandism to show, by the overt public consumption of rare animals: an exercise in conspicuous consumption that puts almost any other in the shade.

It is highly significant that knowledge of foods is so deeply disseminated to the Japanese populace at a *popular* level. It means, in essence, that Japanese cuisine has completed a journey into the creation of a cuisine that is mature: it has broadly disseminated itself into most of the populace, it is welcoming to foreign innovations and introductions, and yet, at the same time, it preserves mechanisms which maintain many of its original features. It is true that massive changes have occurred in food practices in the past one hundred and fifty years. These changes have occurred in *every* institution in Japanese society. Not even the most traditional institutions today are as they have been in Japan in the early Shōwa period, let alone during the Taishō, Meiji or Edo periods. Yet, somehow one is struck by the ability of Japanese to maintain the cores of their traditional culture, however much they have modified their surface expressions.

3 There are numerous women- and girl-oriented *manga*. These deal with themes such as friendship, love, human relationships, work problems and so on. Interestingly enough, the cooking *manga* (at least those we have seen) are largely, in tone, protagonist, and language, male-oriented. We would suppose that most of their reading audience are males.

win

Travel the World Contest – Please list 5 globe symbols below, as shown on page 49. *(There are at least 5 globe symbols in this issue.)*

PAGE # 20 69 8 ____ ____

free advertiser information

Please circle the numbers (below) of the advertisers from whom you would like to receive more information. Listings are found on pages 62 and 63.

name ______

title/occupation ______

company ______

address ______

city/state/zip/country ______

phone ______ e-mail ______

1	11	21	31	41	51	61	71
2	12	22	32	42	52	62	72
3	13	23	33	43	53	63	73
4	14	24	34	44	54	64	74
5	15	25	35	45	55	65	75
6	16	26	36	46	56	66	
7	17	27	37	47	57	67	
8	18	28	38	48	58	68	
9	19	29	39	49	59	69	
10	20	30	40	50	60	70	

Card expires April 30, 2001. Entries received after expiration date will not be processed.

WT 2/2001

Remove this bookmark and take it with you for a quick reference to pit stops on the information superhighway. **Turn to the BOOKMARKS special section on page 55.**

book|**MARKS**

FTD
www.ftd.com/nwa

ONCONTACT SOFTWARE CORPORATION
www.oncontact.com

TELEPOST, INC
www.telepost.com

UNIVERSITY OF MICHIGAN EXECUTIVE EDUCATION
www.execed.bus.umich.edu

VICTORY CIGARS
www.victorycigars.com

WWWRRR
www.wwwrrr.net

ZF LINUX DEVICES, INC.
www.zflinux.com

Remove this bookmark and take it with you for a quick reference to pit stops on the information superhighway. **Turn to the BOOKMARKS special section on page 55.**

book|**MARKS**

FTD
www.ftd.com/nwa

ONCONTACT SOFTWARE CORPORATION
www.oncontact.com

TELEPOST, INC
www.telepost.com

UNIVERSITY OF MICHIGAN EXECUTIVE EDUCATION
www.execed.bus.umich.edu

VICTORY CIGARS
www.victorycigars.com

WWWRRR
www.wwwrrr.net

ZF LINUX DEVICES, INC.
www.zflinux.com

Remove this bookmark and take it with you for a q reference to pit stops on the information superhigh **Turn to the BOOKMARKS special section on page**

book|**MARKS**

FTD
www.ftd.com/nwa

ONCONTACT SOFTWAF CORPORATION
www.oncontact.com

TELEPOST, INC
www.telepost.com

UNIVERSITY OF MICHIG EXECUTIVE EDUCATIO
www.execed.bus.umich.e

VICTORY CIGARS
www.victorycigars.cor

WWWRRR
www.wwwrrr.net

ZF LINUX DEVICES, I
www.zflinux.com

PLACE
STAMP
HERE

NORTHWEST AIRLINES

WORLD Traveler

9655 SW Sunshine Court, Suite 500
Beaverton, OR 97005

NORTHWEST AIRLINES

WORLD Traveler

NORTHWEST AIRLINES

WORLD Traveler

See reverse side for a quick reference to pitstops on the information superhighway.

Tear it off and take it with you!

NORTHWEST AIRLINES

WORLD Traveler

8.3 *THE* MEIBUTSU *CULTURE*

"WHAT ARE THE *meibutsu* (famous products or specialities) of this town?" asked a group of Japanese students overseas, when discussing a proposed trip. This question – 'what are the famous foods/products' – is one that occupies a great many hours in Japanese books, travelogues, discussions, and television programmes. The interest illustrates some important conceptual differences in the ways Japanese and others see their own, and other cultures.

The idea that special products are best, or are finest, from some specific source is of course common throughout most culinary cultures. Dumas (1958) among others, records details of local specialities. Bedouin in the Sinai will drive fifty kilometres through rough terrain with empty water containers to secure some water from the granite-fed streams of the monastery of St. Catherine's, and wine-lovers can recite the names of varietal grapes and where the best of them grow.

The Japanese idea of *meibutsu* transcends the idea of localism, transforming it into a medium of social exchange as well as an economic element. With the emergence of 'tourism' under the guise of pilgrimage in pre- and early-modern Japan, specialities of particular places started emerging into national consciousness. Many of these derived from the religious nature of the touristic momentum: water from holy springs, the fruit of particular mountains, the products of towns on major pilgrimage routes. However, as tourism became more and more a popular phenomenon, and as Japanese started exploring their country to a greater extent, there was more demand for specific local products which would provide the purchasing traveller with a bona fide identification that he had "been there." A large number of books and magazines now identify and catalogue the *meibutsu* of various areas in Japan (and some outside it) to the point that the production of new *meibutsu* has taken off as a minor industry. Many of these *meibutsu*, perhaps the majority of them, are articles of food, either foodstuffs (tea, rice, saké, sweets, and fruit are very common) or ready-to-consume foods, including *bentō* (box lunches). Many of course do provide in and of themselves signs to the origin of the food. These might be by association, direct or indirect, or through actual iconisation: Yuzawa, in which a festival celebrating Akita dogs takes place every winter, sells *meibutsu* in the shape of white dogs made of *mochi*.

The importance of *meibutsu* as an element in "Japanese-ness" has grown because of the growing homogenisation of Japanese society. Since at least the fifties, and starting even earlier, much of the local character of the Japanese countryside has been swamped by the growing power of the metropolitan centre. This can be seen in all fields of life. Partly this is the effect of modernisation, and particularly of the growing power of the centre, mainly Tokyo and its government and economic offices, over the countryside. Partly it is the effect of communication, writ large. Communication allows young people (and older ones too) to travel to the metropolis – the vast urban and cultural sprawl where most Japanese live – and return from there with new, non-local ideas.

Communication in the form of the media – printed material, television, radio – usually presents the central (as opposed to the prefectural/rural) point of view and elements of culture. Partly the effect derives from demographic movement as younger people leave the periphery and head for the large cities and population areas to make a living. A net result has been a decline in the population of smaller and more rural areas, and, in many cases, a loss of their sense of identity. Local authorities and individuals have countered this tendency by a variety of means, ranging from the provision of services through maintaining ties with "expatriates." Certainly, one important way has been providing support for, and even inventing *meibutsu*, some with historical connections that imply great antiquity. This is true of the numerous new forms of *bentō* that have emerged in the past few decades, as well as attempts by rural areas to revive their connections with city people by the provision of special local foods (Knight 1996) and produce. This has meant that a growing number of local communities have been searching, some desperately and hopefully, others with more certainty, for foods and other items that will represent them to the national public. Of course, there is an economic element here, and some manufacturer or other, as well as shops, benefit from the commerce generated. Far more significant, however, is that the creation, regeneration, or sale of a *meibutsu* provides a rallying point for local feelings and local pride. Some of this is also engendered by other means, such as the creation or support of local festivals, shrines, and special events. The creation of a *meibutsu*, however, is similar to the production of that other icon of tourism, the photograph. Gifts from afar, brought back by one's acquaintances, particularly when they are accompanied, as they often are, with a note about provenance and locale where they were bought, provide graphic, tactile, sensual testimony to the quality and goodness, the rich cultural heritage, the ancient history, of the place from which they came. They also generate publicity. The local places become the equivalent of other places throughout Japan, a place with a name that has been noticed.

Paradoxically, this move is in a sense doomed to failure. The natural progression of modern economics foils this attempt simply because it submerges any attempt to be individual and noticed, into a large sea of similarly inclined efforts. Thus the Japanese postal system produces several times a year catalogue books from which one may order delicacies from many places in Japan without ever having been there, or having spent any money there except that for the item itself. Thus *meibutsu* from numerous places can be acquired without the main purpose – identifying the place they come from to those from the outside, and by doing so making it special – ever occurring. Many *meibutsu* also become so famous, that they become discrete entities in their own right, divorced from necessary locality associations. What is worse, one can buy them virtually anywhere, possibly limiting the benefits of the *meibutsu* to the local economy. Hokkaido *kegani* (hairy crabs), an expensive local delicacy, can be bought by post, as can Uji tea, or "*domu bentō*" (dome box lunch) named for a particular baseball stadium, now evolved into a staple box lunch at nationwide baseball stadia.

8.4 *CHANGING TASTES: THE WORLD OF FOOD FADS*

In 1856 the Japanese had their second exposure to Europe, and with it, a second surge of Western food fads. The first had occurred when Portuguese traders first contacted the Japanese in 1501. The results of the first contact, culinarily speaking, were the introduction of maize, sweet potatoes, and wheat, largely in the form of sweet dishes (for example, sponge cake, which is known as *kasutera* and is one of the *meibutsu* of Nagasaki), and of a new method of cooking – *tempura* – still popular today. The results of the second exposure were more far-reaching, and this exposure is interestingly viewed as food fads, which, in the Japanese experience, have often been a first step in the Japanisation of foods.

For our purposes, a food fad is a measurable rise in demand for a particular food. Usually this rise in demand is for a food that has been either unknown or largely ignored until the fad catches on. It usually affects one particular segment of the population, and usually ends with the sinking of the food into obscurity. During the fad, new ways of consuming the food emerge, usually based on previously known and utilised modes of cooking, into which the new food is "fitted." Or not. The examples we bring are from different modern periods, and have ended in somewhat different ways.

The arrival of a meat-hungry population of foreigners after 1854 did much to disturb the Japanese. Arguments pro-beef eating (the major preference of both British and American expatriates) went against the strictures of many Buddhist churches, though by no means all.[4] In practice upper-class Japanese, as well as those who lived in the mountains and thus had access to game, had been eating meat in small quantities throughout history. Beefsteak "in the Western style" enjoyed a period of intense popularity from about 1890 to the end of the century. The number of restaurants serving beef had increased since Rengatei opened in 1868 at the Ginza. The well-known Iroha restaurant, dedicated to meat dishes, was opened in 1878. To put this in perspective, the American Navy forced Japan to open its borders in 1854, and the Emperor Meiji had been restored to "power"[5] in

4 One of Michael's friends, a Buddhist priest, entertained him at a *horumon* bar, which specialises in stewed and grilled innards. When asked about the Buddhist doctrine of *ahimsa* (refraining from taking life), he responded airily that that was a different kind of Buddhism "not the real thing."

5 Things were, of course, far more complicated. The decision of the *shogun* to abdicate and return power to the Emperor, a brave and thoughtful political act, for which the seventeenth Tokugawa shogun rarely receives much credit, merely exchanged one group of elderly clan leaders from the Matsudaira clan (from whom the ruling Tokugawa house sprang) for another slightly younger group from the hitherto out-of-power Shimazu, Mori, Satake, and some other clans. *Plus ça change, plus c'est la même chose,* except that the newest bunch of oligarchs soon found themselves committed to modernisation (including adopting Western food) as a means of chucking the foreigners out, rather than just chucking them out, which had been one of the original rallying cries of the Restoration. For more information on the people who ran Japan subsequent to the Restoration, Akamatsu's *1868*, and *The Deer Cry Pavilion* are probably best.

1868, which date marks the beginning of Japan's modern era. Very quickly, the eating of beef became something of a Japanese speciality, a niche food in a culture of niche foods. Some areas in Japan, notably areas around Kobe, Matsuzaka, and a small area in Akita, have specialised in the production of superior beef for the table:

> One does not normally associate steaks with Japanese cooking, so when we ate for the first time at Saitō's steak house in a back street in Yuzawa, we were surprised at the offering – large sizzling iron plates bearing thick grilled steaks in an aroma of charred, perfectly grilled meat. It was served with a knob of herb butter on top, with exquisitely cut vegetables: carrots and a tomato, and some snow peas, and a delicate scoop of mashed potato. Bowls of rice, of course, came separately.
>
> "Was it tender?" the young son of the owner asked anxiously.
>
> We assured him it was, and he relaxed with a satisfied smile.

"Steak should be tender enough to cut with a fork," another friend explained later. "Pink inside, full of juice, but most importantly, soft as butter." The British, who still occasionally eat hung meat (BSE notwithstanding) will understand the sentiment, but the process is completely different, a Japanese adaptation to Japanese taste. Cattle are fattened on a diet of beer or saké lees (and, not coincidentally, the three major famous beef producing areas are also famous for their saké), and massaged repeatedly. This gives the meat a unique flavour, and, more importantly, distributes the fat throughout the meat so that cut against the grain, the meat has a lacy appearance. A British butcher, proud of the milky layer of fat that coats his beef, would probably not accept this as "real" beef, but to the Japanese taste, the permeation of fat throughout the meat ensures the desired *texture* as well as taste.

And Japanese beef is of course expensive. Now that cheap Australian beef is available, some of the heat and price has gone out of the meat debate, though it remains high, particularly for *wagyu* (beef raised in Japan): one hundred grams of the best Matsuzaka beef retailed in 1996 at ¥6,000. Certainly in the early years of the century, the issue was not price: the pro and con parties, on the grounds of religion (Buddhism formally frowns on meat consumption), of Japanese culture, of aesthetics (meat-eaters smell, to the Japanese sensitive nose. "*Bata-kusai* [stinking of butter]" used to be a common anti-European epithet), raged for decades.

Whatever the case, meat eating in Japan has risen quite substantially. At almost all levels and locales, this has meant a *Japanisation* of the meat dishes. Not only the meat itself, as in the case of the more expensive cuts. For example, one major international hamburger chain caters to local taste with the provision of plum jam as a relish: a localisation not practised in most other countries. Meat exporters from the major meat exporting countries such as the US, Canada, and Australia, recognise the importance of such localisation. And, although many Japanese households continue to prefer Japanese beef for reasons of taste, many others will buy foreign beef *if it is cut to fit their preferences and modes of cooking.* That is, the preparation and presentation of meat, whether Western or Japanese recipes, is by the use of Japanese presentation rules. What had started as a fad, an element in the fad for all things Western, has become deeply embedded in Japanese culture.

To illustrate the issue, we can examine one of the categories of foods mentioned here: hamburger. For the Western reader, this, presumably, conveys a particular idea: a patty of meat, with or without garnishing, served in a baked bread bun. In the United States this is the ultimate convenience meal, and indication of "American-ness" (much more so now than apple pie). It is something that defines and exemplifies not only food, but an industrial and commercial idea and ideal. Hostages rescued from captivity, young children, teenagers all crave (at least apparently) this quintessential ideal of Americana.

The Japanese term transliterated here is actually defined and written in two different ways: *hanbāga* and *hanbāgu.* These two foods are, in semantic and culinary terms, indicative of the essential points we have been making above. A *hanbāga* is, like its American original,[6] a meat patty served on a bun, with or without garnishes. Indeed, when "*hanbāga*" is mentioned, the meaning refers almost entirely to the product of one or another of the giant franchise chains that are available in much of Japan's cities. "*Hanbāgu*" on the other hand, refers to a different dish. It is a patty of grilled or fried meat, covered in a brown sauce, served on a plate with rice, possibly pickles, and a bowl of *miso shiru.* It is a matter of choice whether one considered these foods to be related but separate forms (the presence of the meat patty, and their probably similar origin would indicate that) or whether one considers them two different foods: a Western food consumed by Japanese, made to Western (that is, American) standards or presented in a Western manner, and a "Japanised" food style derived from some foreign original.

In the broader context, the *hanbāga* – *hanbāgu* dichotomy exemplifies the issue of food adoption and adaptation in Japan. It indicates how successfully the Japanese have been in incorporating foreign foods, while, simultaneously, erecting compartments which insulate, in a sense, these types of experience and category from one another. They also indicate how Japanese culture "domesticates" foreign cultural elements, blending them into its own preferences, and, in effect, offering a smooth series of transitions from "foreign food" through "foreign food slightly domesticated" to "thoroughly domesticated" to "Japanese food". Moreover, it is precisely these public eating places – restaurants, bars – that provide the domain in which many of these foods begin to penetrate Japanese cuisine while at the same time they undergo a process of domestication.

6 Our own cultural prejudices incline us to accept the claim of Louis' Diner in downtown New Haven that the hamburger was invented there. Whatever the case, there is evidence for the consumption of fried meat patties in New York in the mid nineteenth century. Perhaps the reporter never made his way to New Haven. The food has no connection (to our knowledge) to the city of Hamburg in Germany.

More interesting is the emergence and transformation of another food – curry. Many of the British traders and engineers who arrived on Japanese shores at the end of the nineteenth century to exploit its riches, had arrived in Japan via India. Not unnaturally they had brought with them their culinary preferences, notably a British dish that had evolved in Anglo-Indian homes called "curry." This was a derivative of Indian food tailored to English taste and sensibilities. In Japan the British taught their local cooks to prepare "curry" to their liking, and, not unnaturally, interest in foreign things in Japan being what it was, many of these cooks retired to open their own businesses.

"*Karē-raisu*" – curried rice – became a rage. Restaurants sprang up around foreign-dominated cities such as Yokohama. So pervasive was the demand, and intriguing the taste, that one Japanese newspaperman, carried away, one assumes, claimed that the wonderful food *karē-raisu* would bring civilisation and modernity to the Japanese people. In post World War II Japan *karē-raisu* became a staple of school lunches. Notwithstanding our friend Noto-san's claim that school lunches have ruined the Japanese palate (or perhaps because of it?), *karē-raisu* is a staple in many school lunches and student diners. Its popularity is strongly reinforced by two things. First, the culturally popular mode for "internationalisation" that runs deep in Japan. It means, for most Japanese, the mixing of foreign exotic items into one's daily life, including one's diet. *Karē-raisu* is no longer exotic: indeed, in our survey, most people counted it as a Japanese food, and so it is. Another factor is the growing demand in Japanese society for convenience foods. Modern technology has formed the *karē-raisu* base into chocolate-bar shaped cakes. Mixed with hot water this produces a paste that is redolent of the spices (cinnamon, turmeric, cumin, fenugreek, some chilli) that go into its making. Its consistency, probably familiar to any eater of British curries, is very thick, due to a butter and flour roux (the word is now Japanese [*ru*] thanks to curry recipes). The sauce is enhanced with vegetables and sometimes meat or very rarely, prawns (we never personally encountered any fish *karē-raisu* though this too is probably offered somewhere).[7] Richer, more elaborate *karē-raisu* come in the form of *katsu karē-raisu*: with a deep fried pork cutlet. The thick curry-flavoured sauce is poured on a bowlful of rice, and a pickle added. This innovation is attributed to many sources, among them the foreign settlement in Yokohama, as well as the Kawagin restaurant in Asakusa which claims their curry-sauce smothered pork cutlet on rice dates from its humble beginning as a mobile kiosk (*yatai*) during the early Taishō period.

Significantly, we see the contributions of a number of factors to the success of imported foods. First, the introduction of a new, exotic food from overseas by importers. Then the broadcasting of this new food in the form of a health or

7 Though not exactly akin to the *hambāga-hambāgu* dichotomy, a *karē-raisu* and *raisu-karē* dichotomy exists. While both terms are fairly interchangeable in restaurant and roadside diner menus, the distinction is that the curry sauce may sometimes come in a separate container, usually a ceramic sauceboat, for *raisu karē*.

health-related and supposed virtue (in the case of *karē*, modernisation). Additionally, the input from the food industry, which is quick to capitalise on the product, via institutional forms (school lunches) and product differentiation (apple *karē*, Vermont *karē*, honey *karē*), and disseminate it far and wide. Throughout this process we also see the gradual assimilation – in form, texture, flavour, serving – of the food into the daily life of people.

In 1979, living in a small northern town we wanted to make a special dessert for some friends, and scoured the town, unsuccessfully, for cream cheese. Half a year later Jeanne was surprised to find one local supermarket with 4 packages, and promptly stocked up. It was then that we became aware, through friends in the metropolis and through journal publications, of the *reya chiizukēki* fad.

There is a belief, common in the West, that Asians, notably Chinese and Japanese, are unable to digest milk, and that therefore their diet lacks that particular food. This is of course not true. Lactase deficiency is the result of weaning from milk, and most people (excluding those of whatever culture who have a genetic lactase deficiency) can digest milk or milk products *provided* they have continued to consume cow's milk after natural weaning. Traditionally of course, lacking the wide grazing areas needed for proper dairy culture, neither Chinese nor Japanese rice farmers raised cattle. Until the mid 70s, it was difficult to find milk products in Japan, though milk production, particularly in Hokkaido, Nagano and Chiba, near Tokyo, had taken off and milk was supplied regularly at all shops and even sold from automatic dispensers.

The origins of *reya chiizukēki* popularity are obscure, but by the summer of 1980, it had become a fad. There were recipes in all the women's and cooking magazines, and several food journals ran multi-paged spreads on the "best" recipes, and the "best" confectioneries for the food. One can trace the fad certainly to the renewed passion of the Japanese for things foreign and its confluence with re-established economic confidence after the 1973 oil shock.

The food is still very common, and indeed, we argue that *chiizukēki* has become a Japanese food as much as *karē-raisu* is. Some of the housewives in our sample simply thought of it as another Japanese food, one for *oyatsu*, in line with other Japanese foods that they would eat on a daily basis. In fact, when asked to name kinds of cake, it is usually the first or second (after chocolate) that most of our respondents, young and old, named.

One indication of the degree to which this fad has become a regular unremarkable element of the diet, are the variations, some of them specifically Japanese, that have emerged:

> Shimo-Kitazawa used to be a sleepy neighbourhood, situated at the intersection of two commuter train lines. Since the seventies, it has become the hub of an entertainment and shopping district for the young and trendy. Incorporating clothes and knickknack shops, modern bars and night-clubs, and fashionable food shops, it offers everything for the young.

> The coffee shop we enter is by no means exceptional, not even if compared with shops outside Shimo-Kitazawa. With several small tables, and a long counter with glassed refrigerator, one can eat in or take-out. The display, as are all Japanese food displays, is mouth-watering. Cream cakes in a variety of colours, an array of biscuits and dried baked things, some made on the premises, others purchased from other sources, some imported. The coffee shop is one of three in a chain. Trying to decide what to sample, on the basis of looks alone, is exhausting and frustrating. A greenish cake topped with the familiar sweet purple-brown *daizu* beans catches the eye. It is a tea-flavoured cheese cake – a fluffy soufflé-type cheese cake infused delicately with the taste of powdered green tea (*matcha*), more usually confined to Tea ceremony use. Cream cheese filling between layers has been flavoured with a very light touch, and the topping of whipped cream is finished with crunchy bits of sweet beans, tasting salty, sweet, and rather chocolaty (perhaps due to the dark brown colour of the azuki beans) at the same time. The contrast of textures and flavours is of course intentional. A mocha cake we also try, it too garnished with beans, conveys much the same contrast, with different degrees of mocha flavouring in the batter and the cream, and the beans adding a unique Japanese character to the Western cake.

The development of *chiizukēki* from gourmet fad to everyday dish is a process worth commenting upon. Significant factors in its transformation are the intrinsic qualities of cream cheese, its physical presentation as a cake, and the associations linked with it when first introduced. The interest in dairy products such as cheese and yoghurt was very limited at first. "Cheese" was generally understood to be the processed, individually wrapped product and mostly given to children for snacks. Yoghurt was easier to market to the adult population, due to the successful television campaign featuring long-lived peoples whose main diet was yoghurt. Cream cheese from the US, Australia, New Zealand, and the Scandinavian countries started appearing in supermarkets towards the end of the 70s. Because it is soft and not strong-flavoured nor yet strong-smelling, it came across as a not overpoweringly "milky" product. Significantly, the texture of gelatine cheesecake is not too asimilar to several Japanese dishes, such as soft tofu. Also, cheesecake allows itself to be presentable in ways acceptable to the Japanese canon. For example, that it could be cut in clean lines due to the gelatine base probably helped, as well as the possibility of applying subtle pastel shadings to the cheese. This means that the food could be presented *in Japanese aesthetic terms*. Cheesecakes can thus be presented in Japanese style, on Japanese utensils as well as Western ones, as indeed became the case. Finally, cheesecake was promoted, and served initially, in places that catered to a particular clientele: young and sophisticated women. Thus coffee shops that catered largely to women were the first to promote *reya chiizukēki*, and, of course, the features on them were mainly in magazines that had female readership: home and fashion, rather than purely food foci. This was significant. Japanese women "tend to be more open to trying Western foods, particularly those foods not associated with liquor," as one informant, himself the head of a cooking organisation noted. And, in Japanese society, it is women who, reputedly, eat more sweets. This is true of traditional *wagashi* (Michael always attracts odd looks from the female clientele of tea-shops when he indulges in his favourite sweet bean-soup), as of Western confectionery (*yōgashi*). Indeed, as time progressed throughout the eighties, *reya chiizukēki* became an item of common consumption, and, in their attempt to win more customers, confectioners departed from the international image (or, more properly speaking, interpreted it in truly international ways) and gave the food a Japanese twist, as in the coffee-shop we described, where powdered green tea was added to the mix.

The conversion of *chiizukēki* is merely one of a long string of such successful incorporations of foreign tradition in foods, foods which turned from "localised" fads, – whether the Heian court's choice of Chinese modes, the Meiji intelligentsia's choice of beef, or the modern diner's liking for cheesecake – into daily food. But not all such fads become successful. This raises several questions: how do food fads occur? And why do some fads settle and become assimilated into the local cuisine, while other vanish? The question is interesting because it allows for a test of one of our main theses: that Japanese cuisine exhibits a sort of overall unity, one which allows great flexibility and change.

Aloe vera, a succulent, became a major fad during the years 1996–1997. It could be found in a variety of forms on supermarket shelves as well as in cafes and homes. We identified aloe vera drinks (mainly yoghurts), cakes, and a large number of recipes published in women's and cooking magazines. At least one book has been published concerning the cultivation, use, and benefits of the plant.

The year before, a popular Philippine food called *nata de coco* had been extremely popular. *Nata de coco* is made of coconut water that has been allowed to ferment, resulting in a thick crust of a hard-jelly consistency. It is used in desserts, and for many years had been a cottage industry, with some limited industrial manufacture, until its popularity in Japan stimulated investment in larger-scale production. By the summer of 1996, however, *nata de coco* was off the shelves. It was almost impossible to find, except at a newly built gourmet supermarket in Shinjuku and at the bargain section of a department store in Shibuya. Few customers seemed to show any interest in eating or trying it, even at bargain prices.

To understand how these food rises and falls come about, it is useful to examine and compare *nata de coco* and aloe vera. Both of these foods are very similar in culinary terms, though their origins are different. When bought, normally each of these is a translucent whitish cube, less than one centimetre to a side. The texture is that of hard jelly, or, more appropriately, the texture of *kanten*, the Japanese jelly used in *wagashi*. These three foods (*kanten* included) are bland, almost flavourless, and, from anecdotal evidence, their main attraction is their texture.

At this point, however, they begin to diverge. *Kanten* has a long culinary tradition in Japan. It has been used for the making of traditional sweets during the current century and before. Its uses, though restricted mainly to sweet dishes, are connected to the sweet accompaniments for the Tea ceremony. This, essentially, provides the background for *nata de coco* as well. That is, we would argue, it was the similarity of *nata de coco* to *kanten* which made possible the transition from a Philippine dish to a Japanese fad. In the first place, *nata de coco* fits the Japanese canons of taste, in terms of its colour, texture, and taste. Two other factors added to *nata de coco*'s attraction. The growing number of Japanese going abroad has meant a growing interest in foreign foods, as we have noted before. In addition, the import of *nata de coco*, mainly, apparently, handled by small trading firms (since in the Philippines, manufacture was a cottage industry, and thus of little interest to the large *sōgo shōsha*) meant that a trading "feeding frenzy" of small trading firms occurred. This was bolstered by the fad-generating function of the Japanese youth media, which encourages quick "turnover" of teenage and young adult fads. The fact that the food was associated with "young" culture was not incidental: the name fits the canons of "cutesie" names of which Japanese young women are extremely fond, and which attract their attention (and considerable buying power): cute kittens, real or in cartoon format, little boys in dungarees, and other "*kawaii*-mono" (cute things) are crucially important for marketing to this consumer segment. "*Nata de coco* has a cute sound," confessed one informant. "That's what made it attractive." The confluence of culinary appropriateness, media interest, and quick trading profits meant a sudden boom in the sale of the food. The reverse of these processes spelled the end of the fad. The media lost interest, the profits for the small trading companies shrank as rationalisation set in, and larger firms started getting interested, and manufacturers started taking shortcuts and adulterating the *nata de coco*, as the daily press discovered.

For aloe vera the same process occurred, but with one additional feature. Aloe vera has been used as a cosmetic base for several decades, and some major cosmetic companies market aloe vera-based skin preparations. The plant has a proven record as an attractant for the health-conscious (whether it has indeed the qualities ascribed is a separate, pharmacological issue). In the West, particularly the US, aloe vera has been marketed as a health food. It is not surprising therefore, that aloe vera became a focus of intense interest not only because it fit the food canon, but also because it had an added dimension – health.

At the time of writing, the aloe vera fad was in full swing. It is difficult to tell whether it will survive, or fall as *nata de coco* has. We rather suspect that, possessing a stronger base in the form of its supposed healthy benefits, the possibility of raising the plant, and utilising it on a household basis (which several of our informants do), is more likely to mean that the plant, and some of its uses, will be incorporated into Japanese cuisine. One magazine featured aloe vera *sashimi*, the translucent green slices laid on an elegant plate, and served with the usual accompaniments of soy sauce and horseradish. This is not to mean that it will continue riding the wave of popularity it enjoyed in mid-1996, but rather that, like *karē-raisu* it may gradually be incorporated into Japanese cuisine whether as a sweet or neutral tasting drink (such as Calpis, Oolong tea, or *saidā*,[8] have been), as a health-food drink among the many variations now entering the market (e.g., aluminum-packed carrot-celery-parsley, tomato-apple), as an additive to sweet or savoury yoghurts, as a sweet jelly somewhat like *kanten*, or even, as a salad vegetable or strikingly coloured sauce.

8.5 *INVENTION AND INNOVATION IN THE JAPANESE KITCHEN*

As THE FOOD fads seem to indicate, Japanese culture has justifiably earned its name as an imitative culture. After all, some critics argue, there is only one Japanese scientific Nobel prize winner, but thousands of derivative patents based on work done in other cultures. The things Japanese are famous for – cars, videos, computers – were invented elsewhere, but improved and brought to perfection in Japan, runs the argument. Putting aside for a moment the idea that being able to improve rather than invent is no bad skill to have, it is useful to consider the process of innovation, particularly of food innovation, from the Japanese point of view, in this case, the owner of a traditional *ryōtei*:

> Over the past three generations food preferences have definitely changed. These days there are new cooking methods, with electricity and ovens, that we never used before. We are thus able to adapt our cooking, make it more streamlined, than we could in the days of charcoal fires. And, of course, because Japan is now a world power, at least economically, we have a wide variety of choices from overseas. New information about foods comes from reading books and journals and watching TV. I, or one of my employees, or someone in my family might see a new thing in the media, and decide to give it a try. We also see new things in the supermarket and try them out.
>
> There is a very clear and specific local preference, and local people, whom I serve every day, pride themselves on being gourmets, and on having good palates. They know and express a knowledge of local delicacies, seasonal quality, and local items, and they often demand that they be served these things, which they consider exceptional. In order to

8 Calpis is a drink made by the fermentation of milk. It derives, ultimately, from the Mongolian (alcoholic) drink called *kumis*, though without the alcohol. It has a slightly sourish-sweet taste, rather tart and refreshing. Oolong tea, imported from China, has recently (in the nineties) become an important drink in Japan, though it was present before, preferred particularly for its supposed health benefits. "*Saidā*" is of course a Japanisation of the English "cider" though in Japan the term has come to mean a carbonated lemonade of artificial provenance, with only a bare nod in the direction of a real fruit extract. A similar drink, copied from Victorian lemonades, is still sold (mainly in rural areas) in old-fashioned Victorian bottles with glass stoppers under the name *ramune* (that is, "lemonade").

> try a new food, therefore, we have to keep these things in mind. We try to arrange the new foods and prepare them in such a way that they will fit into local conceptions of good taste and arrangement, and that they fit the quality and nature of the more familiar foods.
>
> Our locals do not like to be surprised by foods, and they quite often prefer to stick with the tried and familiar. That is why when we do introduce new things – whether it is a new dish I have thought of, or an import – we introduce them a little at a time, adapting the new to fit old patterns. We arrange foreign foods in a Japanese manner, or prepare it by Japanese methods.
>
> Avocado is one example. I like the colour of it – the bright green shading to yellow – as well as the smooth texture. To start with, we made it in the form of a *tempura* about five or seven years ago. At first, people were very surprised and somewhat suspicious. Either they asked what it was, or they did not try it at all. Eventually we found that people did not like it in that form. We used it in lightly vinegared salads (*sunomono*) and tried different dressings with it until it took on, and now it is a commonplace thing.

The introduction of a new food into the Japanese kitchen depends, to a very large degree, on the points of similarity Japanese diners and cooks can make between the introduced food and those which they are familiar with. A new food can be conceived of as an item with many sensory characteristics in many dimensions. It has shape, colour, texture, size, in addition to taste. Just so long as several of these dimensions, in concert, fit Japanese characterisations of a food of some category, the foreign food is likely to be accepted.

Like artists everywhere, Japanese cooks – at least the best of them, and those with sufficient independence, financial and spiritual – experiment with new modes of expressing themselves and pleasing their customers. The owner of the *ryōtei* cited above, as well as many others we interviewed, particularly at the upper end of the scale, were constantly looking for new ways to prepare foods, new and innovative foods and menus. Here too, the degree to which a food is likely to enter into the repertoire is dependent on public acceptance, and that in turn is dependent on the tension between familiarity with at least *some* of the characteristics of the food concerned, and newness in other dimensions of the same food.

Since utensils and dishes are an intrinsic part of Japanese food, foreign foods which can fit (aesthetically speaking), and which can be placed on a Japanese (-style) utensil, are much closer to acceptance than others. Of course, utensils are evolving as well, as craftsmen and artists try out new techniques and styles, and as cooks, in the home and in public, try to fit themselves to foods that have already arrived, or are already a part of the food canon. The artistic development of both food and utensils is an intertwined phenomenon: new ideas for both spring from the mind of the artists, and are stimulated by foreign examples and ideas. Neither can, in the Japanese case, evolve and grow without the other, so intimate is the relationship.

Learning to be Japanese, is a lengthy process as Hendry (1986) points out. Among other elements, it implies learning to eat like a Japanese, and this, in turn, is both a process and an end result. The elements in this process start from a fairly early age, as the young child is inculcated, through the world of the school lunch as well as the provisions of his or her household, into the eating *expectations* that others have. Mother is taught how to make a proper *bentō*, the child is taught the importance of rice, of being as others are, of eating properly in the right time and place. But it is also a life-long process. Adults are taught that food is culture by a variety of means, ranging from their office mates and the process of social drinking and eating that are inevitably part of *nemawashi*, through a variety of media such as *manga* which demonstrate to people of all classes, what the virtues of Japanese *are*, certainly when it comes to food. There may also well be a behavioural training element inherent in part of the process. Certainly the association of "Japanese virtues" with "good food" as can be seen in the *manga* and other publications, reinforces the inherent ideology of *nihonjin-ron* as well.

The end product, however, at least in terms of an understanding of Japanese cuisine, seems to be the creation of a food culture. By this we mean that the average Japanese is highly aware, as members of many other cultures may not be, of the subtlety and some of the implications of their foods. Within modern Japanese culture, being knowledgeable about food is, for a number of reasons – national pride, age distinctions, conspicuous consumption – a desirable social ability and accomplishment, much as it may be in France, China, or any other country in which food plays a very forceful element of national identity. As a consequence, many Japanese practice an awareness of their own foods: it becomes a part of their cultural self-identity, both as Japanese, and, often, as residents of a particular part of Japan. Japanese relationship to food is to something that is unique and uniquely pleasurable, subtle, varied. And they relate themselves, as Japanese, to the foods they consume.

READINGS FOR CHAPTER 8

Anderson, Jennifer L. 1991 *An Introduction to Japanese Tea Ritual.*

Arima, Takeru 1987 *Michizure Bentō.*

Ashkenazi, Michael 1989 "Japanization, internationalization and aesthetics in the Japanese meal".

Tagawa, Yasushi 1985 *Hōchō Mushuku.*

White, Merry I. 1993 *The Material Child.*

9 The Art of Dining

DINING AS A ritual – the actions involved in a meal – is worth examining as a whole in its social, cultural and sensory aspects. To do so, we consider two dining experiences. The differences between these cases highlight the elements of dining in its Japanese form. None of these meals was particularly unusual; in one form or other they are easily accessible to anyone. No special or exotic ingredients were involved, no great expense, and anyone could have access to the public meal. These are neither the elaborate dinners of the rich, nor the simple dinners of the poor, but fit somewhere, comfortably, in the vast midst of the "average." The differences and similarities between them illuminate the personal and the public elements of Japanese food culture. We start with dinner at the house of one informant:

> There were seven diners at the house in a middle-income area of a large city. The hostess had laid the table with a place setting for each diner which included a hand-painted menu on Japanese paper, a *hashioke* (chopstick holder or rest) in the shape of a vegetable, and a pair of disposable chopsticks. For each course, the hosts added a flat plate – ceramic, glass, or lacquer as necessary – on which to place the food. These were not distinguishably "Japanese": they were examples of contemporary, well-made tableware such as can be found in any middle-class modern household, virtually anywhere on the globe. In the middle of the table was a large lazy-susan, and the courses were brought to the table in bowls or plates, and were distributed from there.
>
> The meal started with a round of beer served in small coloured glass goblets. With these came two sauce bowls slightly larger than tea-bowl size, one a deep pink, with cottage cheese and mustard seed; the other blue-grey, containing cream cheese with anchovy paste. A large flat oblong plate contained sliced fat green asparagus. Each diner helped him or herself from the bowls, onto a flat individual plate.
>
> The following course was crisp-fried duck. The duck had been marinated, then fried until crisp in a large wok. This was eaten with *shaopin* (the hostess used the Chinese word for these thin wheat pancakes), sliced Japanese leeks, and *hoisin* sauce somewhat like Peking duck, each guest

assembling his own duck roll from the condiments on the table. The dish, as with its kin, Peking duck, is one of the marvels of the kitchen: a marriage of flavours and textures where the whole that emerges is really greater than the sum of its discrete parts. Any unctuousness of the duck is cut by the sharp bite of the fresh leek, and the warm, soft pancake holds all the rich flavours in, ready to be released undiluted into the diner's mouth with each bite.

Next came a large plain cedar tub full of *chirashi-zushi* (mixed sushi). This is often the way Japanese households make sushi, since it is less fussy than the rolled or shaped varieties. It is essentially a rice salad. Here, thinly sliced seafood, raw and cooked, red carrots and brown shiitake mushrooms, chopped green trefoil stems and leaves, fine-sliced omelette, and green and black nori made it very colourful. The rice was delicious, hearty and slightly saltier than it would be at a commercial sushi shop. To accompany it were *tempura*-fried scallop *(hotate)* chunks, much like *kaki-age*, the mixed "fritter" finale of a tempura course at a restaurant.

The *hotate* were followed by a dish of two fried *tai* (sea bream). Bream are adored by the Japanese both for their delicate flavour, and because the name of the fish "*tai*" is homonymous with the Japanese word for congratulations. The fish had been prepared Chinese style (our hostess had worked for some time in China) – the flesh sliced in fillets, leaving the bone, head and tail in one piece, and all fried separately. The entire fish is re-assembled before serving on a big flat plate, then sweet/sour onions and carrots in thickened *katsuo*-based stock poured on top.

One of the guests was a potter, and her strong fingers and shoulders (developed from kneading clay) were called upon to help in the making of buckwheat *(soba)* noodles from scratch. Buckwheat dough is much stiffer and thus harder to work with than an equivalent measure of wheat dough. Even the addition of about ten percent wheat flour did little to make the kneading easier. The dough was kneaded for ten minutes in one batch, then divided and kneaded again in two batches. This process enhances the flavour.

The dough was then rolled thinly, and folded over after it had been lightly floured, then cut with a large knife. The noodles were boiled in water. They were placed in a large tub, after cooling, and each diner was supplied with a small cup filled with dark, salty, slightly sweetish dip *(tsuyu)*. In the centre of the table the hostess placed a wide shallow basket with tempura of small Japanese aubergines, sliced sweet-potatoes, and *piman* (small Japanese green peppers). The colours of the vegetables – purple, bright orange, bright green – peeped from the golden tempura batter to complement the sombre brownish grey of the noodles. Slices of green onion and *wasabi* on a plate were for flavouring the *tsuyu*.

Finally, the last course was slices of watermelon and melon, coffee or tea (green or Western).

Our hostess and her husband were both well-travelled, slightly more, perhaps, than the average Japanese. They lived in a newly built semi-detached house in a Tokyo ward with their one child. The couple both worked, and fitted comfortably within that broad classification of "middle class" to which about 80% of Japanese society belong. The dinner, though elaborate, was not extravagant, and it contained a mixture of standard foods, foods that represented or reflected the family's particular interests, and a desire to put oneself out for a guest: we had discussed the making of *soba* noodles some weeks before.

Suzuya was a serendipitous find. We had gone to see an exhibition of ceramics and pottery, and on the way back, stopped to look for a place to eat in a large office and shop complex. We were not looking for any specific style of food in particular so we looked at all the restaurants in the building. It was not difficult to make up our minds. We chose a bright and cheerful *tonkatsu-ya* (pork cutlet restaurant) which looked out onto the inner and outer gardens of the complex.

> The walls had been decorated with pottery from various kilns in blue-grey and red glazes (the owner's personal collection, we were later to discover). The kitchen was open to view, bright, polished, the people working in silence but for their occasional obligatory "*irasshaimase.*" Most *tonkatsu-ya* have a standard set of condiments on the table: "*sōsu*" a derivative of "Worcestershire sauce" and mustard. The tables at Suzuya were graced by several different condiments: an in-house *sōsu*, mustard, several kinds of pickles. Calling *tonkatsu* pork cutlet does not do it justice. It is really a thick moist lean pork steak, with no fatty bits at all anywhere. It is usually served as a *teishoku* or set meal, with rice and *tonjiru* (miso soup with pork). Suzuya's offering was unique in three ways. First, the menu includes a large exhortation *not* to indiscriminately use the sauce or any other condiment. "The taste of our *tonkatsu* should be enjoyed for itself. It is the best pork, fried in fresh oil. Why cover its taste with a sauce?" The second is the restaurant's speciality, *tonkatsu ochazuke* (pork cutlet tea soup), whose history, qualities, and methods of preparation are narrated in an explanatory sheet at each table. Third, the restaurant made its own pickles and six varieties came in a compartmented tray. The quality of the food – no more expensive than anywhere else – was indeed superb, the flavours carefully balanced, and care taken in the cooking. It was also evident that the ingredients used – the meat and vegetables – had been very fresh.

It is the conceptual harmony that pervaded Suzuya that we wish to explore here. We have already noted that Japanese food is a multi-dimensional experience, in which the dimensions are balanced in ways that make the food and the act of eating it unique. This argument can now be extended to the entire dining experience. The good host, the aesthete Rōsanjin indicates, does his best to ensure that the entire *experience* of dining presents a uniform quality: that is what making good food means. Suzuya is a successful chain of restaurants headquartered in Shinjuku. We were unaware of this fact prior to reading the shop's "literature" which explained the owner's philosophy about the ingredients used throughout the business. The atmosphere of the Suzuya branch at which we ate did not seem at all to be part of a restaurant chain. It had none of the overslick standardisation that occurs when several places have to conform to a set of requirements. In fact it appeared to be a medium-sized pleasant restaurant, with a museum-like ambience from the pottery and other folkcraft displayed on shelves, and the attentive yet unobsequious demeanour of the staff reinforced the feeling that this was the only one of its kind and that the manager was also the proprietor. We were then all the more impressed that the owner of the business has managed, through a concentration of several elements, to ensure that *his* aesthetic vision of a pleasant dining experience has been strongly expressed throughout, from the setting to the food to the attitude of the staff.

Both the meals described – in a private home and in a restaurant – *seem* to be without a temporal context. Yet, as we shall see, all meals have a place in two domains: that of time – at what hour, day, year – they take place, and that of *ritual*: the realm of codified, repetitive and formally elaborated practices. While neither of these show overtly in the two meals discussed, they were present there as well.

9.1 *DINING AND RITUAL IN DAILY LIFE*

RITUAL, IN ANY form of dining, is inescapable. That we, as humans, seek certain foods and disdain certain others, is most often a part of deeply felt ritual activity, which is related to religious feeling, but which, in a far deeper and more fundamental sense of ritual, provides us with order in our lives. By putting up borders of ritual action, ritual exclusions and permissions, we are defining ourselves in one of a myriad of ways as "human." This definition may intend to juxtapose and contrast ourselves with the holy (as Durkheim would have it), or contrast ourselves with wild and savage nature (as Levi-Strauss has stated), or simply to distinguish ourselves from other tribes of humans (one of Douglas's main points). Whatever the case, we surround the process of fuelling our bodies with multiple layers and uses of ritual.

As noted earlier, the religious/spiritual life of Japan is a paradox. It is a country in which most people claim not to have a religion, and yet in which the total number of people affiliated to religious organisations exceeds the total population by about fifty percent. It is also a nation that has been surprisingly open to foreign religious ideas, and yet in which one of the most powerful of those – Christianity – has, after a century of effort, only a handful of not very intense believers.

Part of the key to this paradox lies in the tremendous interweaving of ritual and daily life. Not only is much of Japanese life highly ritualised, including interpersonal interaction, from speech to letter writing – but rituals that derive from religious experiences carry on into daily life. It has been argued (mainly by

Shintō theorists) that Shintō is so highly integrated into Japanese life that it can no longer be viewed as a religion, and must be considered and defined as the essence of Japanese culture, in perhaps much the same way that Judaism, the religion, is very hard to divorce from Jewish culture. Though the claim must be taken with more than a grain of salt, it is nonetheless true that, at least in the realm of food research, there is a high degree of connectivity between religious perceptions (from Shintō and Buddhism alike) and food perceptions.

Japanese religion (in all its elements) is, like many religions, strongly influenced by the agricultural cycle. This has become refined, partly by aristocratic pretensions (a Heian-era lady was convinced peasants were a different species than herself, and yet happily celebrated agricultural events), partly for ideological reasons during modernisation. What has come down to modern life is an intermixture of ritual cycles of several sorts. Very roughly speaking, these can be divided into nation-wide *traditional* dates, nation-wide *national* dates, and local dates. The traditional calendar includes dates of both religious and (in this day and age) secular practices.

All the calendrical cycles begin with the most important single holiday of the year: *Oshōgatsu*, or the New Year. The New Year is itself an amalgam of several ideas: for example, it is now celebrated during the "civil" (Gregorian calendar) new year, on January 1. Traditionally, the Japanese used the Chinese lunar calendar, and the new year would have been celebrated around February. A series of more or less well-marked dates follow. Some of these are of clear religious origin, some of national origin, others mixed. Some are well-known outside Japan, such as Girls Day (March 3rd, originally, third day of the third lunar month) and Boys Day now Children's Day (5th May), and lesser known ones such as *Hatsu Uma* (the First Day of the Horse, 15th February),[1] or Constitution Day. In parallel to the national cycle, there are local cycles of festivity and ritual: local shrines, communities, temples celebrating particular annual events that are important *for them* but may not be important, or even marked by their neighbours two streets away.

Most of these events have particular foods associated with them. These may be highly traditional foods such as the "demon's horns" served on Children's Day (glutinous rice steamed in cones – hence the name – of bamboo leaf), which are supposed to evoke terror (of demons) and the ability to overcome it. They may also be "traditional" in the sense that a *type* of event is expected to be accompanied by it. Festivals and fairs are incomplete without the smells and tastes of street stalls selling hot corn, grilled squid, and corn-dogs in summer, or hot sweet *amazake* and *mochi* in winter.

1 The traditional Japanese calendar follows the Chinese pattern of zodiacal animals in a twelve-day, twelve-month, and twelve-year rotation. This is mixed with other cycles such as the five-element and dyadic (yin and yang) Daoist cycles. *Hatsu uma* is the first day of the zodiacal sign of the horse in the old calendar, and marked by many Shintō shrines as a day special to Inari, the *kami* (deity) of rice and trade, and by some Buddhist temples and Shintō shrines as a day special to Battō Kannon (Horse-headed Kannon), patroness of animals, carters and so on.

The reasons people eat festival and celebratory foods are complex but fairly self-evident: in traditional societies they provide a break from monotony, they appear in the form of newly harvested foods, and they are items of display and conspicuous consumption. Their appearance in the *modern* world, however, is a different thing. Here they represent what is *not.* Corn, squid, grilled chicken, shaved ices are available year round from the shops. But they *also* represent a Japan-that-was, a nostalgic, sometimes politicised harking back to supposed unity, supposed purity, supposed greater consciousness of who the participants are, which are particularly emphasised in festivals and fairs. Families that nowadays rarely see each other, because they are scattered throughout the country, if not the world, can get together and consume *zōni* (New Year rich soup), and by doing so, feel that they are participating not only in their immediate family surroundings, but a family surrounding bolstered by history and custom, ancestors and stability. Doing so once a year reaffirms not only these bonds, but also deeply held desires (common to any population) for regularity and recursive order.

9.2 *DINING ORDER: THE JAPANESE COURSE*

THE RELATIONSHIP OF meals to annual cycles of order leads inevitably inward: to a discussion of the internal order of Japanese meals. It is useful to start with a contrasting example: the case of the European course, which is probably familiar to most readers. In the European dining tradition which emerged from the French revolution, and evolved after the French restoration, certain rules became evident. Roughly they consisted of a progression, from appetite providers – canapés – through a series of courses to a sweet, and finally a savoury course. Each course consisted of a number of dishes, and an entire formal event could take a whole day.

In middle- and lower-class households, this progression of dishes, particularly in the twentieth century, was revised and edited, effectively into anything from one to about four or five courses, taken in strict order. Murcott (1982) notes the importance, in Britain, of the regular constitution and progression of the central meat course, consisting of a cooked meat and starch, normally potatoes and cooked vegetables. There is thus an almost inevitable order about a European dinner, one that demands particular progressions and is scrutinised with great care by the participants.

In contrast to the European meal, of which the French-influenced British meal is a sub-set, Japanese rice-events, even where there is a progression of dishes, retain their orientation towards the rice.

> Late one year, two days before the New Year, we were driving slowly from Kyoto back to Tokyo around Lake Biwa. A snowstorm forced us to seek shelter for the night in a small fishing village on the northern shore. The inn was hesitant to admit us at first, because the cook had gone on holiday.

We replied that it was mainly shelter that we needed (and a very hot bath) and the innkeeper's wife apologised in advance for the poor quality of our evening meal. We had been duly warned, so we proceeded to enjoy the only luxury the inn offered, the enormous baths. When we returned to our room, we were so thoroughly refreshed that we did not mind the prospect of dried fish and pickled vegetables that we were certain was our lot.

The serving maid called us to eat, and slid the adjoining doors to the neighbouring room. There were four footed lacquered trays on the tatami floor. No table. Each tray held several containers, most were lidded bowls of lacquer and ceramic, and it was impossible to see immediately what they contained. It was quite clear then that cook or no cook, the inn was not going to let us go to bed hungry.

One shallow black lacquer bowl, bigger and wider than that used for miso or clear soups, revealed *chawan-mushi.* Often defined as a soup, it is more than that, because it consists of two layers, a savoury custard one, and a clear soup. Based on *dashi* and eggs, this steamed concoction includes vegetables (here, trefoil, shiitake mushrooms, and gingko nuts) and sometimes meat (in this case, tiny shrimp and pieces of red bream), which cluster close to the bottom with the rich stock that separates from the custard once it is cooked. The custard was a warm yellow, shot through with the green of the leaves, cream flesh of the fish, the old ivory of the gingko nuts, and the darker brown of shiitake mushroom.

A bowl for *sashimi* included *toro*, the fatty tender tuna's belly, and some shellfish. *Toro*, the favourite Japanese cut of tuna, is paler and has a softer texture than the rest of the tuna, and the flavour is more delicate. In two bites, neither of which evokes the sensation of a real *bite*, the slice is finished, and the palate is awake, expecting more. The shellfish, with a stronger flavour and even a slight crunch, made a wonderful complement. A small, grey-glazed bowl held two king-crab legs. They floated on a transparent dip of light rice vinegar. Each red cylinder had been pre-cracked, so that the flaky white, almost translucent flesh could be picked with chopsticks, dipped in the vinegar, and eaten.

In the centre of these dishes, given pride of place, was the pièce-de-résistance. A small ceramic charcoal brazier was placed before each diner. On it rested a shallow, wide, covered dish. The cook had sliced the meat off a duck, and placed it, with some young leeks, in a broth of seaweed, slightly flavoured with *katsuo-bushi.* This had been allowed to simmer gently on the fire while we ate the rest of the meal. Eaten with small bowls of rice the duck provided a perfect closure to the meal.

We can only dream of what we might have been given if the cook had not been on holiday.

The order of a meal circles around the provision of rice. Since the meal was a more elaborate one than most (we were the only guests), rice was peripheral.

Fish, meat, and what could be termed "starters" were served together. When order comes, it comes as a social comment, even a social command:

> After the final practice session, we all went to a *kompa* (drinking party). We all had to drink a toast in beer, and, as the party progressed, with plates of grilled chicken, snacks, and other food on the table, we became merrier and merrier. The OBs (graduated members of the club) ordered saké, and had each of the junior-most members (including myself) drink a water glass of saké with them. After two hours, most of us (excluding the OBs who had drunk more than the rest of us, but who, in their sixties, presumably had more experience) were tottering dizzily about the room in the *ryōtei* where the party was being held. Then the deputy manager announced that the party was to end. Immediately the waitresses brought in bowls of rice swimming in a pale green liquid scattered with sesame seeds. I remember peering at it blearily and wondering why were we being given sesame seeds. The liquid was, I soon discovered, tea: not my favourite drink. I was not, however, too drunk to notice the sudden change that came over my peers and seniors as the *ochazuke* (the name I only learned many months later, as my Japanese improved) was consumed. Like throwing a light switch, the signs of drunkenness and levity were shaken off, sprawled postures were straightened, and even Sakai, whose face was red, and who had been curled giggling happily in a corner for the past quarter of an hour, was up with the rest of us. We juniors filed downstairs to stand at attention and bow and bid farewell to all the seniors, all signs of drunkenness gone.

Drinking parties are important to Japanese social customs: they allow an important informal channel of communication in a society that formalises practically all aspects of life. One aspect that emerges consistently when examining such events is that Japanese drinking parties follow an almost invariable routine: formal seating; a formal toast; eating and drinking; a round of "drinking visits" when participants leave their seats to talk with and toast others in the party; and a formal, almost sober parting. The drinking and eating are made subservient to the social requirements via a set of known and socially enforced rules. Moreover, the acts of drinking and eating, in themselves presumably pleasurable, are subjugated to the needs of the social event, in which participants make strenuous efforts to create an uninhibited, pleasurable, and "rule-relaxed" atmosphere, paradoxically, within the framework of a rigid rule set. The formal ordering of food events, notably those on the more formal end of the range, that is, peripheral-rice meals, seems to follow the same vein.

For Japanese society this ability to switch from one social sub-set of rules to another is of great importance, and perhaps no less crucial to individual life. Relations between individuals are strongly hierarchical and very rule-bound. The language makes grammatical provision for expressing relative rank and position, as well as "proper" politeness levels. Individuals are virtually forced into confronting these relationships in their daily lives. True, for many individuals in many instances this is comforting: there are preset rules for everything, and one need not project much more than conventional expressions of regard. Everyone's position is maintained and retained in social intercourse.

On the other hand, being bound into a set of predefined rules of behaviour and of positions from which there is no appeal, is irksome, even perhaps dangerous, as disjunctions between the formal position of an individual and his actual situation become apparent. Given the fact that individuals interact fluidly, and that they are *individuals*, that is, have wants, desires, preferences and habits, these disjunctions are inevitable. Many authors have commented on the fact that the fluid, liminal stages of drinking parties allow the release of some social tension between formal superiors and formal inferiors. It is while one is drunk that one can tell the boss to his face, that he is an idiot, and suffer few socially acceptable repercussions for it. Management trainers sometimes counsel superiors to play the fool during such interludes, to ignore juniors' remarks, and to otherwise manipulate these situations to the ultimate benefit of the group, that is, of the manager.

In a larger sense, therefore, and in parallel to whatever foods have been served, there is also an order of behaviours, which dictates the states of communication within the participants at a drinking party. There is a formal stage (no food) in which participants are seated formally, and if they drink, the drinking is ritualised, with toasts and attentive handling of cups and liquor. This is followed by a formal stage (with food) in which food is present, people indulge in eating, but are still seated in the formal position in which they have started. Both formal stages are in a sense pauses between the realities of the group of participant's external relations (that is, outside the food event) and the social "play" they are about to embark on. An informal stage then follows. At this point people rise and move about, cluster in discussion groups, juniors make sure, if at all possible, that they speak with all seniors present. In terms of food, this is a point at which the diners help themselves and others to titbits (in contrast to emptying their plates or bowls), fill one another's cups and play drinking games. In other words, this is a stage of relaxation, a stage in which communication is at its most relaxed and fluid, and in which this fluidity is indicated (and perhaps encouraged) by the mixing of foods, drink, and individuals in an incoherent, or at least aggregated manner.

Finally, there is a return to order. In the *kompa* described above, as in many other parties, whether more raucous and drink-related, or more formal, this is indicated by the presence of that most serious and demanding of foods: rice. It is not therefore surprising to find that many Japanese believe that *ochazuke* is a sovereign remedy for over-indulgence. In a social sense, it is that indeed: it puts paid to indulgence by signalling an end to the stage of unlimited drinking. And with the seriousness of the appearance of rice, the formal social relationships that had existed before, come back to re-establish themselves.

The "order" of a Japanese meal is thus of a completely different character to that of the European one. It is designed (if one can call the evolution of a human practice "design") for completely different purposes under completely different circumstances. As many other Japanese behaviours and customs, it is far more concerned with how to circumscribe and deal with human relations, than with the food itself. As individuals, people enjoy food, taste it, appreciate texture and taste and colour. As members of a group indulging in a common activity, the circumstances of the activity are intended to support the activities and aims of the group, whether that group is persisting or ephemeral.

9.3 *THE EPITOME OF TASTE: THE TEA CEREMONY AS A FOOD EVENT*

Being a conformist culture in many ways, Japanese are subject, from early childhood, to instructive media – mothers, teachers, television, and so on – that inculcate the proper and appropriate way to do, to see, to feel, to express oneself. Quite naturally, food is a major focus of these instructions. Much instruction in Japanese society is non-verbal, implied rather than stated. And the school-age child learns much by example of his peers, teachers, parents, and older siblings. This expresses itself in such items as school lunches and food boxes, which, as del Alisal (1999) notes, are expected to be prepared and arranged in appropriate fashion, with proper regard to colour and placement.

The apex of aesthetic appreciation of food is in *kaiseki ryōri*, the cooking that is part of the full Tea ceremony. The importance of the Tea ceremony reaches into the interstice of tradition and consumerism. Both of these terms are multi-valued, no less in the Japanese case. "Tradition" is a human construct: a socially engendered reconstructed memory of how things 'ought to have been' rather than what they really were. Tradition is manipulable, allowing individuals and groups to justify their actions on the basis of what "has been before." In the broad swathe of Confucian[2] cultures, from Japan through Korea, China, and Vietnam, including the Chinese diasporas, tradition plays a more conscious role than it does in the West. Also relevant is the issue of "consumerism" which has been attracting more attention as a field of study for East Asian specialists. Offered a wide range of goods, consumers in Japan can use style templates engendered and formalised through centuries of tradition, at least at the level of the exterior appearance of those goods and perhaps the service that accompanies transactions in those goods.

2 Japanese formal ideology, of whatever stripe, usually includes a large component which can be accounted for by the rather wide and varied ideological and socio-political position called "Confucianism." One element of that position is the view that the present is a poor image of an ideal past: surely the hallmark of a "traditional" view.

The Tea ceremony is a locus of both these features – tradition and consumerism – because it encompasses within itself the essence of style and tradition, and because it is, at an important fundamental level, about consuming valuable goods.

The *chashitsu* (tea room) is one of the rooms of the elegant new house of Mrs. Sato in a quiet suburb. The room, about eight *tatami*, looks out onto a small garden with raked sand and a few rocks. Through one sliding door one enters the living room where we were received. Another door leads to the corridor to the rest of the house. We sit in a row, the *tokonoma* with a scroll and a flower arrangement to our right, the window at our backs. Mrs. Sato enters the *chashitsu* from the corridor entrance, and bows. We respond, and she rises to her feet, pads over to the *irori*, and switches it on. The electric fire glows under the iron *nambu*-ware pot. From a wooden frame which holds the Tea implements she procures a water dipper, ladling it into the iron pot in the *irori*. It boils quickly, and she then prepares a tea bowl, rinsing, drying, putting in the green powder, pouring in water, finally frothing the tea with unhurried movements. Her movements are very hieratic, like Noh or a Shintō priest's rituals: every movement is deliberate, nothing is left to chance, every movement is completed in full, with a minute, almost unnoticeable pause as punctuation before the next action commences.

While making the tea she instructs her daughter to serve us the *kaiseki*, the food that comes with the tea. Because this is only a light tea, the repast consists of cubes of *yōkan* (stiffly jellied sweet bean paste). The daughter approaches the first guest, lowers herself to the tatami, sets the plate of sweets in front of the guest, and bows. The guest bows in turn. Then, taking a folded paper napkin (which we were each given, with a wooden toothpick, upon arrival, but which most Tea guests supply themselves upon receiving an invitation to Tea) and placing it on the *tatami* floor immediately in front of his knees to use as a receiving plate, the first guest takes a sweet with a wooden toothpick and places it on the napkin. The first guest then passes the sweet plate to the next guest and bows. Each subsequent guest bows in turn, and serves him or herself from the sweet plate. When all have been served, the first guest receives a signal from the hostess and we all begin to eat. The *yōkan* is extremely sweet, so the astringent, slightly bitter, frothy thick tea that follows is a welcome change.

The offering and bowing that occurred with the sweets is replicated for the tea bowl. Each of us in turn first examines the filled tea bowl as it is offered to admire it. The bowl is turned in the hand three times, so that one does not drink from the decorative "front" which was initially presented for our examination. Then each imbibes the contents in three sips. The first is a short one, the second slightly longer, the last longest, and the head is allowed to tilt back elegantly (as each action has been) to drain the tea bowl and to show one's full savouring of the green fluid.

There are a great number of dimensions that come into play in a Tea ceremony on the material and consumption side. To fully participate, one must be conscious of, and have some familiarity with pottery, painting, fabrics, architecture, and food, though it is not about flaunting one's connoisseurship in a glaring manner. The Tea ceremony, which has developed from an aristocratic pastime into a mass-practised one (many women take a course on Tea before marriage, either on their own or sponsored by local civic culture halls or their employers), has also, inter-alia, introduced many people to the most "refined" aspects of Japanese culture. This is reflected in consumer attitudes, as for instance, in the use of images from the Tea ceremony to promote elegant goods on television. This would be akin to using classical opera in a Western advertising context: it conveys an image of traditional, "high" culture.

The Tea ceremony itself has an economic and historical dimension that is worth exploring here. Disregarding aesthetics for the moment, participation in the Tea ceremony requires an artistic sensibility, that is, the participant must be able to respond appropriately, in public, to a number of different stimuli: a knowledge of classical Japanese gardening and architecture, proper personal deportment, an ability to comment on and publicly appreciate painting (every Tea room has a *tokonoma* niche with a scroll hanging in it) and flower arrangement, which in turn means some understanding of the implications of seasonality in Japanese culture. A participant might be expected to comment on, or respond to, classical allusions, fabrics, metal-work, and most certainly the pottery used. Now, all of these items, beyond their aesthetic or artistic value, are also economic items. Pottery and fabrics must be bought, not just made.

The Tea ceremony in Japan is thus also, whatever else it is, a major economic segment. The average cost of setting up as a Tea practitioner runs into several hundred thousand yen, not counting the cost of building a *chashitsu* or *chaseki*, even a modern one that is part of a house. The commercial proposition implies that the channels by which taste is learned *include* commercial ones. Thus, the influence of the Tea ceremony, whose participants must become knowledgeable in a large number of aesthetic fields, is one that permeates, to a certain degree, the whole fabric of Japan's socio-economy. The heads of the various Tea schools have the potential of setting new canons of taste, and putting their imprimatur on products in categories such as food, where they otherwise do not have a direct influence. There is a danger in that – Sen-no-Rikyu, codifier of the Tea ceremony in the sixteenth century, and founder of one of the major Tea schools, Ura Senke, was executed for, among other things, rigging the value of Tea utensils. The danger is not so much to the current head of the school – there is no longer a ruler who will demand execution – as to the public who will suffer from attributed worth.

The Tea ceremony is not the only arbiter of quality, but it represents, in its most pure form, the ways in which the aestheticism of Japanese cuisine permeates throughout Japanese society. A Tea aficionado or practitioner is more likely to use traditional aesthetic standards based on previous knowledge to judge foods, than would someone not trained in that fashion. Several million people in Japan participate in tea ceremonies one way or another, as regular or irregular practitioners, and, inasmuch as most of these are women, the permeation of aesthetic standards is very great.

9.4 *SUSHI*

To THE OUTSIDE observer (that is, the foreigner) sushi is perhaps the eponymous Japanese food. It evokes raw fish, and epitomises the strangeness of Japanese food. Conceptually and historically this is a mistake. Sushi is, above all things, pickled (or preserved) *rice*. Sushi originated as a food of scarcity and travel. It was originally one of the methods for preparing cooked food for travellers. Its real place in the Japanese cuisine is therefore with the large spectrum of fermented products: one of the major means (drying and smoking being the other two) by which the human civilisation has, throughout its history in different cultures, preserved foods in times of plenty for later consumption, or for periods of dearth.

Sushi is traced to several origins. One is *narezushi*, which consisted of fresh fish gutted but kept whole and stuffed with rice until it fermented. Only the fish was eaten; the fermented rice was disposed of. This style of sushi is still around, examples are *kaburazushi* and *funazushi*. It is also thought that the process of preserving rice by fermentation may have been brought along with the process of rice cultivation from Southeast Asia. This process was applied to preserve fish. The sour taste imparted by fermentation to preserve fish, gradually developed into a desirable taste. By the 18th or 19th century, the long-pickled fermented ancient process had developed into the instant-pickled dish much closer to the sushi we know today – of cooked rice mixed with a natural vinegar or mild acid, in which was embedded some form of pickled vegetable matter, presumably to act as both a sponge, and, apparently in the case of *umeboshi* (pickled plum), further help in preserving the rice.

For ease of carrying, the preserved rice was made into either compact balls, or stored in wooden boxes, usually cedar, which has a preservative effect in that it is known popularly to deter insects. The addition of other substances, presumably largely for flavouring, came about as a natural development. The need for a way of preserving rice was combined, probably some time in the late Japanese Middle Ages, with the growing demand for sea fish in the Japanese interior. Here too, the demand for food, supplemented by food chemistry, helped in the creation of a new taste. Given the slow modes of transport of the time, limited almost completely to animal and human backs, it is not surprising to find that inland communities could not avail themselves of sea fish. Goody (1982) has commented on the fact that food scarcity tends to increase its value in any society, and therefore, with the growing merchant and aristocratic wealth in that period, demand for luxuries such as sea food grew. The demand for fish was so great that the good burghers of Osaka, as well known for their business acumen as for their love of good food, developed a food in which lightly pickled fish and lightly vinegared rice were combined in a wooden form to create blocks of rice-and-fish sandwiches, which were called *hakozushi* or *oshizushi* (boxed or pressed sushi). This allowed both fish and rice to be preserved for several days, for the benefit of inland dwellers and thrifty housewives. This sushi was an extension of the preserved rice balls (*onigiri*) which were eaten throughout Japan for centuries. Sushi soon became popular in the capital Edo. There, however, the population was led by *bushi* (warrior) households, aristocrats who demanded the best of everything, and for whom one-day old fish were *not* a desirable commodity. In Edo the rarity of a food stuff, in this case perfectly fresh fish – something fishermen, but few others have daily access to – led to the creation of a more refined version of sushi. Fresh fish were substituted for pickled, and because this sushi was to be consumed on the spot, it was not pressed into a box mould, but shaped by hand. Thus its name today, *nigirizushi* ("grasped" sushi). And, in distinction to Osaka-style box-moulded sushi called *battera* (from the Portuguese word "little boat" which the mould resembled), hand-shaped sushi are also referred to as *Edomaezushi*.

This more luxurious variety of sushi is what most non-Japanese recognise as sushi. The principle of pickled rice is maintained, but the topping shows luxury not by pickling the fish, but, on the contrary, by often presenting it raw. More than anything else, the difference between *Osakamaezushi* and *Edomaezushi* exemplifies the historical antecedents of modern Japan: austere merchants preserving their fish and extravagant rulers demanding theirs fresh in a delightful paradox: the merchants had the money and were, in private, extremely lavish while preserving public rectitude. The samurai were often penurious, but needed to keep up a front.

Besides the preparation of the rice base, the modern art of sushi consists primarily of choosing the fish and cutting it. Cut properly, of the right size and freshness, it constitutes the most famously unique of Japan's dishes. Preparing sushi of any kind is a skilled and exacting job. Though sushi is made and eaten at home, it is a quintessential *public* food, one that is consumed most "naturally" in a specialist sushi bar setting:

> Jeanne sits down at her favourite sushi bar in Tokyo. The counterman, after the obligatory "*Irasshaimase!*" waits for her order. In the meantime he prepares the setting: wide green bamboo leaf, a small mound of pink sliced sweetish pickled ginger. A large mug of hot tea. A warm *shibori* towel. All of these are placed on the slightly inclined broad wooden slab of the bar.
>
> "*Saa, mazu, kohada.*" [Let's see ... *kohada* for starters]. Jeanne is following an Edokko tradition.
>
> The counterman, all ready for the decision, flashes his hand to the lightly pickled shad. He cuts off a slice with one quick motion. Left hand into the rice bin to emerge with a patty of rice. There is an audible pop as

> he shapes the rice. Tiny smear of *wasabi* horseradish. Place the fish precisely on the rice handful. Repeat. Lean down and place two pieces on bamboo leaf plate, pieces slightly off alignment for a pleasing asymmetry. First bite. First sip of scalding tea from a giant handle-less mug.
>
> "*Kyō-wa, nani ga ii kanaa* [What's good today]?" And today's best bet might be *maguro* (tuna), *himeji* (yellowtail) or the all time favourites, *uni* (sea urchin) or *amaebi* (raw sweet shrimp).
>
> There are, as any even casual diner at a sushi bar knows, different shapes of sushi. Open-faced (*nigiri*), cone-shaped (*te-maki*), and roll slices (*maki*). The selection of shapes is determined largely by the nature of the fish or other topping, and a diner can choose by flavour, by colour, by texture, in any preferred order. The Edokko preference is to begin with *kohada* and end with sweet omelette or, again, *kohada*.

A sushi meal is in effect a peripheral-rice meal. It is the taste of the fish, the underlying flavour of the rice, the skill of the presentation, the act of presentation, that is the locus of the meal event. So "pure" is the meal supposed to be, that specialist shops strip the experience of all distractions. In one case we experienced, to the point of excluding all liquor "so that the customers will come to taste the sushi, not to get drunk, and so that their taste buds will be fresh for the taste of the food," the proud sushi chef explained.

Sushi exemplifies, perhaps more than any other Japanese dish, the cultural ability to find the essence of an activity, or object, and to employ only slight handling to produce an effect. The minimalism of some Japanese arts – dance, ink-brush painting, calligraphy, flower arrangement – became known in the West in the nineteenth century, and influenced such artistic greats there as Van Gogh. No less is true of Japanese cooking in which, in many of the cooking forms, minimalism of expression is the height of art. This is more true of sushi than any other preparation, because sushi allows the artist very few materials to work with. There are no sauces, no variation in the carbohydrate, and little possibility of even changing presentation and materials, new fish (e.g. from Antarctic waters) and California roll notwithstanding. "Avocado?" sniffed one sushi chef. "What *is* that? And why put it on sushi?" California roll is now just as popular as squid-mayonnaise roll in Tokyo, especially in lunchbox stands near railroad stations. Moreover, while many chefs *do* experiment with new sushi substances, there is a large pool of conservative demand and supply, in which the basic minimalist principles are maintained, even enshrined.

The basic elements of sushi are rice, fish (including seafood), condiments (*wasabi* and *shoyu*), and vegetables (*nori*, cucumber, ginger). To the sushi bar, one needs to add the counterman, as an element in the experience. Within each of these categories, as we have seen when we discussed the schematic meal, things can be expanded, contracted, and changed.

The rice used for sushi is, generally speaking, the best the place can afford, though we have not encountered cases in which *shinmai* (new rice) is used. This is for a simple reason: rice for sushi falls into the flavoured rice category, like *sekihan* eaten at weddings. Elaborating on the exquisite flavour of new rice, which has no need of it, would be sacrilege. Each sushi bar makes rice to its own closely-guarded recipe, flavouring the steamed rice with rice vinegar (milder than standard Western vinegar at about 3% acidity), sugar, and salt. The water used for cooking the rice may have been flavoured during cooking with *konbu* (kelp) stock *(dashi)*. More luxurious (and expensive) bars will use *dashi* they make themselves, others buy it ready made. Mirin (sweet rice liquor) or saké may even be added. Sugar has an additional function, other than seasoning. It keeps the sushi rice from getting hard too soon, especially when the rice is kept for the following day. In general, Osaka sushi rice is flavoured sweeter than Edo sushi rice. Rice for raw toppings will also be flavoured with a lighter touch than that intended to accompany more highly flavoured toppings, such as pickled fish and grilled eel.

"Rice is the soul of sushi," said one counterman. A well-made rice base can go far to spread the reputation of a sushi bar. The actual preparation of sushi rice is a closely guarded secret by most respectable sushi bars. Once cooked, it is turned out of the cooking pan into a shallow tub, made of light wood. The rice is piled high, seasoning vinegar poured over, and then rapidly mixed throughout while gradually levelling the pile and cutting through the rice with a flat wooden spoon. When cooled rapidly with a fan or breeze, it develops its characteristic lustre. For *chirashi zushi* ("rice salad"), the ingredients are added to hot rice to blend the flavours. The rice needs to be fairly warm to be hand moulded for Edo sushi. For box-pressed Osaka sushi, cold rice is used.

Most sushi bar owners select their own fish from fish wholesalers, and, particularly in smaller fishing ports, will buy them during the morning auctions straight off the fishing boats. In one such auction we witnessed, the sushi bar owners in a small town were given the first pick of the catch. This was accompanied by a structure of ritual and personal exchanges, as all such arrangements in Japanese society. Obviously, for larger fish, such as tuna, and a giant two-meter grouper we saw displayed in the food department of a major Tokyo department store, a single shop cannot possibly buy all. In such a case there might be co-operation between shops, or a middle-man will sell desirable portions (*toro*: belly, or *maguro* usually, fillet) to the shops. Tsukiji market, in Tokyo, and its retail "satellites" fill much of the demand.

The fish need to be prepared on the premises. Most, of course, are eaten raw, and the art consists of cutting the fish in precisely the right way to enhance flavour, not an easy thing to do. Some fish must be prepared before presentation, and the preparation varies from fish to fish. Plain prawns and mantis shrimp are cooked, beheaded, peeled, and de-veined. This is not true of *ama ebi* (sweet shrimp) which are cleaned but not cooked, preserving their delicate sweet flavour. All shellfish must be shucked and cleaned. *Kohada*, which tastes somewhat like a delicate version of Michael's Lithuanian-born grandmother's pickled herring, is pickled in vinegar and brine. Here too, the precise means of preparing the fish are a secret, and no sushi chef was prepared to vouchsafe the precise recipe. Octopus is pickled and cooked.

Freshness is obviously an issue, no less today than when sushi was invented and perfected. Refrigeration, as well as clever ways of freezing and thawing make a difference, and create the possibility of "layers" of quality among sushi bars, the top reserved for those who serve freshly caught sea fish, cut open before the diner's eyes, then those who raise their fish in saltwater tanks and do the same, those who buy directly at the port, those who buy cooled or refrigerated fish, those who use flash frozen and thawed. Prices obviously do reflect this hierarchy (or should, rather, modern commerce being what it is, and "in" places being as common in Japan as elsewhere).

The condiments used in sushi preparation and consumption are also minimalist. Two essentials are *wasabi* (Japanese horseradish) and soy sauce (*shoyu*). *Wasabi* is rarely used as a freshly grated root in sushi bars. It is made from the powdered form, which includes Chinese mustard powder, mixed with water to a green paste. Soy sauce, of course, comes in a wide variety of flavours and types. *Tamari*, a more robust-flavoured soy sauce than regular soy, is ideal with sushi, as it does not take too kindly to heating. In sushi jargon, soy sauce is called *murasaki* (purple). While *wasabi*[3] is an essential element, its bite enhancing the flavour of the raw fish, and is, consequently put on by the chef or counterman as he makes the food, how much one uses of *shoyu* is a matter of personal taste. Open sushi are reversed by the diner and the fish dipped into the sauce plate, so that the rice ball with not disintegrate or be further seasoned.

Except in Buddhist vegetarian sushi, vegetables play a minor part in Edo and Osaka sushi, with one exception – *nori* – which is both a garnish for sweet omelette and a casing in all rolled sushi. Its flavour is very evocative of the sea and its texture – which should be crisp – provides a contrast to the tender fish. Its greenish-black colour likewise gives a striking contrast to the white of the rice and the various hues of the fish. Fresh cucumber, stewed dried gourd, stewed shiitake mushrooms, and, more recently, avocado and radish sprouts (*kaiware daikon*) are most commonly used in rolls. And as seasonings or garnishes – green perilla (*shisō*) leaves and flower buds, the roots and young shoots of fresh ginger, *myōga* (ginger relative), pickled plums (*umeboshi*), and green onions. As well, there is pickled ginger (rarely made on the premises, usually bought from specialists) which serves as a taste-bud refresher, to prepare the palate for the next serving.

The progression in eating sushi is flexible, unlike in *ichijū sansai.*

> "There is no set order for eating sushi. While Edokko (people of long ancestry in Edo, or Tokyo), are known to favour *kohada* to start and end with, there are those who usually leave it up to the chef to decide, depending on the day's freshest items. Those who have a sweet tooth prefer

3 As mentioned before, *wasabi* is not only treasured for its taste but also for its bactericidal properties, particularly against ptomaine. The same can probably be said for ginger as well.

to end with something sweet: omelette or sweet shrimp. The essence of eating sushi (at the counter) is the ability of the diner to choose her or his own menu, depending on the freshness, the season, personal preference.

> *Ajï* (horse mackerel) are now at their peak, as are other dry-fleshed fish. Older people like fish such as *tai*, *hirame*, *buri*, which are at their peak in the winter since they are fattier fish."

It is up to the counterman, within the limits imposed by the sushi canon, to improvise, to tease the diner into new experiences.

> "I make this *kaiware-daikon* (daikon sprout) sushi, because the astringent flavour pleases the mouth, particularly in summer, and the crispness provides a new sensation."

Others have introduced different variants, though, as one of our informants stiffly said, "I would never try things like two-fish sushi (in which two different kinds of fish are combined on one rice base)." Indeed, the very adherence to commonly accepted, or at least perceived canons of "proper" sushi creation are what can make an establishment.

Most reputable sushi chefs learn their profession through a long period of apprenticeship and practice. It takes at least five years to master the basics of the craft, though modern sushi academies promise to provide these skills in far less time. Most sushi chefs have also to learn another skill of major importance to their profession – the art of observing customers:

> "I don't cater to customers' whims, but knowing what the customer wants, perhaps even before the customer does, is the second most important skill. I practically provide food directly to the customer's mouth, what could be more intimate? The customer has to trust me implicitly, and therefore I have to have complete confidence in myself. There are things I won't do, like using cheap fish, or mixing two types of fish in a serving, but within the rigid limits of preparing good food, good sushi, it is important that the *customer* knows that he has been properly served. That can only be learned through practice and observation, over a long time of intimate interaction within a sushi bar. *That* is why all these new-fangled sushi academies are no good: their graduates come out technically proficient, but lacking in the ability to handle human relationships which are at the base of good sushi.

Most sushi bars – *sushi-ya* – are long, narrow areas with a wooden counter about thirty centimetres wide fronting the customer. In modern Japan the eating area is topped by an arched glass barrier about twenty centimetres high behind which are ranged the foodstuffs,.

The working area allows access to the various sushi ingredients: a low refrigerated glass case holds raw fish, seafood, garnishes from which the customer chooses the toppings. It also serves as a see-through divider between customer and chef, through which the customer can observe the chef's skills. A large rice steamer usually stands beside the wide wooden counter used for sushi preparation and cutting. Below the counter are shelves for plates, tea cups, and various paraphernalia.

> We started with *kohada*, a semi-sweet, slightly vinegared shad. Each shop makes its *kohada* slightly differently. This one was very mildly vinegared, and on the sweet side. After the *kohada* we had *tako*, the chewiness of the octopus contrasting nicely with the texture of the rice. This was followed by *ama-ebi* (sweet shrimp). The shrimp is raw, a reddish-pink in colour and remarkably sweet. The texture is yielding, and there is a slight astringency (almost unnoticed in truly fresh *ama-ebi*, but there nonetheless) to balance the sweetness. Pink-and-red slices of *hamachi* (yellowtail) followed, their flavour almost smoky, the flesh soft and yielding. After the *hamachi* we had *kaiware-daikon* (radish sprouts) which taste like mustard cress, crisp and slightly peppery. This is an innovation of the past ten years and used as a mouth refresher (*kuchinaoshi*). The green and white sprouts are in a bundle, bound to a rice ball scattered with *katsuo-bushi* flakes by a strip of *nori*. Then we had *toro* (tuna belly), pinker than the red *maguro* cut, and preferred by many Japanese – it was soft as butter. To follow we had *akagai* (red shellfish) whose chewiness contrasted with the tenderness of the *toro*. We ended with a favourite: rich sea urchin roe (*uni*), whose yellow creaminess is an acquired taste, but once acquired, difficult to ignore.

Sushi represents one end in the continuum of "Japanese food." It relies, essentially, on simplicity in terms of the elements used and their preparation, absolute freshness (in theory at least), on a visual and sensory display, and on an interplay of textures as well as tastes. It is also remarkably attractive to non-Japanese diners, even those who do not eat much fish if they are introduced to it unknowingly, as we have found out by experiment. The order in which the sushi are consumed is unimportant: the ambience, setting, and quality are. Certainly sushi perhaps more than any other Japanese food, exemplifies the issue of the use of other senses than taste. And, as well, more than in any other area of food, *shun* – the two weeks at which a particular food is at its peak – is important.

A customer entering a sushi bar is greeted by "*irasshaimase*". This greeting assures the customer that the establishment is open for business, and the connoisseur, of the quality of the establishment: the more vigorous and enthusiastic the greeting, the better the care taken with customers.

A good sushi chef is also an artist, and is likely to suggest, or advise not to try a particular fish to valued customers simply because it is not at the height of its season. Preferences for sushi are extremely varied (Gaishoku kenkyū sentā 1997). Some people have sushi for breakfast (though there is no indication whether the respondents meant *Edomaezushi*, *Osakazushi* or *chirashi zushi* (in Western terms, a rice salad). About 20% of the population have sushi at least once a week. Favourite fish include *toro* (tuna belly flesh); *uni* (sea-urchin roe), *ebi* (prawns), maguro (tuna), *anago* (conger eel), *amaebi* (sweet shrimp), *ika* (squid), shellfish, *hirame* (flounder), and *ikura* (salmon eggs). This choice reflects a change in Japanese dietary and trading patterns, as well as social demographics. In the Edo period, tuna was considered a low-class fish (much as oysters had once been in England), and the samurai class was ashamed to be seen eating it. Salmon, including its roe, was a hardship and winter food: some of our informants in northern Japan could recall when salmon came to spawn in local rivers and most people would be out harvesting. Today, *toro*, the pinkish, fatty belly of the tuna is considered one of the most desirable sushi toppings. The same has become true of a variety of "new" fishes, which the Japanese have been importing from distant places such as the Antarctic fisheries, and which fish merchants have been promoting as alternatives to traditional ones.

A sushi bar is as much a performance as a food locus. On view to his audience at all times, the chef at the counter displays his expertise, all the while attending to his audience's preference and stomachs. His actions are so studied as to appear natural, the highest and most difficult-to-attain level of performance. The intimacy between clients and chef that is established by this performance, artificial though it may be, is one replicated in many small eating and drinking establishments that offer this intimate home-like atmosphere. Making the sushi – fish selected and sliced, hand into the rice pot, rice moulded, *wasabi* smeared, fish placed, *nori* selected and wrapped – is an entrancing show when performed by an expert. There is also a clear correlation between performing in public and price: in cheaper sushi places one is less intimate with the cook, one does not see the full preparation, only the end result, and the prices are accordingly lower. This smooth expertise, perhaps more than any other quality, defines the good professional cook in Japan. Moreover, as in most other cases of clear expertise, it is there to be seen and to be evaluated, because it also defines the quality of everything being served. In Itami Juzo's film, *Tampopo*, two noodle shops are compared: an inexpert one, in which the staff are lackadaisical about their performance (they call out their "*irasshai*" without energy, they execute movements clumsily), and the expert one, in which two cooks make a ballet of the simple action of moving a pot of water. The message is clear: shape and form, perfect action, are what define not only good service and thus good food, but perhaps Japanese perceptions of selfhood and appropriateness as well. This is not to say that everyone achieves that. We commented to one sushi chef on the unusually large size of his helpings.

> "Of course," he said. "This is a quality establishment, as you can see from the queues. In those places where they have a sort of endless chain going around, and you help yourself, the servings are much smaller. They are *gakusei ryōri* (student cooking) places, where quantity in terms of numbers and lower price are more important than quality."
>
> "And are they proper sushi places?"

> "Look, they are there to make a living, and, incidentally, supply a need for people who like sushi but can't afford it. Later, when they are established in life, these same students will come to enjoy *my* sushi, so those places are important too."

The price continuum of sushi bars throughout the industry is important, because it socialises people into sushi culture, in a broader sense, into Japanese food culture, and in an even broader sense, into being Japanese. The positioning of sushi and other food establishments up and down the entire price range, assists in this process because it makes even the most elaborate of cuisines accessible to those at the lower rungs of the consumption ladder.

The price range is also affected by the degree the master chef is willing to divide his attention between supervision and actual preparation. Thus, most good places are relatively small, so that the customer will be sure of being served, insofar as possible, by the master himself. In the example above, the shop goes through twenty to thirty kilograms of fish a day. About ten kilograms of that are of tuna, six are of shellfish of various kinds. With three assistants and the daily need to go and shop at the wholesale market in Tsukiji, the master figures he can keep his own on the all-important (to him, as well as to his customers) quality front. This means that up to ten people can be served at a time. Working at a comfortable speed, a counter chef alternates between orders so that as one customer is partaking of his current order, the other customer's choice is being made. Customers may state their choice of topping one at a time or several at once. Or, may choose a set, which is then made up and served all at once on a small footed wooden tray.

The importance of the relationship with the customer raises a related question: what role does the customer play in the nature and structuring of a food such as sushi? The high-class sushi chefs cited here, as well as other chefs, are dealing with an "ideal" customer. On the purely financial side, of course, one wants a customer who spends well. But from the point of view of one's art, one's performance as a chef, one needs a partner or at least a complement: a connoisseur. What, then, is the nature of connoisseurship? How does connoisseurship in the limited area of food relate to the broader issues of the nature of Japanese culture?

The connoisseur is after all a critic, someone with an informed knowledge of the process, value, and relative place of the art in question, but one who is primarily indulging the self. A connoisseur is also someone whose pleasure depends on knowing the rules that are part of the act. Finally, the connoisseur is also privy to secrets unrevealed to non-connoisseurs. Sushi jargon – words and phrases used in sushi bars by staff, such as special counting terms and denotative words for particular foods (*ote* "The Hand", for octopus) – becomes an inner language the connoisseur can communicate in. The multi-dimensional response of the connoisseur to the total environment complements the chef's efforts and helps spur along his art.

> "It is not just the flavour," said one man at a sushi bar. "It is the smell. Hmmm, draw breath as you enter. You sense the faint hint of the freshly cooked rice and fresh fish. Then the silky feel of the counter and the sound ambience as orders are accepted and presented "*Omachidosama*" as a bamboo leaf or dish is laid before you. Then there is the quick flick-flick of the chef preparing the rice ball, the sure but fast flash of the knife. You catch that unconsciously, until and if a chef makes a mistake. But in your favourite bar, he does not make mistakes, at least ones you can detect, else it would not be your favourite sushi bar. Then it is placed before you, still quivering. Glistening with freshness. Then the texture, which in many cases, say *ika* (squid) and *toro* (tuna belly) hit you before the taste. Then of course the mixture of tastes to flood your taste buds, and before you can be satiated by the taste, another, different one."

One can see a similar expression of sentiment in the opening scenes of Itami's *Tampopo* where the idea of perfect *learned* enjoyment is taken to ridiculous, but not at all inaccurate extremes by the old Professor of Noodles. And, as Itami seems to be saying, this connoisseurship permeates the whole of Japanese society, taking in not only the rich, but also truck drivers whose noodles must be chewy and soup hot, to beggars, who complain about the deteriorating quality of the restaurants whose bins they scavenge. This is not self-indulgence, or a criticism of hedonism: it is an honest expression of a cultural imperative.

The connoisseurship of sushi relates directly to the sushi chef who transforms the fish from foodstuff to food. It is this relationship that is critical, and is critically mediated by a sharp blade. The essence of sushi preparation is a sharp bladed knife, and this popular conception is reinforced both by interviews with chefs and individuals, and by the almost mystical relationship between Japanese and blades.

In the modern era, one tends to forget how important a piece of sharpened steel can be for survival. Having proceeded to computers, we have forgotten our more traditional, and far longer lasting implements. Some of this reverence for the blade is still retained in Japanese society. In public scenes that have been seen or at least noted around the world, an ultra-rightist assassin kills a political victim by stabbing him with a sword. Yukio Mishima, writer, mystic, and reactionary nationalist, makes much of swords, posing with, and eventually dying by one. Nowadays such things are the province of political extremes, but the mystical idea is still there, live, under the surface. Michael's sword teacher emphasised that sword cuts were "to cut out the wielder's bad heart." Jeanne's flower teacher emphasised the need to spend as much time as necessary choosing the right flower cutters, for otherwise the arrangement would fail. And one of our informants, a veteran sushi chef, spent thirty minutes demonstrating and emphasising the importance of a properly honed blade.

> "The cut," said Takeda-san, who has been a sushi master chef for over forty years, "must be absolutely precise. First, the chef must know his tools,

and the first years of apprenticeship are simply devoted to that – knowing one's tools, and one's fish. You have to learn to sharpen your own knives, how they are made, and what the personal characteristics of your hand are. If you balance a blade on your thumb, you can see that a properly sharpened blade will cut into your fingernail, even when you hold the fingernail at a slope, and even if the only weight is that of the blade. A knife that merely *looks* sharp, will slide off.

The cut itself is something that takes a great time to master. The piece of fish must have a smooth surface, and as much surface as possible, to enhance the taste. An amateur merely cuts straight through the piece, a professional will cut creating facets.

There is no 'mystery' to sushi. Those chefs who make a mystery of it are probably merely intent on their reputations and pockets. But it *does* have to do with a great deal of skill and an expertise that cannot be hurried, but must be learned through patient application. Of course, nowadays, people are less ready to work hard for that sort of thing. I do not know if all these new "sushi academies" produce good sushi chefs. If they do not, it is probably because these young men (and some women) go out into the world thinking they know how to do it, but without the experience."

The use of the knife (*hōchō*) is so important in Japanese cooking that it deserves, and has received, a number of treatments of its own, both technical (e.g. Tanaka 1976 *Hōchō nyumon [An introduction to the cooking knife]*, and popular (the comic book *Hōchō Mushuku*, roughly "Restless knife"). Kitchen knives come in four named classes: *usuba* (thin blade), *deba* (carver), *sashimi* (fish), and *tokushu* (special) knives. All of these knives were traditionally made by the welding and folding process which characterised Japanese swords. In this process, alternating bars of tough carbon steel and soft iron are welded together then folded over a number of times. Eventually, one such hardened bar would be welded to a softer bar to provide resiliency combined with toughness and edge (Joly and Inaba 1964). In kitchen knives, a wider steel bar is welded finally to a narrower soft-iron bar. The result is a single-edged blade with an offside cross-section.

Within each class are numerous knife sizes and forms, according to preference of smith and cook. Unsurprisingly, a great deal of attention is paid to maintaining and preparing the knives, as well as to the elegant product they form. Two are significant here: the cutting of fish for sushi and for *sashimi*, and cutting vegetable and other material shapes.

All this attention to traditional manufacture is not a dreamy wish to turn the historical clock back. But it allows most Japanese to connect almost directly, with what they conceive of as the simple virtues of the past: as if Alexander's solution to the Gordian knot were possible today. And this of course expresses itself in the popular press too: *Hōchō mushuku* the comic book is, as its title suggests, *about* knives. Knives, moreover, that relate to aesthetics (in quite a few episodes the hero must compete in cutting the fish to best convey its intrinsic taste) as well as to history (they are made in the same fashion as pre-modern Japanese swords.)[4]

Another element must also be considered: knives are boys' toys. This expresses itself in many ways, and may help explain why so few women are sushi chefs. The popular belief is that women's basal temperature is slightly higher, thus affecting the degree of freshness. The probable real reason is, as usual, the fact that men have arrogated to themselves the better paying and higher status occupations in society. Mediating between these explanations is the fact that the whole cult of the blade is historically more a male occupation and preoccupation than a female one.

To return to the issue of connoisseurship in Japanese culture, one can find it at all levels of society *precisely* because it is closely associated with nationalism and *nihonjin-ron*. The delicate cut of the knife that embodies and delineates the flavour of raw, freshly caught (and sometimes live) fish does not need any garnish. Notwithstanding the currently high price of sushi and *sashimi*, it is also the kind of elegance that anyone, whatever his station in life, can enjoy *and can be an expert in.* Moreover, because the act of preparing sushi is a *public act*, spectatorship is definitely part of the food process, and thus of connossieurship. There is no delicate blending of spices or meticulous sauce-making involved. The only secrets are those of the *okusan* (lit. "the one behind [the scenes]", also in standard language, "wife"), responsible for all the preparations, or those of the performance itself, i.e., the art of the knife, cutting at the right angle, doing it with the swift economy of the protagonist in *Hōchō mushuku*, or of your neighbourhood sushi chef. The larger-than-life greetings, boisterous talk and macho atmosphere of an Edomae sushi bar relates closely to other blade-related male pursuits. It is perhaps not coincidental that a recurrent theme in some *manga* is that of self-harm with a blade: echoes of Yukio Mishima and *yakuza* fingers. As Moeran (1986) has indicated, in Japanese culture, mixing pleasure with some elegantly executed violence adds spice to both.

9.5 *THE RITUALS OF EATING*

What tends to differentiate "dining" from "eating" is that the former is characterised by greater ritualisation. All of the meals we have described in this chapter share in this quality. The ritualisation they embody, however, is of several kinds. The careful balancing of a *kaiseki* meal, or a gathering of friends is characterised, each in its own way, by a careful balancing – an elaboration – of

4 Japanese swords were made by a process of folding hard and soft steels and beating them into a layered sandwich. The result was a blade that could hold a very sharp edge, yet was flexible enough to overcome the steel's tendency to shatter. They are still unequalled in terms of tensile strength, utility (for what they were supposed to do), beauty, and indeed price.

decisions about taste, foodstuffs, utensils to be used. Sushi meals are ritualised by the careful exclusion of extraneous effects, as well as by the attention to minutiae. *Tonkatsu* eaten in a restaurant is carefully embedded in a context of the owner's aesthetic preferences and his attempts to regulate his clientele's dining processes. *All* of these events make what could be a simple process of ingesting foodstuffs into events laden with conscious and unconscious elaborations of rules: the essence of any ritual system.

It is precisely this ritualisation that ensures the continuity and richness of Japanese cuisine. It does so by presenting the participant (essentially, anyone partaking of Japanese food) with a code of elaborate rules. At one extreme is the formality of *kaiseki* and meals of the same sort such as *shōjin ryōri.* In such meals the rules are complex, demand great elaboration and high allocation of precious resources – time and materialle – all of which are evident *to those who know the rules and background.* At the other end are meals, such as the *kompa* and the social gathering, whose ritualisation is focussed on, and occasioned by, the social relations that have "caused" the event to come into being: people are eating because they are hungry, but they are dining because they are establishing or maintaining social relations. Commensality is universal in all human societies. In Japanese society it has taken a special localised colouration.

The "semi-rigid" ordering of Japanese meals is the consequence of this desire to ritualise events, combined with the componential nature of much of Japanese culture. The bare bones of the meal structures seen fully-blown in *kaiseki* and other formal meals can yet exist in other meal forms as the components are adjusted, tinkered with, modified as the social and aesthetic circumstances dictate, and as the cook chooses.

READINGS FOR CHAPTER 9

Anderson, Jennifer L. 1987 "Japanese tea ritual: Religion in practice".
Befu, Harumi 1974 "An ethnography of dinner entertainment in Japan".
Bourdieu, Pierre 1984 *Distinction: A Social Critique of the Judgement of Taste.*
Cooper, Eugene 1986 "Chinese table manners: You are how you eat".
Goldstein-Gidoni, Ofra 1996 *Packaged Japaneseness: Weddings, Business and Brides.*
Ishige, Naomichi 1987 "(Table) manners makyth the man".
Palmer, Elizabeth 1988 *Ikebana: The Art of Japanese Flower Arranging.*
Tanaka Tsuneo 1976 *Hōchō nyumon [An Introduction to the Cooking Knife].*

10 Japan's Food Culture: Dimensions and Contradictions

THE OBJECT OF this chapter is to attempt to draw together the disparate threads of what has been said about Japanese food into a coherent comprehensible cultural whole. To do this, it is necessary to reiterate some of the points that have been made previously. Discussing Japanese food culture must be done, effectively in parallel, at a number of levels. Analytically we can separate these levels, but in practice they coexist and impinge on one another. First, at the most basic level is the level of the foodstuffs that are consumed. These foodstuffs are best viewed at a nexus – the Japanese meal – where consumption of food is bound most noticeably by rules of presentation and preparation that produce a cuisine. The presentation and preparation of foods in meals (and other food events) is meaningful in that it is related to events that occur within Japanese society and within the experiences of its members. This relates to a spectrum of behaviours in Japanese society, from the niceties of domestic life and the family and household, to the proprieties of Japanese public life and the individual's place in it. There is also a dynamic dimension: Japanese society is one undergoing constant change, and it has the reputation of being able to absorb and "domesticate" that change. This is as visible in food as in other aspects of culture. In the changes in the food of Japan in the past century we can find echoes of the changes that have overtaken Japanese society, as well as of the detailed mechanisms by which many of these cultural changes have happened.

10.1 *DIMENSIONS IN JAPANESE FOOD*

A QUALITATIVE DEFINITION of Japanese food culture would be a subjective set of propositions. However, as we have seen, there is one major difference between Japanese food culture and others, which finds expression in a number of different ways. This fundamental difference – in degree rather than type – we can call "dimensionality." For Japanese food culture emphasises to a great degree more dimensions than do most other food cultures. Three obvious such dimensional differences are to be found in the realms of individual sensation, social participation, and consumer choice.

The neophyte non-Japanese diner often complains of the blandness of Japanese food, but compliments its appearance. Even Japanese, such as Tsuchiya, tend to overstate the importance of appearance over flavour. What is obscured by these statements is that the two issues are connected. Rather than "bland", Japanese food *flavours* are necessarily subtle, so as not to obscure other aspects of the food, primarily its fresh, intrinsic taste. These aspects grow in importance, perhaps one could say, at the expense of "loud" dominating flavours.

But the richness of the sensory impact of Japanese food does not end only with the immediate sensations of mouth, eye, nose, teeth. It also encapsulates a heightened awareness of the *context* of the consumed food. "*Shun*" does not just mean that a food must be eaten at the right time, though, undoubtedly, for many Japanese, it is little more than that. *Shun* also means that other triggers – the smell of the season's flowers, the weather when a particular food is eaten, the cloudiness of the sky – are operating in concert to make a food appropriate. The variations chefs allow themselves serve as an enhancement of the various acts of eating by reminding the diner, subtly, of the holism that is implicit in Japanese food culture. That modern Japanese (and their peers around the world) who demand off-season luxuries as of right are actually unable to participate in all these dimensions is true, but the cultural dynamic is there to be partaken of.

This sensing of the total experience includes, unquestionably, the dimension of the social. Social expression cushions the Japanese diner in situations that are acknowledged and signified by the foods eaten and the styles available. The unmediated contact with the chef in a sushi or tempura or other food bar style weaves itself into the fabric of Japanese society because unmediated personal contact is one valued form of interaction in Japanese society. Other forms of contact are represented by the convivial informality inherent in table-top cooking, and by the quiescent formality of *kaiseki*. Here too, the Japanese participant in Japanese food culture is at an advantage because the links to these social issues of desired empathy, childishness, quiescence can be forged through other routes in the culture. That many individuals do not actually enjoy unspoken empathy nor possess the ability to shed class and status restrictions is immaterial: cultural desiderata are models *for*, not models *of*. One strives to achieve them, but they are not guaranteed.

The social dimension also links to more distant, more abstract, more global issues. Japanese are fully conscious, as many are not, of their cultural borrowing from others. They find that borrowing made obvious in their daily food, in the names and materials used for it, in the very shapes of the plates and utensils with which they eat. Food intimately links them to other cultures and other times. Dining is, in a sense, a lesson in history, geography, economics, and marketing, one that easily becomes conscious since there are so many cues laid in the process of eating itself. At the same time, they are also made aware of the innovations achieved within their own culture, of the fact that they are able not only to import ideas from outside, but also to enhance and to imbue these with their own embellishment, so that the end product becomes indistinguishably "native". This state of affairs has been aided by the fact that the Japanese socio-economic pyramid is more of an upside-down turnip than a pyramid: it bulges in the middle. It is not that Japan does not have either the very poor or the very rich, but that it has fewer of those, and more of the people who fit in the middle, even the lower middle. The almost infinite span of consumer choice in food in Japan is an indication to an outsider and to a member of Japanese society of the existence of relative economic fairness (£100 for a single perfect melon notwithstanding).

10.2 *THE ECONOMIC WORLD OF THE JAPANESE GOURMAND*

In increasing the range of options for Japanese diners to choose from, Japan has often exhibited an insensitivity to others that it itself complains about. "Here in Japan, one such as myself, even living in this small northern town, can get anything, literally anything, to eat or drink, simply by lifting a telephone," is how one friend put it in a remote town in Hokkaido. Indeed, in contrast to the limitations of two decades ago, let alone the lean years after the war, Japanese can, with little effort, supply themselves with any foodstuff they desire. Given both the wealth of the country and the intense interest in things foreign, most foreign things are, *pari passu*, more accessible to the common person in Tokyo than in London, Paris, or New York. The reason is not because the Japanese are richer, but because they are more intensely interested in other possibilities, and they are more intent on keeping their eyes on the Joneses, even foreign ones.

In considering the economic issues, we must remember that there are several elements at play here simultaneously which affect one another. Three are prominent: the nature of the market in Japan, the role of media in the formation of modern consumer culture, and the deleterious effects of the Japanese search for more and exotic foods.

The Japanese market has been characterised by lengthy middleman chains that have increased the cost of consumer goods. In the past decade, it has changed, with the emergence of more "rational" shopping and marketing patterns. This of course has coincided with the rise of opportunities of employment for those who would, otherwise, may have become middlemen, as well as coinciding with the growing demand by Japanese customers for lower prices.

In the realm of food this pattern has become more and more noticeable, as customers come to recognise the possibilities inherent in different forms of marketing. One establishment that we studied provided the services of the major fish market at Tsukiji, Tokyo, to neighbourhood housewives and even local tradespeople. For the owner, no less than for the shoppers, this was a keen move. Local fish consumers who had been at the end of a long line of suppliers, found themselves at the end of a shorter one, where they benefited in "Little Tsukiji" as the shop is known, from the economies of scale. The sheer variety of fish and marine products, all of which were moving through the store at an astonishing pace, was enlightening. Shoppers had a vast array of marine products to purchase, many of which had come directly from the fishing boats or importers, rather than going through several middlemen.

There is of course a cost. Much of the personalised service is gone. Customers have to cope with large quantities or even entire fish without the intervening services of a local fishmonger. Rather than the cultural desiratum of personal attention and empathy given by a local shop whose owner lives in the community, the consumer is exposed more and more to the intrusion of impersonal and industrial mercantilism as it strives to create and maintain new markets.

As in any modern society, advertising plays a major role in determining people's exposure to, and pursuit of, foods. Japanese advertising media are extremely diverse. In addition to nation-wide advertising through journals, television, and radio, much of which is handled by major metropolitan agencies, there is no shortage of community efforts. Most shops issue flyers that feature that week's specials or bargains. These monochrome or coloured flyers are inserted into newspapers or are distributed door-to-door. Local salesmen, especially in more remote areas, pass by and are delighted to fill any order.

This exposure to a vast array of advertising, much of which is concerned with food, integrates food demands as well as broadens the possibilities of exposure to new and different foods. The commercial benefits are very clear to consumers and vendors. The former have their choice of purchases and range of prices increased several fold. As Clammer (1999) shows, Japanese housewives, the primary purchasers of food, evaluate their purchases carefully in economic, prestige, and availability terms. The provision of several media of advertising offers them an opportunity to be canny about their purchases, to compare shopping, and to distance themselves from the vendor's ideal: the captive customer. In fact, and notwithstanding the personalised service ideal, Japanese housewives, says Clammer, have far less brand loyalty than would be expected. In more sociological terms, much of the "ideal" Japanese values of loyalty and reciprocity is lost in the light of contemporary shopping behaviour. Traditional Japan is far less powerful than market forces, and these market forces extend further than the borders of traditional Japan.

The economic impact of the Japanese search for the novel and the exotic resounds worldwide, mainly because of its bulk purchasing of food items and its importation of expensive rarities (rarity is, of course, a relative term). The volume of Japanese imports in say, wheat, rice, pulses and meat is such that quite a few manufacturing nations have tailored their production to Japanese demand. Rice that conforms to Japanese preference, i.e., short-grain, is being grown in potential export economies, notably the US and Thailand. The attractiveness of this foreign-grown rice to its commercial target is doubtful. Americans insist that their rice is as good, even better than Japanese rice, and of equal consistency and flavour. Japanese consumers still insist – whether as a matter of pride, of cultural demand, or because of real, if intangible and indefinable issues of taste – that it is not.

Meat is another issue in which Japanese influence has been notable. The Japanese preference for soft, fat-laced beef has led Australia, a major beef producer, to change its feed and raising patterns to fit Japanese demands. Here the exporters to Japan are on surer ground: the small quantities of meat raised in Japan are more expensive, and the best Australian can match the taste. Nevertheless, there remains a lingering distrust of the quality of foreign beef.

What however is significant in all of this is less the Japanese dependence on foreign foods, and more the growing *interdependence* of Japan and its food suppliers. In other words, the sheer volume of food that is shipped, by any one of these countries, to Japan, implies that they are very heavily dependent on the Japanese market for a smooth economic existence. This of course affects the consumers in those countries as well as others. The willingness of the Japanese consumer to pay top price for what he or she considers the best quality, means that lower prices for other types of the same good – meat and rice in particular – are less attractive to the farmers concerned, resulting in decreased production intended for local consumption. This in turn creates a corresponding increase in food prices for the local consumer. Thus, the Japanese food market and its demand for more, better, and cheaper, pulls along consumers in other countries.

Whether we are prepared to accept the fact or not (and many are not), maintaining an ecological balance is a delicate act. This has become particularly noticeable in the realm of marine produce. For millennia, fishing (at least outside immediate coastal waters) was open to all who could – Europe's herring fleets and Japanese fishing fleets went wherever the fish were; Portuguese and Basque fishermen hunted cod off the North American coast. With the advent of industrial fishing, however, this balance – which was maintained because there *was*, most probably, a certain play in the ecology – was broken. Within four decades after World War II (when industrial fishing really took off) both herring and cod stocks, even in such legendary fishing areas as the Grand Banks, were completely, or almost completely, depleted. Japanese fleets were at the heart of this process because they had the technology, and the industrial patience, to invest in deep sea fishing, to a degree that was unprecedented. The technology, on the one hand, and the processes of consumption in Japanese society on the other, meant that Japanese fishermen were forced to effectively vacuum the sea for marine products.[1] As Japan's populace became wealthier, so too did the demand increase for marine products that before had been luxuries. Japanese rivers which had yielded harvests of salmon ceased doing so not only because of pollution but also because salmon were hunted during their breeding season: salmon roe, *ikura,* is a desirable luxury coveted particularly during New Year. The

1 Lest it be assumed that we are purposely excoriating only the Japanese here, it ought to be kept in mind that Norwegians, Koreans, Russians, and Americans were doing the same thing, only later than the Japanese did, or with less technological and financial backing.

same is true of cod roe, as well as other immature fish. The demand for such marine products, which Japan could supply for itself, without paying for much more than set-up and operating costs, has continued to increase. Large sections of the economy, from ship-building and electronics through fish wholesalers and purchasers, have been involved.

However, much of this "wild" harvest is at the expense of others. Whether seen in an ecological perspective, or seen in an economic perspective, fishing (as practised today by most fishing nations) is a predatory, rather than husbandry (to use an old term) activity. One hunts, and what one hunts and catches, is denied to the environment, and denied to others. In essence, it is a return to a primitive past, when yields were a function of natural availability. In farming, on the other hand, the farmer actively promotes a crop, protects it, and fosters its growth.[2] Neither of these processes is necessarily moral or immoral. But hunting/gathering (of animals, fish, or timber), however suitable it is for small Neolithic populations, is unsuitable for large urban ones. Farming, which creates a surplus, allows for a modern, urban, and industrial lifestyle, for good or ill.

The economic lure of a free lunch, which is implicit in fishing activities, is too great to forgo, with what appear to be catastrophic results on the world's fish resources. This is noticeable economically in both Japan and its neighbours. As fishing resources around Japan have dwindled, Japanese fleets have gone further and further abroad. So too have Japanese buyers, paying premium prices for desirable fish like tuna, with consequent costs to local housewives and fishermen, as well as to the fish themselves. In Japan, some forms of produce that had been native, such as seaweed, *matsutake* mushrooms, and dried squid, are now coming largely from overseas. Of course, foreign economies do benefit to a point, but since these products are largely wild, they are also largely non-renewable. The question of what will happen to the economic niches these countries – Indonesia, Korea, the Philippines – have bought so dearly when the fish or timber, or mushrooms run out, is left unanswered. Moreover, Japanese food culture has displayed great insensitivity to ecological issues, or to the sensitivities of others. A major television network has featured meals of tiger meat in a show in which celebrities competed in eating and identifying *getemono*. The station's excuse – the tiger had died of natural causes – was more self-serving than an attempt to deal seriously with the issues arising, ultimately, from Japanese gourmandism.

10.3 *NATURAL FOOD AND REVIVING THE COMMUNITY*

THE ABUSES OF the Japanese search for gourmet lifestyles have brought about countervailing forces in Japanese society as well. These forces have not set

2 Farming, of course does impose many restrictions on the wild biome as well. It is however inarguably more efficient, and, when large populations are combined with technology, hunting very soon exhausts all prey species, whereas farming, at least, requires annual renewal.

themselves up as champions of the abused outside the borders of Japan. For internal, very Japanese reasons, two popular movements (in the informal sense) counteract the demand for more and more external content to Japanese foods. On the one hand is the movement which is still small, for the purchase and consumption of natural foods. Supporting this movement in some ways, opposing it in others, is the need to revive local (rural) confidence and local economies and population, a problem that is facing many small and farming communities in Japan, which we have discussed to some degree above.

The natural food movement, as in other developed countries, is an outgrowth of growing information and growing concern among consumers, notably mothers. Such movements (and fads) are not unusual in Japan. As in many fad movements, the movement was soon hijacked or at least co-opted by larger, more efficient economic actors. Within Japan there are today several suppliers of organic foods, as well as several chains that specialise in organic foods, some of which are suspiciously close to flogging panaceas and nostrums.

Moreover, the natural food movement in Japan cannot be wholly disassociated from some of the less attractive aspects of Japanese nationalism. There is a small but growing number of advertisements and sale devices that indicate openly, or hint, that *Japanese* natural food is the solution for modern Japan's modern illnesses. In other words, it is the foreigners, suppliers of non-Japanese foodstuffs who are to be blamed for the variety of weaknesses and problems that have afflicted modern Japanese. As Ohnuki-Tierney (1993) has pointed out, precisely the same process was a feature in the cultural understanding Japanese have of rice, articulated directly and early by Motoori Norinaga.

In contrast to the nationalistic side, however, the natural food movement has also spawned a large number of small entrepreneurs who *are* going back to the ideas and ideology of self-manufacturing of foods, both Japanese and Japanised. One of our informants, a visionary tofu-maker, had taken a life-cycle route that emulates, knowingly or unknowingly, that of many Japanese religious and artistic innovators. An ambitious businessman, he had succumbed to a form of cancer. Resigning his successful career, leaving his wealth behind, he had retired to try and cure himself. After some years of study, he had hit on the idea that he had become ill through wrong eating. Several years of meditation and study later, he had developed a special kind of tofu, which he now makes by hand and sells to the neighbourhood. He claims that the quality of his tofu and its natural ingredients are responsible for the remission of his cancer. When we met him he was in the process of accruing a band of disciples, users, eaters, and admirers of tofu, who imbibed the implicit message – the health-restoring power of simple natural ingredients – that the master espoused. In less complicated, but nonetheless entirely culturally-acceptable ways, one can find throughout Japan similar craftsmen making their own bread from local wheat and making miso or soy sauce from locally grown soybeans, growing their own rice without pesticides, reviving local production of grain, legumes and other foodstuffs. In some cases, stimulating local cultivation where previously there had never been any.

Attempts to revive village life, successful or not, that have been documented by a number of observers (Smith 1978, Knight 1999) have aspects that relate strongly to food, and relate to the natural food movement as well. Over the past century, Japan has moved from being a predominantly rural country (albeit with a strong and vibrant urban tradition: Edo, now Tokyo, had over a million residents by the eighteenth century) to being a predominantly urban one. This has been accompanied by a gradual degradation and dissolution of the small community identity that many Japanese (and, of course, others) enjoy and desire. The effects of the metropolis – particularly Tokyo and Osaka – have created a homogeneous "Japanese" nation out of what had been culturally, and to a degree linguistically, a cluster of sub-cultures. Local dialects, dress, food, customs – all recognisably Japanese, yet all subtle variations on the same theme – have gradually slipped away to be replaced by common idioms and icons controlled by the metropolis.

In the past two decades, however, villages and small towns have woken up to the fact that they are losing not only their individual identifies, but also their population and economic bases. To counter that trend, these small, sometimes remote rural communities have come up with a number of strategies intended to reverse their fortunes. Collectively these are known as the *furusato undō* (village or countryside [revitalisation] movement). Strategies vary. New foods may be invented, based on local specialities, such as for instance, the newly created *ikura donburi* (salmon-roe rice bowl) which is now a hallmark of Hokkaido, or specific new lunchboxes (*ekiben*). More sophisticated attempts to merge the interests of urban dwellers with those of country-people are also used. Schemes to have urban people adopt trees or parts of natural forests, or to provide them with food "fresh from the farm" and news about their adopted communities, or sale of *meibutsu* items through the mail. These have a particular appeal in the Japanese context, for what the villages and small towns are "selling" is a renewal of the "traditional" social bonds that have held Japanese together for centuries. And part and parcel of this movement is the concept of food, its production and its social consumption. In fact, Knight's material suggests that villagers are consciously creating a situation in which "production" in the Marxian sense, is shared, the farmers doing the actual work, the urban people supporting them, working through their sense of participation and interest in the procedures and material generated.

Both of these kinds of reactions – the natural food movement as well as the *furusato* movement – combine to renew and preserve the shape of Japanese cuisine. They may or may not also claim to preserve the traditions of Japanese (food) culture. In practice, they probably are creating and recreating new forms of Japanese cuisine, some of it borrowed from what remains of traditional Japanese practices, some of it borrowed from abroad and modified to Japanese tastes. The reality appears to be that these two tendencies – preserving a tradition by reviving and adapting it, and combining that with adopted items and practices from abroad, are the very essence of Japanese tradition, more so than the evanescent shape of a *kimono* or taste of a particular food.

10.4 *JAPANESE FOOD AND WORLD FOOD: JAPAN AS A MODEL*

JAPAN PROVIDES AN interesting and admirable example of a food culture. It is and has been a model of a society and economy managing, largely by its own internal efforts, to transform itself into a modern power, while retaining a great deal of the uniqueness that is the gift of any culture. It is a model of the introduction of new social, technical, economic, managerial, and other techniques into the insular, self-satisfied, and imperialistic European and American cultures. It is a model of an alternative mode of co-existing in a crowded world: not one everyone should adopt, and one that has many flaws, but a successful model nonetheless.

So too, in the realm of food and cuisine, Japanese has much to teach, much that can serve as an example. This is notably true considering two processes that the human species is undergoing: our numbers are growing, and we are living in one another's pockets to a growing degree; and much of our individual uniqueness (of persons and of cultures) is homogenising, blending, McDonaldising. Both of these processes are a result of our own lack of control and socio-intellectual processes, which means that both are not inevitable, but they certainly are occurring. So we can ask ourselves how Japanese cuisine responds, and has responded to similar classes of process.

For all that the Japanese have done a great deal to destroy the natural biome, and for all the complaints against Japanese companies (and individuals) raping the environment, it is necessary to keep in mind that the Japanese have used their food resources well. Not necessarily in the eyes of economists, who can, with cold-eyed dispassion and great cultural ignorance, examine the financial costs associated with rice or *mikan* protectionism, but certainly from the point of view of food studies.

The Japanese kitchen, as we have seen, is capable of using its resources parsimoniously, of utilising many different resources, all the while producing foods of excellent dietary quality and great aesthetic appeal. Moreover, by and large, the Japanese have made a virtue of restraint in the kitchen, whether in the use of spices, or in the delicacy of presentation and preservation. Certainly, in the latter half of the modern century, Japanese have done well in a related area: they have distributed the benefits of their cuisine well throughout their population. This implies that they have dealt with the problem of resource distribution – income and consumption – in (by and large) a better way than other countries. It also means that sources of communication – the media, literacy, education – are also well distributed throughout the population, keeping the strands of the food culture together in a cohesive way.

As a lesson for other cultures, this is of enormous value. Simply put, where resources are distributed poorly, cuisines appear to be both limited and restricted as well: to certain areas, certain classes, certain ages, certain ethnic groups. Being able to not only feed people, but make them aware of what can be good, and making this good potentially available to all, is perhaps the greatest positive intellectual example the Japanese model can provide.

As in all modern societies, many Japanese participate in the world of food as an exercise in conspicuous consumption. A simple traverse of any *sakariba* can demonstrate this fact, as expense-account *sarariman* swarm into restaurants and bars, often for little more than the opportunity to show that they *have* an expense account. But Japanese culture, as a whole, often exhibits another, more positive understanding of food enjoyment, one that is Epicurean, in the philosophical sense.

The Epicurean idea – that life is measured by enjoyment, and that experience must be immediate – is similar to many ideas that have been prevalent in East Asia, and which have been formative influences on Japanese society. All sensory dimensions of food – shape and colour, texture, context – are explored and enjoyed, not only taste and smell. Small size, delicate differences, fit with the natural world, all of these are what makes up Japanese appreciation. Above all, something that other cultures might do well to emulate, is the appreciation of the subtleties and pleasures inherent in the simple, whether it be an old rice bowl, now chipped and cracked, or a single piece of tofu floating in an absolutely transparent broth.

Where European sensibilities searched first for *quantities* of food, and only later were tamed into the realm of taste and restraint, never really losing the preference for great masses of food and grandiose gastronomic statements ("I'm a real steak and potatoes man," "A *thick* steak", "A dozen oysters") Japanese preference has always been for a great variety (if possible) of small items, prepared as naturally as possible, and presented elegantly. None of these preferences are solely the province of the elite. They are the preference of the large majority of Japanese who are able to appreciate, and often create themselves, subtle uses of everyday, commonplace foodstuffs.

Higuchi (1974) argues that Japan's "genius" is in inventiveness, contrary to the popular image, in the West at least, of Japan as mainly an imitative and derivative culture. Without debating the many (mainly nationalistic) points Higuchi makes, in the realm of food, at least, Japanese culture, without government directive or intervention, has structured itself to create two effects. On the one hand, the end result of the processes we have documented has brought about the preservation of old styles of cooking and of old tastes and foods. On the other, the atmosphere that has been created, of innovation-within-a-framework, in which certain basic rules are agreed upon by all, has led to a spirit of innovation and renewal in Japanese cuisine. And that spirit is continually being reaffirmed whether by the creation of a new restaurant such as Suzuya, which serves traditional fare but with an eye to modernity, or in the form of the creation of a new "traditional" dish which is within the realm of acceptable Japanese high cuisine.

The structure of Japanese cuisine, with its multifarious social and culinary loci, its literate and common access to the ways others have been doing things, the ideology that demands constant study and restudy, not only by experts but by *anyone*, ensures that the traditions of Japanese cuisine are kept alive. In other words, Japanese cuisine's strength lies in the social arrangements that underlie it (and much of Japanese culture), reinforcing both continuity and change of cultural forms.

The implications of this are, at the very least, the need for culinary education. The distinction, in the UK at least, between the culinary sophisticated elite (some of whom, following cooks such as Gary Rhodes and Jane Grigson, have been returning to the gourmet's delights of an earlier British life) and the fish-and-chips/hamburger/meat and two vegs culinarily limited mass, is a recipe for the disappearance of a cuisine. And a cuisine so battered by the industrial revolution, war, and McDonaldisation, is not likely to return to its previous levels of variety and taste.

In contrast, Japanese cuisine, through a system of combined government education and popular self-education, has created a self-sustaining popular cuisine that adapts and reinvents itself constantly, within the framework of acceptable and accepted canons of taste, of preparation, and of aesthetics. The basic elements seem to be four things: a readiness to accept foreign inputs, as they are adapted for Japanese preferences; a well-educated populace, which is also at the same time, economically affluent, or at least not impoverished; a coherent set of aesthetic ideals, shared by most levels of the populace and interpreted and transmitted through a variety of popular and dedicated channels (such as, for example, television and Tea ceremony schools); and finally, a great flexibility in adapting specific elements – traditional and new, foreign and specifically local – to different sub-populations.

If the Japanese can assume the title of greatness for anything cultural, it is for the inherent cultural ability to absorb and adopt new things – processes, material goods, techniques – and make them their own. A large majority of the foods and techniques we have discussed above are not originally of Japanese natural provenance. They have been imported, and in the importation, adapted to Japanese needs and preferences. Paradoxically they have retained a sense of their origins while adopting a new guise as Japanese foods or Japanese techniques.

Notwithstanding the negative aspects of this gourmandising which we have discussed above, it has a positive side to it. It means that Japanese individuals are far less likely than many Europeans to turn up their noses at new culinary experiments and pleasures. It means that, in this dimension at least, Japanese are certainly more international-minded, with all it implies, than are Europeans or Americans. Whether this sort of open-mindedness can be translated to other areas, such as social relations is another matter, one that, perhaps, can be pursued with a sophisticated understanding of how culinarily, at least, the

Japanese *have* become true *kokusai-jin* ("internationalists"). It also means that food innovations that arise indigenously will be accepted by some portion of the population or other, while still having to compete (a healthy thing, as any capitalist will tell you) within the marketplace of ideas and concepts.

10.5 *FINAL WORD*

"WILL JAPAN CONTINUE its position as an economic giant?" is a question that has troubled a decade of economic and political commentators. Will it be a food giant as well is a parallel, and related question that concerns us more here. Whatever the economic outcome, the culinary outcome of the current century has been that Japanese cuisine has been enriched, and has enriched others. In the nineteenth century it was Japanese painting and aesthetic vision that helped remould European art. To some extent, it has been a superficial knowledge of some of the aesthetics, particularly the presentational ones, that have contributed to the (late? Certainly unlamented) nouvelle cuisine. But the lessons of Japanese cuisine go far deeper, as we have shown above.

In the future, we shall not be able to expect miracles. The countervailing brutish tendencies of conspicuous consumption and of exploitation are too deeply embedded in the human psyche, for us to expect the Japanese only, to dispose of them. Undoubtedly, if Japan continues to be an economic power, it will continue to exploit those around that are weaker than her. In the realm of cooking and food, however, we can expect that at least some of the lessons the natural food movement, *kaiseki ryōri*, and other positive aspects of Japanese food culture are trying to teach will sink in: the ideas that link human health and human aesthetics, though not obvious, are there to be learned and absorbed. Japanese cuisine, in which strands of luxury and limitation, the aesthete and the voluptuary are inextricably entwined, may yet find a way to adapt itself to a world in which exploitation, culinary or otherwise, is unacceptable. In such a case, Japanese food culture in which a bowl of rice with a small plate of pickles and some soup is not merely food, but cuisine, will be able to flourish. And flourishing, will have much to teach others as well.

Glossary of terms

THE TERMS NOTED here are those that have been mentioned in the text. The reader interested in a complete dictionary of Japanese food terms is directed to R. Hosking's *A Dictionary of Japanese Food*, which is probably the most comprehensive source in English.

Term	**Definition**
aji	Horse mackerel. *Trachurus symmetricus*. Eaten raw or salt-grilled. A small (30–40 cm long) fish.
akagai	A shellfish; *Anadara broughtonii*. Commonly eaten as sushi.
ama ebi	Sweet shrimp. *Pandalus borealis*. A medium-sized crustacean eaten usually as sushi or *sashimi*. Flesh is translucent with a sweet edge to the flavour.
amazake	Sweet thin rice gruel with a low alcohol content sold hot. It is a common street food during festivals, and is also served at home during the Doll's Festival.
an	A bean "jam" made of azuki beans boiled with sugar syrup, dark purple in colour. It is a major component of a great many Japanese sweetmeats.
awabi	Abalone. *Nordotis* sp. A large, fleshy mollusc caught off Japan's seacoast by female divers called *ama*.
ayu	Sweetfish. *Plecoglossus altivelis* A small river fish. White fleshed with a delicate almost sweetish taste.
bakufu	The military government of the Shogun. Normally refers to the Tokugawa shogunate (1600–1868).
bentō	Box lunch in a compartmented tray. (See *ekiben*). There are hundreds, if not thousands of types. They normally contain cooked rice and a selection of *okazu* for which the *bentō* may be named. Some *bentō* have become special local products. Certainly, consuming *bentō* bought from a local station as the train passes through the countryside is one of the better ways to travel.
buri	Yellowtail. *Seriola quinqeradiata* Medium-sized fish of the jack family.
bushi	Warriors. The governing and military class in pre-modern Japan. The classes during late medieval (to 1868) times were caste-like. The *bushi* were the upper rung of society, responsible for defence and government. Samurai – the retainers/soldiers/administrators of baronial houses and the shogunal government – were all drawn from this class.
chawan	Literally tea bowl, it is used to refer to bowls for rice as well.

chawan mushi A savoury custard of eggs and *dashi* with bits of seafood (usually prawn), mushrooms, gingko nuts, and trefoil (*mitsuba*), steamed and served in a small tea cup, hence the name, literally "tea cup steamed".

[o]chazuke Tea over rice. Originally, this was simply a way of finishing one's bowl, by rinsing out the remaining rice grains with tea and drinking the lot. In a process of upgrading, this has become a style on its own, in which *dashi* flavoured with tea is poured over a bowl of rice, and various garnishes – *umeboshi*, fish, salmon-eggs, vegetables – are added. As most styles do, there are specialist restaurants for the dish.

chirashi zushi Mixed sushi. Flavoured rice is mixed with seafood and bits of *nori* and vegetables.

chorogi Chinese artichoke. A small, crisp whorled tuber, shaped like the (old) Michelin man. Made into a pickle in the Tohoku area.

daikon Giant radish. Long (20–50 cm) thick (2–10 cm) white roots. *Raphanus sativus*. Eaten grated raw for garnish with *tempura*, or cooked and pickled.

demae Home delivery of food. Most low and middle range restaurants in Japan will deliver dishes to houses and offices. They will often circulate their menus to surrounding neighbourhoods. The food is delivered in the restaurant's dishes, which, after the meal has been eaten, are left outside one's door for later pickup.

[o]den A stew of mainly vegetarian items (*kamaboko*, *daikon*, seaweed, *konnyaku*, potatoes) and boiled eggs simmered in a fish broth. Normally eaten off barrows that appear late at night around *sakariba*.

eda mame Green soy-bean pods. Boiled briefly in salted water, they accompany beer and other drinks in summer.

Edokko A resident of old Tokyo. Normally refers to members of working class families from the *shitamachi* (downtown) neighbourhoods of pre-modern Edo. They have a distinctive working class culture and ethic.

Edomaezushi Edo-style sushi, in which raw or lightly cooked fish top a rice ball shaped by hand. This is what most non-Japanese think of when sushi is mentioned.

ekiben A lunchbox *(bentō)* sold on trains or train stations in disposable containers. There are countless varieties featuring local specialities. Some of the famous ones are *kamameshi* (vegetable hotpot) *bentō* in a distinctive clay pot (now supplanted by plastic, alas) and Kanazawa sushi. New varieties are being created all the time, the latest being paella *bentō*, bought at Tokyo station.

fu Wheat gluten. Normally comes in the form of dried disks, which are resuscitated by hot water. Fu absorbs food dyes well, and is often used to fashion colourful symbols, such as those for New Year or Children's Day.

fugu Blowfish. A family of small fish (*Tetraodontidae*) caught off the Japanese coast. The liver is full of tetradotoxin, a nerve poison, traces of which exist throughout the flesh. Only specially trained cooks are allowed to prepare the fish, and their license must be prominently displayed. Contrary to opinion (at least outside Japan), few people have died from eating *fugu* in the past half century, and those who did ate the fish prepared by amateur cooks. The flesh, as *sashimi*, is a translucent delight.

fuki Sweet coltsfoot or Japanese butterbur. *Petasites japonicus*. A long (to 150 cm) green stem topped by an umbrella-like broad (to 80 cm) leaf.

The young stems are peeled, parboiled, then used in *aemono*, *sunomono*, or for sweetmeats.

furikake — Garnish of dried ingredients, usually *nori* flakes and freeze-dried granules of fish stock, horseradish, or pickled plum, which is scattered over rice at breakfast or at the end of a meal, as a savoury. When hot green tea is poured over, the resulting dish is called *ochazuke* (q.v.).

getemono — "Odd" foods, usually offal, that are eaten largely for supposed health benefits.

ginnan — Ginkgo nuts. The seeds of the gingko tree (*Gingko biloba*). Skewered and grilled, or cooked in *chawan mushi* (q.v.).

gobō — Burdock root. *Arctium lappa*. Treasured for its aromatic flavour and texture. Most popularly used in *kimpira gobō*: julienned *gobō* and carrots with sesame seeds.

gori — Sculpin. A river fish *Cottus pollux*. A small, rather ugly fish with a pleasantly flavoured white flesh, usually set in aspic.

[o]hagi — A sweetmeat made of grilled *mochi* (q.v.) coated with *an* (q.v.) bean "jam".

hakusai — Chinese cabbage, Chinese leaf. *Brassica rapa var pekinensis*. Pale-green leafed, white stalked cabbage popularly used in pickles, *hitashi*, and *aemono*.

halohalo — Philippine sweet made of alternating layers of fresh and preserved tropical fruit, gelatine cubes, sweet red and white beans, topped with crushed ice, milk, custard, or ice cream, served in a tall parfait glass. Similar in concept to Japanese sweets *mitsu mame* and *an mitsu*.

hamachi — Young yellowtail. *Seriola quinqueradiata*. A fish of the jack family.

hamo — Conger-eel. *Muraenesox cinereus*. Usually served grilled.

harumaki — Spring rolls. Crisp fried rolls filled with cabbage, bean sprouts, and (sometimes) meat, flavoured with ginger and garlic.

hashi — Chopsticks.

hassun — A rectangular plate used mainly in presentation of *kaiseki* meals.

hata hata — Sandfish. *Arctoscopus japonicus*. A small fish popular in Akita prefecture; The flesh is somewhat dry. Eaten grilled or used to make *shottsuru*, (q.v.).

hirame — Flounder. *Paralichthys olivaceus*. Medium-sized flatfish prized for its delicate flavour and texture.

hiyayakko — A block of chilled tofu garnished with shavings of dried bonito, ginger, chopped green onion, and soy sauce. The same dish, served warm, is called *yu-dōfu*.

hōchō — General name for Japanese kitchen knives.

hokke — Atka mackerel. *Pleurogrammus azonus*. A herring-sized fish with a somewhat oily texture. Served fried or grilled.

horumon — "Hormone" meaning offal meats: hearts, liver, lungs, spleen. These are usually "male" foods, served in drinking places either grilled or in *motsunabe* (innards stew).

hotate(gai) — Scallop. *Patinopecten yessoensis*. Versatile mollusc, eaten as sushi or *sashimi*, fried, steamed, butter fried, etc.

ichijū sansai — "One soup, three vegetables." The (modern) standard meal structure of rice, soup, and three *okazu* dishes. The older standard was only one accompanying dish and soup: *ichijū issai*. Rice is taken for granted, only the variation in side-dishes is characterised.

imo — Generic name for many root vegetables including potatoes (*jaga-imo*), sweet potatoes (*satsuma-imo*), yams (*yama-imo* or *yamato-imo*) and taro (*sato-imo*).

irori — Hearth. Usually a square form of half a *jo* in size (90 × 90 cm) filled with sand on which charcoal is burned. Rural households had larger ones with a step for warming the sitters' feet. Now, alas, not as common as they used to be, and totally absent in modern households.

ishigarei — Rock turbot. *Kareus bicoloratus.* A small delicate flatfish.

ito-uri — Spaghetti squash, *Cucurbita pepo.* A variety of squash whose flesh forms thin, long threads when ripe.

izakaya — Literally "saké shop". A Japanese-style bar, usually with a mix of bar stools and Japanese *tatami* places for patrons. *Izakaya* normally try to convey a Japanese atmosphere in choice of food, drink, and décor.

jingizu-kan — A style of cooking in which thin slices of meat and vegetables are cooked on a domed rimmed griddle, each diner grilling his food for himself. Named because of the assumed resemblance to a Mongol warrior's helmet, thus the Japanese pronunciation of Ghengis Khan.

kabocha — Japanese squash. *Cucurbita moschata* or *C. maxima.* Sweet orange flesh and green skin. Used in *tempura*, or steamed, candied.

kaiseki ryōri — Cuisine that accompanies the Tea ceremony. Now served on its own (i.e., without the tea ritual) as an elaborate, multi-course meal in restaurants.

kaki — Persimmon. *Diospyros kaki.* Orange fruit, with flattened, square shape and crisp, sweet flesh. Sold in the UK as "Sharon fruit." Often sold in dried form in Japan whereupon it tastes somewhat like dried dates.

kakiage — A fritter. Usually of chopped vegetables and sea food in *tempura.*

kamaboko — Fish paste cake. Manufactured from the flesh of several kinds of white fish (cod, flatfish) to which starch and sometimes vegetable protein is added, moulded, and steamed. Normally moulded on a small wooden slab so that slices are demi-lune shaped. The convex side is often dyed pink or red. *Kamaboko*, like tofu, is extremely versatile, and is shaped, pressed, and cut into a variety of shapes. Each region processes *kamaboko* differently.

kami — The object of worship in Shintō. A deity. The divine.

Kansai — The area of Kyoto and Osaka. The word literally means "West of the Barrier (mountains along the Tōkaidō coastal road)." Kansai cooking is characterised by the use of paler *miso* and sweeter seasoning.

kanten — A gelatine (agar agar) seaweed. It sets at room temperature, and much harder than animal-derived gelatines.

Kantō — The area of the plain surrounding and north of the present city of Tokyo. The word literally means "East of the Barrier (mountains along the Tōkaidō coastal road)." Its cooking is characterised by darker miso and saltier flavouring.

kara-age — Deep fried Chinese style. Before being dipped in batter, ingredients are dipped or marinated in a sauce of ginger and soy, sometimes wine. Sometimes the batter is flavoured instead. Usually refers to chicken cooked in this style.

karē-raisu — Curry rice. A dish of thick roux-based sauce flavoured with mild curry powder or cubes. It owes its origin to British expatriates in Yokohama and Kobe during the nineteenth century.

[o]kashi — Sweetmeats, confectionery. In conversation one might refer specifically to *yōgashi* (Western confectionery) or *wagashi* (Japanese confectionery). The latter are usually made on the basis of *mochi* (q.v.) and *an* (q.v.). *Kanten* jelly is used either on its own or as a binder for *an.*

kasutera — A sponge cake. Of Portuguese origin, the name derives from "Castilla", ancient Spain. It has become a specialty of Nagasaki, Kyushu where Western cultural influences stretch back to the Portuguese arrival in the sixteenth century, and the Dutch factory in Deshima, the sole European outpost during the Edo-era.

katsuo — Bonito. *Katsuwonus pelamis.* Medium-sized variety of fish related to the tuna. This is, probably, the most important fish to Japanese cuisine. It is eaten as *tataki* (charred *sashimi*) and in a number of other forms, but its greatest use is for the making of *katsuo-bushi* from which most *dashi* are made.

katsuo bushi — Dried *katsuo.* The fillet of the fish is boiled, dried, smoked, fermented, then dried again to produce, after a year, a hard, woody object resembling a brown, petrified banana. This is shaved when needed (nowadays bought shaved), and the shavings steeped in hot water to make the basic stock used in Japanese cooking.

kegani — Hairy crab. *Erimacrus isenbeckii.* A heavy, thickset crab with hair-like protrusions over its shell and a delicate white flesh. It is a speciality of the northern seas around Hokkaido and considered a great delicacy.

kibi — Millet. *Panicum milleaceum.* Before the introduction of rice to Japan in proto-historic times, it was one of the mainstays of the population. *Kibi* offerings are still important in some Shintō shrines. For most modern Japanese it is memorable because Momotarō, the hero of a fairy-tale/fable, took *kibi dango* (millet balls) along with him on his adventures.

kimchi — A spicy Korean pickle. A staple of Korean cooking, most often made of *hakusai* cabbage (q.v.), chilli peppers, salt and small shrimp. It has become a popular pickle in Japan as well.

kohada — Young gizzard-shad. *Clupanodon punctatus.* Lightly pickled, the fish is used in Edo sushi.

kompa — A drinking party. Normally accompanied by large masses of food.

konbu — A seaweed or sea-ribbon: a wide, thick strand (*Undaria pinnatifida*.sp. *Laminaria*). Usually sold dry. Soaked in water, it expands from a leathery, dry strip to a slippery thick vegetable strand with a strong sea smell. Used to make basic stock (*dashi*).

konnyaku — Devil's tongue root. *Amorphophallus konjac.* It is made into a thick relatively hard jelly. Normally translucent grey with black specks, it can be dyed by the addition of nori to a bright green. Eaten as a vegetarian *sashimi*, or as an ingredient in *oden.*

konomi-yaki — Lit. "cook as you like it": thin pancakes of vegetables and sea-food, cooked on a metal hot plate. An inexpensive food popular with students.

maguro — Tuna. *Thunnus sp.* A large fish most often eaten raw as sushi or *sashimi.* Because of the size of the fish (one to three meters), one rarely sees it whole except at the Tsukiji or similar wholesale fish markets. In the Edo period it was considered a low-class fish, but since then its star (and price) have risen in line with its growing rarity.

maki — A roll. A kind of sushi in which the rice is wrapped in a sheet of *nori* (q.v.). The filling may be any fish such as *maguro* (q.v.), seafood or fresh or pickled vegetables. California *maki* of avocado and crabmeat, invented and popular in the West, is now also served in Japan.

maneki neko — A small (the largest we have seen was about 80 cm high) statue of a beckoning white cat with one paw upraised. This is supposed to draw in customers. It is a common decoration in the lobbies of restaurants, along with a picture or figurine of the *shichifukujin* (seven lucky gods).

matsutake — Pine mushroom. *Armillaria matsudake.* An expensive wild fungus that grows in pine forests. Comparable in price and esteem to truffles in French cooking. A single cap and stalk of *matsutake* can fetch 10,000 yen.

meibutsu — Lit. "famous things." The special product of an area which travellers buy as presents to bring home. Many have been historically famous. In recent years, with the desire to differentiate communities and maintain their separate identities, new *meibutsu* have been created as marketing ploys, capitalising on real or created local resources.

menrui — Noodles. Generic name.

mirin — A sweet alcoholic liquor used only for cooking. Made from a mixture of alcohol from rice infected by a rice fungus (*Aspergillus oryzae*) and *shochu*, a sweet-potato derived spirit.

miso — Bean paste. A seasoning made by fermenting soy beans with a grain-carried fungi and salt. Used to flavour soups and other dishes, as a pickling medium, and for eating as *moromi miso* (q.v.). Each region has its distinctive *miso*, either light or dark. Pale coloured *miso* is favoured in the Kansai region. It can take up to a year for *miso* to mature. Some *miso*, mixed with a heavy proportion of fermenting agent and grain, are ready in two weeks and have a sweetish flavour. Grains used can be rice, wheat or barley.

miso shiru — A soup based on a *dashi* (q.v.) base, which has been mixed with *miso* paste. Traditionally one blended several kinds of *miso* to achieve a preferred balance of flavours. Vegetables, small clams, and tofu are often added.

mitsuba — Trefoil. *Cryptotaenia japonica.* An aromatic leaf used commonly to flavour soups and custards. Sometimes called Japanese parsley in the West.

mizu-shobai — Lit. "water-business." The entertainment and hospitality business including bars, restaurants, *geisha* and so on. The term derives from a Buddhist concept of the mundane world as a "floating" world, that is, transient and impermanent.

mochi — Glutinous rice, steamed, pounded, and shaped. Used as ritual offerings. A celebratory food. When mixed with sweetened beans or bean paste, forms the basis for Japanese sweets (*wagashi*).

monjya-yaki — A kind of *konomiyaki* (q.v.) that evolved in Tokyo during and after World War II. A thin batter mixed with vegetables, pickles, and sometimes meat or fish is fried on a metal griddle. The crust is scraped off periodically by the diners and eaten immediately. The name is said to derive from *moji* (letters), in reference to the batter which was so thin you could almost use it to write with.

moritsuke — Dishing up, piling up: the arrangement of food on a plate or tray.

morohēya — Molokhia (Ar.) *Corchorus olitorius.* A green leaf, used in Egyptian, Middle Eastern, and Philippine cooking, valued as a thickener in soups. Became popular in Japan about 1996.

moromi miso — Dipping *miso* usually served with cucumbers as a saké accompaniment. *Moromi* is saké must or the solid mass from soy sauce making.

mugi — May refer to wheat or barley, though generally meaning barley. *Mugi-cha* is a refreshing infusion of roasted ground barley often drunk cold during the summer.

murasaki — Sushi terminology for soy sauce.

myōga — Japanese ginger. *Zingiber mioga.* Buds and shoots are both eaten, though the root is inedible. The pink buds are used fresh, finely shredded, or

	both buds and shoots may be lightly vinegared. Its aroma is a lemony-fruity variant of the true ginger.
nanban	Southern barbarian (that is, European). Methods of cooking now associated with the southern island of Kyushu (where Europeans first landed in the sixteenth century). *Nanbanzuke* is escabeche, a marinade of vinegar, onion, sweet and chilli peppers in which fried fish is left to pickle for a few hours or more.
nashi	Asian pear. *Pyrrus serotina.* Crisper and juicier than its Western equivalent.
nasu	Eggplant, aubergine. The Japanese variety is smaller (about 15 cm or less, and about 5 cm thick), sweeter, and firmer than the Western equivalent. Some varieties are so sweet they can almost be eaten raw. A summer delicacy. Tempura-ed, stewed, grilled, also often pickled.
nata de coco	The result of fermenting coconut juice, which is then infected with a bacterium to create a curd. The curd is repeatedly scalded during processing, the end product is sweetened, and cut into small (1 cm) translucent, jelly-like cubes. Used in the Philippines as a sweetmeat or addition to tropical fruit salads. Became a fad food in Japan during the mid-90s.
natto	Beans fermented in a straw wrapping. A breakfast speciality of Eastern Japan. Also used in sushi rolls, miso soup and stews.
nigiri-zushi	"Squeezed" sushi. The type-model of sushi (at least for non-Japanese). A ball of lightly vinegared rice topped with a slice of raw or lightly cooked fish or seafood.
nimono	Simmered things. Vegetables and other foods simmered or poached in *dashi* (q.v.).
nori	Laver. *Porphyra sp.* Sheets of dried seaweed, shiny green-black in colour. Normally bought in standard-sized sheets. Toasted, they acquire a greeny-black colour. In sheets, *nori* is used to make *maki* (q.v.). *Ajitsuke nori* is flavoured *nori* individually packed for breakfast. Shredded, flaked or powdered nori is used as a garnish (see *furikake*).
norimaki	A kind of sushi. A roll wrapped in *nori* (q.v.), filled with sushi rice together with fish or seafood or vegetable (such as cucumber). Shaped with a rolling mat (*makisu).* Cut into small, bite-sized cylinders and served cut-end up to reveal the colourful pattern made by the filling. *Futomaki* (lit. "fat rolls") are rolls with more filling. *Temaki* are hand-rolled (i.e., without a mat) and are ice-cream cone-shaped. Other carbohydrates such as grated yam or noodles may be used instead of rice.
omuraisu	Omelette rice. A popular children's food. Cooked rice is fried with ketchup, then enclosed in an omelette.
osaka-zushi	Osaka-style sushi. Sweetish vinegared rice, lightly pickled fish (usually mackerel [*saba*]) and pale coloured seaweed placed in a wooden mould, pressed and cut into rectangular blocks. Called *saba zushi* or *battera,* after the Portuguese term for "small boat", which the mould resembles.
ponzu	Juice of a small bitter orange or citron, mixed with soy sauce. It is used as a dip or marinade.
rāmen	Chinese style noodles. Usually made of wheat flour, thinly cut or hand-pulled. They are a popular snack dish.
robata-yaki	A style of cooking in which fish, vegetables, and meat are grilled before the diner, often stuck on skewers which are placed vertically in a sand bed on which the coals glow.

ryōtei — A traditional form of eating place in which parties of diners eat in separate rooms, usually a table d'hôte meal featuring seasonal delicacies in a series of courses at different price levels.

saba — Mackerel. *Scombrina.* Usually eaten salt-grilled, since this is a very oily fish, stewed in *miso*, or pickled in rice vinegar, e.g., *shimesaba.*

sakariba — Entertainment areas usually around commuter train stations. They have a high concentration of bars, coffee-shops, tea-houses, nightclubs and so on. Most *sarariman* stop at their favourite bar to unwind, and groups of *sarariman* often undergo bouts of bar-hopping within the same *sakariba,* which extend both horizontally and vertically onto several floors of buildings, both above and below ground.

saké — Liquor. In colloquial usage refers to *nihon-shu* (Japanese liquor), an alcoholic beverage pressed from rice that has been infected with a mould (*Aspergillus oryzae*). The resulting mash is pressed in bags, then filtered. This yields a natural "beer" of about 22%abv. By Japanese law, this is watered down to between 18.5 and 16.5%abv. There are numerous varieties, roughly falling into dry and sweet categories. Dry may be drunk cold, sweet is always drunk warm.

saké — Salmon. Traditionally this was salted (*shiozake*), then grilled for breakfast. It is more rarely prepared as sushi. There is also a thriving smoked salmon industry in northern Japan based on Scottish recipes. Pronounced "*shaké*" in the Tokyo area.

sakoku — Lit. "closed country". During most of the Edo-era, from 1637 to 1856, Japan was closed to foreigners, who, except for the Dutch at Dejima, Nagasaki, would be imprisoned upon landing. Japanese were forbidden to go abroad on pain of execution. This period of isolation did play an important part in keeping Japan free from European colonial domination.

sanbo — Raised footed trays used to present offerings in Shintō rituals.

sanma — Saury. *Cololabis saira.* A small, long and thin fish. Eaten in a variety of ways but more usually salt-grilled.

sanshō — Japanese pepper tree (prickly ash) *Zanthoxylum piperitum.* A very versatile spice. The young leaves, *kinome,* are used as garnish in *sashimi*; in clear soups (as *suikuchi,* "aromatic sipper") for spring *kaiseki.* The flowers, green and mature fruit, and bark are all used for flavouring. A *tsukudani* (soy sauce simmered savoury) of the leaves and fruit is a Kyoto speciality. The *sanshō* fruit's most popular use is as a ground spice sprinkled on *kabayaki* eel. Closely related to Szechuan pepper, it is a component of seven-spice powder (*shichimi togarashi*).

sato imo — Taro. *Colocasia antiquorum.* A small (5 cm long) round root vegetable. Often appears in *nimono.*

sechi ryōri — The traditional foods for the New Year – spiced saké (*toso*), soup with glutinous rice (*zoni*), and assorted boxed foods made well in advance. Colourful arrangements of (usually) cold food offered guests on the New Year. Red and white coloured foods, symbolic allusions predominate.

sekihan — Red rice. Rice that has been cooked with beans. The rice acquires a deep pink tint and rather stiff consistency. A traditional food marking auspicious occasions.

senbei — Crackers or biscuits. These are normally savoury but sometimes sweet. There are countless variations of shapes and flavours. Usually made of rice, some are famous regional specialities.

shiitake Popular dark-brown tree mushrooms. *Cortinellus shiitake.* Widely used fresh or dried in stews, soups, hot-plate cooking, sukiyaki. Dried, it is reconstituted for making stock, especially in Buddhist vegetarian cooking.

shimeji A smallish, white mushroom. *Lyophyllum aggregatum.* They are often a component of dishes such as *nabemono* stews.

shinmai New rice. Rice newly harvested, which is considered particularly tasty. A major gourmet item.

shiruko A sweet soup made of *an* poured over toasted *mochi.* One of the many popular *okashi* (q.v.).

shisō Beefsteak plant, perilla. *Perilla frutescens.* The aromatic leaf looks like stinging nettle, but tastes slightly like basil. It comes in green (*ao-jiso*) and purple (*aka-jiso*) varieties. Both leaves and flower buds are eaten, often as garnishes to sushi and *sashimi* (q.v.).

[O]shōgatsu New Year. The single most important event in the Japanese religious and secular calendar. Most shops and businesses close down for several days. Special foods – *osechi ryōri* – are prepared to offer to guests. Many households still maintain specific household rituals. In modern Japanese *shōgatsu* there is a mixture of elements, religious and secular, Japanese and Western.

shōjin ryōri Buddhist vegetarian cooking. Designed to follow the strict rules of monastic sects, no foods of animal origin are allowed, not even eggs. Protein sources are nuts, wheat gluten and soybeans in various forms: *miso* bean paste, fresh bean curd (tofu), fresh and dried bean sheets (*yuba*), fried bean curd (*abura age*), freeze-dried bean curd (*kōya dōfu*). A lot of imagination goes into making even the simplest vegetarian meals.

shottsuru A fish sauce made by fermenting small fishes such as sardines. An element in Akita and other northern prefectural cooking. In Edo period Japan it was as common as soy sauce as a condiment. It is similar to Southeast Asian fish sauces such as the Vietnamese *nuoc-mam* and Philippine *patis.*

shun The perfect season for a given food.

soba Buckwheat. *Fagopyrum esculentum.* A grain used in Japan mainly to manufacture noodles. By extension, even Chinese noodles, made of wheat flour, are called by the same name (e.g., *chūka-soba*).

sōsu A contraction for *oosta sōsu* or Worcester Sauce. The Japanese version, however is thick and sweetish, somewhat like HP sauce. Used as a condiment for *hanbāga* and *tonkatsu* (q.v.).

sunomono Literally vinegared things. Foods that have been prepared by light salting and vinegaring, including fish, seafood, seaweeds, and vegetables.

surume Dried squid or cuttlefish. Normally eaten as *otsumami* (q.v.). It can be bought either whole, looking like a cardboard cutout of a squid, or shredded into strips.

suzuki Sea bass. *Percina.* A white-fleshed medium-sized fish often served as *sashimi.*

tachiuo Cutlass-fish. *Trichiuridae.* A long, vertically flattened fish looking somewhat like an eel.

taho Very soft unmoulded tofu usually eaten with caramel syrup as a sweet snack. Philippine street/peddled food.

tai Bream. *Sparidae sp.* Several species are eaten. Considered to be one of the most delicious of fish. The name "tai" is homonymous with *medetai* (congratulations) and it is therefore the preferred fish for celebrations such as weddings.

takuan — Pickled *daikon*. This is one of the most common Japanese pickles, alas, in the modern world, often artificially dyed a vile yellow. Normally it is made by drying peeled daikon, which are then pickled in rice bran. In Northern Honshu (Akita) they are also smoked after pickling.

tamago zushi — Literally "egg" but in sushi it refers to a kind of sushi made of a thick, cooled omelette made with *mirin* (q.v.) so the end product is sweetish and moist. Edokko who are supposed to have a sweet tooth are particularly fond of this sushi, also called *datemaki*.

tamari — A light soy sauce which is the residue of *miso* making. In traditional *miso* breweries, a pail with small holes was inserted into the *miso* and the liquid collected was sold separately as *tamari*.

tataki — To pound or chop. A method of preparation involving chopping, cutting into, or kneading vegetables, such as burdock root and cucumber, and marinading in ginger, sesame or vinegar. The same term refers to *katsuo*, beef fillets, and other fish/meat seared at high heat, leaving the centre raw, and seasoned with green onions, ginger, vinegar and soy sauce. A speciality of Tosa, a former clan on Shikoku Island, said to be derived from steak tartare.

tatami — Straw mats which floor traditional Japanese rooms. They are of standard size, usually 90 × 180 cm.

te-maki — A cone-shaped *norimaki* (q.v.). *Nori* is wrapped around sushi rice, a fish, seafood or vegetable filling, then rolled into a cone by hand. Fillings are similar to sushi toppings but include those that don't hold their shape, e.g., pickled plum paste, perilla leaf, shredded raw squid, sea-urchin roe.

tempura — Deep fried, lightly battered vegetables and fish. Usually served with a sauce of soy, stock, grated ginger and grated radish, or plain/flavoured salt. May have originated in the Portuguese word "tempero" (condiments), or Spanish "tempora" (fasting food).

teppan — Griddle or iron plate. A flat metal surface heated for grilling (usually self-cooking) meat or vegetables. Small electric ones are a common utility in Japanese houses. May have originated from the practice of cooking food over heated flat stones.

tokonoma — The niche in a traditional Japanese room used for a restrained display of a seasonal flower arrangement, a scroll (determined, traditionally, by the owner's mood and the occasion), or piece of pottery.

tonjiru — A miso soup based on a pork and vegetables stock. Normal accompaniment to *tonkatsu* (q.v.).

tonkatsu — *Ton* = pork and *katsu* = cutlet. Another importation from Europe. A slice of deep fried battered and crumbed pork. Normally served with finely shredded cabbage, mustard and some *sōsu* (q.v.). Accompaniments are pickles and *tonjiru* or *miso* soup. Yokohama claims to have developed *tonkatsu* from British expatriates' pork cutlets.

toro — Tuna belly meat. Eaten exclusively as sushi or *sashimi*, it is softer, more delicately flavoured than the *maguro* cut. Containing more fat, its colour is pink, highly prized, and priced accordingly.

tororo — Grated yam (*yamaimo* q.v.).Other yams used are *nagaimo* and *yamatoimo*. A delicacy of mountain regions. A slightly astringent, frothy and "slippery" sauce added to soup or poured over rice.

tsukemono Literally "pickles" which hardly does justice to the concept. There are countless varieties, flavours, ingredients. Most commonly used are saké lees, *miso*, and salt fermentation for long pickles, and vinegar and/or just salt for short (one-hour or one-day) pickles. Traditional housewives took great pride in creating elaborate and complex *tsukemono*, e.g. stuffed pickled gourd with swirl-patterned, vari-coloured stuffing.

tsukudani A savoury of vegetables (burdock root, mushrooms), seafood and small fish simmered down in soy sauce and sugar until almost caramelised. Often eaten as a breakfast or after-dinner (now rare) relish.

tsukune Balls of chicken meat or fish. May be simmered in stock, or grilled *yakitori*-style.

[o]tsumami Drinking foods. Snacks. These may range from peanuts and pickles, to elaborate concoctions of grilled food, fish, etc. Also called *saké no sakana*.

tsuruna New Zealand spinach. *Tetragonia expansa*. Greens favoured for their delicate texture and flavour for soups, cooked salads (*hitashi*), stir-frying.

udo A plant, both cultivated and wild, treasured for its crisp texture and distinctive flavour and scent. *Aralia cordata*. Invaluable in *sunomono* (vinegared salads) and *nimono* (stews).

udon Wheat flour noodles, dried or fresh (*te uchi* "hand cut"). Names abound for variants of this noodle, distinguished only by their diameters. *Himokawa* (also called *imokawa*) *udon* are the thickest; less thick are Nagoya's famed *kishimen*. Vermicelli-thin *sōmen* and the slightly thicker *hiyamugi* are summer treats, served chilled on ice and dipped in cold sauce, horseradish and chopped green onions. Udon's capacity for absorbing flavours makes it ideal for long-simmered *nikomi udon* (simmered in flavourful stock) and table-top cooked *nabeyaki udon*.

umeboshi Pickled "plums" (actually the fruit of the Japanese apricot *Prunus mume*). They are usually dull or bright red, more rarely dull green, the size of an olive or a quail's egg. May be crisply-textured, or soft and mushy. In either case they are extremely salty. Used to make *hinomaru bentō* (Japanese flag lunchbox) where the *umeboshi* serves as the roundel in the middle of the white rice. Reputed to stop rice going bad, hence their inclusion in *bentō*.

uni Sea urchin. *Echinoidea sp.* The gonads are eaten. They are a delicacy in sushi, an orangey yellow sweet cream that melts on the tongue. Also served steamed, preserved in salt or saké, used as a seasoning sauce or topping in *aemono* (salads flavoured with a thick, richly flavoured dressing, not vinegar).

wakame A type of seaweed. *Undaria pinnatifida*. Mainly used to make *dashi* (q.v.) and as garnish, salads.

warabi Fiddlehead ferns. *Osmunda japonica* or *Pteridium aquilinum*. One of the wild greens or mountain vegetables (*sansai*), though cultivated since the end of the Meiji period. Young shoots of a bracken pickled or scalded for stews, *aemono* (thickly dressed salads), and *hitashi* (cooked salad). The raw greens have to be soaked in lye or baking soda and rinsed thoroughly before using. Believed to contain a carcinogen, but at normal dietary amounts, considered safe.

wasabi Japanese horseradish. *Wasabia japonica*. An essential flavouring in most sushi, its fiery effect is skull-tingling and nose-clearing. Usually comes as a green powder (sometimes adulterated with mustard) which is mixed with water to make a green paste. The grated plant root, where available, is more flavourful. It is alleged to prevent ptomaine poisoning as well.

yakimono Roasted or grilled things. The word in Japanese subsumes a variety of cooking methods including grilling over charcoal, pan frying, and *teppan* (q.v.) grilling.

yakitori Chicken bits – meat, gizzards, skin – and vegetables – sweet peppers, asparagus, mushrooms – on small skewers grilled over charcoal. A popular [*o*]*tsumami* (drinking food), it is also served on its own as a separate style in stalls and dedicated restaurants.

yamaimo Mountain yam. *Dioscorea esculenta.* A large, broad root vegetable. One of several yams used to make *tororo* (q.v.).

yamamomo Arbutus. *Arbutus unedo.* A small (2–3 cm) strawberry-coloured globular fruit full of sweet-sour juice. Grown mainly in Kochi and Tokushima (as well as China and Okinawa) but rarely seen in shops because it does not travel well.

yatai A street stall. Most often, these sell foods, which may range from dishes of *oden* (q.v.) through sweets and candy apples.

yōkan Jellied *anko* made with *kudzu* or some other gelling agent.

zōni A vegetable soup based on *dashi* in which *mochi* balls have been floated. One of the three elements of *osechi* cuisine for the New Year. Most households have their own preferred recipe, and there are innumerable variations.

References

REFERENCES IN ENGLISH AND OTHER WESTERN LANGUAGES

Allison, Anne 1991 "Japanese Mothers and Obentos: The lunchbox as ideological state apparatus" *Anthropological Quarterly* 64(4): 195–208.

Anderson, Eugene 1980 "'Heating' and 'cooling' foods in Hong Kong and Taiwan" *Social Science Information* 19(2): 237–68.

Anderson, E. 1984 "Heating and cooling foods re-examined" *Social Science Information,* 23(4/5): 755–73.

Anderson, Eugene N. 1988 *The Food of China.* New Haven: Yale University Press.

Anderson, Jennifer L. 1987 "Japanese tea ritual: Religion in practice" *Man* 22(3): 475–98.

Anderson, Jennifer L. 1991 *An Introduction to Japanese Tea Ritual.* Stonybrook: State University of New York.

Angulo, Julio 1987 "Three meanings of food: The psychological, ecological and symbolic perspectives" *Transformations* 2(2–3): 33–7.

Appadurai, Arjun 1981 "Gastropolitics in Hindu South Asia" *American Ethnologist* 8: 494–511.

Appadurai, Arjun 1988 "How to make a national cuisine: Cookbooks in contemporary India" *Comparative Studies in Society and History* 30(1): 3–24.

Arnott, Margaret L. (ed.) 1975 *Gastronomy: The Anthropology of Food Habits.* The Hague: Mouton.

Ashkenazi, Michael 1989 "Japanization, Internationalization and Aesthetics in the Japanese Meal" in A. Boscaro et al. (eds) *Rethinking Japan.* London: Paul Norbury.

Ashkenazi, Michael 1993 *Matsuri: Festivals of a Japanese Town.* Honolulu: University of Hawaii Press.

Ashkenazi, Michael 1991 "From tachi soba to naorai: Cultural implications of the Japanese meal" *Social Science Information* 30(2): 287–304.

Asquith, Pamela J. and Arne Kalland (eds) 1997 *Japanese Images of Nature: Cultural Perspectives.* Richmond: Curzon.

Australian Bureau of Agricultural and Resource Economics 1988 *Japanese Agricultural Policies: A Time of Change.* Policy Monographs #3. Canberra: Australian Government Publishing Services.

Barer-Stein, T. 1979 *You Are What You Eat.* Toronto: McClelland & Stewart.

Barlosius, Eva 1987 "Riechen und Schmecken-Riechendes und Schmeckendes. Ernahrungssoziologische Anmerkungen zum Wandel der sinnlichen Wahrnehmung beim Essen, dargestellt an den Beispielen der grande cuisine Frankreichs und der modernen Aromenherstellung [Smell and Taste-Substances That Smell and Taste. Notes on the Sociology of Food and Changing Sense Perceptions in Eating: The Examples of French Grande Cuisine and Modern Flavor Manufacturing]" *Kolner Zeitschrift fur Soziologie und Sozialpsychologie* 39(2): 367–75.

Barlosius, Eva and Wolfgang Manz 1988 "Der Wandel der Kochkunst als Genussorientierte Speisengestaltung. Webers Theorie der Ausdifferenzierung und Rationalisierung als Grundlage einer Ernahrungssoziologie [The Change in the Art of Cooking to Enjoyment-Oriented Meal Creation. Weber's Theory of Rationalization and Differentiation as the Basis of Nutritional Sociology]" *Kolner Zeitschrift fur Soziologie und Sozialpsychologie* 40(4): 728–46.

Bates, Marsten 1967 *Gluttons and Libertines: Human Problems of Being Natural.* New York: Random House.

Batstone, Eric 1983 "The hierarchy of maintenance and the maintenance of hierarchy: Notes on food and industry" in A. Murcott (ed.) *The Sociology of Food and Eating.* Aldershot: Gower.

Befu, Harumi 1974 "An ethnography of dinner entertainment in Japan" *Arctic anthropology* XI-suppl.: 196–203.

Bella, Balint 1982 "Scarcity of resources and social action" *Social Science Information* 21(6): 901–13.

Ben-Ari, Eyal 1989 "At the interstices: Drinking, management and temporary groups in a local Japanese organisation" *Social Analysis* 26: 46–65.

Blofeld, John 1985 *The Chinese Art of Tea.* Boston: Shambhala.

Bourdieu, Pierre 1984 *Distinction: A Social Critique of the Judgement of Taste.* London: Routledge & Kegan Paul.

Brillat-Savarin, Jean Anthelme 1978 *The Physiology of Taste.* (MFK Fisher Trans.) New York: Harcourt Brace Jovanovich.

Bryant, Carol A., Anita Courteney, Barbara Mankesberry and Cathleen DeWalt 1985 *The Cultural Feast: An Introduction to Food and Society.* St. Paul Minn: West Publ. Co.

Calnan, Michael and Sarah Cant 1990 "The social organisation of food consumption: A comparison of middle class and working class households" *International Journal of Sociology and Social Policy* 10(2): 53–9.

Casal, U. A. 1958–59 "Salt" *Monumenta Nipponica* 14: 61–91.

Cassel, John 1977 "Social and cultural implications of food and food habits" in D. Landy (ed.) *Culture, Disease, and Healing.* NY: Macmillan Publishing Co., Inc.

Chang, K. C. (ed.) 1977 *Food in Chinese Culture: Anthropological and Historical Perspectives.* New Haven: Yale University Press.

Cherulnik, Paul D. 1991 "Reading restaurant facades: Environmental influence in finding the right place to eat" *Environment and Behavior* 23(2): 150–70.

Chiva, Matty 1979 "How a person is built through eating; Comment la personne se construit en mangeant" *Communications* 31: 107–18.

Clammer, John 1999 "The global and the local: Gender, class and the internationalisation of consumption in a Tokyo neighbourhood" in M. Ashkenazi and J. Clammer (eds) *Material Culture in Japanese Society.* London: Kegan Paul International.

Clark, Priscilla P. 1975a "Thoughts for food, I: French cuisine and French culture" *French Review* 49(1): 32–41.

Clark, Priscilla P. 1975b "Thoughts for food II: Culinary culture in contemporary France" *French Review* 49(2): 198–205.

Cobbi, Jane 1978 *Le vegetal dans la vie Japonaise: L'utilisation alimentaire de plantes sauvages dans un village de montagne, Kaidamura.* Paris: Publications Orientalistes de France.

Cobbi, Jane 1984 "Tradition et adoptions: Cuisines du Japon", *Revue des Amis de Sévres, No. special: Cuisines et culture*: 16–22.

Cobbi, Jane 1987 "Don et contre-don" in A. Berque (ed.) *Le Japon et son double: Logigue d'un autoportrait.* Paris: Masson.

Cobbi, Jane 1988 "Le doux et le fort (Japon)" *Journal d'agronomé tropicale er de botanique appliquée*, No. special: Le sucre et le sel, 35: 267–79.

Cobbi, Jane 1991 "Dieux, buveurs et ancétres gourmands" *L'Homme* 118(5): 111–23.

Cooper, Eugene 1986 "Chinese table manners: You are how you eat" *Human Organization* 45(2): 179–84.
Creighton, Millie R. 1992 "The Depaato: Merchandising the West while selling Japaneseness" in Joesph J. Tobin (ed.) *Re-Made in Japan: Everyday Life and Consumer Taste in a Changing Society.* New Haven: Yale University Press.
Cwiertka, Katrinjka 1995 "To what extent is foreign food adoption culturally determined – an example of Japan in comparison with Europe" *Appetite,* 24(3): 272–80.
Cwiertka, Katrinjka 1998 "A note on the making of culinary tradition – An example of modern Japan" *Appetite* 30(2): 117–28.
Dalby, Liza C. 1983 *Geisha.* N.Y.: Vintage Books.
Dale, Peter N. 1986 *The Myth of Japanese Uniqueness.* London & Sydney: Croom Helm.
Davis, Winston 1984 "Pilgrimage and world renewal: A study of religion and social value in Tokugawa Japan" *History of Religions* 23(3).
De Garine, I. 1976 "Food, tradition and prestige" in D. N. Walcher, N. Kretchmer, and H. L. Barnett (eds) *Food, Man, and Society.* N.Y.: Plenum Press.
Del Alisal, Maria 1999 "Japanese lunch boxes: From convenient snack to the convenience store" in M. Ashkenazi and J. Clammer (eds) *Material Culture in Japanese Society.* London: Kegan Paul International.
Delamont, Sara 1983 "Lobster, chicken, cake and tears: Deciphering wedding meals" in A. Murcott (ed.) *The Sociology of Food and Eating.* Aldershot: Gower Press.
Douglas, Mary 1971 "Deciphering a meal" In C. Geertz (ed.) *Myth, Symbol & Culture* N.Y.
Douglas, Mary and Jonathan Gross 1981 "Food and culture: Measuring the intricacy of rule systems" *Social Science Information* 20(1): 1–35.
Douglas, Mary 1982 "Food as a system of communication" pp. 82–124 in M. Douglas, *In the active voice.* London: Routledge & Kegan Paul.
Douglas, Mary (ed.) 1984 *Food in the Social Order: Studies of Food and Festivities in Three American Communities.* N.Y.: Russell Sage Foundation.
Douglas, Mary J. 1984 "Standard social uses of food: Introduction" in M. Douglas (ed.) *Food in the Social Order.* N.Y.: Russell Sage Foundation.
Douglas, Mary (ed.) 1985 *Constructive Drinking.* Cambridge: Cambridge U. Press.
Dreyfus, Hubert L., Steward E. Dreyfus with Tom Athanasiou 1986 *The Mind of the Machine: The Power of Human Intuition and Expertise in the Era of the Computer.* Oxford: Blackwell.
Dumas, Alexandre 1958 *Dictionary of Cuisine* (Louis Colman trans. and ed.) N.Y.: Avon Books.
Eckstein E. F. 1980 *Food, People and Nutrition.* Westport, Conn: AVI Publications.
Elias, Norbert 1982 *The Civilizing Process.* New York: Urizen Press.
Embree, John F. 1939 *Suye Mura: A Japanese Village.* Chicago: University of Chicago Press.
Facciola, Stephen 1990 *Cornucopia: A Source Book Of Edible Plants* Vista, Ca: Kampong Publications.
Farb, Peter and George Armelagos 1980 *Consuming Passions: The Anthropology of Eating.* N.Y.: Washington Square Press.
Fernandez, Doreen G. and Edilberto N. Alegre 1988 *Sarap: Essays on Philippine Food.* Manila: Mr. & Ms. Publishing Co.
Ferro-Luzzi, G. E. 1977 "Remarks on D. P. McDonald's 'Food taboos'" *Anthropos* 73: 593–94.
Fiddes, Nick 1991 *Meat: A Natural Symbol.* London: Routledge.
Fieldhouse, Paul 1986 *Food and Nutrition: Customs and Culture.* London: Croom Helm.
Fine, Gary-Alan 1987 "Working Cooks: The Dynamics of Professional Kitchens" *Current Research on Occupations and Professions* 4: 141–58.
Fischler, Claude 1980 "Food habits, social change, and the nature/culture dilemma" *Social Science Information* 19(6): 937–53.
Fischler, Claude 1988 "Food, self and identity" *Social Science Information* 27(2): 275–92.
Fisher, M. F. K. (Mary Frances Kennedy) 1976 *The Art of Eating.* New York: Vintage Books.

Fisher, M. F. K. (Mary Frances Kennedy) 1992 *Conversations with M. F. K. Fisher.* (Edited by Davis Lazar). Jackson Miss.: University Press of Mississippi.

Fitzgerald, Thomas M. 1986 "Dietary change among Cook Islanders in New Zealand" pp. 67–86 in L. Manderson (ed.) *Shared Wealth and Symbol: Food Culture and Society in Oceania.* Cambridge: Cambride University Press.

Flores, Toni 1985 "The Anthropology of Aesthetics" *Dialectical Anthropology* 10(1–2): 27–41.

Forster, R. and O. Ranum (eds) 1979 *Food and drink in history.* Baltimore: Johns Hopkins University Press.

Freeman, M. 1998 "Culture food for thought" *Royal Geographical Society Magazine* 70(4): 46–51.

Fujita Den interview, 1992 *The Japan Times Weekly International Edition* (March 23–29).

Fukutake, Tadashi 1974 *Japanese Society Today.* Tokyo: University of Tokyo Press.

Gayn, Mark 1976 "Food demonstrations and MacArthur's warning" in J. Livingston et al. (eds) *The Japan Reader* – vol. 2. Harmondsworth: Penguin Books.

Geertz, Clifford 1966 "Religion as a cultural system" in M. Banton (ed.) *Anthropological Approaches to the Study of Religion.* London: Tavistock Publications Ltd.

Goode, Judith, Karen Curtin, and Janet Theophano 1984 "Meal formats, meal cycles, and menu negotiation in the maintenance of an Italian-American community" pp. 143–217 in M. Douglas (ed.) *Food in the Social Order.* N.Y.: Russell Sage Foundation.

Goody, Jack 1982 *Cooking, Cuisine, and Class.* Cambridge: Cambridge University Press.

Goldstein-Gidoni, Ofra 1996 *Packaged Japaneseness: Weddings, Business and Brides.* Richmond: Curzon.

Grignon, Claude and Christiane Grignon 1980 "Styles d'alimentation et gouts populaires [Food Habits and Popular Tastes]" *Revue francaise de Sociologie* 21(4): 531–69.

Gross, Jonathan 1984 "Measurement of calendrical information in food-taking behavior" in M. Douglas (ed.) *Food in the Social Order.* N.Y.: Russell Sage Foundation.

Grosser, Arthur E. 1981 *The Cookbook Decoder, Or, Culinary Alchemy Explained* New York: Beaufort Books.

Guichard-Anguis, Sylvie 1999 "Cultural heritage and consumption" in M. Ashkenazi and J. Clammer (eds) *Material Culture in Japanese Society.* London: Kegan Paul International.

Harris Marvin, and Eric Ross 1978. "How beef became king." *Psychology Today*, Oct. 1978: 88–94.

Harris, Marvin 1987 "Foodways: Historical overview and theoretical prolegomenon" in M. Harris and E. Ross (eds) *Food and Evolution: Toward a Theory of Human Food Habits.* Philadelphia: Temple University Press.

Harris, Marvin and Eric Ross (eds) 1987 *Food and Evolution: Toward a Theory of Human Food Habits.* Philadelphia: Temple University Press.

Harris, Marvin 1988 *Good to Eat: Riddles of Food and Culture.* New York: Simon and Schuster.

Hartley, Dorothy 1969 *Food in England.* London: Macdonald.

Hayashi, Junichi 1984 "Foreign confectionery transformed into Japanese treats", *Asian Culture* 36.

Hendry, Joy 1986 *Becoming Japanese: The World of the Pre-school Child.* Manchester: Manchester University Press.

Hendry, Joy 1990 'Food as social nutrition: The Japanese case' in Chapman, Malcolm and Macbeth, Helen (eds): *Food for Humanity: Cross Disciplinary Readings.* Oxford: Centre for the Sciences of Food and Nutrition, Oxford Polytechnic.

Hendry, Joy 1993 *Wrapping Culture.* Oxford: Clarendon Press.

Hendry, Joy 1997 "Nature tamed: Japanese gardens as a microcosm of Japan's view of the world" in P. Asquith and A. Kalland (eds) *Japanese Images of Nature: Cultural Perspectives.* Richmond: Curzon.

Herpin, Nicolas 1988 "Le repas comme institution. Compte rendu d'une enquete exploratoire [The Meal as an Institution. Report of an Exploratory Survey]" *Revue francaise de Sociologie* 29(3): 503–21.

Herrigel, Eugen 1953 *Zen in the Art of Archery.* New York: Pantheon.
Herrigel, Gustie 1958 *Zen in the Art of Flower Arrangement.* London: Arkana Paperbacks.
Hirai, Michiko 1997. 'An appetite for homegrown food'. *Look Japan* 43(495): 14–5.
Hosking, Richard 1996 *A Dictionary of Japanese Food: Ingredients & Culture.* Totnes: Prospect Books.
Hsu, Francis L. K. 1975 *Iemoto: The Heart of Japan.* N.Y.: John Wiley.
Huizinga, Johann 1955 *Homo Ludens.* Boston: Beacon Press.
Irvine, Judith T. 1979 "Formality and informality in communicative events" *American Anthropologist* 81 (4): 773–91.
Ishida, Eichiro 1974 *Japanese Culture: a Study of Origins and Characteristics.* Honolulu: University Press of Hawaii.
Ishige, Naomichi 1979 "Meshi ... The staple" *Aji Communications on Japan's dietary culture* 1.
Ishige, Naomichi 1980 "Sashimi ... A gorgeous way of tasting seafood" *Aji Communications on Japan's dietary culture* 4.
Ishige, Naomichi 1980 "Sukiyaki ... A new tradition at the table" *Aji Communications on Japan's dietary culture* 2.
Ishige, Naomichi 1980 "Sushi ... Now it's instant" *Aji Communications on Japan's dietary culture* 5.
Ishige, Naomichi 1980 "Tempura ... Another usage of lamp oil" *Aji Communications on Japan's dietary culture* 3.
Ishige, Naomichi 1981 "Moritsuke ... A Japanese garden on the table" *Aji Communications on Japan's dietary culture* 8.
Ishige, Naomichi 1984 "Civilization without models" *Senri Ethnological Studies* 16: 77–86.
Ishige, Naomichi 1987 "(Table) manners makyth the man" *The Unesco Courier* May: 18–21.
Ishige, Naomichi 1990 "Développement des Restaurants Japonais pendant la périod Edo (1603–1867)" in Joseph Berchoux (ed.) *La Gastronomie ou l'homme des champs a table.* Grenoble: Editions Glénat.
James, A. 1993 "Piggy in the middle: Food symbolism and social relations" *Food Culture and History* 1: 29–48.
Japan External Trade Organization 1997 *Survey on Actual Conditions Regarding Access to Japan: Processed Foods.* Tokyo: JETRO.
Jelliffe, D. B. 1967 "Parallel food classification in developing and industrialized countries." *American Journal of Clinical nutrition* 20: 279–81.
Jeremy, Michael and M. E Robinson 1989 *Ceremony and Symbolism in the Japanese Home.* Manchester: Manchester University Press.
Johnston, Francis E. (ed.) 1987 *Nutritional Anthropology.* N.Y.: Alan R. Liss. Inc.
Joly, Henri L. and Inada Hogitaro 1963 *Arai Hakuseki's The Sword Book in Honchō Gunkikō and the Book of Samé Kō Hi Sei Gi of Inaba Tsūriō.* New York: Charles E. Tuttle.
Jussaume, Raymond A. Jr. 1991 "The growing importance of food safety to Japanese consumers and its implications for United States farmers". *American Journal of Alternative Agriculture* 6(1): 29–33.
Kanagaki, Robun 1968 *Aguranabe; Ushiya zodan; ichimei, Doronken. Meicho fukkoku zenshu kindai bungakkan.* Tokyo: Nihon Kindai Bungakkan. (translated as "The Beefeater" in Donald Keene (ed.) 1956 *Modern Japanese Literature.* New York: Grove Press.
Kanai, M., N. Fujita, T. Hasebe, Y. Sawada, Y. Aita, S. J. Hiemstra and L. Deaton 1993 "Changing patterns of food-consumption in Japan" *American Journal of Agricultural economics,* 75 (5): 1293–7.
Kanehisa, Tching 1983 "Whiskey et saké: La publicite façon japonais [Whiskey and saké: Publicity Japanese style]" *Recherche* 14(146): 998–1001.
Katz, Solomon H. 1990 "An evolutionary theory of cuisine" *Human Nature* 1(3): 233–359.
Kawamura, Yojiro and Morley R. Kare (eds) 1987 *Umami: A Basic Taste.* New York & Basel: Marcel Dekker Inc.

Khare, R. S. 1980 "Food as nutrition and culture: Notes towards an anthropological methodology" *Social Science Information* 19(3): 519–42.

Kimura, M. 1974 "Geographical distribution of local traditional cuisines in Japan" *Geographical Review of Japan* 47(6): 394–401.

Kline, Stephen 1988 "The theatre of consumption: On comparing American and Japanese advertising" *Canadian Journal of Political and Social Theory* 12(3): 101–20.

Knight, John 1994 "The Spirit of the village and the taste of the country: Aspects of rural revitalisation in present-day Japan" *Asian Survey* 34 (7): 634–46.

Knight, John 1999 "Sharing Suzuki's rice: Commodity narratives in the rural revitalization movement" in M. Ashkenazi and J. Clammer (eds) *Material Culture in Japanese Society.* London: Kegan Paul International.

Kondo, Dorinne 1985 "The Way of Tea: A symbolic analysis" *Man* 20(2): 287–306.

Krondl, M. M. and G. G. Boxen 1975 "Nutrition behaviour, food resources, and energy" in M. Arnott (ed.) *Gastronomy: The Anthropology of Food and Food Habits.* The Hague: Mouton.

Kuper, J. 1977 *The Anthropologists' Cookbook.* London: Routledge and Kegan Paul.

Lacey, Richard W. 1994 *Hard to Swallow: A Brief History of Food.* Cambridge: Cambridge University Press.

Laderman, C. 1981 "Symbolic and empirical reality: A new approach to the analysis of food avoidance" *American Ethnologist* 8(3): 468–93.

Larkcom, Joy 1991 *Oriental vegetables.* London: John Murray.

Lehrer, A 1969 "Semantic cuisine" *Linguistics* 5: 1–192.

Levi-Strauss, Claude 1969 *The Raw and the Cooked.* New York: Harper and Row.

Lindenbaum, Shirley 1977 "The last course: Nutrition and anthropology in Asia" in T. K. Fitzgerald (ed.) *Nutrition and Anthropology in Action.* Amsterdam: Van Gorcum.

Linhart, Sepp 1986 "Sakariba: Zone of 'evaporation' between work and home?" in J. Hendry and J. Webber (eds) *Interpreting Japanese Society.* Oxford: JASO.

Loveday, Leo and Satomi Chiba 1985 "Partaking with the divine and symbolizing the societal: The semiotics of Japanese food and drink" *Semiotica* 56(1/2): 115–31.

Lu, Yu 1974 *The Classic of Tea.* F. R. Carpenter (trans) Boston: Little Brown.

Lunsing, Wim 1999 "Prostitution, dating, mating and marriage: Love, sex and materialism in Japan" in M. Ashkenazi and J. Clammer (eds) *Material Culture in Japanese Society.* London: Kegan Paul International.

Lupton, Deborah 1996 *Food, the Body and the Self.* London: Sage Publications.

Manderson, Lenore 1981 "Traditional food beliefs and critical life events in Peninsular Malaysia" *Social Science Information* 20(6): 947–75.

Manderson, Lenore 1986 "Food classification and restriction in Peninsular Malaysia: Nature culture, hot and cold?" in L. Manderson (ed.) *Shared Wealth and Symbol: Food Culture and Society in Oceania.* Cambridge: Cambridge University Press.

Manderson, Lenore, (ed.) 1986 *Shared Wealth and Symbol: Food, Culture, and Society in Oceania and Southeast Asia.* Cambridge: Cambridge University Press.

Mars, G. Mars, V. 1993 "Two contrasting dining styles: Suburban conformity and urban individualism" *Food Culture and History* 1: 49–60.

Masuda, K. 1975 "Bride's progress: How a yome becomes a shutome" in D. Plath (ed.) *Adult Episodes in Japan.* Leyden: E. J. Brill.

Matsuyama, T. 1981 "Nut-gathering and processing methods in traditional Japanese villages," in S. Koyama & D. H. Thomas (eds), *Affluent Foragers: Pacific Coasts East and West.* Senri Ethnological Studies 9. Osaka: National Museum of Ethnology.

McDonald's Company (Japan), Ltd. 1991 *20 Year History of McDonald's Japan.* Tokyo: McDonald's Company (Japan), Ltd.

McFarlane, Alan 1997 *The Savage Wars of Peace.* Oxford: Blackwell.

McMillan, Charles 1989 *The Japanese Industrial System.* Berlin: Walter de Gruyter.

Mennell, Stephen 1985 *All Manners of Food.* Oxford: Basil Blackwell.
Mennell, Stephen 1987 "On the civilizing of appetite" *Theory, Culture and Society* 4(2–3): 373–403.
Mennell, Stephen 1996 "Identity and culinary culture: England, France and tomorrow the world" *Food in European Literature* 2(4): 9–16.
Messer, Ellen 1984 "Anthropological perspectives on diet" *Annual Review of Anthropology* 13: 205–49.
Metraux, G. S. 1976 "Of feasts and carnivals" *Cultures* 3(1): 7–12.
Mintz, Sidney W. 1985 *Sweetness and Power.* N.Y.: Viking.
Mintz, Sidney 1996 *Tasting Food, Tasting Freedom: Excursions into Eating, Culture, and the Past.* Boston: Beacon Press.
Mock, L. M. W. 1994 "The gardens of Hikone, Japan: Studying people-plant relationships in another culture" in J. Flagler, R. P. Poincelot, (eds) *2nd People-Plant Symposium: People-Plant Relationships: Setting Research Priorities.* N.Y.: Food Products Press.
Moeran, Brian 1981 "Yanagi Muneyoshi and the Japanese folkcraft movement" *Asian Folklore Studies* 40(1): 87–99.
Moeran, Brian 1984 *Lost Innocence: Folk Craft Potters of Onta, Japan.* Berkeley: University of California Press.
Moeran, Brian 1986 "The beauty of violence: Jidaigeki, Yakuza and 'Eroduction' films in Japanese cinema" in David Riches (ed.) *The Anthropology of Violence.* Oxford: Basil Blackwell.
Moeran, Brian 1986 "One over the seven: Saké drinking in a Japanese pottery community" in J. Hendry and J. Webber (eds) *Interpreting Japanese Society.* Oxford: JASO.
Morimoto, M. T. 1994 "A woman's place is in the kitchen of knowledge: Premodern and postmodern representations of food (for thought) in Japanese film" in Masavisut, N. Simson, G. Smith, L. E. (eds) *Gender and Culture in Literature and Film, East and West: Issues of Perception and Interpretation* Vol 9: 260–72 Honolulu: University of Hawaii Press.
Murcott, Anne (ed.) 1983 *The Sociology of Food and Eating.* Aldershot: Gower.
Murcott, Anne 1982 "On the social significance of the 'cooked dinner' in South Wales" *Social Science Information* 21(4/5): 677–96.
Nakane, Chie 1970 *Japanese Society.* Berkeley: University of California Press.
Nakatsuka, H., M. Kasahara, T. Watanabe, S. Hisamichi, H. Shimizu, S. Fujisaku, Y. Ichinowatari, Y. Ida, M. Suda, K. Kato and M. Ikeda 1988 "Urban-rural differences in food-habits in Northeastern Japan" *Ecology of Food and Nutrition* 21(1): 77–87.
Nicoll, Ruaridh 1998 "Chilling the soup, the wine – and the profits" *The Guardian*, Wednesday, April 15 1998.
Noguchi, P. H. 1994 "Savour slowly: Ekiben – the fast food of high-speed Japan" *Ethnology* 33(4): 317–30.
Norge, Jerome 1975 "On determining food patterns of urban dwellers in contemporary U.S. society" in M. Arnott (ed.) *Gastonomy: The Anthropology of Food Habits.* The Hague: Mouton.
Ohnuki-Tierney, Emiko 1988 *The Monkey as Mirror.* Princeton: Princeton University Press.
Ohnuki-Tierney, Emiko 1990 "The ambivalent self of the contemporary Japanese" *Cultural Anthropology* 5(2): 197–216.
Ohnuki-Tierney, Emiko 1993 *Rice as Self: Japanese Identities Through Time.* Princeton: Princeton University Press.
Ohnuki-Tierney, Emiko 1997 "McDonald's in Japan: Changing manners and etiquette" in James L. Watson (ed.) *Golden Arches East: McDonalds' in East Asia.* Stanford: Stanford University Press.
Ortner, Sherry 1975 "Gods' bodies, gods' foods: A symbolic analysis of Sherpa ritual" in R. Willis (ed.) *The Interpretation of Symbolism.* London: Malaby Press.
Owen, S. 1973 "Introducing children to food and table manners in Java" *Food Culture and History* 1: 61–73.

Pachter, Michele 1981 "Sociologie de la cuisine; Sociology of Cooking" *Cahiers Internationaux de Sociologie* 28: 356–8.
Palmer, Elizabeth 1988 *Ikebana: The Art of Japanese Flower Arranging.* London: Quintet Publishing.
Passim, Herbert and John W. Bennett 1943 *Social Process and Dietary Change.* Washington: National Resources Council Bulletin #108.
Pimentel, David and M. Pimentel 1979 *Food, Energy, and Society.* N.Y.: Wiley.
Powdermaker, Hortense 1932 "Feasts in New Ireland: The social function of eating" *American Anthropologist* 34: 236–47.
Rappaport, Roy 1967 "Ritual regulation of environmental relations among a New Guinea people" *Ethnology* 6(1): 17–30.
Raz, Jacob 1976 "The actor and his audience: Zeami's views on the audience of the Noh" *Monumenta Nipponica* 31(3): 251–74.
Revel, Jean Francois 1984 *Festin En Paroles.* [Culture and cuisine: A journey through the history of food. Helen R. Lane, Trans.] N.Y.: Da Capo Press.
Richie, Donald 1985 *A Taste of Japan: Food, Fact, and Fable.* Tokyo, N.Y. and San Francisco: Kodansha International Ltd.
Ritzer, George 1983 "The "McDonaldization" of Society" *Journal of American Culture* 6(1): 100–7.
Ritzer, George 1993 *The McDonaldization of Society: An Investigation into the Changing Character of Contemporary Social Life.* Thousand Oaks, Calif.: Pine Forge Press.
Robertson, Jennifer 1991 *Native and Newcomer: Making and Remaking a Japanese City.* Berkeley: University Of California Press.
Robson, J. (ed.) 1980 *Food, Ecology, and Culture: Readings in the Anthropology of Dietary Practices.* N.Y.: Gordon & Beach.
Ross, Eric B. 1980 "Patterns of diet and forces of production: An economic and ecological history of the ascendancy of beef in the US diet" in E. Ross (ed.) *Beyond the Myths of Culture.* N.Y.: Academic Press.
Rowlandson, J. 1993 "Food and the fellwalker, the symbolism of eating in wild places" *Food Culture and History* 1: 17–28.
Rozin, Elizabeth and Paul Rozin 1981 "Some surprisingly unique characteristics of human food preferences" in Alexander Fenton and Trefor Owen (eds) *Food in Perspective.* Edinburgh: John Donald Publishers.
Rozin, Paul 1987 "Psychobiological perspectives on food preferences and avoidances" in M. Harris and E. Ross (eds) *Food and Evolution: Toward a Theory of Human Food Habits.* Philadelphia: Temple University Press.
Seligman, Lucy 1994 "The history of Japanese cuisine" *Japan Quarterly,* April–June.
Sen, Sōshitsu 1972 "The Tea ceremony and Kaiseki" in K. Tsuji *Kaiseki: Zen Tastes in Japanese Cooking.* Tokyo: Kodansha.
Shelton, Allen 1990 "A theater for eating, looking, and thinking: The restaurant as symbolic space" *Sociological Spectrum* 10(4): 507–26.
Shibusawa, K. 1958 "Food and drink" in K. Shibusawa (ed.) *Japanese Life and Culture in the Meiji Era.* Tokyo: Tōyō Bunko.
Shimizu, Kay 1993 *Tsukemono: Japanese Pickled Vegetables.* Tokyō: Shufunotomo.
Simoons, Frederick J. 1991 *Food in China: A Cultural and Historical Inquiry.* Boca Raton: CRC.
Smith, Robert J. 1978 *Kurusu: The price of progress in a Japanese town.* Stanford: Stanford University Press.
Statler, Oliver 1984 *Japanese Pilgrimage.* London: Pan Books.
Suzuki, Daisetz 1959 *Zen and Japanese Culture.* New York: Pantheon.
Tan, M. et al. 1970 *Social and Cultural Aspects of Food Patterns and Food Habits in Five Rural Areas in Indonesia.* Jakarta: National Institute of of Economic and Social Research.
Tannahill, Reay 1973 *Food in history.* N.Y.: Stein & Day.

Terasaki, Gwen 1976 "Hunger in the mountains" in J. Livingston et al. (eds) *The Japan Reader – Vol. 1*. Harmondsworth: Penguin Books.
Tokoyama H. and F. Egaitsu 1994 "Major categories of changes in food consumption patterns in Japan 1963–91" *Oxford agrarian studies* 22(2): 191–202.
Tsuchiya, Yoshio 1983 *A feast for the eyes: The Japanese art of Food Arrangement*. Tokyo: Kodansha.
Tsuji, Kaichi 1974 *Kaiseki: Zen Tastes in Japanese cooking*. Tokyo: Kodansha.
Twigg, Julia 1983 "Vegetarianism and the meaning of meat" in A. Murcott (ed.) *The Sociology of Food and Eating*. Aldershot: Gower Press.
United States Department of Agriculture 1969 *Food For Us All*. Washington, D.C.: U.S. G.P.O.
Varley, H. Paul and George Elison 1981 "The culture of Tea: From its origins to Sen no Rikyu" in George Elison, and Bardwell Smith (eds) 1981 *Warlords, Artists and Commoners: Japan in the Suxteenth Century*. Honolulu: University Press of Hawaii.
Veblen, Thorstein 1965 *The Theory of the Leisure Class*. N.Y.: Random House.
Voss, Joachim 1987 "The politics of pork and the rituals of rice: Redistributive feasting and commodity circulation in Northern Luzon, Philippines" in J. Clammer (ed.) 1987 *Beyond the New Economic Anthropology*. London: Macmillan.
Walcher, D. N., N. Kretchmer & H. L. Barnett (eds) 1976 *Foods, Man and Society*. N.Y.: Plenum Press.
Warde, A. 1997 "Consumption, food and taste: Culinary antinomies and commodity culture" *Keele Sociological Review* 45(4): 714–7.
Watson, James L. 1987 "From the common pot: Feasting with equals in Chinese society" *Anthropos* 82: 389–401.
White, Merry I. 1993 *The Material Child*. N.Y.: The Free Press.
Wilson, C. Anne 1973 *Food and Drink in Britain*. London: Constable.
Wilson, Christine 1986 "Social and nutritional context of 'Ethnic foods': Malay examples" in L. Manderson (ed.) *Shared Wealth and Symbol: Food Culture and Society in Oceania*. Cambridge: Cambridge University Press.
Woronoff, Jon 1981 *Japan's Wasted Workers*. Tokyo: Lotus Press.
Yoneda, Soei 1982 *Good Food from a Japanese Temple*. Tokyo: Kodansha.
Yoneyama, Toshinao 1967 "Kaminosho: A farm village suburban to Osaka in South Central Japan" in J. Steward (ed.) *Contemporary Change in Traditional Societies*. Urbana: University of Illinois Press.
Yoshida, Mitsukuni & Sesoko, Tsune 1989 (eds) *Naorai: Communion of the Table*. Hiroshima: Mazda Motor Corp.
Young, M. W. 1971 *Fighting with Food: Leadership, Values, and Control in a Massim Society*. Cambridge: Cambridge University Press.

REFERENCES IN JAPANESE

Abe, Kiyoei (ed.) 1997 *1997 Annual – Japan statistical survey*. Tokyo: Kokuseisha.
Ado, Hiroki 1992 *International comparison of food culture*. Tokyo: Tokyo Gas Tōshi seikatsu kenkyujouhen.
Aiba, Hitoshi 1964 *The World of sensation*. Tokyo: Kodansha.
Akioka, Yoshio 1992 "About Japanese food containers: Evidence of differences in food cultures from food vessels" *Vesta* 12: 22–7.
Aoba, Takashi 1982 *Japanese Vegetables*. Tokyo: Yasakashoboh.
Aoba, Takashi 1991 *History of Vegetables in Japan*. Tokyo: Yasakashoboh.
Arasaki, Makoto 1991 *Japanese Culture of Saké*. Tokyo: Kadokawashoten.
Arima Takeru and Kiri Kiriko 1987 *Bentō Travel Companion Vol 2: Oshizushi Trip*. Tokyo: Ridosha.

Chin, Shunshin 1976 "Edo and the refined palate" *Taiyou Special* 14: 175–80.
Ego, Michiko 1991 "Local food cultures: Kyushu sweetmeats" *Vesta* 12: 66–71.
Ehara, Kei 1976 "Japanese cooking and chefs" *Taiyou Special* 14: 159–66.
Fukuda Ichiro and Yamamoto Eiji 1992 *The Folk-life of Rice.* Tokyo: Chuoshinshou.
Furukawa, Hideko 1985 *Aspects of Sensory Examination of Goods.* Tokyo: Shojinsha.
Gaishoku sangyō sōgō chōsa kenkyū sentā [Eating-out industry survey research center] 1998 *Eating-Out Industry Statistical Data Compilation: 1997.* Tokyo: Gaishoku sangyō sōgō chōsa kenkyū sentā.
Harada, Nobuo 1991 *Rice and Meat in History: Foodstuffs and the Emperor.* Tokyo: Heibonsha.
Hataa, Akemi 1991 "Food and colour" *Vesta* 7: 63–6.
Higuchi, Kiyoyuki 1987 *The History of Japan's Foodstuffs: The History of Diet.* Tokyo: Shibata Shoten.
Hokkaido Suisanbu 1990 *Hokkaido Fisheries Today: 1990 Marine Industries White Paper.* Hokkaido: Hokkaido Suisanbu.
Hosking, Richard 1993 "Karē-raisu and Worcester sauce: A British point of view" *Vesta* 17: 70–7.
Iguchi, Kaisen 1978 *Introduction to Kaiseki.* Tokyo: Tankōsha.
Ishige, Naomichi 1980 *People, Food, Culture: Food Culture Symposium '80.* Tokyo: Heibonsha.
Ishige, Naomichi 1982 *A Theory of the Civilization of Meals.* Tokyo: Chuo Koron-sha.
Ishige, Naomichi 1985 *Studies in the Eating Cultures of East Asia.* Tokyo: Heibonsha.
Ishige, Naomichi 1986 "'Gyosho' in N.E. Asia: A study of fermented aquatic products" *Kokuritsu Minzokugakku hakubutsukan kenkyū* 11(1): 1–14.
Ishige, Naomichi 1986 "Narezushi in Asia: A study of fermented aquatic products (2)" *Kokuritsu Minzokugakku hakubutsukan kenkyū* 11(3): 603–68.
Ishige, Naomichi 1989 "Origins and distributions: A study of fermented aquatic products" *Kokuritsu Minzokugakku hakubutsukan kenkyū* 14(1): 199–250.
Ishige, Naomichi 1990 "The cultural range of taste" *Vesta* 3: 4–13.
Ishige, Naomichi 1992 "Tendencies in ethnological research concerning food culture" *Vesta* 1(10): 4–14.
Ishige, Naomichi, Komatsu Sakyō, and Toyokawa Hiroyuki (eds) 1989 *The Food of the Shōwa-era* (Proceedings of the Food Culture symposium '89). Tokyo: Domesu Shuppan.
Ishige, Naomichi and Inoue Chuuji (eds) 1991 *Modern Japanese Households and Dining Tables: From meimeizen to chabudai.* Osaka: Kokuritsu minzoku hakubutsukan kenkyū hōkoku.
Iwabuchi, Michio 1996 *Eating-out Industry Report: Eating Out Competition and Growth.* Tokyo: Norintōkeikyōkai.
JETRO 1991 *U.S. and Japan in Figures.* Tokyo: Nihon Bōeki Shinkōkai.
Joshieiyōdaigakushuppanbu [Women's Nutrition University Publication Department] (ed.) 1965 *Twelve months' obentō.* Tokyo: Joshieiyōdaigakushuppanbu.
Kanda, Hiroshi 1991 *Cooking Edo-style.* Tokyo: Kyoikusha.
Kariya Tetsu and Hanasaki Akira 1985 *Oishinbo.* Tokyo: Shōgakkan Big Comics.
Kawabata, Shouko 1990 "The tastiness of mochi" *Vesta* 2: 48–53.
Kawabata, Douki 1990 *Confections Kyoto.* Tokyo: Iwanami Shōten.
Kawakami, Kouzou 1976 "Edo period gourmet" *Taiyou Special* 14: 117–24.
Kishimoto, Shigenobu 1993 "On my love for beef" *Vesta* 16: 2–3.
Kitaoji, Rōsanjin 1980 *Rōsanjin's Cookery Kingdom.* Tokyo: Bunkashuppankyoku.
Kogawa, Hiro 1990 *The Man Who Made Koshihikari.* Tokyo: Shinchosha.
Kogawa, Zenio 1991 "Has the basis of eating habits changed?" *Vesta* 6: 10–20.
Kōkawa, Aya (ed.) 1991 *Standard Tables of Food Composition in Japan.* Tokyo: Joshi eiyō daigaku shuppanbu.
Kondo, Shin 1993 "Food, sound, and brightness: An inquiry into food and environment" *Vesta* 17: 38–46.
Koyanagi, Kiichi 1976 "Records of foods and foodstuffs" *Taiyou Special* 14: 181–7.

Kumakura, Isao 1976 "From regular dinner to kaiseki" *Taiyou Special* 14: 85–92.

Kumakura, Norio 1992 "Taisho, Showa local food cultures" *Vesta* 13: 12–22.

Kusama, Toshio 1992 "Yokohama: The reception of Western food culture (1): Late Edo-Early Meiji core" *Vesta* 14: 64–9.

Maruyama, Hiroshi 1990 *Inquiry into the Basis of Eating Habits*. Tokyo: Nohbunkyo.

Masunari, Takashi 1992 "A comparative perspective on food culture" *Vesta* 12: 14–20.

Matsumura, Machiko 1992 "The culture of English fish eating" *Vesta* 12: 58–65.

Matsushita, Sachiko 1991 *The Food Culture of Celebration*. Tokyo: Tokyo-bijutsu.

Minami, Hiroko 1990 *Tea, Tea, Tea*. Tokyo: Tankohsha.

Mistushoku, Seikoshou 1976 "Early royal cooking" *Taiyou Special* 14: 53–60.

Miyahara, Shuuji 1993 "School lunches today and tomorrow: The food culture of food lunch" *Vesta* 17: 4–10.

Miyake, Makoto 1991 *The Study of Fish-Eating Cultural Resources Throughout the World*. Tokyo: Chuo Koronsha.

Nakamura, Takao 1976 "History of bowl and chopsticks" *Taiyou Special* 14: 167–74.

Norin Suisansho. (Keizaikyoku). Tokei Johobu [Ministry of Agriculture, Forestry and Fisheries. Statistics and Information Department] 1997 *Report on findings of the 1995 census of agriculture in Japan*. Tokyo: Norin Suisansho.

Oda, Susumu 1991 *The Dining Table of Powerful People: An Ethnology of Taste*. Osaka: PHP Laboratory.

Ōtsuka Chikara 1976 "Civilisation and Western food" *Taiyou Special* 14: 133–40.

Ōtsuka, Shigeru 1990 *The Cultural History of Taste*. Tokyo: Asahi Shinbunsha.

Ōtsuka, Shinichiro 1992 "On the evaluation of foodstuffs from 'Theory of foodstuff evaluation'" *Vesta* 11: 30–7.

Ōtsuka, T. 1960 *Foodstuff Food History*. Tokyo: Yuzankaku.

Ozaki, Michio 1990 "The oral literature of South-East Asia: Fermented coconut foods" *Vesta* 2: 22–6.

Ozaki, Michio 1990 "The oral literature of South-East Asia: Fermented coconut foods" *Vesta* 4: 21–7.

PiaMAPgurume 1996 *Pia gourmet map 1996*. Tokyo: Pia Inc.

Segawa, K. 1964 *Japanese Livelihood*. Tokyo: Kawade shobo.

Sen, Sōshitsu 1985 *Morning Tea Utensils: Furō Compilation*.

Setagaya Art Museum 1996 *Creative Tradition: The Ceramics of Rosanjin and Masterpieces of the Past Which Influenced Him*. Tokyo: Setagaya Art Museum.

Shibata, Takeshi 1990 "The language of food: Rice balls" *Vesta* 5: 55.

Shimada, Akiko 1992 "Thinking about rice: Food culture from the viewpoint of food science" *Vesta* 4: 38–44.

Shinoda, Touchaku 1993 *Chinese Foodstuff History*. Tokyo: Shibata Shoten.

Shinoda, Touchaku 1978 *About Sushi*. Tokyo: Shinshindo.

Shinoda, Touchaku 1993 *The Book of Sushi*. Tokyo: Shibata Shoten.

Shirasaki, Hideo 1971 *Kitaoji Rōsanjin*. Tokyo: Bungei Shunju.

Suminoe, K. 1962 *Japanese saké*. Tokyo: Kawade Shobo.

Suzuki Soukou, Shiraishi Kazuko, Ego Michiko and Yamaguchi Takashi 1995 *Well-made Japanese Confections*. Tokyo: Shinchosha.

Tae, Ta-sho 1992 *Japan and Korea in the Context of Food Culture*. Tokyo: Kodansha Gendai Shinshou.

Tagawa, Nobuyuki 1985 *Hōchō mushuku*, Goraku Comics. Tokyo: Nihon Bungeisha.

Takagi, Kazuo 1993 "An inquiry into food culture" *Vesta* 14: 36–41.

Takahashi, Gikou 1976 "Opinion – Rethinking food" *Taiyou Special* 14: 29–36.

Tanaka, Seiichi 1991 *Encyclopaedia of Chinese Food*. Tokyo: Shibata Shoten.

Tanaka, Tsuneo 1976 *Introduction to the Kitchen Knife*. Tokyo: Shibata Shoten.

Tsuchiya, Ei 1981 *Home Cooking Encyclopedia*. Tokyo: Sekai Bunkasha.

Tsuda, Yoshie 1992 "American nutrition education information" *Vesta* 4: 73–7.
Tsukazaki, S. 1962 *Food of the Japanese*. Tokyo: Iwasaki Shoten.
Uchino, Choko 1992 "Food consumption patterns: Regional attributes" *Vesta* 1(10): 40–8.
Watanabe, Tadayo 1993 "Mochi culture range dispersal and food habits" *Vesta* 16: 4–15.
Yamada Saburo 1992 "Economic development and changes in food culture" *Vesta* 14: 26–34.
Yamashita, Shigeru 1970 *Japanese Cooking*. Tokyo: Kōbunshoin.
Yanagi, Soetsu 1926 [1955] *The Way of the Potter*. Tokyo: Nihon Mingeikan.
Yanagimo, M., S. Ohya and T. Yanagimo 1987 "The trend of seasonality of processed food consumption in Japan by a new statistical method" *Journal of the Japanese Society of Food* 34(10): 647–53.
Yanagita, Kunio 1962 *Food and Belief*. Vol 14 in K. Yanagita Teihon: Yanagida Kunio Zenshu. Tokyo: Chikuma Shobo.
Yoshida, Yasuo 1990 "Statistical data on changes of food culture" *Vesta* 3: 14–22.
Yoshida, Yoshiko 1989 *Tropical Foods in Japan*. Tokyo: Rakū Shobō.
Yoshikawa Makototsugi 1992 "The story of bentō, past and present: A brief history of present and past bentō box contents" *Vesta* 1: 58–65.

FILMOGRAPHY

Tampopo Directed by Itami, Juzo 1987. Toei.
The Colonel Comes to Japan Produced, written, and directed by John Nathan. Boston, Mass.: Enterprise (WGBH) 1981.

Index